The Mature Metropolis

The Mature Metropolis

Edited by

Charles L. Leven
Washington University

Lexington Books
D.C. Heath and Company
Lexington, Massachusetts
Toronto

The Institute for Urban and Regional Studies is an interdisciplinary unit of Washington University (St. Louis) which organizes and administers research projects and other scholarly activities.

Mercantile Bancorporation, Inc. is a regional multi-bank holding company headquartered in St. Louis.

Library of Congress Cataloging in Publication Data

Main entry under title:

The Mature metropolis.

   Contains essays commissioned by the Institute for Urban and Regional Studies, Washington University, St. Louis, for a symposium held in St. Louis on June 6-8, 1977.
   1. Cities and towns—Addresses, essays, lectures. I. Leven, Charles L., 1928-   II. Washington University, St. Louis. Institute for Urban and Regional Studies.
HT153.M395   301.36   77-10363
ISBN 0-669-01844-9

Copyright © 1978 by D.C. Heath and Company.

All rights reserved. No part of this publication may be reproduced or transmitted in any form or by any means, electronic or mechanical, including photocopy, recording, or any information storage or retrieval system, without permission in writing from the publisher. This book was based on a symposium organized by the Institute for Urban and Regional Studies, Washington University, under a grant from Mercantile Bancorporation, Inc.

Published simultaneously in Canada.

Printed in the United States of America.

International Standard Book Number: 0-669-01844-9

Library of Congress Catalog Card Number: 77-10363

Contents

	Foreword, by *Donald E. Lasater*	vii
	Preface	ix
Part I	Overview of the Mature Metropolis	1
Chapter 1	**The Emergence of Maturity in Metropolis**—*Charles L. Leven*	3
Part II	Origins of Maturity	21
Chapter 2	**The Current Halt in the Metropolitan Phenomenon**—*William Alonso*	23
Chapter 3	**Social Processes and Social Policy in the Stable Metropolis**—*James S. Coleman*	43
Part III	Extent of Maturity	63
Chapter 4	**The Declining Metropolis: Patterns, Problems, and Policies in Britain and Mainland Europe**—*Peter Hall* and *David Metcalf*	65
Chapter 5	**Metropolitan Development in Poland and Implications for America**—*Piotr Korcelli*	91
Part IV	Functions of the Mature Metropolis	107
Chapter 6	**The Central City in the Postindustrial Age**—*Harvey S. Perloff*	109
Chapter 7	**Tomorrow's Agglomeration Economies**—*Norman Macrae*	131
Part V	Physical Organization of the Mature Metropolis	147
Chapter 8	**Transportation and Land Use in the Mature Metropolis**—*Alex Anas* and *Leon N. Moses*	149
Chapter 9	**Environmental Problems in the Mature Metropolis**—*Edwin S. Mills, Daniel Feenberg,* and *Randall Zisler*	169

Part VI	*Governmental Organization of the Mature Metropolis*	187
Chapter 10	Metropolitan Governance and the Mature Metropolis—*Alan K. Campbell*	189
Chapter 11	The Role of Neighborhoods in the Mature Metropolis—*M. Leanne Lachman* and *Anthony Downs*	207
Part VII	*Public, Private, and Human Investment in the Mature Metropolis*	225
Chapter 12	Public Sector Investment Strategies in the Mature Metropolis—*Dick Netzer*	227
Chapter 13	"Basic" Economic Activities in Metropolis—*Harry W. Richardson*	251
Chapter 14	The Economically Disadvantaged in the Mature Metropolis—*Marcus Alexis*	281
Part VIII	*Policy for the Mature Metropolis*	303
Chapter 15	Agenda for the Mature Metropolis—*Robert C. Holland* and *Charles L. Leven*	305
	About the Contributors	313
	About the Editor	319

Foreword

Mercantile Bancorporation Inc., as a major regional bank holding company, is committed to economic development and community involvement in the extensive Midwestern region which we serve. This commitment led us to underwrite a three-day symposium in June 1977 addressing "Challenges and Opportunities in the Mature Metropolis," conducted in St. Louis by the Institute for Urban and Regional Studies of Washington University.

The major, mature metropolitan areas comprise a significant portion of the human, physical, and intellectual resources of our country. These concentrations of resources, from which so much of the progress and spirit of America has emanated, are undergoing dramatic changes.

The present and future nature of that change is having and will continue to have a tremendous impact upon a vital area of the basic fabric of America. Our nation's ability to cope with this change, let alone manage it for the betterment of our way of life, depends on understanding the change and developing various means of using that change to the common advantage of all. If, based on that understanding, strategies for more effective public and private participation in the future development of our older cities can be even vaguely envisioned, then the symposium will have been worthwhile.

Mercantile hopes the symposium and the publication of this volume will in some way act as catalysts enabling other things to happen through public and private sector reaction to the information, concepts, and ideas presented here.

Donald E. Lasater
Chairman of the Board
Mercantile Bancorporation Inc.

Preface

Since the end of World War II, the anatomy of metropolis has undergone more rapid change than at any time since the spurt in growth in the late-nineteenth century. Superimposed on these trends is a new and somewhat baffling phenomenon: the ceasing of significant population growth for large metropolitan areas as a whole—cities and suburbs combined.

The phenomenon of decline raises complex issues for the future development of our large metropolitan areas. One set of issues concerns the durability of these trends and the conditions under which they would be reversed. While there is considerable interest in trend reversal, such efforts are not likely to be successful without a deeper understanding of the metropolitan process. Moreover, a deeper understanding would also be needed to uncover challenges and opportunities for development in the mature metropolis, even without significant further population growth. It is toward that understanding that this volume is dedicated.

Under a grant from Mercantile Bancorporation Inc., the Institute for Urban and Regional Studies, Washington University, St. Louis, commissioned thirteen essays which are presented as Chapters 2 to 14 of this volume. These essays were especially commissioned, as much as a year in advance, for a symposium held at the St. Louis Exhibition and Convention Center on June 6-8, 1977. The luncheon speaker at that symposium was Robert C. Holland; his prepared remarks form much of the basis for Chapter 15.

The authors who have contributed to the symposium and this volume have established scholarly eminence, substantial experience as policymakers or advisers, and deep technical skill in various facets of the urban economic experience. Out of this experience, the material in this volume will analyze the sources of present trends in metropolitan development, explore the alternative paths to which these trends might lead, identify the critical factors on which our metropolitan future depends, and point out the opportunities for effective adaptation to the emerging metropolis.

Ultimately, the decisions that will guide metropolis must be made by private and public bodies intimately concerned with particular places and familiar with the details of their problems and prospects. It is hoped that this volume will provide a more meaningful and more deeply thoughtful agenda for those concerned with metropolitan development over the next several decades.

Needless to say, the number of people who should be thanked for their contributions to the organization of the complex of events underlying this volume is large indeed, but space prevents naming everyone who made the organization of the symposium and the preparation of this volume so much easier as well as rewarding for me.

Most special thanks are due to Donald Lasater and other members of the

Executive Committee of the Board of Directors of Mercantile Bancorporation Inc. for their vision in seeing the importance of the symposium topic, not only to St. Louis but to all of the mature metropolitan areas of the modern world, and their confidence in the ability of the Institute to carry out this assignment. Mercantile also assumed responsibility for most of the physical arrangements for the symposium event itself; I would like to express my personal thanks to Leigh Doxsie, and June Ellison of Mercantile, and Charles Lipton of Ruder and Finn, Inc., for numerous helpful suggestions as well as just plain help.

Carol Martin, then Special Projects Coordinator at the Institute, was responsible for presymposium arrangements with all the authors as well as for coordinating them, their papers, and their arrivals and departures with Mercantile's plans. Probably nothing at all would have occurred without her efforts, and the help to her in staffing the symposium event by Candace Harper, Adele Reilly, and Mark Platt.

My colleagues in the Institute and in the Department of Economics at Washington University surely must have found the subject matter of this volume progressively less fascinating as I solicited their reactions during the editing process. Most of them would probably just as soon forget the whole thing, but at least James Little might want, and certainly deserves special thanks, for his consistent encouragement and helpful technical comments.

Publication arrangements were handled by Candace Harper, the Institute secretary, and very substantial thanks must go to her and to Mary Proemsey for typing the manuscript and keeping up my spirits.

Perhaps the biggest thanks of all must go to the contributors of the papers that make up this volume. Surely, they do not need me to accept responsibility for what they have said; but I do agree with almost all of it.

Finally, I would like to thank my wife, Dorothy Wish Leven, for her forebearance as well as for entertaining a lot of visiting firemen.

Charles L. Leven

Part I
Overview of the Mature Metropolis

1

The Emergence of Maturity in Metropolis

Charles L. Leven

In 1958, not very long ago in terms of the way we look at historical trends, a volume titled *Exploding Metropolis* attracted widespread attention.[1] In a sense, it reflected the increasing awareness of the emergence of large, more-or-less continuous "megalopolitan conurbations" like "Bos-Wash" and "Chi-Pitts" and the problems connected with this new social phenomenon called "megalopolis."[2]

On the one hand, private gains available to people willing to move there were seen as almost limitless, stemming mainly from the comparative advantage of the large metropolis in production, especially of goods and services that were the most technologically advanced and often the most profitable. On the other hand, the continued stream of net in-migrants was seen as leading to growth in scale and density of metropolitan population that was imposing substantial increases in unit costs of providing public services and social costs of dense urban living. The "challenge" in this setting was seen as finding some combination of more imaginative, and more efficient, management of local public services and land-use planning, together with attempts at retaining in nonmetro areas as many people as possible, or at least slowing down the speed at which migration to metropolis took place. The "opportunity" was the chance to make the supposedly more attractive "Gotham-on-Hudson" life-style available to an increasing proportion of Americans.

Less than twenty years later, in 1976, we saw the appearance of *The Urban Predicament*, which dealt with the economic and social policies occasioned by the onset of apparent malfunction in many large-scale metropolises.[3] Instead of a crisis of physically accommodating economic agglomeration, we find a crisis of disappearing industrial jobs; instead of a crisis of critical shortages in public service capacity, we find an inability to finance local government; instead of a crisis engendered by bottlenecks in subdividing suburbia, we find a crisis of physical decay in central cities.

It is true that we live in an era of rapid change, both in ideas and technology. Changing attitudes toward what constitutes normal family life and sexual behavior no doubt produce changes in relative demands for differing life-styles. The coming of the computer revolution in information processing and message transmission, and shifts in energy costs no doubt change the advantages of locating different economic activities in different locations. In fact, the major purpose of this volume is to explain in detail the underlying factors producing the recent shift in metropolitan development.

There are two important and fundamental reasons for wanting to understand this change in so much detail. First, there is a need to understand the factors underlying change if effective strategies for reversing (or accommodating) trends are to be formulated; all too often, proposed strategies are no more than restatements of the problem itself. For example, a policy of "attracting more industry" really provides little beyond a reminder of dwindling manufacturing employment as a problem. It only restates an objective; if decline is to be reversed, just why it has occurred must be understood in some detail.

But the foregoing is fairly obvious. The second and more important reason for knowing the details of change is the need to place these trends in the perspective of time and place. All too often, those responsible for policy formation for a particular metropolitan area feel themselves caught up in somewhat mysterious forces which they perceive as being of sudden origin and largely unique to their area. Thus, another purpose of this book is to indicate that the factors underlying change, even in specific metropolitan areas, are an outgrowth of understandable historical processes, and that policies to alter or accommodate to current trends can be forged out of an understanding of the more basic underlying causes.

Factors Underlying Metropolitan Maturity

The forces leading to metropolitan maturity can be categorized as being of three types: those related to basic changes in the economics of production, those stemming from underlying demographic trends, and those related to shifting societal goals. These sets of factors will be discussed in turn with an understandable emphasis on economic factors, but with due consideration to factors associated with demographic change and shifting societal goals as well.

Economics and Metropolitan Maturity

The economic forces associated with maturity in metropolis are directly related to the emergence of the modern metropolis in the nineteenth century, when the driving economic phenomenon was the rise of the factory system, with its attendant economies of scale: economies related to production in larger-scale individual units (mainly to economize on the high fixed costs of establishing steam power), and economies related to the congregating together of a large number of complementary production activities (mainly to economize on transport costs).

As indicated, the major technical forces behind the efficiency of large urban concentrations were the nonhuman motive power—first steam and later electric—and the growth of intercity railroads, which permitted vastly lower costs of shipping goods over almost any route. Other forces followed, first intensifying the initial trends toward urban concentration, but later leading to maturity in metropolis and the declines now emerging. The role of economic forces in the birth, growth, and maturity of the industrial metropolis will be discussed to some extent in almost every chapter to follow, since it is at the very heart of the phenomenon of maturity.

In the nineteenth and into the twentieth century, the steam engine and the intercity railroad made it both possible and profitable to initiate large-scale manufacturing efficiently located at or between raw materials and markets. But compared to the present, industrial technology at that time used a vast bulk of raw material, as indicated in Chapter 8. Coupled with the fact that intracity movement of goods was very expensive compared to the cost of moving people, and coupled with the relatively high cost of utilizing steam or even electric power, very far from its source, the early industrial metropolis contained pressures for compactness as well as for scale.

As the twentieth century progressed, a variety of technological developments produced metropolitan sprawl and what we came eventually to recognize as stagnation, or "maturity." The private passenger car was one of these developments; but perhaps even more important, if less well recognized, was the motortruck. It vastly reduced the cost of internal movement of goods compared with the horse-drawn wagon that it replaced, permitting work places to spread out from central terminal areas. With the passenger car, it allowed both residences and work places to be free of locations proximate to fixed rights-of-way, permitting still more spread which in turn permitted even greater scale. These basic technological forces were enhanced by two kinds of government action in the early post-World War II period: the building of high-speed urban expressways wherever projected traffic demand seemed to be in prospect, and the ready availability of mortgage credit at preferential terms for new single-family detached suburban housing.

More recent technical developments have made locating economic activities near the core of an urban area, or even within a metropolitan area at all, much less important. Probably more significant has been the steady reduction in the bulk of raw materials associated with most workers' occupations. With the expansion of the service sector, it turns out that at least two-thirds of American workers are not involved with any raw materials at all; and even for the remainder, there has been a fairly steady drop in bulk-to-value ratios for most commodities. At the same time, since the extent of economies of scale at the establishment level is much more limited for services than for goods, the need for large individual production units has been reduced. Finally, technological developments in information storage, retrieval, and transmission have reduced the need for closely related activities necessarily to be located near each other.

All of this adds up to a powerful reduction in the hold of the central city, or even the **SMSA** (standard metropolitan statistical areas), on economic activities.

Other contributing factors also can be identified; for example, the more widespread use of air-conditioning has led to more dispersal of economic activities regionally, though not necessarily away from metro areas within a region. On the other hand, things like television and nationally standardized eating places and discount stores have reduced the cultural isolation of smaller cities and towns substantially, adding to the ease with which an increasing variety of economic activities find it feasible to escape the higher public service and congestion costs of metropolis.

Demographic Trends Underlying Metropolitan Maturity

The demographic trends associated with contemporary metropolitan change make one very important aspect of that change abundantly clear, namely, that the kind of economic changes indicated above are neither as abrupt nor as recent a phenomenon as is popularly supposed. In fact, the number of people moving away from SMSAs has been greater than the number moving to them, at least since the early 1960s; for larger, older SMSAs, net out-migration dates from even earlier in the postwar period. This relative trend away from metropolis was not generally noticed until recently, however, because up until about 1970 the excess of births over deaths exceeded out-migration, and SMSAs continued to show continued absolute growth in population for all SMSAs combined and, with rather few exceptions, for individual SMSAs as well. The high rates of natural increase in metro areas were partly due to high, if dwindling, birthrates, and partly due to the heavy representation in metropolitan populations of women in their childbearing years.

The long-term trend directing economic activities progressively away from metropolis has been revealed dramatically by the precipitous decline in the birthrate since 1970. As Alonso points out in Chapter 2, "The principal reason for the decline in metropolitan population is simple: the rate of natural increase has plummeted." And it might be noted the change in the rate of natural increase is almost entirely due to the fall in birthrates. It is this factor more than any other which has produced the unprecedented phenomenon of absolute declines in metropolitan population since 1970; before 1960 no large SMSA had ever lost population; between 1960 and 1970 only one area, Pittsburgh, showed an absolute loss; between 1970 and 1975 ten SMSAs showed absolute decline, and several more showed only nominal rates of population increase.

But the economic forces promoting out-migration from large SMSAs have been with us for at least ten and more likely twenty years as has a complex of migration flows between metropolitan areas themselves. Again in Chapter 2, Alonso remarks, "When such small rates of population increase are coupled with continuing differential exchanges among metropolises, it is a mathematical certainty that many of the metropolitan areas will experience population loss."

It should be stressed as strongly as possible that the emergence of metropolitan population decline since 1970 is not a reflection of some underlying sudden change in the economic viability of metropolis. If anything "sudden" has occurred, it is the drop in the birthrate, which in the mid-1970s stood at 1.8 per female—below the equilibrium replacement rate of 2.1—compared with a rate of about 3.7 as recently as the late 1950s.

In part, the apparent population losses in metropolis reflect the spread of rather than a turning away from metropolis; that is, they reflect the sprawl of population beyond the official boundaries of SMSAs, with some time lag to be expected before the boundaries are adjusted outward. This indeed is part of the story; but for two reasons one should hesitate from concluding that this then means that nothing much of real consequence has happened. First, counties well beyond metropolitan hinterlands are growing in significant numbers for the first time in this century, and such growth is occurring in almost all sections of the country. Second, even to the extent that it represents a spreading out of existing metro areas, the more recent patterns of spread are producing an organization of metropolitan life which may be as different in kind as it is in degree.

The basic reason for spread of SMSAs is the progressive outward shift of job locations which then permits residential locations to bound one more commutation jump outward, and so on. But we now find that job growth is not following a course of continuous suburbanization, but one of leapfrogging development to outlying exurban sites. Thus, any attempt to draw metropolitan boundaries that would include this outward development would not only catch large amounts of nonmetropolitan activity in its boundaries, it also, at least in the more populous parts of the nation, would give us metro areas which virtually exhausted all existing space. We are rapidly reaching a situation where we would find that virtually every county in states like, say, Ohio would be within one of a few SMSAs, if SMSAs really were defined inclusively. *It is not so much that metropolitan life is being forsaken for a return to a small town or rural existence, but rather that metropolis is actually moving to the countryside.* Increasingly, individuals and families can be participants in economic, informational, and even cultural and social aspects of metropolitan life without actually having to live quite in metropolis in the sense that we know it.

One recent trend that might give the appearance of renewed population growth vitality in metropolitan areas is the record volume of new suburban construction just at the time when central-city property decay and abandonment, if anything, seem to be abating. In part, this reflects some upgrading and replacement demand of ordinary dimensions. But it also reflects a curious feature of the underlying demography, namely, that even with a falling total population we can experience a rise in the number of dwelling units, as single individuals and unmarried adults form separate households. But numerically, such a trend cannot continue once a substantial shift has occurred. Also, without immigration from abroad—which most experts feel far exceeds the officially reported rate of a little over a million a year—large metropolitan area population figures would be still more depressed.

Social Values and Metropolitan Maturity

It should be emphasized that the economic and demographic factors underlying metropolitan population decline are pervasive and likely to be quite persistent. This does not mean that the population declines we have witnessed in mature metropolitan areas were quite inevitable, or that it would be impossible to reverse prospective future declines in the near-term future. But as might be suspected from the strength of the underlying forces producing maturity, what might be required for trend reversal could come into sharp conflict with some other very important societal objectives.

At an individual level, it is obvious that proximity to a metropolitan area or its center brings certain advantages—mainly easier access to work, shopping and trading, and cultural and institutional facilities. Distance from metropolis traditionally brought less of these things but greater assurance of space, privacy, and safety. And, as Coleman points out in Chapter 3, at least up until 1950 "it was always the same; people remained on the land or moved to the city if work existed there for them."

Since about 1950, however, it has been less necessary to go to metropolis to find work in nonrural pursuits, and the communications revolution has lowered the cultural and informational advantage of metropolis. At the same time, it appears that the "safety" advantages of distance from metropolis may have increased substantially until, as indicated in Chapter 3, "the much lower crime outside the city may allow the nonmetropolitan resident *greater* participation in cultural life and entertainment outside the home than the city resident." And as there may be conflict for individual families as between living in metropolis or not, there may be conflicts for the larger society between maintaining population growth trends in metropolis and fostering other ends. Four examples of this kind of conflict are pointed out in Chapter 3.

First, out of the belief, about the late 1940s, that a housing shortage of massive proportion was in prospect, we erected an entire system of home finance calculated to spur the effective demand for new units. We paid little attention to the fact that the technical characteristics of this system made residential investment in central cities rather unattractive. And even to the extent that this might have been noted, the stimulation of new construction was serving a social goal that simply was seen as more important than preserving the inner city, though the ultimate ramifications of central-city decay for lagging metropolitan growth probably were not noted.

Second, maintaining a large and growing output of passenger automobiles was seen as very important in the postwar period. Partly, this served to maintain a brisk aggregate demand for the product of one of the nation's more politically potent industries; but it also did meet the objective of catering to a popular desire for a much preferred personal transport mode. That stimulating and maintaining this demand took the form of heavy underwriting of urban expressways (which also lowered the access value of central-city locations) also was incidental to the larger social goal of putting America on wheels; but whether intended or not—no doubt it was unintended—it certainly stimulated escape from the central city and reduced the comparative advantage of metropolis as a whole.

Third, the increase in crime really has been substantial in metropolitan areas, and perhaps more important is the growing belief that no one seems determined to do anything about it. Between 1960 and 1970 the population of prisons actually went down, even though the crime rate had more than doubled for a bigger population; the rate of imprisonment fell from 6 per 100 FBI indexed crimes committed to 2 per 100. Over the same period, of course, the rights of the accused became substantially better protected. Perhaps on balance, this strengthening of civil rights was to the good and even worth the increased feelings of vulnerability to crime which resulted. But more germane to this discussion, however, is that it certainly did result in increasing the value of distance from metropolis.

Fourth, policies explicitly have been aimed, not just at ending racial discrimination but specifically at achieving integration, particularly in public schools. Here, too, it is not for us to argue that the achievement of integrated schools may not be more important than the preservation of the attractiveness of metropolitan areas as places to live, but we cannot escape observing that school integration attempts and out-migration rates are related.

In all four of these examples, it seems reasonable to assume that policies would not have been carried out so as to conflict as seriously with the attractiveness of metropolis, had they been decided on at the local level rather than substantially by federal authorities. We cannot say whether this would have been better in some total social sense or not (better for whom?), but we certainly can say that the attractiveness of nonmetropolitan areas relative to the large SMSAs probably would not have increased so markedly as we have seen in the early 1970s.

The Pervasiveness of Maturity

Often, metropolitan community leaders may view population stagnation or decline as a peculiar misfortune which they, almost alone, have had to face. And they may cling to this view despite the fact that, while different metropolitan areas have had and will have different growth experiences, "slowdown" is a generalized phenomenon related to very basic factors in our national experience.

In fact, the phenomenon is even more pervasive than that, as indicated in Chapters 4 and 5.

The similarity of the emergence of metropolitan maturity in much of West Europe (in particular in Britain) and in the United States is striking in terms of timing, extent, and apparent causes. In Britain, for example, the population of the largest metropolitan areas declined by 7 percent from 1961 to 1974, while the rest of Britain experienced a 14 percent gain; and as in the United States, the core cities showed much greater rates of decline than did suburban areas.

Again, as in the United States, the leading edge of the drop in demand for labor in large metropolitan areas was the very sharp relative decline of manufacturing employment. The seven largest conurbations in Britain showed 1961-71 losses in manufacturing employment, ranging from 7 percent in Tyneside to 25 percent in Greater London. And in Greater London only about a fourth of the loss in manufacturing jobs was due to actual establishment relocations to sites outside of London. The major part of the loss was due simply to a much greater excess of firm closures over new firm establishments in Greater London, along with some shrinkage of employment in existing establishments.

Still another parallel with U.S. experience is that out-migration from major metropolitan areas was occurring over a longer period than was apparent, with the real extent of the shift not fully realized until after a sharp fall in the natural rate of increase of population, again stemming from a drastically falling birthrate. Though data are less readily available for continental countries, reasonably similar scenarios could be worked out for the Netherlands and Scandinavia, in particular, and for most of Northern Europe, in general. Except for some dramatic population losses in Paris, however, population decline has yet to impact on metropolitan areas in Southern Europe. In the discussion in Chapter 4, Hall and Metcalf attribute this to differences in preferences for very dense apartment living and simply to a lower stage of economic development.

For much of West Europe, however, almost the same story can be told for metropolitan development since 1960 as for the United States (and the story is more the same, than different, for Canada). But what makes this all the more interesting is that, while metropolitan leaders were trying to attract economic activities over that period in the United States, at least in Britain there were explicit policies aimed at deliberate attempts to relocate economic activities away, mainly from London, but from other major conurbations as well. Realized trends were much the same both where public policy, at least outwardly, was to resist the change as where public policy was to facilitate it. In Britain and the Netherlands, we should have expected less local incentive to stimulate population growth; local public services are much more directly a function of automatic national allocations, and much tighter land-use controls preclude speculative developmental profits at anything near the level possible in the United States. But despite these differences, the manifest experiences were very much the same as in the United States; this seems highly consistent with the view that the underlying economic and demographic forces are strong indeed. In fact, even in East Europe, where national control is still more powerful, much the same scenario also can be seen, though at a different stage in the developmental cycle.

Many contrasts can be cited between Poland and the United States, besides the obvious differences in their political systems. Poland entered the postwar period as a rural nation and despite very substantial urbanization remains over 40 percent rural today. For a period during the 1960s, there were explicit policies aimed at preventing in-migration and restricting growth into the larger Polish cities. But it turns out that in a very real sense they were suppressing the kind of urban buildup that had occurred in the United States in the 1950s. This led to a reversal of the growth restriction policies by the end of the 1960s, with more rapid growth in large metropolitan areas since then.

For the 1950-75 period as a whole, however, the growth rate of Polish cities of over 200,000 was less than the growth rate for smaller places. The more rapid growth of manufacturing in the smaller urban areas at the expense of the larger ones also can be observed, as can the masking of this trend until recent sharp declines in the birthrate. Finally, as stated in Chapter 5, "In long-range perspective it is possible to envision a slackening of growth rates ... within Poland's large metropolitan areas as an effect of demographic trends and an evolution of locational preferences." The same general scenario, again!

Thus, we conclude that *strong and widespread forces are working to disperse what we think of as metropolitan activity far beyond what we think of as metropolitan areas.* Later, we will suggest that this is neither necessarily bad nor good, nor is it inevitable or irreversible. At the same time, it reveals a contemporary metropolitan dynamic vastly different from that of the 1950s, and the danger of forming contemporary metropolitan development policy out of a 1950s understanding.

If the best is to be made of the newly emerging metropolis or even if wise decisions are to be made as to where we should try to reverse trends, and where accommodate to them (and how?), we must understand the dynamic of the new metropolis. In the next section, we look at what has happened to traditional functions and what may be the emerging functions both for the central city and for metropolis as a whole.

Economic Functions in the Mature Metropolis

Why it seems unrealistic to expect rises in manufacturing employment in the mature metropolis has already been discussed; in fact, in the aggregate, further declines are likely. This raises the obvious question of what kinds of economic activities will find a congenial location in the large metropolis. This question is addressed mainly in Chapters 6 and 7, and also in Chapter 13.

Much of the economic basis for the decline of metropolis translates into a necessarily conservative view as to its manufacturing prospects, at least in the near-term future. While this is the conclusion generally reached by the symposium, in a limited sense some manufacturing possibilities are realizable. As Macrae points out in Chapter 7, "one factory or warehouse in five within twenty miles of Marble Arch [the center of London] is now vacant; at some point this trend should produce some cost advantage." Also, the likely development of general-purpose jigs—what are loosely referred to as "industrial robots"—will brighten prospects for the kind of small-scale industrial establishment which historically was attracted to central-city locations. And, at least according to Macrae, "the degree of trade unionization will be less in new industries in the declining cities than it may become in the expanded outer areas."

Notwithstanding some positive aspects of the industrial future of the central city, most experts would look to the service sector as holding the greatest prospects for future growth or even viability of the central city and metropolis. It is certainly the case that services have shown most of the employment strength in the large metropolis during the past two decades; and within service, the major expansion has been in the so-called FIRE group (finance, insurance, and real estate) and in public services. There are reasons for expecting growth in those sectors to diminish in the future, but also reasons to expect them to grow.

Probably the most serious limitation on service expansion is the dependence of public service employment on local fiscal resources, which have dwindled even more rapidly than metropolis itself. Also, many of the expanding private service sectors are linked to the information industry, and as pointed out in Chapter 7, "Brain-workers can already more easily dispatch their work to their offices than dispatch themselves." If this is so, the age of telecommuting may be upon us and would still further warp the geographic correspondence between metropolitan activities and metropolitan areas. Finally, to the extent that it is the high-technology services which have bright prospects, the match between labor demand and the unskilled, often minority, labor available, at least in the inner city, may not be fortuitous. More will be said of that problem later.

According to Perloff, the real future of metropolis, and especially central cities, is intimately bound up in the prospects for "new" services. For example, if we look at the 1950-70 period, we see the emergence of whole new occupations; while the number of physicians grew by 31 percent, the increase in nurses and therapists was 125 percent and in health technologists and technicians, 238 percent. The most likely outlets for the emergence of new activities related to metropolis are those catering to (1) head office and knowledge technology activities, (2) recreation and tourism, (3) arts and cultural services, and (4) health, learning, and other personal services. However, realizing substantial growth in these activities will require not only a rethinking of the role of metropolis but, as indicated in Chapter 6, "the development of organizational capacity for encouraging the emergence and growth of those services which are particularly fitting to the central city in the postindustrial age." The organizational challenge may be as great as the technical one.

Physical Environment of the Mature Metropolis

In large metropolitan areas, the number of commuters from the suburbs to the central city has grown slowly in recent years, while the number commuting from the city out to the suburbs—though still smaller—has grown at a much more rapid rate. There has been a sharp rise in the number of workers with both home and work place in the suburbs, and a sharp drop in those with both home and work place in the central city. Overlying this pattern is a very rapid increase in the number of workers commuting from residences inside to working places outside the SMSA. These conclusions, as reported in Chapter 8, also strikingly underscore the blurring of the distinction between metropolitan area and metropolitan activity.

Anas and Moses (Chapter 8) see little likelihood of a continuation of historic metropolitan development patterns; that is, a creeping suburbanization with dispersal of population and employment in a regular and continuous fashion. They also see little likelihood of substantial reconcentration of population within mature areas, along existing or even new public transport rights-of-way. Rather, they see as most likely, "the development of truly multinucleated metropolitan areas in which there are a relatively few, large secondary employment centers . . . that draw a considerable portion of their labor from nearby areas in which population is dense." In essence, the kind of land-use pattern which seems to be emerging is quite consistent with the increased importance of information-based and other new services stressed in Chapter 6, and at least to some extent, with the kind of telecommuting world noted in Chapter 7.

The future metropolis is not likely to look too much like the conventional metropolis of yesterday, with a concentrated major core and steadily declining population and employment density out to some SMSA boundary. Rather, it is likely to consist of a loose federation of smaller and fairly compact residential-employment centers, with the system itself being very large—perhaps even a few hundred miles across—but with very few people engaged in any long-distance commuting on a regular basis, and with much, or most, of the land area still used for nonmetropolitan pursuits such as agriculture or mining.

The shape of metropolis also will be molded by changes in demography. For reasons cited earlier, the average size of household will surely decline so that even though the overall population of the mature metropolis is likely to fall, there will be a need for more housing units—but smaller units, more typically in multifamily dwellings. Some obvious economies are possible if these units are built at fairly high density. This, along with the desire for privacy and social distance pointed out in Chapter 3, with the possibility for work place dispersal and with a higher cost of fuel, again point to a future metropolis with a number of fairly dense nodes separated in space. This trend should be reinforced by an expected fall in the quality of the urban road network. As noted in Chapter 8, "The costs of road maintenance have risen dramatically ... and the funds needed for maintaining ... roads are simply not available. New York ... surely ... has less urban highway capacity ... lower in quality than it was ten years ago."

Paradoxically, the cost of personal travel may rise more rapidly than the cost of moving goods. Thus, the era of the major shopping center drawing customers from very large distances may have reached its peak, with future patterns calling for much more dispersed patterns, rather like neighborhood shopping of years back, though with inventories being kept and merchandise being distributed from more central depots.

It is the case that local environmental problems may emerge at a "neighborhood" level in the mature metropolis, with residences and work places more closely coordinated in space and commuting distances shorter. Also, we might be inclined to conclude that the mature metropolis may have more serious environmental problems, since the older metropolitan areas currently seem to have more degraded environments. In part, though, as pointed out in Chapter 9, "mature metropolitan areas tend to have relatively poor environmental quality because they tend to have relatively old capital equipment." In consequence, it seems that unless the government requires retrofitting (which currently they are not), environmental quality in mature metropolitan areas may continue to be somewhat lower in the large than in newer developing areas. But as Mills et al. indicate in Chapter 9, this is simply an inherited by-product of the characteristics of the mature metropolis, and there is nothing in current trends toward maturity, or toward the multinucleated settlement pattern, that would put any particular additional strain on the environment.

Governing the Mature Metropolis

As noted in Chapter 3, until sometime fairly recently in our history, it was the case that the city was where people came in search of better opportunities than those available in rural areas. And it was the government of the city that mostly took care of their needs for public services as well as figuring out how to tax them for the needed revenue. As more workers came to the city, the size of the settlement grew, but the city's boundaries were extended more or less along with settlement, so there was close correspondence between (1) the area enclosing the community of interrelated producers of manufactured goods and services, (2) the area of more-or-less continuous dense urban settlement, and (3) the relevant community for decisions about local public goods. Interest in reform, such as that of the muckrakers at the turn of the century, was related to bossism and corruption but not to spatial organization, as pointed out in Chapter 10.

Somewhere around World War I this situation changed, with central-city boundaries no longer following the path of urban settlement and, in the minds of a few social scientists, the issue of "too many" governments surfaced in the 1920s. By the 1950s, "balkanization" was seen as a national malady of serious proportion. But if the suburbs were too many and too small, at least for some purposes, the central city was seen as too big and too imperialistic, with too little opportunity for the preferences of particular neighborhood groups to be felt effectively. By the end of the 1960s, conventional wisdom was lined up pretty heavily in favor of a two-tier system of local government a la Toronto, with economic development, major transport, and other large system decisions made at a metro level, and decisions about particular public services such as parks and neighborhood streetlights made at a smaller scale.

The applicability of this two-tier model to the contemporary situation is an important issue. In a real sense, it may be that for the mature metropolis, the notion of regional government is an idea whose time has come and passed. It is not that the notion of regional decision making is any less appealing. It is rather that with metropolis moving to the countryside in a somewhat helter-skelter fashion, it may be that the only choice is between defining the region so narrowly that we miss many important spillover effects, or defining it so broadly that if we insist on a contiguous area definition, we would have something like a fourth or a third of a large state. Also, given the rate at which change is occurring and the political resistance to changing boundaries, it may be that presently existing cities and states are about as close as we could hope to come anyway. As Campbell notes in Chapter 10, "The fact is, there is no internally consistent theory which can be used to guide either the placement of governmental functions or the design of a system in which to place those functions."

This is not to deny the coordination advantages of regional government, and even its potential for achieving greater efficiency in the provision of public goods. In those metropolitan areas which are still growing, the establishment of regional government might actually provide some extra insurance against economic decline; though where the central city has begun to decline, the resistance of the suburbs to regional government might well be insurmountable. According to Campbell, "metropolitanization as a structural change will offer small relief for those areas where decline has spread from city to suburb."

As the pressure for regional government seems to have abated in the mature metropolis, experimentation with geographically decentralized government inside the central city is growing. Usually, this has been in response to a perceived lack of responsiveness of the central city to the felt needs of particular neighborhood groups. Also, as the central city becomes increasingly proletarian, one might expect the pressure for neighborhoodism to grow since, as stated in Chapter 11, "neighborhoods in lower-income and working-class residential areas appear to have more positive social interaction . . . than those in middle-income and upper-income residential areas."

But the "neighborhood," especially within the central city, forms a peculiar polity. On the one hand, migration rates of 35 to 50 percent a year are not uncommon in such areas, especially if they are heavily composed of renters. At the same time, even in highly transient neighborhoods, a significant portion of the population may be quite long-term residents. This presents the problem of either finding a basis for defining common interests by other than neighborhood geography, or developing techniques for insulating much of the neighborhood population from the tyranny of a small group of entrenched long-term residents.

Finding a viable neighborhood administrative structure inside central cities is important in achieving greater economic efficiency and more equity in the meeting of citizen needs. It is also important for another reason, incidental to the geography of metropolis but vital to its survival, namely, the physical decay of residential and commercial buildings which is a neighborhood phenomenon. As Lachman and Downs stress in Chapter 11, "we are passing the equilibrium point and are building excess housing in many metropolitan areas ... we have reached the point now where a large proportion of the cast-off units are in habitable structures in livable neighborhoods." Recent sharp rises in the cost of new housing have strengthened older near-suburb and inner-city neighborhoods. At the same time, the near-record levels of new suburban housing starts should lead us to a calculus of extreme caution. In the mature metropolis, it must be that the number of new family units and the replacement housing demand cannot consist of large numbers. This means that record construction of new housing inexorably must lead to eliminating some housing from the stock somewhere. Given the critical role of livability of neighborhoods *as perceived by their residents* in determining a neighborhood's viability, it does seem important that those responsible for attitude formation at a neighborhood level be part of the system for community decision in metropolis.

Economic Development in the Mature Metropolis

We have described the onset and nature of maturity in the large metropolis and the problems associated with the onset of maturity. Obviously, it would take little imagination to see that reestablishment of earlier growth trends could solve many of them. But the urging of a return to growth is simply another way of stating that maturity brings problems; stating the desirability of new growth does not tell us how to make it happen and, throughout this volume, substantial arguments will be developed to indicate that the reestablishment of past growth trends in the near-term future is not likely on a general, or widespread, basis.

Whatever particular opportunities for expansion might exist in particular places should be exploited. But exploiting these opportunities or, what is more likely, building the quality and profitability of personal, public, and corporate life without growth in numbers will require some combination of strategies resulting in increased output. Given the limited prospects for population expansion, this points to a need for increasing output per worker.

Greater output per capita could come about through increased capital formation in the private sector—essentially, expansion of the economic base of the metropolis; it could come about through improvements in the human capital resources of metropolis itself; it could come about through improved public services or simply an increased capacity to absorb labor by the local public sector. In the remainder of this chapter, we will briefly indicate development possibilities in these three dimension; more detailed discussion will be found in later chapters.

The Local Public Sector in the Mature Metropolis

Through the 1950s and even more into the 1960s, one of the fastest growing sectors in the American economy was local government. In fact, until recently, substantial increases in public service employment in the mature metropolis masked much of the underlying decline in industrial employment. Unfortunately, the prospects for continued expansion in public employment are weak indeed.

Much of the recent increase came as a result of massive increases in federal aid to state and local governments during the 1960s but, as pointed out in Chapter 12, "the increase in federal aid . . . will be far smaller over the next decade than . . . from 1956 to 1976." The budgetary leeway for major departures in federal programs will just be too limited in the near-term future. Also, at least under existing revenue systems, the mature metropolis will suffer disproportionately. At least two-thirds of state and local revenues are generated by taxes on material things, and the economic mix of the mature metropolis is turning progressively away from a focus on goods toward a focus on services. The one bright spot on the revenue side of the accounts is the rise in state aid to big cities. As further stated in Chapter 12, "If these cities are shortchanged today, the data do not reveal it."

But the gloomy forecast indicated above essentially rests on the notion that the system for providing local government revenues will not materially change. But might it not be the case that service needs and spending pressures will be so great as to force an expansion of the local government sector somehow, in some way? This is unlikely. First of all, the current population declines produce a tendency to think small, economically, on the part of the taxpayer. This tendency is reinforced by two additional developments.

First, the real costs of public services have skyrocketed due to increased personnel costs. Sharp rises in personnel costs probably were necessary as part of the process of attracting a rapidly increasing number of workers into the public sector during the 1960s. But as Netzer argues in Chapter 12, recent strong resistance to wage, pension, or other fringe benefit increases "is not a result of the sudden inclination to be mean-spirited on the part of elected officials," but rather a reaction to extreme fiscal pressure and, in part, only to be expected in a situation where the local public sector can easily afford to—indeed, must—shed some of its work force.

The other reason for abatement of the pressure to spend more money at the local level comes from disillusion with the ease of achieving the aims of the Great Society. Most sensible and humane people probably see as great a need for public policy to cope with urban poverty now as in the past, but at least in Netzer's view, "most sensible and humane people also are convinced that local and state governments do not have the financial capacity to finance . . . costly income redistributive public services, . . . and they lack the capacity to manage such programs."

Indeed, it seems likely that some of the redistributive functions will be absorbed by the federal government, but the discussion in Chapter 12 concludes, "it would be unwise to expect this kind of federal rescue at an early date." We are left, then, with the conclusion that the kind of fiscal debacle seen in New York is most unlikely to afflict other mature metropolises; but the very safeguards that seem sure to be employed against it, will prevent the local public sector from providing for any substantial growth in employment or service levels.

Business Investment in the Mature Metropolis

Increased business investment in any metropolitan economy depends on the profitability of increased output or the substitution of a superior technology in the basic activities of metropolis. Basic activities essentially are those in the specialization of which the rationale for the very existence of metropolis can be found.

Traditionally, the basic activities of metropolis have been thought of as being more or less the same as its manufacturing activities. Increasingly, however, metropolitan areas have shown specialization in the production of services which serve a national or large-scale regional market: such activities as research and development, central offices, large-scale record and information processing activities, and even metropolitan specializations in cultural, educational, and tourist facilities.

It is fortunate that basic activities have become less intimately identified with manufacturing, since the prospects for manufacturing in the mature metropolis are not at all bright. First of all, manufacturing employment is declining nationally so that even an area "holding its own" can expect some fall in employment. Moreover, as indicated earlier, the mature metropolis is experiencing ever-stiffer competition from smaller metropolitan areas. Obviously, there are particular exceptions to this. Both Anaheim and San Jose have larger than average fractions of their employment in manufacturing and have shown larger than average growth in total employment. But the fact remains that for most of the mature metropolises, manufacturing is not a bellwether sector. Traditionally, much of the manufacturing employment in the large metropolis has been close to the "new product end of the spectrum," leaning heavily on the ability of metropolis to serve as an incubator for innovation. This special advantage, too, is likely to be weakened by the geographic spread of the knowledge industries, the easier transmission of information, and the geographic homogenizing of culture and the labor force.

The prospects for nonmanufacturing basic sectors certainly are brighter than for manufacturing sectors, though some warnings must be given. In Chapter 6, Perloff sees not only some real opportunity for the mature metropolis but also the necessity for the metropolis to capitalize on newly emerging occupations for that promise to be realized; and in Chapter 7 we are warned of possibilities of even more substantial dispersion in the high-technology service industries than we have seen in the past in manufacturing. But in a sense, the "law of opposites" may apply to the mature metropolis, and according to Richardson in Chapter 13, "conditions in the large metropolitan areas may have to get worse before they can get better." And, Richardson goes on to say, "the site advantages of the big cities, the quality of their infrastructure, the adaptability and reliance of their populations, and their contribution to civilization are too valuable to be thrown away."

Human Resources in the Mature Metropolis

The implication of the latter quotation from Richardson is that ultimately, it is on the quality of its human resources that the future of the mature metropolis rests. If there is anything special about the human resources of the mature metropolis, it is the overrepresentation in its population of people whose training, experience, and apparent skill characteristics are badly matched to the needs of emerging metropolitan activities. Indeed, as metropolitan activities spread to the new "spaceless" metropolis of the countryside, they leave behind them in the old metropolis a residue of the economically disadvantaged who cannot compete effectively.

Especially in its central cities, but even in the SMSA as a whole, the mature metropolis has been characterized by growing proportions of minority and female-headed households. These particular groups are the most likely to be in poverty and to have low confidence in their prospective success. And low confidence leads to low motivation to achieve success: what Banfield has characterized as excessive "present orientedness."[4] Alexis points out in Chapter 14 that as recently as 1972 only 2.6 percent of the nation's businesses were black-owned and they accounted for only 1.7 percent of business receipts. This is especially unfortunate since, according to Alexis, "a viable black business community is important to the life of the central city not only because of the additional income that it might generate but because there are skills to be acquired which are difficult if not impossible to gain elsewhere."

At the same time that meaningful business experience is difficult to achieve for blacks, for the uneducated young, for the products of the female-headed household, the schools, "Unfortunately ... concentrate on preparing students for college and a life which they and the school know will not be theirs," as noted in Chapter 14. Surely we need to maintain or perhaps even improve conventional education (though let us remember that claims on local public resources will be harder to satisfy), but it seems that, along with Alexis, we should recognize "an essential goal of schools should be to provide a set of habits, skills, and attitudes which make it possible for young people to function in an adult world once their schooling is complete."

To some extent, the human resource mismatch problems of the mature metropolis will be self-equilibrating. As the more routine industrial and construction jobs which can use unskilled labor leave the mature metropolis, some of the less-skilled work force may follow, and at least those seeking such opportunity are less likely to come to the mature metropolis. So, too, will those seeking improved health and welfare services find the mature metropolis a less attractive destination than in the past, as support levels will be poorer than before or, depending upon the federal government's role, may increasingly be neither better nor worse than in smaller towns or even in rural areas. Also, as noted earlier, at some stage vacant land and vacant factories and warehouses can be sufficiently available in the central city as to foster a rebirth of activities with low labor skill requirements. But we should not be sanguine about how rapidly this self-adjustment might occur, or about the human losses and forsaken business opportunities that will be missed in the meantime. More effectively linking the human resources of the mature metropolis to its developmental opportunities without waiting for metropolis to "hit bottom" means that we will have to seek more imaginative ways of utilizing human beings, and more effective techniques for giving the disadvantaged what they need to compete. And we must do this within the fiscal limits of the mature metropolis. Such a reconsideration of the management of human resources in the mature metropolis would stand high on its agenda for concern, which will be discussed in Chapter 15.

Notes

1. Editors of Fortune, *Exploding Metropolis,* New York: Fortune Magazine, 1958.

2. See Jean Gottman, *Megalopolis,* New York: Twentieth Century Fund, 1961.

3. W. Gorham and N. Glazer, eds., *The Urban Predicament,* Washington, D.C.: Urban Institute, 1976.

4. E. Banfield, *The Unheavenly City Revisited,* Boston: Little, Brown, 1974.

**Part II
Origins of Maturity**

2

The Current Halt in the Metropolitan Phenomenon

William Alonso

The 1970s have already seen a number of startling societal changes. There have been, of course, the energy crisis and the changed awareness it symbolizes of man's relation to the material environment. Within American society itself, profound and rapid changes have been manifested in the role of women as people and as workers, the modes by which individuals organize themselves into families and households, the frequency with which they change these arrangements, and in a lowered rate of reproduction. In our human geography, for the first time we see a net migration out of metropolitan areas to more rural ones and, indeed, for the first time an absolute decline in population in a great many metropolitan areas, especially among the largest. These changes are not unrelated. This chapter will focus on the changes in the human geography, but also will try to signal a few of the connections to other changes.

Metropolitan Growth and Policy Debate in the 1960s; Changes in the 1970s

Up through the late 1960s, the national pattern of growth of metropolitan areas seemed clear and well established. The major metropolitan areas were all growing in population at about the nation's pace, give or take a few percent, carried by the momentum of their intricate economies. Some of the medium-sized metropolitan areas, especially in the West and Southwest, were growing faster and beginning to take their place as national, rather than merely regional, urban centers. The smaller metropolitan areas, having economies that were not only smaller but also more specialized in particular activities, showed a much greater variety of growth rates; some were growing very fast indeed and some losing population according to their economic fortunes. Meanwhile, nonmetropolitan areas continued to send their young to the metropolises as they had for the two centuries since the industrial revolution. The South, that special region, continued to send its youth, both white and black, to the North and increasingly to the West.

In this context, the federal government instituted some programs in the U.S. departments of agriculture and commerce to promote development in the lagging rural areas and in small nonmetropolitan cities. Many observers, moreover, were concerned not only with the decline of these rural areas but also with the population explosion in the nation and its crowding into urban areas, as indicated in Chapter 1. Influential individuals, organizations, and government officials from the president down worried about such overconcentration ("human anthills" was a common epithet) and called for national policies of population dispersion. The U.S. Department of Housing and Urban Development established a program to assist the developers of new towns. To these views, many students of urbanization replied that the existing trends were firmly rooted in demographic, economic, and technological realities, and that trying to stop the trend was akin to King Canute's commanding a stop to the swelling ocean tide.

Those who favored decentralization policies replied that by the end of the century there would be an additional 100 million Americans, and asked, Where shall they live? They pointed to well-established policies of population decentralization in the major European countries as possible models for our own. The others replied that the European experience illustrated their point, because after more than two decades of effort neither France nor Britain had made much of a decentralization dent. Further, those politically to the right viewed the establishment of such a policy as another incursion by government into personal freedom, while those politically to the left viewed it as a form of escapism to avoid facing the cruel difficulties of the problems of the cities, most notably those of poverty and race.

And so it went. There were some national commissions and White House conferences which addressed these subjects, some bills of great sweep introduced in Congress, and, as has been mentioned, some legislative action and operational programs instituted both under Republican and Democratic administrations. But no great departures were made, whether or not they would have been wise. The country became preoccupied with the Vietnam war, with Watergate, and with the economic difficulties of stagflation and resource crises. A national urbanization policy seemed far less urgent, and it was put on a backburner, perhaps even taken off the stove.

Meanwhile, the past few years have witnessed some startling changes in the trends in this country's territorial development. What some had viewed as inevitable, and others as a dreadful fate which called for vigorous action if it was to be avoided, now seems a very doubtful outcome. These changes are the subject of this chapter, as they affect the patterns of growth and decline among metropolitan areas and between metropolitan and nonmetropolitan portions of the country.

The changes are many and become fascinating in their richness as one enters into details, but some of the broad outlines may be suggested. Metropolitan population has slowed its growth, and for the first time a great many metropolitan areas, including many of the largest, are experiencing a decline in population. This applies to entire metropolitan areas, not just to their central cities. Most of the vigorous population growth is taking place in the Sunbelt, and many areas of chronic distress and population loss have turned around and are growing faster than the nation in both respects. Most startling, rural to urban migration has reversed, and the balance of migration now goes from metropolitan to nonmetropolitan areas. One may even note that, whereas in the past, population was shifting out of the center of the country and concentrating within fifty miles of the ocean shores, since 1970 even this trend has reversed, and the interior of the country is growing faster than its marine periphery.[1]

These changes result from a variety of causes, many of which are not yet understood. Moreover, as will become clear upon examination, some of these are not changes at all but continuations of long-standing trends which were not sufficiently recognized, such as basic demographic changes, changes in the location and sectoral composition of economic activity, the rise in the importance of transfer payments, and changes in life-styles.

The Nature of Metropolitan Decline

Before proceeding to discuss the details of metropolitan decline, some definitional cautions are necessary. Of necessity we perceive complex societal events through the lens of statistical data gathered according to certain conventions and definitions. Therefore, we often err when we assign a commonsense interpretation to these numbers. When we say that a metropolitan area has X number of people, the image leaps to the mind that all of these are urban, and that they live in the central city or in the suburbs; but this is not the case.

The principal data we will use are gathered by SMSAs (standard metropolitan statistical areas), which are essentially defined as a central city of no less than 50,000 population and its surrounding counties if they meet certain criteria of continuity of urbanized development and commuting patterns. The other principal classification of data is by "nonmetropolitan areas," which are merely the areas which are not included in SMSAs.

While, in general, we will equate SMSAs with urban areas, or metropolises, and nonmetropolitan with rural districts and small towns, the realities encompassed in these definitions are not so simple. For instance, on the whole, only one-tenth of the land within SMSA boundaries is urbanized and the rest, rural. About one-third of the nation's rural population lives within SMSA boundaries, and they produce an even larger share of agricultural production. On the other hand, within the nonmetropolitan areas about two-fifths of the population is urban and nearly one-fifth of the country's urban population lives in nonmetropolitan areas. Finally, the image of rural people as agricultural is misleading. Only 4 percent of the nation's labor force is engaged in agriculture, forestry, or fishing; while as of 1970, 26 percent of the population was rural, indicating that about 85 percent of the rural population earned its living in pursuits other than agriculture, such as running shops and gas stations, working in factories, and teaching in schools and universities.

For convenience we will often use terms such as "metropolitan" or "large urban area" for SMSA, and "rural" for nonmetropolitan, exercising due care to make clear where other meanings or definitions are involved. But the reader should keep in mind the nature of the underlying statistical bases.

Metropolitan Population Decline

It had been rare in the past for metropolitan areas to decline in population. Some of the small ones sometimes have, as a result of local economic adversity, but large urban areas have tended to grow from their own momentum, based on larger, more diversified, more adaptable, and more innovative economies. If one economic sector suffered a reverse, another was likely to be growing in compensation.[2] Indeed, a common pattern for areas such as Boston and New York was to specialize in innovation in electronics, fashion apparel, professional services, and the like. When these new activities matured, they tended to move to other areas, while the metropolis developed new activities. Such metropolises, while always losing industries to others, based much of their economic vitality on this seedbed function.[3] Hence, all of the large metropolitan areas tended to grow at rates that did not differ markedly from the nation's. Only Pittsburgh among the large urban areas lost population in the 1960s, and it is notable for being a metropolis specialized in traditional industry.

In recent years, however, the number of metropolitan areas which are losing population has increased markedly, as pointed out in Chapter 1. One-third of the nation's metropolitan population now lives in areas which experienced population decline in the 1970-74 period. Overall, one-sixth of all metropolitan areas lost population from 1970 to 1974; in the last year of that period the proportion increased to over one-fourth, so that the trend is accelerating.[4]

Our history has conditioned us to take metropolitan population increase for granted, but by now, in terms of the number of people exposed, metropolitan population decline is as common as growth. The consequences of this novel condition are hard to anticipate, both because it has been a rare one in the past and because it was not foreseen and so little thought has been devoted to it. Neither formal theories of academics nor practical rules for action of worldly men are at hand to deal with it. Both theorists and doers have assumed until now that the arrow of time always pointed to increasing numbers. While population growth will still be the common case in terms of numbers of areas until the turn of the century, more and more people and metropolises will find the arrow pointing the other way.

Many have associated the phenomenon of metropolitan population slowdown or decline with the unexpected reversal of rural to urban migratory flows which has occurred since 1970. While this reversal, on which more will be said later, is both startling and important, it should not be thought the sole, or even the major, reason for the decline in metropolitan population growth; there are two other more important reasons. One, the most powerful, is the decline in the national rate of population growth. The other is the continuing flow of people from one metropolitan area to another, which redistributes population among metropolitan areas to the gain of some and the loss of others.

Decline in Birthrate

The principal reason for the decline in metropolitan population growth is simple: the rate of natural increase has plummeted. It is still positive on the whole, but a great many metropolitan areas now have yearly rates of natural increase of only one or two-tenths of 1 percent. Three metropolitan areas actually had fewer births than deaths. Two of these (Sarasota and Tampa-St. Petersburg) are in Florida and are in fact growing briskly through immigration. But many of these migrants are old, and have few babies and high mortality. The third is more typical of what will become more common; it is an area called Northeast Pennsylvania, and encompasses Scranton and Wilkes-Barre-Hazelton. Here persistent out-migration has reduced the number of fertile young people and left behind an aged population. Ironically, some of the economic changes described later have resulted in a small net immigration in the past few years, so that this area has grown a bit in population.[5]

When very small rates of natural increase, to say nothing of decline, are coupled with continuing differential exchanges among metropolises, it is a mathematical certainty that many of the metropolitan areas will experience population losses, even in the absence of the reversal of rural to urban migration.

The decline in the natural increase of the U.S. population has begun to be noticed by the public and termed the "baby bust" by contrast to the "baby boom" which followed World War II; but the magnitude of this decline has not sunk in. The crude birthrate now stands below fifteen yearly babies per thousand population, a historic low. By comparison, the birthrate at the top of the baby boom in the later 1950s was over twenty-five per thousand. Thus, taking account of deaths, the natural increase in the U.S. population, which had reached 1.6 percent per year, stands now at less than 0.6 percent.

This drop in the crude birthrate is dramatic in itself, but a further look suggests that the intrinsic change is even greater. The crude birthrate is a measure of the current rate of reproduction, but it can mislead as to long-term trends, because there can be temporary increases in the numbers of potential mothers, as is the case now as a result of the maturing of the children of the baby boom.

Let us look at the total fertility rate. It is the lifetime number of children per woman which would be expected if women continued to have children at current rates for particular ages. A rate of 2.1 children per woman would replace the population exactly in the long run. The fertility rate was as high as 3.7 in the late 1950s, but now stands under 1.8, well below replacement levels.

Further, it seems plausible that 1.8 may be an overestimate of the actual number of children per woman which will be borne by today's young women during the course of their lives. The manner of computing this rate attributes in the future, rates of childbearing to today's young women, which are based on today's rates for older women. But younger women today are remaining unmarried in larger numbers, and the intentions of those who are married as to how many total children they intend to bear show a strong decline. It is reasonable, therefore, to expect that total births will continue to decline in the coming years since there will be fewer women in prime childbearing ages and they appear to want fewer children.[6]

In short, given a slight decrease in the death rate and a sharp decrease in the birthrate, the rate of natural increase is only slightly above one-third of what it was in the late 1950s, and bids fair to continue to decline. As the benchmark of natural increase comes closer to zero, metropolitan areas as a whole will grow more slowly, and the influence of forces which differentiate among them will ensure that negative population growth will be commonplace.

In other words, the experience of continued population growth in the past was based on a vigorous rate of natural increase and on a steady stream of rural to urban migrants. By the 1960s, however, the migration rate into metropolitan areas was small, and three-fourths of metropolitan population growth was based on natural increase, and only one-ninth on migration from nonmetropolitan areas, the balance resulting from immigration from abroad. Now the decline in the rate of natural increase has cut the growth rate sharply, and this has been accented by the reversal of net migration into nonmetropolitan areas. Further, now that population growth for all metropolitan areas is so small, the migratory streams along metropolitan areas add up to a zero-sum game, driving many areas into the category of population losers.

Migration into, out of, and among Metropolitan Areas

Out-migration from metropolitan areas was already a common experience in the 1960s, when nearly 40 percent of SMSAs had more people leaving than arriving. The percent of metro areas with net out-migration rose to 44 percent by 1974, as did the overall rate of out-migration. But whereas the high rates of natural increase in the 1960s masked such out-migration, the current low ones reveal it as a receding tide bares the rocks along a shore.

Where do the people who leave metropolitan areas go? Many would have it that they are going back to rural America, and this is partially true. But there are rich and complex crosscurrents of people of different kinds doing different things, and the resulting pattern is a complicated one. Some of what is happening may be gleaned from Figure 2-1, which shows the broad outlines of population movements in the United States in the period from March 1975 to March 1976.

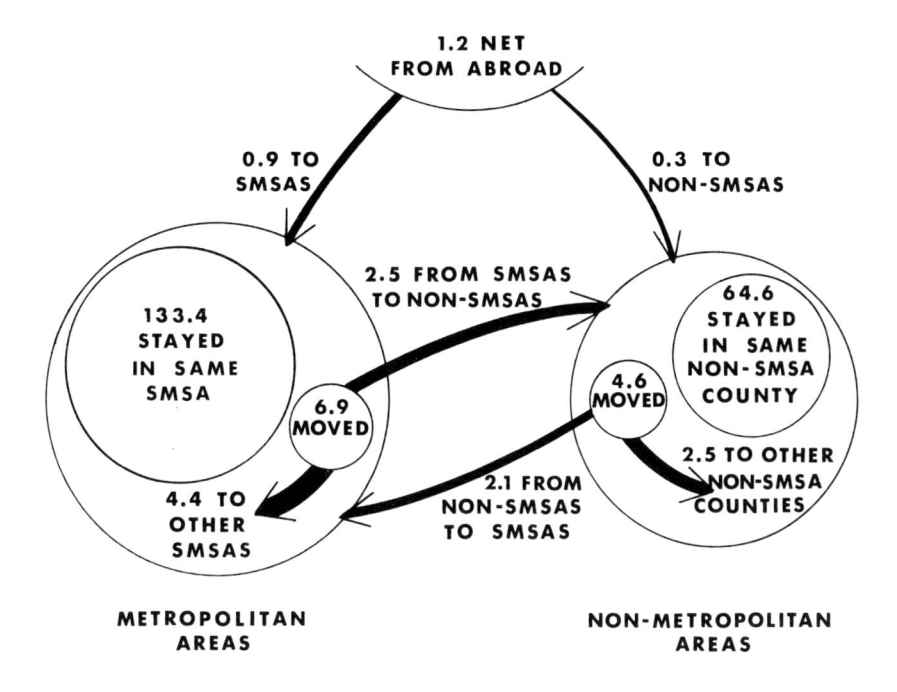

Source: Computed and adapted from U.S. Bureau of the Census, *Current Population Reports*, Series P-20, No. 305, "Geographical Mobility: March 1975 to March 1976," Washington: Government Printing Office, 1977.

Figure 2-1. Population Movements in the United States, March 1975 to 1976 (Numbers in the Millions).

Note that 2,477,000 people left metropolitan areas for nonmetropolitan destinations, and that 2,081,000 went in the other direction, for a net balance of 396,000 in the year in favor of nonmetropolitan areas. But note that total departures from metropolitan areas amounted to 6,877,000, of which 4,400,000 (64 percent) went to other metropolitan areas. By comparison, out of 4,619,000 departures from nonmetropolitan counties, 2,538,000 (55 percent) go to other nonmetropolitan areas.

Thus, taking account of the respective metropolitan and nonmetropolitan populations, in that year 1.8 percent of the metropolitan population moved to nonmetropolitan areas while 3 percent of the nonmetropolitan population moved into metropolitan areas. Simply put, the chances that a nonmetropolitan person will move to a metropolitan area are 1.7 times higher than they are for the reverse move. On the whole, then, the rate of metropolitanization of population is higher than that of demetropolitanization, but the absolute magnitudes of their bases result in a larger absolute flow out of metropolitan areas. It is thus a matter of viewpoint as to which way people are moving: in absolute terms they are moving out of metropolitan areas; in terms of life's chances they are still moving in.

Migration out of Metropolitan Areas

Yet the very fact that there is net out-migration from metropolitan to nonmetropolitan areas is so surprisingly contrary to two centuries of experience here and in Europe, that it has mobilized a great deal of recent research and even found its way repeatedly into the popular press. Some hold that a new millenium has arrived, a profound change in consciousness among millions of Americans who, tired of the pressures, pollution, and crime of the cities, alienated by the corruption of our institutions, and imbued with a new land ethic, leave the metropolis for rural areas in search of a simpler, saner, healthier life.

Undoubtedly some of this is going on. One reads accounts by editors, writers, and other intellectual toilers of the pains and pleasures of their new lives on Vermont farms. One also reads accounts of communitarian agricultural experiments consisting mostly of young people; but two points must be made. First, there is no evidence that such moves amount to anything in particular, either as a gross outflow from urban areas or more particularly as a net flow once the stream of returnees is taken into account. The other point is, to my mind, more important. This is that there is absolutely nothing new in some Americans, with spiritual or intellectual inquietudes, removing themselves to rural areas for awhile or for life. The list of intellectuals who have done so stretches from Thoreau to Edmund Wilson, from Jack London to E.B. White, to stay within the literary vein. Similarly, ideological or religious community experiments are one of the dominant themes of American history from Roger Williams through Shakers, Mormons, Transcendentalists, Fourrierists, and a splendid variety of other creeds. Thus, such returns to the land, whether by individuals or by groups, are as American as apple pie and a continuation of our traditions. They are not an explanation of the reversal.

The explanation for the reversal seems to lie in the coincidence of several distinct effects, which include the geographic extension of the functional field of urban areas beyond the officially defined SMSA, shifts in the location of manufacturing industry, the continued expansion of the recreation and resource industries, the greater numbers of retired people, and the recent recession. It is not clear, however, how much each of these contributes in diverse nonmetropolitan areas.

To some degree, the growth of nonmetropolitan areas is a continuation of the extension of the functional geographic range of urban areas. The eighteenth and nineteenth century cities were extremely compact, based principally on pedestrian ranges of movement. With improvements in transportation, principally the private automobile, the effective range of movement was vastly expanded, giving rise to massive suburbanization and to the metropolitan phenomenon. But especially since World War II, it is not only commuters who have moved to the suburbs, but shops and industry; manufacturing led the way, and now the service sectors are busily suburbanizing. In consequence, only about a fifth of suburbanites now commute to central cities, and the preponderant majority lives and works in the suburbs. The metropolitan phenomenon, then, consists not only of the diffusion of workers' homes but of the formation of strong suburban nuclei for services and employment. Thus, it is possible, and does happen, that people live beyond the suburbs of a metropolitan area (i.e., in a nonmetropolitan area) and commute to the suburbs of the nearest SMSA. Indeed, employment and services, by the same linked processes, can also move beyond these boundaries. These expanding urban fields exceed the boundaries of the SMSA, but are functionally part of the same urban system.

Current estimates indicate that over 60 percent of metropolitan to nonmetropolitan migrants move into counties immediately adjacent to SMSAs. The 1970 census classified nonmetropolitan counties by the percent of their work force which commuted to a metropolitan area. The data show a consistent pattern: counties in which over 20 percent of the work force commuted to metropolitan areas in 1970 had a yearly net immigration since 1970 of 1.5 percent; counties with 10 to 20 percent of commuters had a rate of 0.8 percent; those with 3 to 10 percent had a rate of 0.7 percent; and those with less than 3 percent commuters had an immigration rate of 0.5 percent.[7] It is clear that the expansion of urban fields, washing over earlier censual metropolitan definitions, is a large part of the apparent reversal. To a degree, what is happening is not so much that people are leaving the city for the country as that the city itself is moving to the country. It is worth recalling Louis Wirth's aphorism that "urbanism is a way of life."[8]

This expansion of urban fields is, in a way, the strong tail of a movement from greater to lesser concentrations. Out-migration and population decline are more prevalent among the larger metropolitan areas, while as a group those with populations under three-quarters of a million are still growing substantially, with a net in-migration. The expansion into the nonmetropolitan periphery appears as another form of this general process of population and economic diffusion.

But this is not the entire explanation. Counties well beyond any metropolitan field are, for the first time in memory, experiencing net in-migration. This is true for every region of the country with the exception of the old tobacco and cotton belt extending from the North Carolina Cape to the delta of the Mississippi River.

One principal reason has been the continuing shift of manufacturing production out of metropolitan areas to small cities and rural areas, which is discussed in more detail in Chapter 13. For instance, from 1969 to 1973 personal income in durable manufacturing increased by 46 percent in nonmetropolitan areas in comparison to a 25 percent increase in metropolitan areas; comparable figures for nondurable manufacturing are 33 and 24 percent.[9] This follows a long-standing process whereby production manufacturing has been moving from large to small areas: down the hierarchy of sizes of metropolitan areas and into nonmetropolitan areas. Neither has this process stopped here; this flow of manufacturing production from center to periphery has extended beyond the national borders to the northern Mexican cities, to Taiwan and Korea, and to other countries of low labor costs, as will be referred to again in Chapter 7.

The greatest durable manufacturing increases in nonmetropolitan counties have been in transportation equipment, notably in recreational vehicles, mobile homes, and automobiles. The electrical machinery industry has grown rapidly, and labor-intensive electronics plants continue to move to non-SMSAs in search of low-wage, primarily female, labor in the face of foreign competition. Capital-intensive and engineering-intensive electronics plants have remained in metropolitan areas. In nondurable manufacturing, nonmetropolitan areas have experienced large gains in apparel, rubber and plastics, and leather products. These, too, are labor-intensive industries that locate according to the availability of low-wage, unskilled, and semiskilled labor.

Nonmetropolitan areas outgained metropolitan areas in almost every category of source of income, especially in goods-producing industries; that is, manufacturing, mining, and contract construction. Also, as a consequence of their new economic and demographic vigor, finance, insurance, and real estate (FIRE) are growing very rapidly in these areas.

Recreation also has flourished in nonmetropolitan areas, often in association with an influx of retired people who not only enjoy some of these facilities but often supplement their retirement income by running them. The increased importance of transfer payments, especially to the aged, has made them more footloose. Whether on Social Security or on private pensions, a growing number of older people are increasingly able to move, since their income is not tied to their location; from 1970 to 1975 nearly half a million left metropolitan areas.[10] Some pulled up stakes and went to retirement communities in the Sunbelt, others returned to places where their roots were, so that some of this migration is, in effect, the echo four decades later of earlier rural to urban migrations.

No up-to-date information appears to be available on the expansion of non-SMSA employment linked to resource development and environmental preservation, but it is substantial. This includes coal mining and oil exploration, associated construction and services, water development, land reclamation, construction of atomic facilities and other energy-related activities, sewage treatment facilities, and others. Much of this activity is distinct from other bases for the rebirth of population in rural areas, because it lasts at high levels only for the period of construction, involves to a large degree a population for whom moving from place to place is a way of life, and in the end it leaves the local area. Although it may move on to another nonmetro district, it results in cycles of local boom and bust, with the attendant hardships for the original and remaining population.

Another cause for rural population rebirth appears to be the current recession. If times are hard, many earlier migrants to metropolitan areas go back home, where it is easier to manage and where friends and relatives can help. There is anecdotal evidence that this is happening, and it is suggestive that the only other period when there was something like a reversal of migratory flows was during the Great Depression, but no figures are available to determine its importance. Although the economic cycle may be playing a part, it must be remembered that the reversal began by 1970, when economic times were good.

Finally, just to be clear about it, one thing that is *not* happening is a rediscovery of the joys of working the land and a new ethic leading the young to agriculture. From 1970 to 1976 the farm population declined by 1.4 million or 14 percent, much of the drop taking place in 1975-76.[11]

It must be remembered that national trends are manifested quite differently in different places. A particular area in the South may be seeing labor-intensive industry moving into town, absorbing some of the workers released from agriculture. In another, some whites and blacks who had moved North may be returning, some because they are now retired and find the living cheaper and more congenial where they grew up, and some because the social and economic progress of the South now makes it an acceptable alternative for them. In another area, possibly in the Great Plains, coal mining may have brought boom conditions to a tiny town, with workers moving in, living in trailers, and bringing with them shopkeepers and entrepreneurs of diverse sorts. In yet other areas, the basis of growth may be a new water-based resort, a think tank, an expanded state university campus, a defense installation, or an environmental project. And, of course, a fair number of nonmetropolitan counties are still declining.

The available statistics on the characteristics of the migrants support the picture outlined as to the economic bases for the revival of nonmetropolitan population growth. Those moving from the metropolises to rural areas are younger, better educated, and more skilled on the average than present residents of those areas. But they are older, less educated, and less occupationally skilled than those leaving the rural areas for the metropolis. Thus, though 100 people arrive in nonmetro areas for every 84 who leave, it appears that the nonmetro areas still are losing a bit, qualitatively, sending somewhat better educated and occupationally qualified youth to the metropolitan areas than they are receiving.

Finally, as in most American social phenomena, race must be taken into account. Although for the first time there are important return flows among blacks, on the whole their main direction is still toward metropolitan areas; for every 100 blacks who left metropolitan areas, 142 entered them.

Migration among Metropolitan Areas

As has been noted, migration *among* metropolitan areas is an important factor in their differential growth. Returning to Figure 2-1, note that the number of moves among metropolitan areas was only a shade lower than the number of moves between metropolitan and nonmetropolitan areas. These flows involve a great many moves among pairs of SMSAs, with some coming and some going. The net effect on differential growth, therefore, for the year 1975-76 is far less than the total 4,400,000 intermetropolitan moves. Direct data are not available, but, based on past experience, the contribution to differential metropolitan growth would be in the order of 350,000 to 400,000 net migrations. This figure is comparable to the net loss of 396,000 migrants from metropolitan to nonmetropolitan areas in that year.

It is well known that the SMSAs that are the principal gainers in these exchanges are in the South and West. Of the thirteen SMSAs growing fastest in percentage terms from 1970 to 1974, seven were in Florida, and two each in Colorado, Arizona, and Texas.

Some important differences may be noted within the Sunbelt. Thus, Florida and the metropolitan areas west of Arkansas are growing primarily from migration from the nation as a whole, while metropolitan areas of the South are growing in part from national migration (some substantial portion of it being return migration of Southerners), but also in large part from migration from within their region. One may say that the growth of Southern metropolitan areas, especially in the Southeast, is the result of the urbanization attendant to the return of that region to national parity, while the growth of the areas closer to or in the Southwest is the result of interregional shifts.

No simple generalizations can be made as to the economic bases of the growth of the so-called Sunbelt metropolises. It probably is true that many Americans want a better climate and a new way of life, but except for those who are retired or of independent means this is not enough. Jobs and businesses are needed. And, indeed, for the enjoyment of the climate, so is air-conditioning often needed; and it is becoming expensive.

Some of the economic bases for the observed migration shifts are apparent. Retirement living based on transfer payments is part of the base in Florida, together with the influx and dynamism of the Cuban refugee population. Oil and gas, both as an industry and as a form of Ricardian wealth, is part of the story in Texas. Military establishments and procurements are an important component in California and in Washington. The regional center function is important to certain metropolises of the South which are situated in regions of rapid economic growth, just as the decline of these functions accounts for the decline in growth of some of the metropolises in California's Central Valley and parts of Texas.

Some shifts are visible within the geographic growth patterns of the Sunbelt.

The Pacific coast still has fast-growing areas, such as San Diego and San Jose, but its overall growth has been blunted to a degree, with the Los Angeles and San Francisco SMSAs estimated to have lost population in 1973-74 and Seattle having had a very small increase. The Mountain States are growing rapidly, and so are areas in Appalachia and the Ozarks which had been economic backwaters.

While no comprehensive analysis of the sectoral components of the growth of the Sunbelt is now available, it appears that the growth of its metropolises is broadly based on manufacturing services, growing in part because of competitive shifts from economic activities based in older areas and in part from specialization in economic activities which are themselves rapidly growing.[1,2]

One may guess, but it is only a guess, that the preference for the climate and the life-style among people is complemented by the attraction of amenities to increasingly footloose industries. Try, for instance, asking the young woman who answers for an airline, hotel, or car rental company on an area code 800 number, where she is located. From the point of view of the economics of communications costs, she could be anywhere, but in fact she is likely to be in some Southern or Western city such as Denver.

Thus, in a very general way, part of the Sunbelt phenomenon rests on the shift to the "service," "postindustrial," or "information" economy, which is explored in Chapters 6 and 7. The extraordinary advances in the transmission of information together with the standardization and routinization of the handling of information, which render it subject to economies of scale and the use of semiskilled labor, make it possible to locate an increasing number of economic activities where they are wanted, rather than where they are forced to be. It must be noted, on the other hand, that Sunbelt metropolises are more than holding their own on manufacturing employment by comparison to older urban centers.

Is it then a coincidence of factors for Florida, the South, the Mountain and Pacific States that creates the phenomenon of the Sunbelt? This seems unlikely, and it is probable that some few underlying social and economic tendencies are at the root. They may be as simple as the preference for climate and life-style, aided by technology and sectoral evolution. But there is more to it, though no grand synthesis is at hand.

In a sense, it appears that what is going on is a very long-run equilibration of the national distribution of urban centers, still trying to rectify the original mistake made by the first British settlers when they landed on the upper-right-hand corner of our nation's map. It is worth noting, for instance, that the growth of many of today's Sunbelt centers is not a recent phenomenon at all, but one that goes back at least to the turn of the century or earlier. It was not particularly noticed until now, because the high rates of natural increase everywhere masked this differential growth based on intermetropolitan migration.

Immigration from Abroad

Figure 2-1 shows immigration from abroad of 1,148,000 for the year 1975-76. This must be compared to a reported net civilian immigration of 450,000 in 1975, a year when this figure was swollen by Vietnamese refugees. The difference may be accounted for by returning servicemen, businessmen, and others; and some comparable number may have left our shores to take up temporary or permanent residence abroad. The census publications are singularly silent on the interpretation of this figure, yet it is not trivial since it amounts to more than the sum of the net metropolitan to nonmetropolitan migration and the net intermetropolitan exchange.

Immigration from abroad is the X-rated statistic in American population figures, primarily because it is terribly important and because no one knows much about it; as a statistical as well as a policy issue, it is avoided like a hot potato. It is unlikely that the number shown in Figure 2-1 is accurate; the true number almost certainly is higher. It appears that there is a very great deal of illegal immigration into this country, both permanent and seasonal, but it is quite unlikely that such illegal migrants would have been captured in the sample in the first place or would have replied truthfully if asked.

Various estimates place the number of illegal residents in the United States in the order of 5 to 10 million, and some go higher. Estimates in New York City alone have placed the number of illegal aliens living there at between 0.5 and 2 million. The whole matter of estimation in this case is a mare's nest of special interests, which include the politics of ethnic groups, the interests of labor and of those who hire illegal aliens at cheap wages, and the vital issues of revenue sharing and other modes of distributions of money based on population estimates.

Obviously, if these estimates are anywhere near the truth, the population decline of New York is exaggerated and the population growth of the Southwest is understated. The magnitude of the numbers involved is comparable to that of the natural increase of the population. Therefore, if anything like the number of illegal migrants estimated is a reality, some important aspects of the redistribution of the country's population must be reconsidered. We cannot here resolve these uncertainties, or make up for their studious neglect. They remain a blind spot which is certain to result in errors and inconsistencies in data, in wrong diagnoses for policy, and in political equivocation over figures for dollars.

Metropolitan Population Decline: Its Sources and Meaning

We have said, above, that there are three principal sources of metropolitan population decline. The first two affect the overall rate of population growth of metropolitan areas. The larger of these effects is the decline in the birthrate, and the other is the reversal of direction in the net flow of metropolitan to nonmetropolitan migration. The third force, somewhat smaller than the others, is that of differential growth from intermetropolitan migration, which redistributes metropolitan population in a zero-sum game of losers and winners.

The importance of the decline in the birthrate is not merely statistical. It has not declined by chance, but rather as part of an interconnected set of social developments. These include the sociology and psychology of the redefined sexual roles; the increase in labor force participation of women (which raise the direct and opportunity costs of giving birth to and rearing a child); the social and personal acceptance of the mutability of family and household relationships which is manifested in more people living alone, or in various combinations of single individuals; in a soaring divorce rate and the rising number of single-parent households; and in dozens of other ways which we all experience, some subtle and some brutally forceful. These demographic changes are in turn associated with rising levels of education, with the expansion of the service sector of the economy (which employs more women), with changes in technology which range from contraception to computers and communication satellites, and, in brief, with the ongoing evolution of modern society.

Once one grasps that the experience of metropolitan decline is linked mostly to the decline in the birthrate, and that this is not a matter of fashion or random fluctuation but one of structured relations to other societal changes, then the phenomenon of decline takes on another meaning, distinct from that of the 1950s and 1960s, when it only took place through major out-migrations resulting from severe economic distress.[13] Population stability and decline are now part and parcel of our social change; while they may not immutably be so forever, they are likely to be with us for some while.

For instance, population decline may be consistent with increasing numbers of workers, because more women are working. It is consistent with a lower dependency ratio, both because there are more workers and because there are fewer children, though there may be more older people. It may mean more money per person for the population at large and for particular people. For instance, a man who supports a wife and three children on a $25,000 a year salary results in a household with income of $5000 per capita. On the other hand, two adults living together on salaries of $11,000 and $9000, respectively, result in a household with income of $10,000 per capita. Population decline may be consistent with lowered public expenditures for schools and urban infrastructure, though it must be admitted that institutional pressures thus far have resulted in greater per capita costs for declining areas. It may mean an easier housing market, more room and more freedom, less pressure for development, and more chances to adapt; I know of no reason why less cannot be more for urban areas.

Of course, old industrial plants and established bureaucracies can result in fiscal pressures, and this seems to be what is happening to declining urban areas, so that they are today in greater fiscal difficulties than newer ones; but these may be shrinking pains. Consider, for instance, that crime, which is mostly committed by the young, is bound to go down with the proportion of those who tend to commit it. Indeed, a characteristic of metropolitan areas which lost[14] population during the 1960s was their lower crime rate.

Consider in particular the relation of population decline to the housing market. At first it might appear that the inevitable consequence of decline would be a softer market, and a sharp decline in construction. While it is obvious that, all other things being equal, a declining population will demand less housing than a growing one, this perspective is altered by the fact that the decline results from social changes of which the drop in the birthrate is only one manifestation. Another result is the sharp drop in average household size from 3.3 persons in 1960 to 3.1 persons in 1970 and 2.9 persons in 1976, so that a stable population would have grown by 8 percent in the number of households just from 1970 to 1976.

The decline of household size results in part from there being fewer children in homes, but in large part it results from more adults establishing their own households. This includes more young people leaving home, more people remaining single, and more older people and divorced people maintaining their own households. All of these are manifestations of the same social transformation. In turn, smaller households result in a higher consumption of housing space per person. Even one-person and two-person households need a bathroom, a kitchen, corridor space, and so forth, and household space increases less than in proportion to the number of people in the household.

The increasing number of households and the increased space used per capita more than compensate for current rates of population decline and maintain the demand for housing. Of course, there are other effects from these changes, but this is not the place to discuss them.[15]

To reemphasize the general point being made, it is not as if the current halt in the growth of metropolitan population were occurring by happenstance in the social and economic context of a decade or two ago. The decline is a manifestation of the changes in the social and economic context, and its significance and consequences can only be assayed properly when this context is taken into account. Otherwise, there will be misdiagnoses from the application of stereotypes and pernicious remedies will be attempted. As mentioned at the beginning of this chapter, there has been precious little thought or experience with the phenomenon of population decline, and we need to get smart fast, because it is upon us.

Nonmetropolitan Growth: How Permanent Is the Reversal?

Is the rebirth of nonmetropolitan America an episode, a temporary quirk, or is it here to stay? If the observations in this chapter are accurate, it is likely to continue, if for no other reason than the continued extension of the urban fields of SMSAs beyond their defined boundaries. This diffusion of the functioning urban areas is the natural continuation of the spread from the nineteenth-century central city, fostered by improvements in transportation and communications.

Other factors present a mixed picture. The number of retired people is certain to increase and should continue to contribute to the strength of nonmetro areas. Moreover, if there is a nationalization of welfare, as seems likely, this important form of transfer payments might make it still easier for its recipients to choose nonmetropolitan locations.

The exurban movement of labor-intensive manufacturing may go somewhat further, but it may have crested as to its rate of increase. The number of production workers in manufacturing has increased only slightly since the late 1940s, and the metropolitan areas have already lost much of what they had to lose in this respect. It seems likely that, barring continued economic hardship, recreation will keep growing as an industry. It is hard to judge whether there will be increases in nonmetropolitan employment arising from mining, energy, environmental and resource improvements, and the associated construction; it seems possible, but not likely, to be large, given the capital intensity of these activities. Employment in agriculture is virtually certain to continue to decline.

As we come out of the recession, some of the return migration associated with hard times will reverse again, and some more young residents of nonmetropolitan areas will try their fortune in metropolitan areas. Several of the factors noted above may be modified by the manner of our adaptation to the energy stringency. The expansion of the urban field is based in part on the cost and ease of moving people and goods; the recreation industry is in part based on the facility of travel, whether by car or by plane. And, overall, consumption of gasoline for road use is very substantially higher on a per capita basis in rural areas, most probably because of the large distances involved in travel to work, shopping, and services, and because many of the vehicles need the capacity to carry goods as well as people. Insofar as the energy crisis has effects such as a substantial increase in the price of gasoline, it would disadvantage continued metropolitan growth, both through price effects which would lead to concentration in an effort to minimize distances and through an income effect because the use of gasoline is so large that price increases would in fact reduce income available for other purposes in nonmetropolitan areas, and increase the effective difference in income in favor of metropolitan areas.

In the balance, it seems that for the next decade statistics for SMSA and non-SMSA areas will show a pattern not unlike that seen now. Whether this is interpreted as a rebirth of rural America or as the diffusion of urban areas over the countryside is a matter of degree and opinion, but the remaining chapters in this book will tilt strongly to the latter view.

Notes

1. U.S. Bureau of the Census, Statistical Abstract, Washington: Government Printing Office, 1976.
2. Wilbur Thompson, *A Preface to Urban Economics,* Baltimore: Johns Hopkins Press, 1965.
3. E.M. Hoover and R. Vernon, *Anatomy of Metropolis,* Cambridge, Mass.: Harvard University Press, 1960.
4. Computed from U.S. Bureau of the Census, Series P-25, No. 618, "Estimates of the Population of Metropolitan Areas, 1973 and 1974, and Components of Change since 1970," Washington: Government Printing Office, 1976.
5. U.S. Bureau of the Census, "Estimates of the Population."
6. These matters are discussed in greater detail in William Alonso, "The Population Factor and Urban Structure," Working Paper No. 02, Center for Population Studies, Harvard University, 1977.
7. The following section relies primarily on the data of Calvin Beale, "The Revival of Population Growth in Non-metropolitan America," ERS 605, Economic Research Service, U.S. Department of Agriculture, 1975; and "A Further Look at Nonmetropolitan Population Growth since 1970," *American Journal of Agricultural Economics,* December 1976; Brian Berry and Donald Dahman, *Population Redistribution in the United States in the 1970's,* National Academy of Sciences, Washington, D.C., 1977; Peter Morrison with Judith Wheeler, "Rural Renaissance in America: The Revival of Population Growth in Remote Areas," *Population Bulletin,* vol. 31, No. 3, Population Reference Bureau, Inc., Washington, D.C., 1976; James Zuiches and David Brown, "The Changing Character of the Nonmetropolitan Population, 1950-75," in Thomas Ford, ed., *Rural Society in the United States—Current Trends,* Ames, Iowa: Iowa State University Press, forthcoming (cited in Morrison, above).
8. Louis Wirth, *Community Life and Social Policy,* Chicago: University of Chicago Press, 1956.
9. Data from Bureau of Economic Analysis, U.S. Department of Commerce, "Metropolitan and Nonmetropolitan Non-farm Personal Income: Growth Patterns, 1969-73," *Survey of Current Business,* December 1976.
10. U.S. Bureau of the Census, Series P-20, No. 285, "Mobility of the Population of the United States, March 1970 to March 1975," Washington: Government Printing Office, 1975.
11. U.S. Bureau of the Census and U.S. Department of Agriculture figures, cited in the *New York Times,* April 15, 1977.
12. Zuiches and Brown, "Changing Character of Nonmetropolitan Population."
13. William Alonso, "Spontaneous Growth Centers in Twentieth Century American Urbanization" (with Elliott Medrich), *Growth Centers in Regional Economic Development* (Niles M. Hansen, ed.), New York: Free Press, 1972.

14. Edgar Rust, *No Growth: Impact on Metropolitan Areas,* Lexington, Mass.: Lexington Books, 1975.

15. Alonso, "Population Factor."

3 Social Processes and Social Policy in the Stable Metropolis

James S. Coleman

Over a hundred years ago, when the population of Chicago was about 30,000, a student of American cities wrote,

The proportion between the rural and town population of a country is an important fact in its interior economy and condition. It determines, in a great degree, its capacity for manufactures, the extent of its commerce and the amount of its wealth. The growth of cities commonly marks the progress of intelligence and the arts, measures the sum of social enjoyment, and always implies excessive mental activity, which is sometimes healthy and useful, sometimes distempered and pernicious.... Whatever may be the good or evil tendencies of populous cities, they are the result to which all countries that are at once fertile, free and intelligent, inevitably tend.[1]

The words, "Whatever may be the good or evil tendencies of populous cities, they are the result to which all countries that are at once fertile, free and intelligent, inevitably tend" convey a sense of an inexorable movement.

If all this was true in 1870, why is it no longer true a hundred years later? Between 1970 and 1975 the central cities of U.S. metropolitan areas lost 1,404,000 persons *per year* through net out-migration.[2] If we get some sense of the assumptions implicit in the quotation above, and why they no longer hold, we can at one time obtain a broader perspective on the present condition of cities and a beginning insight into what changes in conditions or in policy might be beneficial to them.

First, however, these words from a hundred years ago should give us pause in considering the present condition of cities, for the very fact that the tendency toward increasing urbanization, once seen as inevitable, has turned out not to be so should lead to some caution about pronouncing current trends in the other direction as similarly inevitable.

If we examine with some care the ideas once held about universal increasing urbanization, we can see that what lay behind it was an assumption that the division of the population between cities and noncities was a division between industry and agriculture. A certain fraction of the labor force was necessary in the production of food, in agriculture. If that fraction was high, as it has been throughout history until the past century, and is still in some areas of the world, a large fraction of the population must live on the land, and only a small fraction is available to live in urban centers and engage in pursuits other than those of producing food from the land. As technological developments took place in food production, allowing the same amount of food to be produced with less labor, labor was automatically freed for other pursuits.

The implicit assumption that lay behind the thesis of inevitably increasing urbanization, with a final stable state realized only when almost the whole population lived in cities, was an assumption that pursuits other than food production and extractive industries must necessarily be carried out in urban centers, or at least are optimally carried out in such centers. Further, the assumption was implicitly made that if those pursuits were carried out there, the persons engaged in such activities must live there.

In recent years, however, both these assumptions have proved no longer to hold, as emphasized by Anas and Moses in Chapter 8. In addition to agriculture and other extractive activities, many pursuits that are industrial or postindustrial are no longer carried out in cities. Industrial plants are now often located outside major metropolitan areas, and expanding nonindustrial activities such as higher education are often located outside metropolitan areas as well.

The second assumption, that persons must live near their work, is equally invalid today. There has come to be a rupture of the connection between place of work and place of residence, so that even if the assumption remained true, even if all occupational pursuits other than agriculture and extractive occupations took place in cities, the cities would not contain all the people engaged in those pursuits. This rupture is sufficiently great that industrial plants which once would have created cities around them by their very existence no longer do so. Their work force remains largely distributed in surrounding rural areas, not as farmers but as a "rural nonfarm" population, with neither the amenities nor the problems of an urban existence.

The failure of these once-held assumptions to be met indicates that it is not correct to conceive of a single unilateral force pushing in either a centralizing or decentralizing direction, with only a matter of time separating the present state from either complete urbanization or complete demetropolitanization. It is instead necessary to think of the relations between cities, suburban areas, and nonurban areas as involving a balance of forces, with some forces acting toward greater locational centralization, some forces toward nucleation on the fringes (suburban development), and some forces toward full decentralization of location. As the balance among these forces changes, there will be net movement into or out of the cities, and into or out of metropolitan areas. If the forces themselves were immutable, and subject to change only by forces outside man's control, our task would be confined to that of observing and accommodating to these forces. But this is not the case. It is true, of course, that forces of centralization and decentralization change in part as a result of technological developments, which are not easily predicted and which have unintended consequences, and in part as a result of demographic changes, which are not easily subject to societal control. But they also change in part as a result of changes in the relation between demand and supply in certain markets, which can push people into nonurban areas or pull them into urban areas.

Examples of the inadequacy of the simple notion of unidirectional and immutable forces can easily be found. It is commonly believed that despite wishful thinking to the contrary, there is an inexorable move of middle classes (first whites, then blacks) out of central cities, and an accompanying inexorable decrease in the socioeconomic level of persons living in the cities. Now while this is true for most American cities, it is not true for all, and in particular it is not true for Washington, D.C. Areas in the central city which were once lower class and black are now middle class and more white than black. Southeast Washington developed this way with the aid of new housing, though one cannot say "because of" new housing, for comparable new housing in other cities has not had a comparable effect. In contrast, the East Capitol area has undergone such a transition without any change in the housing stock whatsoever.

What happened in these and other areas of Washington was simply a change in relative demand from two segments of the population and, as a result, a net exodus of middle classes changed to a net in-migration of middle classes. This example is not introduced to suggest that this kind of change can be brought about elsewhere, or to add to the fanciful wishful thinking that sometimes characterizes urban planning, but only to illustrate that the net flow of people in one direction or the other is a result of a number of forces in both directions, and slight changes in these forces can sometimes change the direction of the net flow. Here we emphasize the precariousness of this balance in a particular situation, much as Alonso emphasized it in general in Chapter 2.

It will be useful, in gaining a sense of the forces which have affected the growth of urban areas, to examine factors affecting the location of two elements: economic activity and residence. For it is the location of economic activity and of residence that taken together affect the growth or decline of urban areas. This will involve repeating some elementary points in the economics of location, but repeating them here will be helpful for what follows.

Location of Economic Activity

Most primary economic activities—activities of agriculture, lumbering, mining, and fishing—constitute a large fraction of the economic activities of primitive and premodern societies. They constitute a small fraction of the economic activities of modern societies.

Most of these primary industries have their location fixed, and tied to the land by nature. And, in general, the geographic distribution of these activities is dispersed. Except for relatively small concentrations, such as mining towns and fishing villages, the location of these activities does not lead to geographic concentration in urban areas. The strongest argument against the historical thesis that Moses and 20,000 Israelites camped for some time on a plain near Mount Sinai in the desert is that the area could not provide the food to support such a concentration. Similarly, few areas, desert or not, can support a concentrated population so long as agricultural technology is so primitive that a large proportion of the labor force must be engaged in growing food. Today there are some large and increasing urban agglomerations in relatively primitive economies (e.g., Cairo will have over 15 million inhabitants by 1985), but these have been produced by two disturbances introduced from developing countries: improved health conditions, leading to greatly reduced infant and adult mortality; and imports of food which have kept large numbers of economically dependent persons alive. If these were wholly isolated economies (i.e., they could not import food in return for raw material or credit), the urban agglomerations could not exist.

As economies came to consist increasingly of secondary economic activities, that is to say manufacturing industry, the location of economic activity became very different. First of all, it was increasingly disconnected from the land, so that urban agglomerations had the opportunity to form, as they did not have the opportunity in economies consisting of primary industry. Second, the interdependence of these industries means that there are great economies of proximity. These economies came about for two principal reasons: transportation and communication. Particularly in heavy industry, but in the manufacture of goods generally, transportation costs between interdependent industrial sectors can be large, and are reduced by proximity. Thus, all sorts of metal fabricating plants sprout up near a steel mill, and all sorts of consumer product plants sprout up near the metal fabricating plants.

The economies of proximity for interdependent industries due to communication are important as well. Specifications for materials, sales negotiations, and all of the detailed communication necessary for economic transactions are more rapidly accomplished at less cost with fewer errors at close proximity. Small-parts suppliers for automobile manufacturers have crowded close to their customers in the Detroit area to facilitate communications and sales. Such concentrations are sometimes found even within small areas of a city to allow quick and easy face-to-face contact. The book and job shop printing industry in the United States has traditionally been located in the East 40s of Manhattan, with printers, stereotypers, engravers, and presses all located in close proximity. But the most extreme example is the stock market, which consists solely of paper transactions with no physical flows, and is located within a small section of lower Manhattan.[a]

These factors were increasingly important as the manufacturing sectors of industry grew. But several developments have taken place to make them less

---

[a]It is likely that the economies of proximity in the stock market are due not directly to communication ease, but to its facilitation of trust, which is of central importance for investment banking.

important. First is the development of the economy into increasingly long chains of production. As the process of production gets increasingly long, with increasing amounts of labor costs embedded in the materials, transportation costs become a diminishing fraction of the total cost of materials, so that proximity to materials sources becomes of lesser importance. The cost of materials used in the manufacture of computer memories, for example, is sufficiently high per pound that proximity to sources of supply does not significantly lower costs and thus offer a competitive advantage.

Second, mature manufacturing processes no longer require the proximity and centralization necessary in their period of development. The huge stockyards and meat-packing industry of Chicago that were once necessary have been replaced by smaller slaughtering, processing, and freezing units near the feedlots in Iowa and Kansas. A mature and technologically stabilized automobile industry is able to have more dispersed manufacturing and assembly plants than in its formative period. Government agencies that require massive keypunching of individual records have this done not in Washington but in rural Appalachia, where workers are less expensive, harder working, and more concentrated. The electronics industry, which in its early days utilized the proximity that the high density of New York City provided no longer required that proximity as it matured, and moved, first to New Jersey, then throughout the country, especially to California, and even to Taiwan and Korea. The conclusions of a study of the economy of New York City are relevant to this point: that New York's economic survival depends upon spawning new industries and new techniques, which require for their initiation the ready proximity of the various intellectual and technical ingredients necessary to such innovation, but that once the infant industry is born, the high labor and other costs of the city make it noncompetitive.[3] To a lesser extent, the same may be said of all large cities; and as the major manufacturing processes mature, they are decentralized or moved out of large urban areas, because the benefits of proximity no longer outweigh labor and other costs.

A third change, interacting with the second, has added to the forces that decentralize economic activities. This is the revolution in communications. Modern long-distance communications, at reduced cost relative to other goods and services, lessen the importance of proximity. Typesetting for books that would have been done until recently in New York is now sent to Europe where labor costs are lower. Western Union, which once had its principal transmission staffs in major cities, now maintains only minimal delivery staffs there, with its principal staffs located in a few rural places, where they are reachable by WATS lines. Long-distance telephone, TWX lines, and document transmission equipment allow decentralization, with plants located in rural areas or small towns that would never have been economically efficient in the absence of present communication technology.

One of the consequences of the freedom of location allowed by transportation and communications technology is an increasing functional specialization of localities. The classical independent town that was functionally diverse has come to be replaced by localities which specialize in one or another activity. Residential suburbs are functionally very specific, covering only housing, education, religion, and sometimes a few other activities, but not economic production. Other suburbs as well as towns outside urban areas complement this with industrial concentration. Still other communities are functionally specialized as resort communities, with nothing but a service industry, on the seashore or in the mountains, or throughout whole states, like Vermont or New Hampshire, which have become states of second homes and vacationers.

In the presence of functional specialization, central cities are something of an anachronism, for they retain much of the economic completeness which characterizes an independent economy. Nevertheless, certain economic activities have left the cities while others have not, so that there has come to be by default some degree of functional specialization of the central city. An examination of the economic profile of cities of different size shows that large cities specialize in governmental activities, services, finance, and wholesale (not retail) trade. They contain manufacturing as well, but in continually decreasing amounts, as manufacturing plants leave the city, and even the metropolitan area.

This functional specialization of localities is part of a change in the organization of society that has been taking place since the end of the Middle Ages, and with special rapidity in the past century: a change away from the total institutions, groups, and communities into which persons are born and in which they live all their lives, and toward voluntary associations which cover only a segment of their lives and only for a limited period of time. It is a change of which the modern city, with its anonymity, its impermanence of association, and its freedom of choice and action was a first manifestation; but it is a change which has moved beyond the functionally complete city as transportation developments have made local specialization possible on a wide scale.

It is still the case that the anonymity and the freedom of choice of the central city are compatible with this continuing secular trend away from encompassing total institutions; but the functional completeness of the central city is not. An obvious implication of this is that the central city has a strong continuing compatibility with the secular trend—but not in its traditional role as a functionally complete locality. This means, of course, that the search for a role for the mature city in the future is not automatically destined for failure, but also that its potential for success is not to be found in the pattern of the past, as discussed by Perloff in Chapter 6.

But all this moves us into the area of location decisions of persons and households and away from the location decisions of industrial units, and so it is to these questions of residential location that we now turn.

Location of Residence

I wrote the first draft of this chapter in view of the walled city of Old Jerusalem. From the time of David's City, over 3000 years ago, until the latter part of the last century, to live within its walls offered so many benefits that houses were piled on top of each other inside, while outside were naked hills. A hundred years ago, Moses Montefiore from England offered each Jew of Jerusalem a pound sterling to live outside the walls, yet many could not bear to remain outside and ran to return to the protection of the walls and the safety of numbers within. This centripetal force, which has operated for all population groups in Jerusalem, has been mostly for protection, but also for the amenities provided by the city's institutions and facilities. The centripetal force of other cities has come from a variety of causes, but largely, since the industrial revolution began, because there was work in the city. It was always and everywhere the same: persons either remained on the land, if doing so was necessary in order to eke out a living, or left for the city, if there was sufficient work there. No alternative existed, and as the nonagricultural jobs increased in number, the urban population did as well.

The move to the city that took place for most families in Western society during the period 1850-1950 was such a move—a move to find work or to find better work. Before the age of affluence, man's location was largely fixed by economic necessity, and his movements were channeled by the goal of economic betterment. Thus economic necessity first dictated a dispersed attachment to the land for most persons, and then with the industrial revolution a concentrated clustering around the large factories and related enterprises of the city. There were other determinants of location as well, such as the protection already discussed, and for smaller numbers of persons, the possibility of a style of life at once freer, more individualistic, and proximate to cultural activities and social events. But the central motive was an economic one.

Residential movement was thus seen as unidirectional, beginning as dispersed on the land, and slowly agglomerating into large clusters of persons and industries, that is, cities. Residential movement in subsequent years has become much more complex. There are a number of patterns and sequences, and it is useful to spell them out. One point characterizes them all, however: as economic necessity becomes less imperative, location of residence is increasingly shaped by other motives. It may become in the extreme highly volatile and subject to minor events, such as the socialite who decides to leave Paris for Antibes because the climate suits her cat's asthma. But even at some distance from this extreme, a whole variety of considerations begin to enter, which have been necessarily suppressed in the name of economic survival: living space indoors and outdoors, climate, children's education, safety, proximity of friends, and many others.

The Sequence of Increasing Affluence

One major sequence which has characterized many families can be described as the sequence of increasing affluence. It consists of these stages: farm to central city, central city to outskirts, outskirts to suburb, suburb to exurb. The first of these steps, toward the center, is dictated by economic necessity, or at least the aim of economic betterment; the remaining moves, away from the center, often entail no change of job, and are not to improve one's occupation but one's conditions of residence. What has made these steps of the sequence possible is a breaking of the connection between work place and residence, a break that is brought about primarily by modern transportation. H.G. Wells, in 1901, when most persons thought the continual growth of cities was inevitable, wrote:

It will be convenient to make the issue part of a more general proposition, namely, that *the general distribution of population in a country must always be directly dependent on transport facilities.*

We have heard so much of the "problem of our great cities" . . . the belief in the inevitableness of yet denser and more multitudinous agglomerations in the future is so widely diffused, that at first sight it will be thought that no other motive than a wish to startle can dictate the proposition that not only will many of these railway-begotten "giant cities" reach their maximum in the commencing century, but that in all probability they . . . are destined to such a process of dissection and diffusion as to amount almost to obliteration, so far, at least, as the blot on the map goes, within a measurable further space of years.[4]

The Life-cycle Sequence

A second sequence is coming to characterize the life cycle of the nuclear family. This is, first, a move to an apartment in the central city after the end of education until about the time the first child arrives. Next is a move out toward the edge of the city, or the suburbs, in a small house; then a move to a larger house further out; and finally, after the children have left, a move back into an apartment in the central city.[5] The result is that the central city contains a higher proportion of young singles and newly marrieds, and a higher proportion of older persons, than do the remaining residential areas.

This sequence of moves suggests the dual forces of high population density: the attraction of proximity to others, and the attraction of distance from others. The first outweighs the second for the young and the old, and the second outweighs the first for adults with families. It is not coincidental that it is those population groups without primary family ties, the young who have left home and the old who have broken up their home, for whom the attraction of proximity to others, and thus the city, is strongest. In the absence of intimate family relations, the importance of relations outside the family increases.

There are, of course, variations upon this life-cycle pattern; it is far from universal. Some of those variations have particular implications for cities, however, and some suggest barriers to city residence. One variation, which appears at first curious, is the initial move not to a city apartment but to an apartment in the outer suburbs, where a number of new apartment buildings have recently come to be occupied by singles and couples. The failure of the central city to attract its "natural" childless residents suggests that in recent years, the city's natural attractions for this age group have been partly overridden by opposing forces. A similar inference follows from the alternative movement of many older couples or persons, not into the city but into a community constructed solely for their age group.

The Diurnal Cycle

Another pattern of movement is that which occurs daily, from residence to work and back. This movement is directly dependent on transportation technology and cost. The journey that once was limited by trolley-car tracks now can easily extend beyond the suburbs into the countryside. The automobile has made it possible, at some transportation cost, to separate the decision about where to work from the decision about where to live. This separation has led to suburbs that are wholly residential, to economic homogeneity of suburbs, and to increased social and ethnic segregation. The interest in escaping the city is evident by the increasing social-class gradient with distance from the city center; those with greatest economic resources, and thus the greatest freedom to live where they like, live furthest out. There are exceptions, indicating that under certain conditions the central city is attractive for those who have the freedom to choose, but the general gradient nevertheless exists. Such a gradient did not always exist, and does not exist now in some countries. But it does exist in almost all metro areas in the United States.

Race is a second measure of freedom to live where one likes, since residential discrimination is the strongest remaining area of discrimination in American life; and the racial gradient with distance from the city center is even greater than the income gradient, indicating again that those with greatest freedom of choice (in this case, whites) live furthest out from the center.[b]

Communications Change and Its Impact on Residential Choice

One of the less recognized changes in the elements that determine residential choice is communications. If we ask the question, what differentiates the quality

---

[b]Even in an Eastern European city like Warsaw, where the gradient has not until recently existed, it has now begun to come into existence with the advent of family automobiles, as those with higher incomes begin to move outside the city. See discussion by Korcelli in Chapter 5.

of life in rural areas from that in urban areas, there is one major communications change in recent years that affects the answer: because of television, and to a lesser extent other communications media such as the telephone and even the CB radio, the rural resident gains much more of the benefits of proximity to others than he once did. Entertainment and leisure pursuits which once required physical presence at movie theaters, football, baseball, and other sporting events, now require only a television set in the living room.

The cultural isolation that once characterized life outside metropolitan areas no longer does so, as an increasingly large fraction of cultural life is not dependent on physical gatherings, but can be experienced as easily by someone outside a metropolitan area as by a person in its center. The cultural attraction of the city and of population density is reduced as cultural activities, entertainment, and the sense of full participation in the culture can be obtained without proximity to others. In short, the revolution in communications technology has meant that the nonmetropolitan resident is no longer isolated from the cultural center of society as he once was. For persons in their late teens and twenties, entertainment and leisure depend more on physical proximity to others, and thus on population density. For them, the disabilities of nonmetropolitan life loom larger. But for young children and for older adults, those disabilities have come to be sharply reduced.

Violent Crime, and the Costs of Proximity

The complement to the change which allows persons to participate in culture from their living room is another which has increasingly confined them to their living rooms. The increase in violent crime, which has been most spectacular in central cities, less so in suburban areas, and still less outside metropolitan areas, has left many persons in cities afraid to leave their homes at night. The difference between large cities and small towns is exemplified by the difference in robbery rates in 1973: 756 per 100,000 in cities over a million in population, and only 61 per 100,000 in cities between 10,000 and 25,000 in size.[6] Thus, the big-city rate is over twelve times that of cities under 25,000 in size. In national surveys, a surprisingly large proportion of city residents report being afraid to go out of their houses after dark. Such a fear, coupled with the presence of television entertainment within the house, completes the destruction of differential cultural opportunities for urban and nonmetropolitan dwellers.

If the urbanite feels a prisoner in his house, then he is excluded by danger from those activities from which the nonmetropolitan resident is excluded by distance. Indeed, the much lower crime outside the city may allow the nonmetropolitan resident *greater* participation in cultural life and entertainment outside the home than the city resident. The logic of the ancient walled city is reversed. If the modern city had walls, persons would flee to the outside for protection, rather than scurrying inside.

The Demand for Proximity

It is useful to conceptualize these centripetal and centrifugal tendencies on the part of persons, and changes in them, in economic terms. We can conceive of proximity to others as containing certain desired goods such as social interaction and the availability of various institutional amenities, and thus of a demand for proximity, which is different for different persons (particularly for different age groups), and also differs as the goods that proximity brings differs. But also we can conceive of distance as containing other desired goods, such as space, privacy, and safety, and thus of a demand for distance. Depending on its demand for the goods brought by proximity and distance, respectively, there will be for any household a net demand either for distance or proximity.

There are several essential points about this net demand for distance or proximity. One is that it can be in different directions for persons who differ in the utility that different goods brought by proximity and distance have for them. Second, the directionality and strength can vary over time, as proximity and distance bring with them differing amounts of their respective goods. For example, the remarks about television bringing cultural life into the living room imply that proximity to others brings far less of that good than it once did. And the remarks about violent crime in the cities imply that distance from others brings a greater amount of safety than it did before that level of crime in the cities existed.

Third, in each stratum of the housing market, there is a particular distance from the city center which minimizes cost, depending upon the housing stock available, transportation costs, and costs of various other amenities. This statement is based on the idea that persons first of all place themselves on a certain social stratum, depending upon income, associations, and aspirations, and then examine housing which they regard as appropriate for that stratum.

Those who have a net demand for proximity are willing to pay more to live closer to the center than the minimum-cost point for their stratum. Those who have a net demand for distance from others are willing to pay more to live farther from the center. Thus, even though it is less expensive for upper middle classes to live some distance from the center than in central-city apartments, some will live in such apartments because they are willing to pay for the proximity such living brings. And even though it is less expensive for low-income persons to live in inexpensive housing near the city center, some who have a net demand for distance will pay to live farther out. For most persons, it appears likely that there is a net demand for distance, and thus they live farther from the center than the minimum-cost point. The major question then becomes, what is the price elasticity of the demand for distance? The importance of this question lies in the fact that the price of distancing oneself from others and from one's work place is steadily increasing, as the cost of energy to transport increases. The redistribution of residential location, and the consequent impact on metropolitan areas, will depend on that price elasticity. If it is very high, increased energy costs will bring people closer to their places of work, and altogether into more compact metropolitan areas than before. If not, there will be little impact of increasing energy costs upon the shape of metropolitan areas.[c]

The income gradient of households moving from the center outward indicates that income elasticity of demand for distance is high: as incomes increase, persons spend increasing fractions of their income in distancing themselves from others. The great post-World War II suburbanization of cities as incomes increased reflects this relationship.

Policies Affecting Development of Urban Areas

To this point, this chapter has developed a conception of both economic enterprises and households locating themselves as a result of a balance between forces that lead to proximity and agglomeration and forces that lead to distance and dispersal. Furthermore, though the balance of forces is affected by costs of distance and costs of proximity, even if these costs were very different there would remain forces pushing in both direction. That is to say, proximity contains certain elements which persons desire and hold as valuable, and distance contains certain elements which persons desire and hold as valuable. It is not the case that nothing but economic constraints keep people from spreading out all over the countryside. Increasing affluence does not necessarily lead to increasing dispersal.

The implications of this for social policy are strong. Because social policy can greatly affect the goods associated with proximity and the goods associated with distance, it can affect the demand for proximity and for distance, and thus the future of metropolitan areas. If, for example, social policy acts in such a way as to make freedom from danger of violent crime more dependent on distance from others, distance becomes more valuable, and dispersal will increase. If, on the other hand, social policy reduces crime in high-density areas or creates powerfully attractive amenities, especially for singles and retired persons, proximity becomes more valuable for some, and metropolitan areas will become denser and more compact. Consequently, despite the very great effect of changes in communication and transportation on the shape of urban areas, social policies can affect that shape as well.

In exactly the same way that H.G. Wells argued that unending movement toward the city was not inevitable, we can point out that unending movement away is not inevitable either. Just as the continued growth of cities was not inevitable, their continued decline is not inevitable. There is a fatalism in the face of technological and demographic change which overlooks the effect of social policy on the demand for proximity and the demand for distance. The question then arises, if governmental policy can, without undue difficulty,

---
[c]The importance of energy-cost changes is analyzed in Chapter 8.

vitalize cities and metropolitan areas that are declining in population and economic purpose, why does it fail to do so? The answer to this question is straightforward: we simply do not, as a collective body, wish to vitalize the cities. If we did, we would do so.

Policy Choices and a Scale of Social Values

When I say that we do not wish to vitalize the cities, I mean quite simply that we desire other things more. We enact policies which aim to accomplish other goals, but which have as an additional effect an increase in the value of distance from others, or a decrease in the value of proximity. I will give a number of examples, and will dwell at some length on one, where the data are exceptionally good.

One classic example of a policy which has, over a long period of time after World War II, acted to increase the value of distance from others, and thus movement from city to suburbs, is federal home mortgage loan policy. Federal policy, through two loan guarantee programs, FHA and GI, made the purchase of a new home very easy by lower-interest rates and lower down payment. This facilitated purchase of suburban housing, since most new construction was in the suburbs. The programs, however, did not equally facilitate purchase of an existing older house—and such houses were mostly in the city.

The benefits to the construction industry of such a differential were great, for it encouraged new home construction. In effect, it provided an economic subsidy to persons to move out from the central city and, thus, a subsidy which aided the deterioration of the central city, and was one of the factors ultimately leading to housing abandonment in the central city as that housing stock became increasingly poorly maintained and no longer economic. Housing abandonments in Chicago, for example, were 2800 in 1976, and demolition of abandoned buildings increased from 143 in 1960 to 2446 in 1976.[7] And Chicago is not the city hardest hit by abandonments.

If we ask the question, how can neighborhoods be maintained, housing in the central city kept in repair, and the exodus of families from the city reduced, the answer is often a despairing one. But the despair is misplaced. Policies already exist, and they provide incentives *not* to maintain the neighborhood, *not* to keep central-city housing in repair, *not* to stay in the city. Collectively, in our legislation, we have placed a higher value on other things, that is, on economic encouragement to the construction industry. If the subsidy had not existed by the differential policy toward old and new housing, this would not have in itself led all families to remain in the city; it would, however, have led some to do so, a difference which might have been important for the progressive development of decay in central cities, encouraged by the implication that old housing was of little value. It is wrong, therefore, to say that we do not know what to do; it is correct to say that collectively we have been unwilling to act so as to maintain cities. Other values have shown themselves greater.

Another area of social policy illustrates the same point: policy in the construction of expressways under the Federal Interstate Highway program. For a number of years in the 1950s and 1960s, until it ran into the civil-rights movement in the late 1960s, the federal highway program was extremely important in changing the relative demand for proximity and distance, for centralization and dispersal. In two ways, this program increased the demand for distance. First, it was able to impede the attempt of neighborhoods to conserve and protect themselves, and of the city to aid their attempts, but cutting through them, with principal power not in the hands of the city or the neighborhood but in the hands of the State Highway Department. Second, it greatly reduced the time and inconvenience of travel between central city and distant suburbs, aiding the disconnection between residence and work.

This highway policy greatly benefited the automobile industry, facilitating the automobile's use and encouraging the two-car family. It also greatly benefited those who wished to reside away from the city while continuing to work inside it. Thus, if we ask with bewilderment, Why cannot effective policies be devised to aid the central city? the answer is already with us: there *are* policies, the policies *are* effective, but they are implementing other values to which we have given greater weight; at least until the highway program came into conflict, in its condemnation of residential areas, with the civil-rights movement, which was even higher on the scale of values. There should be no mystery about ineffectiveness of policies designed to strengthen the city. We are simply unwilling, as a collectivity, to forego certain other policies which weaken the city.

A third use of social policy illustrates the point in a somewhat different way. This is policy toward crime. Increased crime in the central cities, and even moving into the suburbs, is a major contribution to the value that people place on distance from others, the value they see in living in smaller towns or rural areas. Indeed, the effect is so great that even some criminologists propose this as a strategy for reducing crime. For example, Wilson and Boland, in a section titled "Self-Defense" in a recent paper on crime have a subsection titled "Relocation" involving moves from the central city.[8]

In general, social policies relating to crimes in the past twenty years have been designed to protect the rights of the accused, and to protect the interests of the offender. Landmark Supreme Court decisions crystallized those policies, and criminology concerned itself with rehabilitation. Deterrence as a principle in punishment was almost forgotten. In 1970 the year-end prison population was 196,429 persons, *less* than in 1960, when 212,957 persons were in prison, though the crime rate had risen over 100 percent in that period, and the population size had risen as well.[9]

Police lost the informal support of the population in detecting crime and apprehending criminals, and lost the support of the courts in convicting those who were apprehended. The result of all these changes is a low rate of apprehending those who commit crimes, a low rate of convicting those apprehended, and a low rate of imprisoning those convicted. The product of these rates results in an overall chance of imprisonment for someone who commits a crime that is exceedingly low. For example, in 1960 there were 24 arrests for every 100 crimes in the FBI index, and 24 persons sent to prison for every 100 such arrests, giving an overall imprisonment rate of only 6 per 100 crimes. But in 1970 the rate of arrest had dropped to 16, and the rate of imprisonment to 13, giving an overall imprisonment rate of only 2 per 100 crimes reported to the FBI.[10]

Altogether, the society, from its lawmakers and its judges down to its ordinary citizens, held values and chose policies which were designed to protect civil liberties, to reduce errors of punishing the innocent, and to increase individual freedom from legal or normative constraint. There was, of course, a cost: increase in the incursions upon others' rights; an increase in errors of releasing the guilty; and an increasing necessity to substitute self-protection for protection by laws, norms, and the agencies of law enforcement. And one of the further consequences was to increase the value, for most persons, of distance from others, and of residence in localities small enough that informal social controls could substitute for the no-longer-effective legal controls.

This is not to say that social policies were wholly responsible for the change. Most offenses are committed by young men in their late teens and early twenties and the baby boom of 1946 brought many more of them into the population beginning about 1963. And other factors had an effect also, such as the increased use of personal property insurance, which reduced persons' interest in apprehending and punishing offenders. But probably the major force was the pattern of social policy described above.

The point, then, is clear: the balance between concentration and dispersal, between the value of proximity to others and the value of distance from them, has been changed by explicit policy in a way inimical to urban areas. It is not the *absence* of policy, not the "failure to do anything about crime," but the *existence* of policy which carefully protected certain rights (among which are those of criminals) at the expense of others (among which are those of victims) that has had this consequence. If we desired sufficiently strongly to vitalize urban areas, we would change these policies; but other values have been stronger, and this one has suffered as a consequence.

There is despair sometimes voiced that "we simply do not know how to control crime," when policies of increasing the density of police patrols or the illumination of street lights are ineffective in reducing crime. But again the despair is misplaced. We are *unwilling* to take those actions which will reduce crime, though we know how to do so. We have indicated, through our collective actions, that other things are more important. Currently, however, indications suggest that some change in values is occurring. For example, some criminologists are resuscitating the theory of deterrence as a principle to guide law enforcement, and some recent legal decisions have been more attentive to victim's rights and less to those of the accused than in the recent past. It is, however, a long way from these minor changes of direction to a degree of personal safety which will affect residential decisions in metropolitan areas.

Still another area of social policy which shares some of these same attributes is that of school desegregation. Recent policy (since 1970) in the cities in school desegregation has moved clearly away from elimination of de jure segregation toward affirmative integration by eliminating de facto segregation. Busing, which came to be an instrument of desegregation policy for large cities following the *Swann v. Charlotte-Mecklenberg* case in 1970, is almost synonymous with affirmative integration, going beyond eliminating de jure segregation, for busing is an attempt to overcome residential segregation.[d]

These actions in large cities such as Denver, Boston, Memphis, San Francisco, Dallas, Indianapolis, and others, both North and South, have been designed to implement the value of equality of educational opportunity, particularly for black students. They reflect the importance of that value, and of the policy goal of benefiting black students. An indirect consequence of these policies (mostly resulting from court decisions, but others from federal policy pursued by HEW) has been a very sharp increase in the movement of white children out of city schools: most to the suburbs, but some to private schools and some beyond the metropolitan area altogether. In Boston there was a loss of about 4 percent per year of white students before partial desegregation occurred in 1974. In 1974 there was a loss of 16 percent; and in 1975, when Phase II went into effect, there was a further loss of 19 percent. In other cities the increase in losses was less dramatic, but nevertheless strong enough to have serious consequences for the city. In Denver the white student population was almost stable before desegregation, averaging a 1 percent loss per year. After partial desegregation in 1970, the white student loss has been 7 percent per year for the next six years, leaving only 64 percent as many whites in the Denver schools in 1975 as in 1969. In Dallas the loss of white students from the schools was less than 2 percent per year until partial desegregation in 1971; since then, the loss has been about 9 percent per year, again leaving only 64 percent as many whites in the schools in 1975 as in 1970, this time within a five-year evacuation period.[11]

One policy proposed by some in lieu of the present policy which provides a

---

[d]These remedies involving busing to bring about racial balance in cities continue to be justified by judges *as if* they were necessary to eliminate de jure segregation. But what seems to have been the case in a number of big-city cases is that the judge, faced with an aggressive and apparently insatiable plaintiff, who keeps bringing the case back into court, and an ambivalent and consequently nearly dormant defense, turns to complete racial balance through busing as the one remedy which will end the case. See, for example, David Kirp, "Race, Politics, and the Courts: School Desegregation in San Francisco," *Harvard Educational Review*, vol. 46, 1976, pp. 572-611. Another motive of judges in the South, leading to the same result, has been, paradoxically, to protect the rights of whites: to devise a plan which would ensure that no white was ever in a black-majority school.

powerful incentive to leave the central city for the suburbs, is to introduce compulsory racial balance by busing throughout the whole metropolitan area. That policy was initiated in 1975 in Louisville, Kentucky, by introducing busing throughout Jefferson County which surrounds Louisville. One result has been to drive up housing prices and construction in nearby Bullitt County, outside the reach of the court's action. Another result was a sharp loss of white students from Jefferson County schools in 1975, which amounted, for the schools which had previously been predominantly black, to over 30 percent of the white students assigned to those schools. The long-term result, so long as the judge's order stands, seems likely to move people and industries away from the Louisville metropolitan area.

Though it is clear that the policies that have been implemented by court or HEW action have created an extreme incentive for whites to leave the city for the suburbs, and though it is clear that any policy, if it is to be at all attentive to interests of the city, must not treat suburbs and city differentially, it does not follow that an extreme policy of busing throughout the metropolitan area, as in Louisville, will be good for *either* the city *or* the suburbs. What has proved to be a policy for the central city which drives people out of the city seems likely to be a policy for the metropolitan area which drives them out of the metropolitan area itself. Parenthetically, it might be felt that since this reaction on the part of whites is presumably a result of prejudice against blacks, an appropriate policy is to attempt to reduce this prejudice. But data on who leaves cities in which busing is instituted indicate that it is those with higher income and higher education, and *not* those who are more racially prejudiced.[12] Consequently, reduction of prejudice would seem to have little effect on this movement. Rather, the impulse to leave seems more to be due to busing itself and the conditions in the schools to which the child is bused. The two characteristics of families which appear to make the family most responsive to these factors are concern for their child's education, which impels them to leave, and economic level, which gives them the resources to do so.

The school desegregation policies, like the FHA mortgage policy, the Federal Highway Program, and policies toward crime, exemplify again that the problem of metropolitan areas is not a failure to know what to do to strengthen these areas. It is the use of policies that are harmful to metropolitan areas, despite knowledge that they are harmful. The policies are implemented anyway, because they pursue other values that are collectively held to be more important than those of strengthening metropolitan areas.

Another illustration, which is particularly poignant, is given by the consequences of the fact that middle classes through greater market power have been able in Washington, D.C., to push out the poor from housing in which they live. In a comment in Chapter 11, Lachman and Downs mention that at least Washington, D.C., and New York City, through laws such as anticonversion laws against condominiums, have begun policies of "slum preservation." These policies, which we can hope will be unsuccessful, exhibit not only the intrusion of other values but even more a kind of perverse antipathy by political authority, even when the results both aid racial integration and strengthen the city.

We may ask just what kinds of policies will be most likely to be destructive of metropolitan areas. These examples suggest two general properties of such urban-destructive policies, one which is characteristic of all four, and the other characteristic of two. The two properties are policy initiation at a higher level of government and egalitarian-oriented policy; we examine each in turn.

Policy Initiation at a Higher Level of Government

In all four of the policy areas discussed above—mortgage loans, highways, crime, and school integration—the policies described as leading persons to move away from cities, and in the latter two cases, even from metropolitan areas, are largely federal policies. The FHA and GI mortgage policies and the highway program were congressional actions, and the other two are policies largely resulting from actions taken by federal courts. One characteristic of policies made at a city level is that they will be very attentive to city interests. The government of cities tends to be conservative with regard to city structure, that is, to preserve the existing organization. Policy made at the federal level does not. As a result, federal policies will more often sacrifice city or even metropolitan area values in the pursuit of other values—such as the health of the construction or automobile industry, the rights of persons accused of crimes, and the education of the disadvantaged.

What makes this characteristic of policy formation of particular relevance is the further fact that the importance of federal policy relative to local policy is increasing. More decisions affecting localities and their residents are coming to be made at the national level, while fewer are made completely independently of the national level. It is safe to say that in none of the four policy areas would social policy have gone so far in directions that are harmful to cities if it had been made at the local level, subject to interests and pressures at the local level.

Would this have been "better"? Such a question is unanswerable, because it fails to specify better for whom. It would probably have been better for the health of cities and perhaps of urban areas generally; but it would probably not have been better for the health of the construction industry, the automobile industry, persons accused of crimes, and (though this is more problematic, in the case of school busing) disadvantaged black children. The strengthening of cities does not benefit all. There are serious conflicts of interest, simply because the policies that would be attentive to the health of cities would be inattentive to other interests—exactly as the four policies discussed, each of which pursues certain interests are inattentive to the interests of strengthening the city.

Egalitarian Policy

The second property of two of these policy directions, in the area of crime and the area of school integration, is that they are egalitarian policies. This is explicit in school desegregation, which is justified in terms of the equal protection clause of the 14th Amendment; in crime, the connection is somewhat less direct. The policies designed to protect the rights of the accused, to constrain police actions toward suspects, and related policies, are largely directed toward ensuring that the have-nots receive equal protection from the law. They result generally, as in the Miranda case, from intervention on behalf of a defendant who appears helpless, with few resources, monetary or otherwise.

Now perhaps the most interesting point about egalitarian policies in general is that they have the result of increasing the value of distancing oneself from others. In particular, they increase, for those persons with more than average resources (whether money, school achievement, or something else), the value of distancing themselves from those with fewer resources. Thus egalitarian policies, including the two discussed, but also others that have the effect of reducing social distance, will have the effect of increasing the value of physical distance. When social distance is not obtainable at close proximity, persons who have the resources to do so will buy physical distance—that is, they will disperse from the city and from the metropolitan area. The result is ironic, but upon reflection not surprising: egalitarian policies lead to increases in segregation of the haves from the have-nots, and the increase of inequalities in physical location. Jimmy Carter could maintain close proximity to blacks and lower-class whites because of the presumption of inequality in the plantation South; but when that presumption is replaced by policies pushing toward equality, toward lowered respect for position and property, as in the modern American city; the value of distance increases and the city disperses, those with greatest resources leaving fastest.

Such policies, then, whatever their overall impact on inequality (and that is not at all certain, because the boomerang effect may be greater than the direct effect) are damaging to the strength of metropolitan areas and, most particularly, to their central cities. This is not to say, of course, that such policies are, in their overall effect, "bad"; the health of cities and metropolitan areas is not the only yardstick by which a policy should be measured. There are conflicting interests; and the point to recognize is that such policies do affect the interests of the city (and thus its residents, who depend to some degree on its health), and not only the interests of those whom they are intended to benefit.

The conclusion of this examination of policy should be self-evident. It is that the rebuilding and strengthening of urban areas, the revitalizing of cities and metropolitan areas now undergoing decline, is not to be brought about by some brilliant plan which has so far eluded us, nor is the decline an inevitable consequence of technological change. The decline is not inevitable, but the rebuilding of cities will require, if it is to occur, policies which intrude on other values. It may be necessary to decide, for example, between the value of maintaining metropolitan areas and the value of increased protection of the rights of criminal suspects. It may be necessary to decide between the value of racially heterogeneous cities and metropolitan areas having racial imbalance within them, and the value of racially homogeneous cities that are formally egalitarian. Only when we begin to recognize that the city declines simply because we actively pursue ends that bring about the city's decline will we have reached the sober point where serious discussion can begin about what will be gained and what will be lost by strengthening the city and its environs.

Notes

1. George Tucker, *Progress of the United States in Population and Wealth in Fifty Years,* New York: Augustus H. Kelley, 1964, p. 127.

2. *Mobility of the Population of the United States: March 1970–March 1975,* Washington, D.C.: Bureau of the Census, 1975.

3. See Edgar M. Hoover and Raymond Vernon, *Anatomy of Metropolis,* Cambridge, Mass.: Harvard University Press, 1960.

4. H.G. Wells, *Anticipations of the Reaction to Mechanical and Scientific Progress upon Human Life and Thought,* London: Chapman & Hall, 1902, chapter 2.

5. See Philip Hauser, *Population Perspective,* New Brunswick, N.J.: Rutgers University Press, 1961, chapter 4.

6. FBI, *Uniform Crime Reports, 1973,* Washington: Government Printing Office, p. 104.

7. Chicago Department of Buildings figures as reported in *Chicago Tribune,* June 5, 1977, p. 1,b.

8. James Wilson and Barbara Boland, "Crime," in *The Urban Predicament,* W. Gorham and N. Glazer, eds., Washington: Urban Institute, 1976.

9. Wilson and Boland, "Crime," p. 203.

10. U.S. Department of Commerce, *Statistical Abstract of the United States, 1972,* Washington: Government Printing Office, 1972, p. 160.

11. The initial analysis of this data, through 1973, is reported in James S. Coleman, Sara Kelly, and John Moore, *Trends in School Segregation, 1968-73,* Washington: Urban Institute, 1975. Some further statistics, through 1975, are reported in "Response to Professors Pettigrew and Green," *Harvard Educational Review,* vol. 46, 1976, pp. 217-233.

12. See Everett Cataldo, Michael Gites, Douglas Gatlin, and Deborah Athos, "Desegregation and White Flight," *Integrated Education,* vol. 11, 1973, pp. 12-26.

Part III
Extent of Maturity

4

The Declining Metropolis: Patterns, Problems, and Policies in Britain and Mainland Europe

Peter Hall and
David Metcalf

The declining metropolis is not a phenomenon confined to the United States. Population and employment are falling in many European conurbations, particularly in the inner cores of these urban areas. These trends, and their associated problems and policies, are analyzed here. This chapter will discuss population, employment, unemployment, and deprivation in British urban areas. It attempts to tell a story—to get the flavor of some of what has happened to urban Britain in the last twenty-five years. Also, it will refer to experience of urban areas on the European mainland, but these, so far, are less well documented.

Population and Employment Trends in British Urban Areas

The population of the biggest British urban agglomerations, or conurbations, is declining steadily. Between 1961 and 1974 their total population fell by 7 percent. In contrast, the population of the rest of Britain rose by 14 percent. The overall population fall reverses the trend of the century and a half preceding 1950, much as in the United States as described in Chapter 2. There are two main features of this population decline.

First, in each conurbation the central city now accounts for a smaller proportion of the total conurbation population than it did twenty years ago. Thus, the overall population decline experienced by the conurbations is caused disproportionately by the fall in the population in cores. Second, the decline in the conurbation populations is part of a suburbanization process which has been in operation for some time.[1] Conurbations and other urban areas with populations over 250,000 have tended to experience falling populations since 1961, while the smaller urban and suburban areas on the fringes of the larger town and conurbations have increased their populations.

The twin features of declining central cities and suburbanization have recently been thoroughly investigated in a study for the British Department of the Environment which builds on earlier work by Hall and defines 126 metropolitan areas in Britain from 1966 and 1971 census data.[2] For each metro area, two alternative definitions were given: the Standard Metropolitan Labour Area (SMLA), corresponding to the SMSA of the U.S. census, and the Metropolitan Economic Labour Area (MELA), corresponding to the American

OBE regions derived on the basis of the work on Daily Urban Systems. They show that during the 1950s and 1960s, there was progressive decentralization of population and, more belatedly, employment from the core areas to the rings of the SMLAs and, increasingly, to the fringe areas of the MELAs; see Table 4-1.

Standard Metropolitan Areas (SMAs) have been defined for England on a slightly different basis, distinguishing core cities and other cities, urbanized parts and rural parts of rings.[3] The results, shown in Table 4-2, broadly present the same pattern of decentralization. For example, Table 4-2 indicates that between 1951 and 1971, the central city grew in only two of the twelve largest SMAs in England and Wales, while the vast majority of the fringe cities and suburbs increased their populations. The general pattern of outward movement of population between 1961 and 1971 is shown in Figure 4-1.

Employment in Conurbations

In 1971 the conurbations accounted for 35 percent of the total labor force in Britain and 38 percent of total employment. This difference reflects a net flow of commuters into conurbations. Movements in the industrial composition of employment in conurbations compared with the rest of the country are quite remarkable. Manufacturing industry (1968 Standard Industrial Classification, Industrial Orders III-XIX) accounted in 1971 for between one-quarter (in Greater London) of employment in conurbations and one-half (West Midlands). Between 1961 and 1971 the percent *change* in employment in manufacturing industry was as follows:

Greater London	−25
Central Clydeside	−18
Merseyside	− 9
South East Lancashire	−20
Tyneside	− 7
West Midlands	−10
West Yorkshire	−16
Rest of Britain	+11

Thus each conurbation lost employment in manufacturing while the rest of Britain gained manufacturing employment. A similar tendency also occurs for employment in public utilities.

Between 1961 and 1974 Greater London lost almost half a million, or one-third of its manufacturing jobs. During 1966-74 alone, the loss was 383,000. This decline was seven times the national average. The decline in manufacturing in Greater London differs from that in other metropolitan areas, where a large part of the decline can be traced to one or a few dominant industries in the local

Table 4-1
Population and Employment Change in Britain, 1951-61 and 1961-71, by Urban Zone

	Population					Employment				
	Number of Inhabitants (thousands)			Change (percent)		Number of Inhabitants (thousands)			Change (percent)	
	1951	1961	1971	1951-61	1961-71	1951	1961	1971	1951-61	1961-71
Urban cores	25,767	26,253	25,524	1.9	-2.8	13,434	14,337	13,898	6.7	-3.1
Metropolitan rings	12,914	14,635	17,147	13.3	17.2	4,425	4,719	5,429	6.6	15.0
SMLAs	38,681	40,887	42,671	5.7	4.4	17,859	19,055	19,327	6.7	1.4
Outer metropolitan rings	7,808	8,053	8,838	3.1	9.8	3,327	3,313	3,443	-0.4	3.9
MELAs	46,489	48,940	51,509	5.3	5.2	21,187	22,368	22,769	5.6	1.8
Unclassified areas	2,366	2,344	2,312	-0.9	-1.4	1,027	970	963	-5.5	-0.7
Britain	48,854	51,284	53,821	5.0	5.0	22,214	23,338	23,733	5.1	1.7

Source: Department of the Environment, British Cities: Urban Population and Employment Trends, 1951-71.

Table 4-2
Population Growth in the Twelve Largest SMAs in Britain, 1951-61 and 1961-71

	1971 Population (thousands)		Population Growth (percent)							
			Central City			Other Cities			Suburbs Nonrural District	Suburbs Rural District
	Major City	Other Cities	1951-61	1961-71	1951-71	1951-61	1961-71	1951-71	1951-71	1951-71
1. Greater London	7452.3	1621.8	−2.5	−6.8	−9.1	+33.3	+15.6	+54.1	+50.4	+55.5
2. Greater Manchester	543.7	853.6	−5.9	−17.9	−22.7	−0.8	−3.9	−4.7	−24.3	—
3. Merseyside	610.1	948.3	−5.7	−18.2	−22.9	+1.7	+0.7	+2.5	+45.6	+61.1
4. Tyneside	222.2	481.5	−7.6	−17.6	−23.8	+1.3	−4.0	−2.7	+19.7	—
5. Greater Birmingham	1014.7	1621.6	−0.3	−8.6	−8.9	+10.5	+6.0	+17.1	+51.5	+66.5
6. West Yorkshire	496.0	745.3	+1.0	−2.9	−2.0	+1.1	−0.5	+0.6	+13.1	—
7. Southampton	215.1	273.5	+7.8	+4.9	+13.2	−4.9	−1.4	−6.3	+96.6	+53.5
8. Bristol	426.7	84.7	−1.2	−2.6	−3.8	+2.3	+0.7	+3.0	—	+64.4
9. Preston	98.1	215.2	−6.7	−13.4	−19.2	−4.7	−4.7	−9.2	—	—
10. Nottingham	300.6	327.4	+1.3	−3.6	−2.4	+6.7	+3.4	+10.3	+25.1	+40.4
11. Sheffield	520.3	313.0	−0.4	−3.7	−4.1	+1.9	−0.5	+1.4	+9.8	+33.8
12. Cardiff	279.1	112.3	+8.1	−1.7	+6.2	+1.7	+2.9	+4.7	+13.5	—

Source: G. Crampton, *Metropolitan Areas in Britain*, Ph.D. thesis, Cambridge University (unpublished).
Note: For detailed definitions of SMAs, etc., see source. Growth rates are not given for areas of less than 100,000.

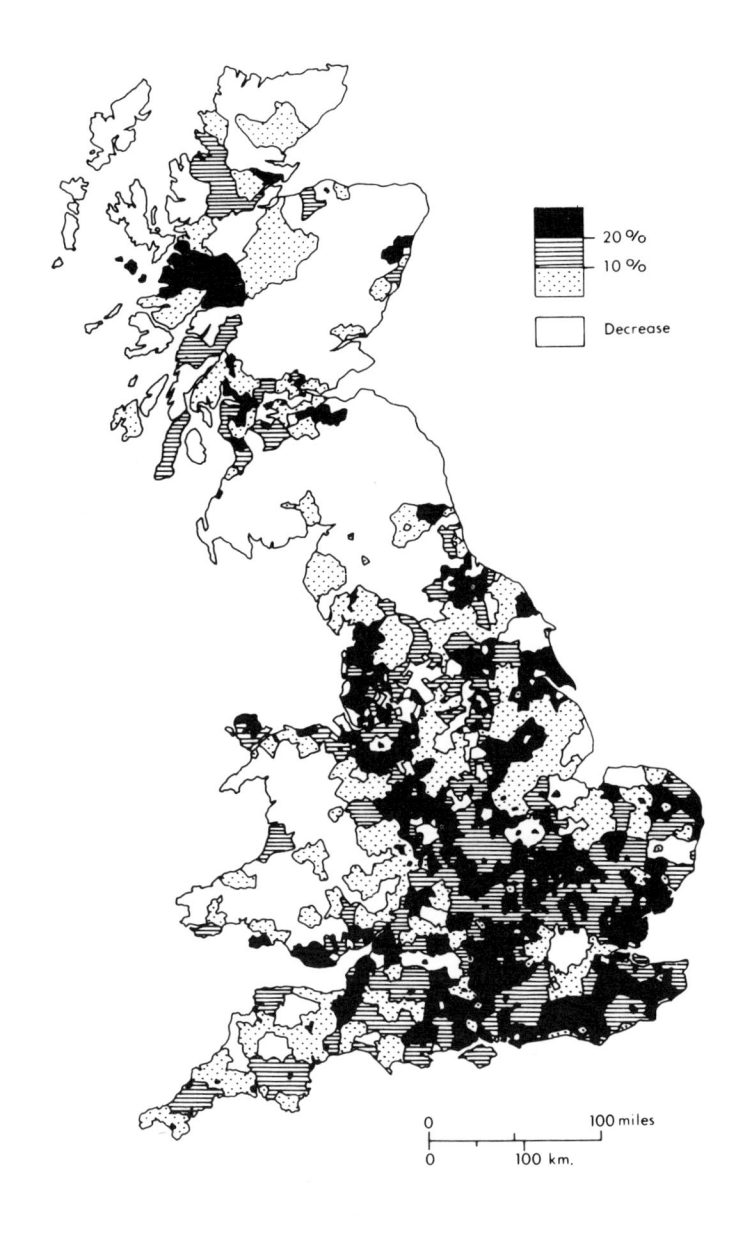

Source: P. Hall, *Urban and Regional Planning*, Harmondsworth: Pelican Books, 1977. © Peter Hall, 1975. Reprinted by permission of Penquin Books, Ltd.

Figure 4-1. Great Britain: Population Change 1961-71.

industrial structure. In contrast, London has many industries which have grown nationally, but even these have declined steeply in London. Had London industries followed the national pattern, manufacturing employment would have grown between 1961 and 1971 by some 13,000 rather than declining by 335,000.

The decrease in manufacturing employment in the conurbations is associated with a reduction in the proportion of skilled, semiskilled, and unskilled manual workers in their respective labor forces, which is larger than the reduction being experienced in the rest of the country. However, there is also clear evidence that the population and employment movements are resulting in a disproportionate number of semiskilled and unskilled manual workers living in the *inner cores* of the conurbations. For example, in 1971 unskilled and semiskilled manual workers accounted for 23 percent of the economically active population of England and Wales, but in the inner areas of Birmingham, Clydeside, Liverpool, and Manchester the corresponding figure was 35 to 40 percent. This has important implications for the spatial structure of unemployment and urban deprivation, discussed in a later section.

There is also a tendency for the loss of jobs in the conurbations to be concentrated disproportionately in inner-city areas. For example, the loss of jobs in inner South East London (Southwark, Lewisham, Greenwich) between 1966 and 1971 was 12.5 percent, while that for the Greater London Council area as a whole was 5.5 percent.[4] A similar rate of decline throughout inner London would largely account for the total fall in the London conurbation. In that area, 74 percent of closures of establishments arose from deaths as opposed to relocation, leading to the conclusion that the direct influence of relocation policy had been very limited. The Department of the Environment's inner-area study of Liverpool showed that between 1961 and 1971 the city lost 28,000 jobs in the port, railways, construction, and utilities; 21,000 jobs in retail and wholesale distribution; and 31,000 jobs in manufacturing industry. The loss of manufacturing jobs has accelerated since 1971. Regional policy has brought 100,000 new jobs to the Merseyside conurbation, but nearly all these have been located on the periphery—often outside economic commuting distance.[5]

LFP Rates of Married Females in Urban Areas

The size of the labor force in Britain rose from 22.6 million in 1951 to 25.1 million in 1971. Much as in the United States, the most distinctive feature of this rise is the dramatic increase in the number of economically active married females, from 2.7 to 5.8 million over the 1951-67 period. The conurbations have each experienced a growth in the number of married females in their labor forces over this period (albeit lower than the growth experienced by the rest of Britain); this is largely the result of higher-labor-force-participation rates among married women.

Not only have married female labor-force-participation (LFP) rates increased, but they also exhibit considerable variation from one urban area to another. In an analysis of married female LFP rates across 106 urban areas of Britain using 1971 census data, the mean married women's LFP rate was 50.3 percent and the standard deviation was 5.16 percent. The LFP rate is positively related to female wages and negatively related to male income. The elasticity with respect to the female wage is larger than that with respect to husbands' income. Thus, holding relative male and female wage constant, a town with a higher female wage has a higher married female LFP rate.[6]

Unemployment and demographic characteristics also are important in explaining the variation in married women's LFP rates across urban areas. A town with a high unemployment rate will tend to have low married female LFP. However, persistent deficient demand in the wider region in which the town lies is associated with a higher-LFP rate. This supports the existence of both discouraged and added worker effects.

Towns with relatively high proportion of foreign immigrants tend to have higher married female LFP rates. This suggests that immigrants have different motivations than native-born residents; in fact, they have a higher-LFP rate at all ages over twenty-five.

Participation is higher in conurbations. Thus, any negative effect on participation rates in conurbations, operating via higher conurbation prices lowering real wage, must be outweighed by cheaper and easier travel to work and generally lowered costs of labor market activity in conurbations.

The higher female LFP rate in conurbations is also demonstrated in a recent Department of the Environment study.[7] The unit of observation used was the smallest spatial unit for which data exist for the whole of Britain—the enumeration district (ED) of the 1971 Census of Population, averaging about 160 households. The aim was to identify the characteristics of the 5 percent of EDs with the lowest female LFP rates. Such EDs are underrepresented in conurbations, as shown in Table 4-3. Thus, London accounts for 19 percent of EDs in Britain but contains only 5 percent of the EDs with lowest (5 percent cut-off) female LFP rates. It is only the Scottish conurbation of Clydeside which has a significant overrepresentation of EDs with low female LFP rates.

The importance of industrial structure (i.e., labor demand) in explaining differences among urban areas in their female LFP rates is indicated by the strong positive association between the proportion of employment in a town in the office/institutional (hospital, university, etc.) sector and the female LFP rate. Further, when explaining growth in female participation rates among the towns, Crampton concludes that "the absorption of reserves of female labour into the tertiary part of the metropolitan economy is a crucial, perhaps dominant, part of the process of change."[8]

These studies of female LFP make good sense. The participation rates in conurbations are higher than those in the rest of Britain. This reflects the interaction of job opportunities, the labor supply response to higher wages in

Table 4-3
Distribution of Female LFP Rates in Enumeration Districts in Great Britain

	% of EDs in Total Number of EDs in the 5% Lowest Female LFP Rate	Number of EDS in Area as % of Total in Great Britain
London	5.0	19.0
Tyneside	2.1	2.0
West Yorkshire	2.4	4.3
Merseyside	2.2	2.7
SE Lancashire	2.7	5.8
West Midlands	3.1	4.8
Clydeside	5.7	4.3

conurbations, demographic factors such as the proportion of immigrants, and general taste factors.

Movements of Labor and Capital and Their Consequences

It has been shown that population and employment are both declining in conurbations and that the decline is more severe in the inner city than in the remainder of the conurbation. There is, as yet, no well-articulated story to explain how these flows are related. All that we can do here is to present some fragments of evidence on the nature of moves by people and firms and discuss the consequences of this urban change.

The Census of Population data for Britain show that individuals in the nonmanual occupations have higher rates of net migration from the conurbations than do manual workers. The reasons for labor mobility have, surprisingly, been little studied. It is worth noting, however, that long-distance moves are strongly associated with employment, while short-distance moves are associated with housing factors. Thus, the relatively high rate of migration out of conurbations by nonmanual workers may reflect, in part, a higher propensity of their particular employment to be decentralized than is the case for manual workers.

The decline in the net number of manufacturing jobs in London between 1966 and 1974 has been broken down into several components (see Table 4-4) by the Department of Industry.[9] Thus, the majority of the reduction in manufacturing employment in London involves plant closures, with no offsetting increases in jobs elsewhere in the country. To the extent that this pattern is repeated for other industrial sectors and conurbations, it is clearly unlikely that the systematic reductions in the population, labor force, and employment

Table 4-4
Decline in Number of Manufacturing Jobs in London, 1966-74

Total loss attributable to movement to new establishments outside Greater London	105,300	27%
To Assisted Areas	36,200	9%
To London overspill policy	26,000	7%
Elsewhere	43,100	11%
Total loss attributable solely to difference between birth and death rates of manufacturing firms	196,300	51%
Employing over 20 people	170,300	44%
Employing under 20 people (estimated)	26,000	7%
Residual (shrinkage of employment at existing plants)	81,800	21%
Total Decline of manufacturing employment in Greater London	383,400	100%

in conurbations merely involved a smooth transition from living and working in conurbations to living and working outside them.

There have been few studies which have thoroughly analyzed the interrelationship between employment and population decrease in connurbations and the consequences of these changes on the welfare of the relevant population. However, the thought-provoking paper by Eversley has produced some evidence on how London has fared in recent years compared with the rest of the South East region.[10]

The decrease in the number of people and jobs in London does not appear to have led to a dramatic increase in labor market hardship in London, relative to the rest of the South East region, or relative to the rest of Britain. Further, other indicators of the quality of life show, broadly, London as improving relative to the rest of the South East.

And other data support the view that the loss of work places has *not* been the leading, independent influence on the decline in employment in London, at least over the period 1960-71.[11] Unemployment did not rise in the GLC relative to Britain, or to the South East region, over the 1960-71 period. Further, the London unemployment rate in manufacturing was always lower than that in other industries. Similarly, adult vacancy rates for males and females in the GLC were higher than those in Britain, making it hard to discern extensive hardship in London resulting from declining population size. Evidence indicates that between 1966 and 1971, as compared with the rest of the South East, London improved its teacher/pupil and doctor/patient ratio; it suffered a smaller increase in crime; its air pollution fell more rapidly. Housing and labor market indicators show London's position deteriorating very modestly relative to the rest of the South East region.[12]

These broad indicators are important but they do not bring out some of the more detailed changes in welfare. In particular, more disaggregated evidence shows clearly that males aged forty and over in London are suffering from geographic dispersal of jobs and population while those under forty are not. Thus, as compared with the rest of the South East, older males experienced a smaller increase in earnings and a bigger increase in employment, while younger men experienced a bigger pay increase and smaller unemployment increase. As has been the case in the past, adjustment problems are falling disproportionately on the older-age groups.

The decline in manufacturing in London has not coincided with a reduction in earnings in London, compared with earnings in the rest of the South East; the index of average gross weekly earnings in London and in the South East excluding London are shown in Table 4-5.[13] Thus the rest of the South East region—which has gained jobs and population—has suffered a larger fall in relative earnings than has London.

The net out-migration of capital and labor from London do not appear to have resulted in London's position deteriorating relative to the rest of the South East on many of the conventional indicators. However, there is little evidence of whether this finding is repeated for other conurbations. Further, this section has dealt with *changes* in the relative position of the conurbation compared with the rest of the region in which it is located. It is necessary also to consider simply the relative position of the conurbation compared with the wider region, and the inner city compared with the outer city. In the next sections we examine the extent and location of urban unemployment and urban deprivation in more detail.

Unemployment and Deprivation

The conurbations account for about one-third of the population of Britain but over two-fifths of the unemployed. In general, the conurbation has a higher

Table 4-5
Average Gross Weekly Earnings in Greater London and the South East[a]

	Greater London		Rest of South East	
	1970	1975	1970	1975
Manufacturing	105.6	104.9	102.8	101.1
Nonmanufacturing	110.8	109.9	98.4	96.3

[a]Great Britain = 100.

unemployment rate than the region in which it is located, and the inner core of the conurbation has a higher rate than the outer part, as indicated in Table 4-6. The male unemployment rate by residence in inner London in 1971 was 5.25 percent, almost twice as high as that prevailing in the outer London boroughs— 2.73 percent. It is important to know whether the higher unemployment rates existing in inner cities compared with outer cities, and in urban areas compared with nonurban areas, occur because of the composition of their respective labor forces or because of location factors. It is well known that unemployment rates are higher for unskilled, single old males than for skilled, married prime-age males. Thus, areas with a high proportion of their residents at risk of unemployment will, because of these composition effects, tend to have relatively high unemployment rates. This was confirmed in a regression analysis of unemployment among the thirty-two London boroughs, which found personal characteristics the dominant explanatory variables.[14] A similar result has been reported for Birmingham; 68 percent of the difference in the unemployment rates in inner Birmingham compared with Birmingham District are accounted for by demographic characteristics.[15]

It is important, however, to recognize that there probably are other influences on unemployment than merely the socioeconomic status of the resident population. The mean of the 1971 census unemployment rate across the thirty-two London boroughs was 4.4 percent and the standard deviation was 1.34 percent. After controlling for the socioeconomic composition of the boroughs' labor forces, the standard deviation in the unemployment rate falls, but only to 0.62 percent. This hints that locational factors play a role in determining whether an individual with given personal characteristics is likely to be unemployed. But it is clear that geographic location is of secondary importance to labor force composition in explaining interborough differences in unemployment.

These results are confirmed in an analysis of 1971 male unemployment across the seventy-eight English county boroughs; the personal characteristics of the towns' respective labor force explains over half the variance in unemployment.[16] But it is also apparent that, other things equal, a town which is employment intensive in declining industry, or located in a region of deficient demand, has a higher unemployment rate. If the risk of unemployment for a person with particular personal characteristics (unskilled, etc.) is identical across areas, there is little case, on either equity or efficiency grounds, for favoring one geographic area over another in allocating funds to alleviate unemployment. The tentative analysis of this problem thus far suggests that the risk of unemployment does vary modestly across areas and there does, therefore, seem to be a case for policies designed specifically to help inner-city employment problems.

Urban deprivation has received much attention recently; it mainly stems from the idea of helping people in specific *areas*, rather than operating via Social Security to alter *individual* welfare. Area-based policies exist in education, housing, and urban renewal. The thesis underpinning area-based policies is

Table 4-6
Regional and Urban Unemployment Rates, January 1977

Region	Unemployment (%)	Metropolitan County	Unemployment (%)	Inner Area	Unemployment (%)
South East	4.3	Greater London	4.3	n.a.	
West Midlands	5.3	West Midlands	6.0	Birmingham	6.5
Yorkshire and Humberside	5.2	West Yorkshire	5.3	Leeds	5.7
North West	6.7	Merseyside	10.7	Liverpool	11.0
North West	6.7	Greater Manchester	5.9	Manchester	5.9
North	7.4	Tyne and Wear	9.0	Wearside	11.4
				Tyneside	8.3
Scotland	7.4	Strathclyde	9.9	Glasgow	9.6

Source: Department of Employment, *Gazette*, February 1977, pp. 154-56.
Note: Unemployment rates refer to registered unemployed (male plus female). Metropolitan Counties are not identical to conurbations.
n.a. not available.

essentially that deprivation (however defined) can be reduced by concentrating resources within well-defined areas, and that this policy does not merely shuffle the problems to another geographic location. It is implicit in this notion that a large proportion of the total number of deprived people live in areas of urban deprivation.

Most of the analysis of urban deprivation has been undertaken using 1971 Census of Population data at the level of the enumeration district (ED). There were 87,578 nonrural EDs in Britain in 1971. The research concentrates on the characteristics and location of EDs which are in the "worst 5 percent of all EDs" on selected indicators, such as overcrowding and unemployment.

It shows that large conurbations have disproportionately large numbers of the worst EDs on many indicators. In particular, Clydeside has a disproportionate amount of nearly all forms of deprivation and inner London has a disproportionate amount of housing deprivation. Deprivation is concentrated in the inner city; in each conurbation, the inner city accounted for a larger share of the conurbations' worst EDs than did outlying EDs.[17]

This is illustrated in more detail in Table 4-7 for the London area. Inner London has 8016 EDs, fewer than the 9226 in outer London. However, it has massively more EDs in the worst 5 percent of Britain's EDs on all indicators of deprivation. For example, 9.2 percent of the worst of Britain's urban EDs on the male unemployment indicator are in inner London, while only 1.3 percent are in outer London. The inner cities also have a greatly disproportionate number of the EDs which suffer multiple deprivation; that is, which are on the worst 5 percent on more than one indicator.

Table 4-7
Distribution by Inner and Outer London of EDs in "Worst" 5% on Selected Indicators

Indicator	Inner London (8016 EDs)	Outer London (9226 EDs)
Severe overcrowding (>1.5 people per room)	8.7	1.8
Shared dwellings	8.8	1.4
Lacking exclusive use of basic amenities	9.3	0.6
Male unemployment	9.2	1.3
Lacking a car	10.0	0.4
SEGs 10 and 11	7.2	2.5

Source: J. Fawcett, "Greater London," *Census Indicators of Urban Deprivation,* Working Note No. 11, Department of the Environment, January 1976.

Trends on the European Mainland

The pattern of urban change in Britain is well documented; the corresponding patterns on mainland Europe, so far, is less so, though partial analyses have been made and a more complete analysis, based on a standard set of metropolitan areas similar to the U.S. Office of Business Economics (OBE) regions, is approaching completion.[18] Up to now, only fragmentary indications of trends are available.

It is possible, however, to say that decentralization of population is occurring throughout most of the larger urban areas of Northern and Western Europe: Scandinavia, the Low Countries, West Germany, and the British Isles. In France, it is occurring in Paris and in one or two other large urban areas. In Southern and Eastern Europe it appears not to be happening so far. This probably is a reflection of different housing patterns; Southern Europeans by preference, East Europeans by policy, and perhaps also by preference, are largely housed at quite high densities within central cities, while Northwest Europeans tend to be spreading out on the Anglo-Saxon model.

The pattern for employment is not as clear, partly because local work place data in many European countries are nonexistent or very partial. There is probably relative decentralization of employment in some larger urban areas of Northwest Europe, in that the growth of jobs in the central city is slow or nonexistent, while in the suburbs it is rapid. This is now the pattern recorded for Paris, for instance, by the French 1975 census. Though total employment in the city still grew modestly between 1968 and 1975 due to the increase in the tertiary sector, the small workshop industry of the east end of Paris is showing a sharp decline, and is presenting a problem for planners.

The tendency to outward movement of population is, however, quite distinct; and, if Anglo-American experience is any guide, it should be followed before long by loss of jobs from the central city. Thus, the city of Paris lost 300,000 people between 1968 and 1975, while the surrounding ring gained 900,000; the city itself now accounts for little more than one-quarter of the total population of the Paris region, 2.3 million out of 9.9 million. The major cities of western Holland, constituting the so-called Randstad (Ring City) Holland, are also losing people to their surrounding suburban areas. Between 1971 and 1974 alone, the three largest cities—Amsterdam, Rotterdam, and the Hague—lost 110,000. Much of this loss passes to contiguous municipalities, but some leads to long-distance commuting by car, which the energy-conscious Dutch want to discourage.[19]

Policies and Powers in Britain and Western Europe

The stagnant or declining metropolis, therefore, is a relatively new phenomenon in Europe. As already indicated above, however, the problem is perceived much as in the United States, at least until recently, as one of the declining inner city—and that only in a limited number of Western European countries. The exception is provided by a few larger urban areas in older industrial regions—Central Scotland, Northeast England, Southern Belgium, the Ruhr—which have experienced a shrinking population and economic base. But this has generally been defined as part of a wider regional problem, not as a metropolitan problem per se.

Accordingly, the policies that have been devised in West European countries in the three decades since World War II have been addressed to rather different issues than the decline of metropolis. First, regional policies have been devised in context of national planning: promotion of the economic growth of lagging peripheral regions vis-à-vis central metropolitan industrial regions. Second, local planning policies have been devised, usually by local or provincial grovernments, to guide the physical pattern of urban growth; frequently, the object has been to impose some determined physical concept of a desired order, usually by limiting the growth of the larger urban areas and promoting decentralization to smaller satellite communities. This "regional-local" planning has in many cases been coordinated and monitored by central government.

There has sometimes been an implicit link between these two policy bundles—especially in Great Britain, France, and the Netherlands. For the general effect of both has been to limit the growth of the major metropolitan regions—London, Paris, the Randstad Holland—both in an economic sense and in a physical sense. The growth potential, that has been thus abstracted, has in effect been transferred to two kinds of location. First, it has gone to the major provincial urban agglomerations, particularly those in the regions where growth is being promoted. Second, it has gone to the satellite communities, including new towns and growth poles, within a limited distance of the major metropolitan center. Thus, though it may never have been expressed as such, the combination of the two bundles constitutes an implicit national urban development policy.

Before looking at the powers employed, and at some results of the policies, it may be worthwhile to emphasize the very different spatial scale. Western Europe as a whole is broadly comparable with the eastern half of the United States. It contains thinly populated and weakly urbanized regions—Northern Scandinavia, the Highlands of Scotland, Western Ireland, the Massif Central of France, much of the Spanish Meseta—which are comparable to the northwoods of Michigan, Wisconsin, and Minnesota, or to parts of the Old South. The main urban concentrations are in a triangle bounded by Birmingham in England, Dortmund in Germany, and Milan in Italy; the southern prolongation of this triangle follows the great Rhine corridor. There are also pronounced coastal urban concentrations outside this triangle: in Southern Scandinavia, Northern Germany, Northern England, and Southern Scotland, and the Mediterranean coasts generally. The urban hierarchy has been greatly influenced by accidents of national history and the location of national frontiers. By definition, national urban policies (including regional policies) work in rather different ways on different national hierarchies. Thus, France has an extremely strong central metropolitan area, and a limited number of much weaker provincial metropolises. Germany, in contrast, since 1945 has had no real central metropolitan area, but instead, a set of extremely strong provincial urban centers.

The Main Policy Instruments

In terms of national policy, the most important policy instruments have been those of national-regional policy. These have been used to secure a limited and defined set of objectives, including, especially, the reduction of unemployment and out-migration in the lagging peripheral regions, as indicated in Figure 4-2; industrial modernization has also been an aim, sometimes conflicting with the first two. Foremost among policies for industrial decentralization have been the provision of incentives to private industry to relocate (or to locate new branch plants) in lagging regions. These may consist of capital incentives in the form of tax relief or grants for buildings or plants; actual building of factories either in advance or to order; and direct subsidies to labor, which have been used for instance in Britain's Regional Employment Premium, introduced in 1967 and abolished in 1977.

Additionally, these lagging regions have invariably received a priority allocation of national investment in infrastructure, both of a direct economic kind (national highways, ports, airports) and of an indirect social kind (housing, hospitals, environmental protection facilities). Such help may come directly from the national government, for instance, in national highway plans, or indirectly through grants to local government or special-purpose agencies, such as public utility undertakings. Finally, in some cases governments have sought directly to create employment in lagging regions, generally by establishing new agencies; an example is the establishment of Britain's new central computerized vehicle and driver license system in Swansea, South Wales.

A less commonly used policy is direct governmental controls on industrial location. Only Britain on a larger scale and France on a more limited scale have employed it to any extent. In Britain, since 1945 all establishment of new industry and all extensions to existing industrial plants above a certain minimum threshold (which has varied over time) have been subject to the award by a central government department, the Department of Industry, of an Industrial Development Certificate (IDC). Since 1965, the same powers have been applied to office facilities through a system of Office Development Permits (ODPs) issued by the Department of the Environment. Industrial controls were applied fairly stringently during the late 1940s and much of the 1960s, but were applied much less strictly in the 1950s, and again in the growth-starved 1970s. Throughout, they have been used to try to steer industry from Greater London

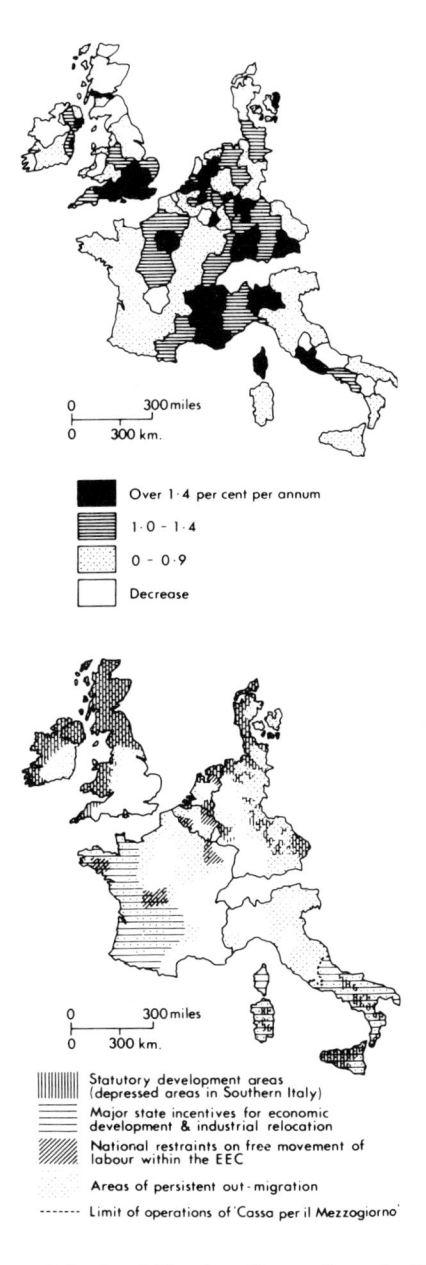

Source: P. Hall, *Urban and Regional Planning*, Harmondsworth: Pelican Books, 1977. © Peter Hall, 1975. Reprinted by permission of Penguin Books, Ltd.

Figure 4-2. European Economic Community: Population Change 1958-68 and Assisted Areas.

and the surrounding South East region (and, to a certain extent, from the Midlands) to the Assisted Areas of Northern England, Merseyside, South Wales, and Central Scotland. Since the mid-1950s, the French have used a similar system of licensing to try to steer industry away from the Paris region, though most of the resulting moves have been to a very limited zone within about 150 miles of the capital.

Through varying combinations of these policies, most European nations have sought to promote their peripheral regions. Britain has developed its older coalfield industrial areas (Central Scotland, Northeast England, South Wales) and also some thinly populated peripheral rural areas such as North Devon and North Cornwall, Mid and North Wales, and the Highlands and Islands of Scotland.

France has sought to aid *le désert français*—the whole area south and west of a line from the Loire mouth to the Rhone mouth; to this end, heavy investment is being made in eight counterweight metropolises (*métropoles d'équilibre*) based on the biggest provincial cities. Similarly, Federal Germany has aided a great variety of thinly populated coastal or upland regions, such as northern Schleswig-Holstein, near the Danish border; the Eifel, next to the Belgian frontier; and the Bayrische Wald-Böhmer Wald, against the Czech frontier. The Netherlands have sought to steer industry and white-collar employment out of their congested Randstad to older industrial areas like Limburg, in the extreme south next to the frontier with Belgium and Germany, or to thinly populated peripheral rural regions like Friesland-Groningen in the far northeast. The Italians have promoted the development of their Mezzogiorno (the southern one-third of the peninsula) which suffers from a degree of regional backwardness barely paralleled in the rest of the European Economic Communities.[20]

These policies have had varying degrees of success; the precise degree is difficult to judge because it is impossible to gauge what would have happened without them. In a very careful statistical analysis, Moore and Rhodes calculated that between 1963 and 1970 alone, the total bundle of British regional policies is estimated to have created 220,000 jobs in the Development Areas that would not have been there otherwise.[21] Regional unemployment differentials have shown some convergence; regional out-migration has been slowed and in one case (Wales) reversed. Both the French and the Dutch have undoubtedly created jobs in certain areas—the French in eastern Brittany and the Loire Valley, the Dutch in Limburg and Groningen—that would not have existed without their intervention. The Germans have created thriving industrial enclaves in small country towns, far from their economic heartland. But in almost all these cases, the problem is that the tides may have been running, at least partly, in these directions anyway; regional policies may merely have anticipated, by accident, the relative decline of the central metropolitan region. To that highly speculative and tendentious conclusion, we will return in the final section.

Regional-local policies start from definite physical planning objectives. To a certain extent in all these countries, but particularly in Britain and the

Netherlands, there is a generally accepted belief that the community has a right to restrict the freedom of the individual to develop land. One particular motive for this is to save the highest-grade, even medium-grade, farmland in the interests of greater agricultural self-sufficiency; this belief, very strong in Britain at the end of World War II, has recently again had increased support. Another motive is to limit the size of large urban agglomerations, which are seen as the source of many social evils, or negative externalities: long, tedious, and expensive commuter journeys, traffic congestion, pollution, high land values, and social alienation. A third motive, particularly pronounced in Britain, is a belief in urban containment for its own sake; the idea that the city and the countryside should be clearly defined and separated from each other. This has been in striking contrast to the development ethos prevalent in the United States.[22] Yet another motive, particularly strong in recent years, has been the idea that planning should result in an economy that put less demand on scarce energy and other natural resources; this has been particularly strong in the Netherlands and now in France. Last, and again very strongly in the most recent period, there has been the notion that planning should seek to promote greater equity, even at the expense of economic efficiency; for example, it should be an aim to guarantee that people are within walking distance of shops and public services, even though that might mean a scale of provision smaller than the economic optimum.

To achieve such extended economic and social objectives, there is a whole variety of instruments, and much national and local variation in their use. Again, as at the larger scale, there are both positive and negative policies. Positive policies include infrastructure provision, especially roads, housing, social provision, and in certain cases industrial plant. The best single example is the British new towns policy, which since 1946 has placed over 1 million new people in twenty-eight planned new communities, each of them funded directly by central government through a development corporation, which in form most clearly resembles Britain's nationalized industry boards. But, admired internationally as they may be, the new towns account for less than 3 percent of the total British new housing program during the post-World War II period.

More recently, France also has put considerable central investment into a new towns program, particularly the 1965 plan for eight major new towns, housing up to half a million people each, arrayed along two major axes in the Paris region. Though this program has subsequently been slowed due to the drastic reduction in forward population projections, this still remains one of the most remarkable schemes of planned metropolitan decentralization at present in progress in Europe. The Dutch, too, have developed a whole series of smaller statellite developments to take the pressure off the growth of their major Randstad cities, chiefly by providing for growth to take place on the outer fringes of the Randstad, where it is less menacing to intensive agriculture.

But such policies cannot alone achieve the desired goals of physical planning. Therefore, most West European countries also placed negative controls on land development. Through their local governments, they have declared explicitly that development should not take place in certain areas or in certain directions. This is, of course, simplest in those rare cases where public bodies already own all or most development land, as in the British new towns or (due to an initiative taken by the municipality at the start of this century) the Stockholm suburbs. Elsewhere—that is, in nearly all the rest of Europe—they depend on general land-use planning powers. Typically, as in the historic British 1947 Town and Country Planning Act, these may depend on the de facto nationalization of land development rights, with payment of compensation to landowners similar to the payments to former railway or coal mine shareholders. The development rights were then in effect passed to local planning authorities, which, thus, now possess much stronger powers over development than those given to local zoning boards in the United States. The British local authorities may, for example, and frequently do, entirely forbid development in a way not possible under the general police power used in zoning.

In using these powers, local authorities clearly have a degree of autonomy. But in a way characteristic of British governmental procedures, their rights are circumscribed by the requirement to submit their plans to the central government for approval or possible modification. Currently, planmaking in Britain is a two-stage process, with broad structure plans made by county planning authorities and submitted to the central government for approval, and detailed local plans (usually made by lower-tier county districts) which require no such approval, but which must accord with the general lines of the structure plan. This central power is used to introduce a degree of coordination and uniformity on the policies of different local authorities; and it is supplemented by a stream of circulars from the Department of the Environment to local authorities, which give policy advice in a way that is normally heeded. Thus, for instance, greenbelts have been drawn around Greater London and the other major conurbations and freestanding cities. This has been done in each case by a number of different authorities, but the net effect is a remarkably tidy and uniform one. Since, in general, all development land within the conurbations has been long since used up, further urban growth has had to leapfrog the greenbelt, being then channelled by local planning policies into small and medium-sized towns and villages on the far side of the greenbelt. A schematic picture of the resulting development pattern is shown in Figure 4-3; it is very different from the pattern of leapfrog development typical of American suburban sprawl in the post-1945 period.

No other country in Western Europe, perhaps, has taken and used such powers quite as stringently as Britain. But the Dutch have created green buffer zones to protect the agricultural green heart of their Randstad, and the French have established zones of special protection around Paris and other large cities, as well as appropriating development land so as to safeguard a large part of the rise in land values for the community. The British 1975 Community Land Act,

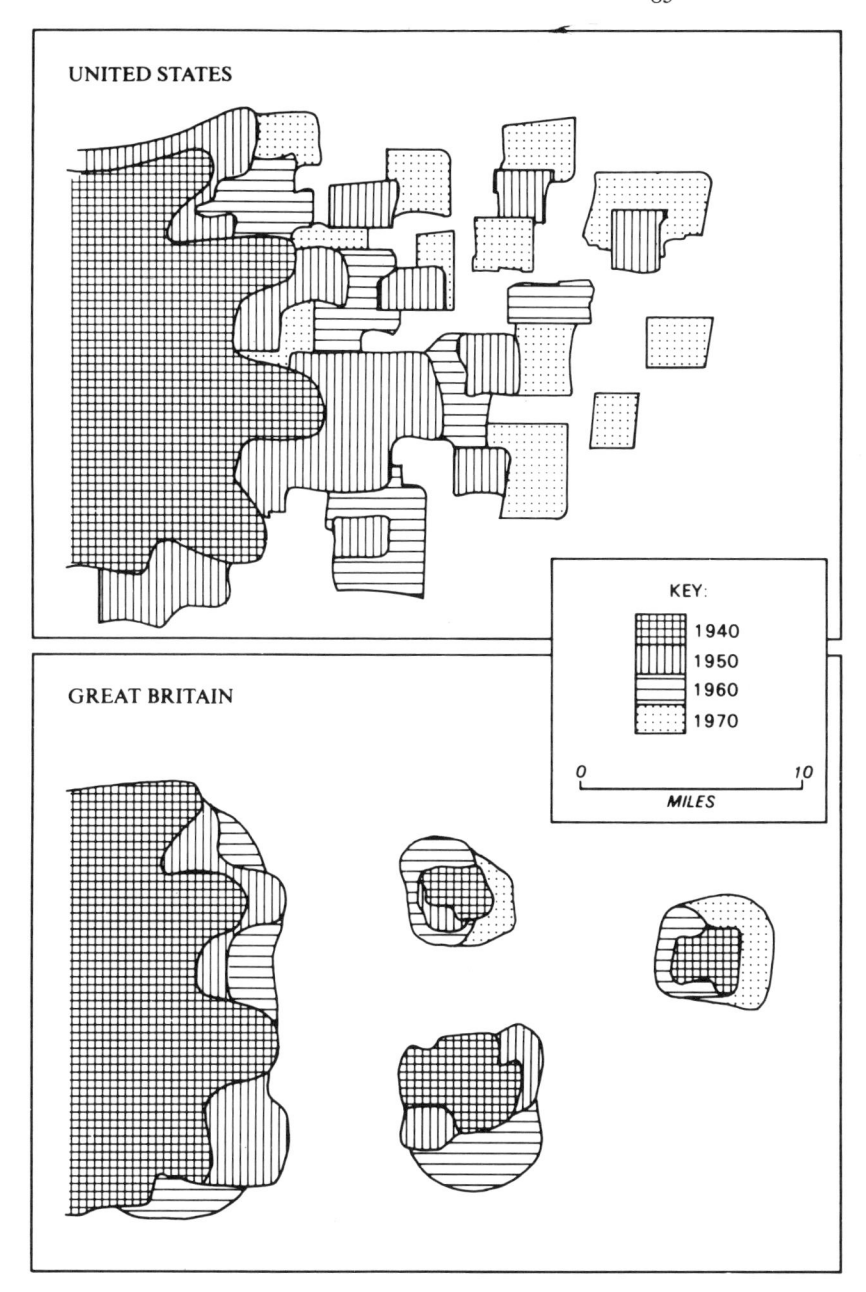

Source: M. Clawson and P. Hall, *Planning and Urban Growth: An Anglo-American Comparison*, Baltimore: Johns Hopkins, 1973. Reprinted by permission.

Figure 4-3. United States and Britain: Schematic Representation of Urban Development in the Postwar Period.

which was supposed to secure the same result in that country, has so far failed to produce any substantial results. In general, however, many European countries have either not taken the same powers, or have used them more laxly. In France and Belgium, for instance, new out-of-town shopping centers (*hypermarchés*) have been built on a very large scale during the last decade. In Britain, due to a very stringent policy of local control supported by central government, such developments are exceedingly rare and shopping remains concentrated in the city centers.

The net effect of these two sets of policies—national-regional and regional-local—may now be summed up. In almost all Northwest European countries, the effect has been somewhat to slow down the rate of growth of major provincial cities; this effect is strongest in Britain, quite marked in France and the Netherlands, and less evident in countries like Belgium or Denmark. In some of these countries, regional policy has also tried to promote the development of a wide spread of smaller country towns in the remoter rural regions; West Germany is notable in this regard. Several countries have tried to decentralize their leading metropolitan region by the development of planned satellites or new towns, supplemented by negative controls on physical development, such as greenbelts. The effect has been to slow down or stop the growth of the central city; this growth has been transferred to a ring around the city, where the new planned developments are concentrated.

Similarities and Contrasts with U.S. Trends and Policies

In Europe, the precise use of national-regional and regional-local powers has been very much influenced by the perceptions of policymakers. In Western Europe, as in the United States, the 1950s and 1960s were in general decades of bouyant demographic and economic growth; the expectation, therefore, was that large-scale physical urbanization would be the order of the day. The American response was typically to give the process over to the private developer, working within fairly loose zoning and subdivision control and aided by a battery of governmental policies, ranging from mortgage finance help to Interstate Highway programs; the result was the familiar pattern of low-density suburban sprawl. The European response was a greater degree of planned provision, including both comprehensively planned new towns and close indirect control on the decisions of private developers. The resulting pattern of development is in some ways different, in others, similar. It is different because it is often more compact, more defined against buffer zones or greenbelts of open country, and built at a higher density. It is similar, because it takes place outside the central city, and depends on commuting to employment in the central city; in a strict meaning of the term, it is suburban. The sole exception is the fully planned new towns, which achieve a balance between residential population and employment; but as already noted, even in Britain these have housed only a small minority of the population.

Thus, in Europe as in the United States, there has been a pattern of decentralization, in which population has moved out from central cities earlier and faster than has employment. We do not yet know the full dimensions of this movement, but we can tentatively say the following:

1. Decentralization is well advanced in Northwest Europe (Scandinavia, West Germany, the Low Countries, Britain); it is only beginning to affect France and has probably not had any pronounced effect on southern Europe.

2. It affects first residential population, leading to lengthened commuter journeys from suburbs to central cities. London's commuter field extended during the 1950s and 1960s and more than half a million enter each day from surrounding areas, about half bound for the Central Business District (CBD). Later, employment too begins to decentralize, affecting especially larger-scale manufacturing and routine office employment; in a later stage, observable in London, headquarters office operations may also move out.

3. It affects the largest metropolitan areas earliest and most profoundly. Here, as for instance in London, the central city now records absolute losses of people and jobs. Further, these move out, not only or even mainly, to suburban areas within the commuter shed of the central city but to smaller, largely self-contained metropolitan areas where employment recentralizes in small central cities. The pattern of employment decentralization is apparently very similar in New York City (to centers like Stamford, Greenwich, Bridgeport, or New Haven) and London (to centers like Reading, Guildford, or Southend).

4. Thus, especially in near proximity to a large declining metropolitan area, smaller metros may still show sharp rises in population and employment; the whole regional system of cities, however, now tends to reach some static equilibrium.

5. An important reason for this is that population growth in metropolitan areas has dramatically slowed, due to falls in the birthrate in all European countries, while employment growth has also ceased, due in part to recession.

Thus, in a paradoxical way, it can be concluded that in most of these countries, national and local policies were aiding and abetting a process that might well have occurred naturally. They promoted vigorous metropolitan decentralization, both to provincial cities and to metropolitan satellites, in order to cope with an imagined future population growth that soon became illusory. Paris planned in 1965 for 5 million extra people by 2000; by 1975 this was cut to 3 to 4 million. Shortly after, South East England planned for 3.5 million more over the same period; this estimate is now cut to 300,000. Meanwhile, the process had sometimes gone further than many policymakers intended; instead of a mere relative shift from the static city, planners were quite suddenly faced with absolute losses of people and jobs, as will be discussed further in Chapter 7. The explanation for this is complex, but two factors have clearly been important.

First, with the very sudden and sharp fall in birthrates in almost every country, out-migration from central cities has no longer been balanced by natural increase. This has been observed in London, Paris, and the Randstad cities. Second, the mid-1970s recession has overlain and exaggerated certain structural tendencies in the Western European economies—notably, the major losses in unskilled and semiskilled work in manufacturing and warehousing, and the closure of many small uncompetitive firms that were traditionally located in inner-city areas.

In many cases, indeed, local planning policies have exacerbated these underlying trends. From evidence in Britain, France, and the Netherlands, it seems clear that wholesale clearance and renewal both thinned out populations and destroyed much employment in older, small-scale industrial premises. Indeed, these were deliberate policies, carried through in the interests of better housing conditions and properly segregated land uses. But with mounting evidence of the results, many planners are now contemplating a deliberate reversal.

In this attempted reversal, they may be participating in, and even helping to bring about, the end of one planning era and the beginning of another. Especially in Britain, and to some extent in all Western European countries since World War II, there has been an all-pervasive idea that physical planning was concerned with the control and guidance of growth. That such growth was occurring at a rate seldom previously experienced, that left to itself it could produce all kinds of social costs, were regarded almost as self-evident facts. Further, implicit in the policies was the idea that growth would be sufficient to allow planning a free rein; if the effect was to remove some potential growth (as for instance when a British industrialist was denied an Industrial Development Certificate), that was a price that could willingly be afforded. In the changed circumstances of the late 1970s, that is by no means a foregone conclusion.

Planning in all countries may now need to be much more focused on generation of growth rather than its control; it may need to be entrepreneurial rather than regulative. There is some experience of all this, in almost every country, in regional development programs. And in a sense, the shift in several European nations toward an inner-city regeneration policy may be regarded just as a new dimension of regional policy. But the new element is that growth overall is so limited. Once, it seemed easy to rob the affluent region Peter to pay the poor peripheral region Paul. But now Peter has all too little to spare, and many advanced industrial nations face the problem of engendering genuinely new economic growth. That is a trick that neither they, nor the United States, have yet quite learned.

Notes

1. P. Hall et al., *The Containment of Urban England,* Reading, Mass.: George Allen & Unwin, 1973.

2. *Urban England* and Department of the Environment, *British Cities: Urban Population and Employment Trends 1951-71,* 1976; as indicated in G. Crampton, "Metropolitan Areas in Britain," Cambridge University, unpublished Ph.D. thesis, 1977.

3. Crampton, "Metropolitan Areas."

4. P. Gripaios, "The Closure of Firms in the Inner City: The South East London Case 1970-75," *Regional Studies*, vol. 11, 1977, pp. 1-6.

5. Department of the Environment, *Inner Area Studies: Liverpool, Birmingham and Lambeth,* London: HMSO, 1977.

6. C. Greenhalgh, "Labour Supply Functions for Married Women in Great Britain," *Economica,* 1977.

7. F. Silkin, "Economic Activity," *Census Indicators of Urban Deprivation,* Working Note No. 9, Department of the Environment, March 1975.

8. Crampton, "Metropolitan Areas."

9. Department of Industry, "The Decline of Manufacturing Employment in Greater London 1966-74," DSPSE (SG) 85, January 1976.

10. D. Eversley, "Rising Costs and Static Incomes: Some Economic Consequences of Regional Planning in London," *Urban Studies,* vol. 9, 1972, pp. 347-368.

11. C. Foster and R. Richardson, "Employment Trends in London in the 1960s and Their Relevance for the Future," in *London: Urban Patterns, Problems and Policies,* eds., D. Donnison and D. Eversley, London: Heinemann, 1973; C. Foster and C. Whitehead, "The Layfield Report on the Greater London Development Plan," *Economica*, vol. 40, November 1973, pp. 442-454.

12. C. O'Cleireacain, "The Earnings of Londoners and Their Implications for Welfare," Centre for Urban Economics, LSE, 1972, mimeo.

13. N. Simon, "The Relative Level and Changes in Earnings in London and Great Britain," 1976, mimeo.

14. D. Metcalf and R. Richardson, "Unemployment in London," in *The Concept and Measurement of Involuntary Unemployment,* ed., D. Worswick, London: Unwin, 1976.

15. G. Barrett, "The Inner City Unemployment Problem: A Framework for Policy Analysis," West Midlands County Council, 1976, mimeo.

16. D. Metcalf, "Urban Unemployment in England," *Economic Journal,* vol. 85, 1975, pp. 578-589.

17. S. Holtermann, "Areas of Urban Deprivation in Great Britain: An Analysis of 1971 Census Data," CSO, *Social Trends 6,* HMSO, 1975.

18. D.R. Vining, Jr., and T. Kontuly, "Increasing Returns to City Size in the Face of an Impending Decline in the Sizes of Large Cities: Which Is the Bogus Fact?", *Environment and Planning,* vol. 9, 1977, pp. 59-62; G. Reigluth, *Urban Development Patterns and National Growth Policy: The European Experience,* Washington: Urban Institute, 1976 (*not* generally published); P. Hall, N. Hansen, D. Hay, and C. Sherrin, *Final Report of the IIASA/Reading European International Urban Systems Study,* Laxenburg: International Institute for Applied Systems Analysis, 1977.

19. P. Hall, *The World Cities,* 2d ed., London: Weidenfeld, 1977.
20. P. Hall, *Urban and Regional Planning,* Harmondsworth: Penguin, 1975.
21. B. Moore and J. Rhodes, "Evaluating the Effects of British Regional Policy," *Economic Journal,* vol. 83, 1973, pp. 87-110.
22. M. Clawson and P. Hall, *Planning and Urban Growth: An Anglo-American Comparison,* Baltimore: Johns Hopkins, 1973.

5 Metropolitan Development in Poland and Implications for America

Piotr Korcelli

Spatial policies are aimed at producing desired spatial forms, but their scope and content are greatly influenced by existing patterns of land use and infrastructure. Thus, effective policies are based on a thorough understanding of processes which are explicitly spatial, such as the search for location, or whose consequences may or may not become clearly expressed over space, for example, shifts in consumer demands. Such processes in turn are frequently shaped by past and present policies producing an interdependence effect between policy and process. In that spirit, this chapter will discuss the development of metropolitan growth policies in Poland, including an overview of trends in urban growth, an identification of the changing place and functions performed by metropolitan areas within the national settlement system. This latter is important, since internal processes have had a greater impact on metropolitan growth trajectories over the past few decades than have their external relations; this seems to be the situation in the United States, but the problem is of a universal nature. This chapter also will discuss major planning problems of Poland's large cities. Finally, selected conclusions from earlier discussions will be put in a cross-national context.

Patterns of Metropolitan Growth and Change

Observed rates of population growth or decline of metropolitan areas are determined, among other factors, by (1) the overall population dynamics of the country or region involved; (2) the function of metropolitan areas within their national and regional settlement systems; and (3) the comparative advantages offered by metropolitan and nonmetropolitan areas in terms of accessibility to jobs and services, and with respect to environmental conditions.

Existing models of settlement systems pay considerable attention to the role of metropolitan areas, and most analysis rests on the premise of a continuous and inevitable expansion of metropolitan areas. Perhaps most characteristic of this approach is "the large-city focused model of city-system development," which portrays the process of circular and cumulative growth of large urban centers.[1] Such centers reinforce their advantages after having acquired a dominant position at an early development stage, since they are able to sustain the old, and generate new channels of goods, people, and information flows, interconnecting them with other similar units in the city system. The intermetropolitan linkage dimension is also heavily emphasized by Dziewoński, according to whom urban agglomerations tend to form a single subsystem in a national settlement system.[2] In yet other typologies, metropolitan centers are treated as dominant components, or "nodal points" within national settlement systems, frequently with a supposed stability of their city rank-size distribution.[3]

It is mostly in the domain of city-region studies that one finds conceptual underpinnings of the alternative paths of metropolitan development. These are reflected in the two polar notions of metropolitan regions and urban fields. The latter concept, unlike the former, accounts for the extensive spatial deconcentration of people and economic activity, actually leading to a reversal of established core-periphery relations. However, this concept has not been highly formalized, and only recently have comprehensive empirical studies on the changing structure of urban regions been undertaken.[4]

One can hypothesize, using an analogy derived from spatial diffusion theory, that urban places of different size categories undergo a growth cycle whose intensity over time can be depicted by an S-shaped curve, that is, a cycle consisting of successive phases of slow growth, rapid growth, and a slow growth again. With a new stimulus, the growth cycle may be renewed.

In Poland, urban growth has been rapid and sustained during the past thirty years. This could be attributed to postwar reconstruction and subsequent industrialization. Yet, owing to economic development, a changing demographic situation, and evolving spatial policies, somewhat different patterns of urban growth were characteristic of each of the consecutive decades. Thus, the 1950s witnessed a much quicker increase of urban population than the 1960s—48 and 20 percent, respectively. During the 1950s, the highest growth rates occurred in places of 10,000 to 20,000 and of over 200,000 population. In the 1960s, on the other hand, the highest growth was in cities of 20,000 to 50,000 and 50,000 to 100,000 inhabitants. The 1970-75 period brought a trend reversal; the highest rates of growth were for places between 50,000 and 100,000 and over 200,000 population. These trend shifts, however, are influenced by shifts in the position of individual units between size categories. For stable cohorts of urban places a somewhat different pattern can be observed, but it shows nevertheless—contrary to popular belief—that the largest cities have by no means been those with the fastest rates of increase over the whole 1950-75 period. In fact, their growth was smaller on average than for total urban population.

A somewhat different perspective is provided by population data for functional urban regions, decomposed into core and periphery.[5] Urban regions have been delineated mostly on the basis of commuting to work, with their boundaries adjusted for administrative status and central-place functions, in such a way that the resulting units cover the whole national territory. The core areas include major urban centers, together with the surrounding second-level administrative units; they are much closer to a metropolitan area than to a central-city definition.

Table 5-1 shows a general trend toward spatial population concentration within core areas over the 1950-73 period as well as a negative relation between the size of core population and total metropolitan change. This regularity holds strictly for the four largest categories, but it still suggests that smaller metropolitan areas were those which grew the fastest in relation to their hinterland. On the other hand, core areas of over a million have not increased their share from 1950-73, and they even declined somewhat relative to their hinterlands during 1960-70. It should be borne in mind that the figures pertain to total population; the growing concentration of population within core areas reflects a rural population that has remained virtually constant in absolute size since 1950, with its share of total population declining from 61 to 46 percent by 1973.

As suggested earlier, the observed patterns should be interpreted from the point of view of demographic structure and change, as well as from the spatial economic development perspective, which under conditions of a planned economy, reflects major policy objectives and their implementation. It is instructive, in this context, to examine the distribution of growth components of urban population from 1950 to 1975. Until 1967, natural increase accounted for more than half of total growth; this was followed by migration and administrative boundary change, each of which accounted for roughly 25 percent. Since 1967, migration has become the dominating factor, contributing about 60 percent of the total change from 1970 to 1975.[6] This shift reflects a rise in rural-urban migrations as well as a fall in the natural rate of increase.

Table 5-2 shows natural growth indexes for Poland's five largest cities. The decline in the values of those indexes has been much more pronounced for all five cities shown than for the country as a whole. Variations between cities reflect their past in-migration patterns and the related age-composition characteristics; variations in fertility level, as evidenced by the gross reproduction index values, are small, all the values falling well below unity.

The marked slowdown of growth of large metropolitan areas during the 1960s has been halted since 1970, owing to new policy directions as well as to the second-generation effect of the postwar birthrate increase—the so-called demographic echo, much the same as the echo for the United States noted in Chapter 2. Since 1970, rural-urban migration has increased by about 50 percent, compared to the 1960s, the main destinations for migration being metropolitan areas and large cities, in general. Also, in terms of urban-to-urban migrations, each of the major size categories of urban places has been characterized by a positive migration balance with respect to all lower-size categories, and a negative balance in relation to the larger-size groups.

Interrelations between population dynamics and the economic functions of cities have been studied in some detail. Generally, it was found that among the large and medium-sized centers, the old industrial cities had low or moderate growth indexes, while the most rapid population increase occurred in those administrative centers of the upper level—such as Kielce and Białystok—which witnessed major industrial expansion. Intersectoral employment proportions for

Table 5-1
Basic Core-Periphery Proportions for Forty-five Functional Urban Regions in Poland

Urban Regions by Population Size of the Core in 1973[a]	Percentage of Population Living in the Core			Percentage of Industrial Employment in the Core			Percentage of Housing Units in the Core		
	1950	1960	1970	1973	1960	1970	1973	1950	1960	1970	1973
Above 1,000,000 (2)	40.0	41.6	41.5	41.6	49.0	52.8	51.0	41.2	43.2	45.5	45.1
500,000-1,000,000 (5)	36.5	39.4	41.1	42.9	59.6	65.0	62.8	37.6	40.8	44.1	45.8
200,000-500,000 (3)	24.4	26.0	31.1	32.5	54.8	56.6	53.9	24.4	27.3	31.2	32.2
150,000-200,000 (3)	18.9	23.9	27.7	29.0	54.6	58.5	57.0	20.9	24.9	29.3	30.2
100,000-150,000 (5)	14.5	16.3	18.2	19.3	22.3	33.9	34.4	15.1	17.7	19.7	20.6
75,000-100,000 (10)	14.7	17.4	19.4	19.6	32.7	41.0	40.4	15.8	17.9	19.0	21.2
50,000-75,000 (8)	11.5	13.7	15.5	16.2	24.9	31.3	31.3	12.9	14.3	16.5	16.3
below 50,000 (9)	5.7	7.7	9.5	10.2	15.7	28.7	28.3	6.9	8.5	10.8	11.3

Source: P. Korcelli, 1977. An Approach to the Study of Functional Urban Regions, International Institute for Applied Systems Analysis, Laxenburg.

[a]Number of places in each class is in parentheses.

Table 5-2
Natural Increase Indexes for Poland's Five Largest Cities

	\multicolumn{5}{c}{Natural Increase Index}	Gross Reproduction Index, 1970
	1950	1960	1965	1970	1975	
Poland total	19.1	12.9	10.0	8.5	10.2	1.064
Warsaw	12.5	7.2	2.2	1.4	3.4	0.617
Łódź	15.0	6.2	2.1	0.9	2.8	0.612
Cracow	11.3	9.3	5.1	5.3	7.0	0.714
Wrocław	31.5	14.0	8.6	7.3	9.4	0.636
Poznań	16.6	7.4	4.2	3.4	5.8	0.676

Source: *Rocznik Demograficzny,* 1967-68, 1971, 1976, Central Statistical Office, Warsaw.

individual cities, in fact, have converged with cities of a predominantly central-place character attracting manufacturing employment and those dominated by industry expanding their tertiary functions.

These trends need to be considered in the light of industrial location and housing policies, which shall be dealt with in the next section of this chapter. However, since such policies pertain to both interurban and intraurban dimensions, it is necessary first to discuss briefly those aspects of the internal structure of cities and metropolitan areas which are vital to their overall growth performance.

Intermetropolitan patterns in Poland can be interpreted as a product of planned development aimed at the creation of an urban environment satisfying conditions of social equity. This development has been superimposed upon, and has had partly to be adjusted to preexisting patterns. Its course also has been determined by economic constraints and technological factors as well as the desire to preserve cultural and historical values contained in urban forms. An example of the latter is the rebuilding of old town districts after the war. Planned development was facilitated by state control over urban land (in Warsaw it involved the communalization of all land within prewar boundaries) and over the housing market, and by the centralization of investment rights. The resulting spatial patterns can be traced in the socioecological structure as well as in the structure of land use and daily human interactions.

Recent factor ecological studies of Polish cities reveal that spatial variations in socioeconomic variables have clearly diminished and the concentric-sectoral patterns predating central planning have blurred.[7] The existing patterns can be described as mosaiclike; in addition to the social transformation involved, a major factor has been a housing policy which favored construction of multiunit blocks, offering more or less uniform standards in terms of equipment and residential density. Furthermore, a relative housing shortage has been a factor discouraging intraurban moves, while migration to metropolitan areas often is of a two-stage nature; that is, it first involves a move to a marginal zone, followed by a move to the city.

As a result of this migration sequence, major spatial variations can be observed between areas of residential development of different age, that is, between those built in the 1950s, 1960s, and 1970s. Areas developed in the form of large housing estates have been populated by families at a certain stage in their life cycle, and now tend to be homogeneous in terms of demographic characteristics. With the frontier of residential development moving outward from the city center toward the periphery of metropolitan areas, one may expect a growing regularity in terms of spatial demographic structure within areas of the same vintage; this structure is now reflected in variations in natural rates of increase. For example, the central part of Warsaw, rebuilt after the massive destruction of World War II, was characterized in the mid-1950s by birthrates somewhat higher than those in the intermediate zone; by the late 1960s, the central zone exhibited an excess of deaths over births.

Along with transforming the social structure of cities, another conspicuous objective of planning has been the division of urban space into residential, working, and recreation zones. Such a separation of major land uses was postulated by Polish planners even before World War II, and now has largely been achieved, accompanied by an expansion of public transportation. Aside from relatively high and uniform residential densities, in fact, the dominance of rapid transit is another characteristic feature of Poland's contemporary metropolitan areas. In Warsaw, for example, over 70 percent and in Łódź nearly 80 percent of all journeys to work are by public transport; the respective figures for commuting from outer zones to central cities are still higher. The overall relation between the number of work trips and distance traveled is unimodal, though the shape of the curve may be largely attributable to the spatial arrangement of trip destinations (i.e., concentration of jobs in central-city districts) and to intrametro population density patterns, rather than to the type of behavior represented by gravity or intervening opportunity formulas. The growing specialization of jobs and skills on the one hand, and the constraints imposed by the housing market suggest, however, that the selection of work place and residence within a metropolitan area are separate and largely independent processes.

Metropolitan Development Policies

When speaking of metropolitan development policies, or more broadly, in the case of Poland, of national urban policies, it should be kept in mind that such policies have both an explicit and implicit dimension. The latter refers to the impact of sectoral planning and resource allocation on the settlement system, and often it is crucial in the shaping of metropolitan forms. Relations between physical and economic planning in Poland have undergone an evolution which has led to the formulation of an integrated planning model. Such a model, based upon the provisions of the Spatial Planning Act of 1961, assumes an iterative procedure of adjusting sectoral decisions to spatial development goals. Owing to regional and metropolitan interdependence, this adjustment must take place at a central level, at least as far as production planning is concerned; it can and should be subject to regional disaggregation, however, with respect to tertiary activities.

Under economic planning, dominant most of the time since World War II, spatial development objectives at the macrolevel have always been clearly delineated. During the 1950s, national policies were aimed at rapid and extensive industrialization of the country, and the general guidelines adopted in locational analyses represented a uniform spatial distribution of productive forces. Due to scale and agglomeration economies, however, industrial development was more concentrated at selected points than planned. Also, given the deficiency of infrastructure in less developed areas, it frequently turned out to be more efficient to expand existing plants then to build new ones, though this trend was partly counterbalanced by diseconomies of congestion. As a result, during the 1950s and early 1960s, we saw both enlargement and spread of existing industrial districts, and the emergence of several new industrial concentrations based on the extraction of mineral resources.[8] The rate of population growth was highly correlated with that of industrial development; the fastest growth was experienced by those cities and metropolitan areas which were getting new, or rapidly expanding, industry. Interregional variations in economic indexes have remained basically unchanged over the 1950-65 period; this applies to the distribution of fixed assets, total investment outlays, and regional product.[9] On the other hand, spatial variations in consumption level diminished, showing the existence of major income transfer mechanisms.

The evident inertia of the spatial structure at the national level precipitated more radical deconcentration measures during the late 1960s. These were intended to limit the growth of large metropolitan areas and to stimulate the expansion of some 100 middle-sized cities. The conceptual basis for this policy was provided by new city planning methods based on economic efficiency calculations, which developed quite rapidly in Poland during the 1960s. Two major concepts applied to the estimation of the cost of urban growth, namely, threshold analysis of city growth and optimum city size, will be briefly discussed.

Threshold analysis of city growth assumes that cities face certain barriers to their expansion.[10] These are (1) natural environment barriers, (2) limitations related to the capacity of utility systems, and (3) the friction involved in a change of the scale of urban forms. When investment outlays per new inhabitant (or per unit of time or area) are plotted against total city population, they yield, it was argued, a curve of a wavelike shape. Modal points on this curve are defined as thresholds. Between individual thresholds, city growth involves relatively low cost, while passing through a threshold requires disproportionately high marginal investments. An analysis of urban development based on this concept makes it possible to compare alternative land development programs for a given city or metropolitan area as well as to appraise such alternatives between areas.

The threshold concept has been criticized on several grounds. First, it was found to be a partial concept and based on technical infrastructure costs only; second, it did not really fit historical data; third, it was claimed that the methods for calculating costs were ambiguous and not fully operational. On the other hand, it has been emphasized that threshold methods really are designed mainly in the analysis preceding the plan-building stage, and cannot be the sole basis for actual land development decisions.

The question of optimal city size has been thoroughly studied in many countries and has generated a voluminous literature of its own. In the Polish context, this question has been mainly posed in terms of a housing production model. It has been maintained that the total marginal cost of housing, technical infrastructure, and public services per inhabitant are positively correlated with city size. Moreover, this relation seems to be independent of the appearance of thresholds. Minimum cost has been estimated to fall between 20,000 and 100,000 population, with costs climbing dramatically above 200,000.

These concepts have been criticized for not accounting for total urban costs and for neglecting the productivity aspects of city size. Nonetheless, they provided a rationale for the so-called "deglomeration" policies carried on during the 1960s. Such policies were known and applied earlier, both in planned and market economies; for example, there were several attempts during the early 1960s to curb the growth of Paris by promoting spatial deconcentration of industry. In Poland, some deglomeration measures were used just after World War II, mainly focused on the industrial conurbation of Upper Silesia. One also has to account for deconcentration, such as involuntary out-migration of industry brought about by urban redevelopment. Generally, however, the term deglomeration would denote urban growth limitation policies rather than "spontaneous" industrial or population deconcentration, such as American-style suburbanization.

As mentioned earlier, the 1950-65 period was characterized by a relative equilibrium between forces of concentration and deconcentration. In terms of total as well as industrial employment, the largest metropolitan areas were growing faster than the national average, though this growth was reflected in an increase of labor-force-participation rates and an extension of commuting range rather than in an expansion of central-city population. Furthermore, investment in manufacturing was expanding faster than capital outlays for infrastructure, with the particular shortfalls in housing and services. To meet the demand for labor, it was necessary either to allow for large-scale migration to metro areas, or to accommodate, somehow, further increases in commutation flows. These solutions seemed unsatisfactory, since they would have involved growing spatial differentials in the level of economic development or the social adjustment problems resulting from mass migration. Under these assumptions the interdependence between costs of urban growth on the one hand, and city size as well as its growth rate on the other, provided conceptual evidence in favor of a policy to limit the growth of large cities. Other bases for that policy were to tap the existing labor resources of smaller urban places and promote their overall development as well as to stimulate the expansion of capital-intensive manufacturing sectors within metropolitan areas.

Urban growth limitation policies which were introduced in 1965 and continued until 1970 pertained to the metropolitan areas of Warsaw and five other large cities: Cracow, Poznań, Wrocław, Łódź and Gdańsk. The main mechanism was administrative control of employment increases in individual enterprises and the identification of enterprises which could be transferred to smaller urban places in the hinterland, or merged with existing enterprises. For example, in Warsaw all enterprises and other labor-employing institutions were divided into three categories: those which were expected to grow, which included national growth industries; those which could develop in the metro area without a further increase in employment; those which should be discontinued or moved to other areas. The latter consisted mainly of plants which were environmentally degrading or which had low productivity.

The policies were generally effective; while during 1960-64, total employment in the socialist sector in the city of Warsaw expanded annually by 3-6 percent (as compared with the national average of 2.3 percent), this rate dropped to 0.7 to 1.9 percent during 1966-70. As a result, Warsaw's share in total national employment fell from 8.5 to 7.3 percent.

Net in-migration to Warsaw also declined, from 12.6 per thousand population in 1960 to 10.4 in 1970. Table 5-1 shows that over the 1960-70 decade, the percentage of dwelling units in the largest core areas of functional urban regions increased by more than their share of total population, thus indicating an improvement of housing standards within major cities relative to their hinterlands.

There were adverse effects of urban growth limitation policies on demographic trends, intersectoral employment proportions, and development patterns of the outer zones of metropolitan areas. As far as demographic structure is concerned, a decline in and a high selectivity of migration in the largest cities has been reflected in changing age composition and in markedly declining rates of natural increase. With regard to employment structure, the shortage of manpower hindered the development of tertiary activities, whose growth already had been lagging behind that of industry. Finally, urbanization phenomena in the zone peripheral to metro areas were much faster than anticipated. A large influx of population into those areas could not be properly matched by the development of housing, local services, and commuter transport.

On the other hand, there also were positive consequences of urban growth limitation policies, including the stimulation of capital-intensive technology and a resultant increase in labor productivity. A number of small and medium-sized towns situated in the metropolitan periphery strengthened their economic base by receiving new industry; in many cases, these were branch or subsidiary plants of large establishments located inside metropolitan areas. Thus the migration of people has to a certain extent been replaced by the migration of jobs.[11]

The socioeconomic policy followed since 1970 has emphasized the need for an acceleration of growth by making full use of existing production capacity, skills, and infrastructure as well as by a comprehensive program of new investment. In this connection, due regard was given to the productivity aspects of large cities and metropolitan areas, resulting in a considerable relaxation of urban growth limitation measures and in the rapid development of housing construction. Starting in the late 1960s, numerous studies of the structure of urban systems and of economies and diseconomies of urban agglomerations have provided new inputs for spatial planning.[12] These studies all emphasized that metropolitan areas should be allowed to grow. In the long run, it was argued, improvements in living conditions in major areas would constitute a major pull factor in overall migration flows besides effecting labor market participation. It was found that manufacturing industries in metropolitan areas were characterized by higher labor productivity when compared to nonmetropolitan areas, and by a more effective implementation of investment programs; as a consequence of smaller average size and older age of plants, however, they were somewhat less capital intensive than was the case elsewhere. In terms of technical innovation diffusion, metropolitan areas accounted for over 90 percent of all patents registered during the 1963-73 period.

The expression of the new spatial policy has been the National Plan of Physical Development for the period up to 1990. Its basic principle has been formulated as "moderate polycentric concentration." The plan stems from the work of the Governmental Committee of Experts on Spatial Development as well as from numerous planning and academic institutions. Its major goals include spatial integration of all regions on the national level, efficient use of existing resources, protection and enhancement of man's environment, and equalization of interregional differentials in the level of living.

With respect to settlement patterns, it is postulated that urban population should increase more than twice as fast as the total population from the early 1970s up to 1990, while the population of metropolitan areas (the eighteen areas defined as "urban agglomerations") is expected to grow even somewhat faster. Thus, socioeconomic development should proceed via the growth of selected centers, including nine "developed" or mature urban agglomerations, nine agglomerations which are not yet fully shaped, and thirty-two other urban places, or clusters, ranging in size from 30,000 to 140,000 inhabitants in 1975. These centers vary substantially in terms of anticipated growth rates, however, with the rate being inversely related to present population size. For metropolitan areas and urban places of over 1 million, 0.5-1 million, 100,000-500,000, 60,000-100,000, and 30,000-60,000, population the respective indexes (1970 = 100) are estimated as 118, 131, 141, 158, and 169, respectively.[13] Selected middle sized cities, rather than large metropolitan areas, are expected to experience the fastest growth rates up to 1990. In this way the polycentric nature of the Polish urban system is likely to become strengthened, while efficiency objectives are to be accomplished via a moderate concentration and functional integration of individual urban places within the national system of cities.

The network of urban growth centers has been planned in such a way as to ensure that services are spatially accessible to all the population. It is recognized that for an urban place to perform higher-order service functions, a threshold population of 80,000-100,000 is required. It is conceivable that zones of intensive daily human interactions centered around cities of that size, and around larger metropolitan areas, will cover the whole national territory by 1990, and that the spatial organization of tertiary activities will conform to the pattern of urban regions. This trend has been supported by a reform of the territorial administrative structure, carried out during 1973-75, which involved a change from a three-level to a two-level hierarchy, with the twenty-two units at the highest level (voivodships) being replaced by forty-nine. And the list of new voivodship capitals closely follows the list of urban growth centers as identified in the National Physical Development Plan. The four largest metropolitan areas (Warsaw, Łódź, Cracow, and the Upper Silesia conurbation) now are each a single administrative region.

Problems involved in the implementation of the proposed spatial change have to be considered within the framework of demographic trends, distribution of manpower, and intrametropolitan structure. Since 1973, the natural increase index for the nation as a whole has risen and long-range demographic projections have been adjusted accordingly. It still remains to be seen, however, whether this change reflects only a shift in the age-related fertility schedule, or a more general evolution of fertility behavior itself. At present, large metropolitan areas do not fully reproduce their population, and this also is true of those rural areas which have recently experienced the heaviest out-migration. One interesting aspect of migration patterns, effecting the regional distribution of fertility rates, is that among migrants, women are more numerous than men. Population projections for the whole country, therefore, have to be looked at from the perspective of a regional decomposition of migration origins and destinations.

A related problem is that of intersectoral manpower balance and the spatial distribution of manpower. The modernization of agriculture, projected for the next fifteen years or so, will require a thinning out of agricultural population, but it also will require retaining in rural areas those who will carry on the technological and organizational changes. Thus migration controls have to be differentiated at a regional scale. A lower than anticipated level of rural-to-urban and of interregional migration might result in a locational pattern of economic activity less concentrated than originally estimated.

Finally, expansion of metropolitan areas and other major urban centers will require substantial adjustments and transformations of their spatial patterns, which will require the allocation of considerable resources; and the situation will vary in areas of differing population size. Recent growth has brought about a consolidation of built-up areas within the largest agglomerations, but future population increase will make their marked further territorial expansion inevitable.

Implications for Recent Metropolitan Trends in America

There are two aspects which are important in a comparative view of recent metropolitan trends: one relates to the spatial concentration-deconcentration phenomenon itself, and the other to actions intended to control the direction of change. As far as the former aspect is concerned, one can speak of common characteristics of the late 1960s and of diverging growth patterns in the early 1970s. In a long-range perspective, it is possible to envision a slackening of growth rates followed by stability of population in Poland's large metropolitan areas, mainly as an effect of national demographic trends and, perhaps, of an evolution of locational preferences. The course of this evolution will depend highly on future transformations of intrametropolitan patterns and environmental conditions prevailing within metro areas.

The second aspect of the comparison, however, seems to be more basic in the present context. It has been demonstrated that different socioeconomic conditions produce different urban forms as a consequence of the pursuit of different development goals—what Friedmann and Wulff refer to as variations in the "shape of relevant decision space for each of the phenomena observed."[14] Under centrally planned socialist economies, this space is delineated by such elements as the integration of physical with economic planning, the interaction between plan design and plan implementation, the absence of formal land rent mechanisms, and a clear correlation between the extent of metropolitan areas and the national territorial administrative structure. Keeping this in mind, it still seems possible to point to certain general effects of observed development trends and of the efforts to control them. As far as urban growth limitation policies are concerned, for example, four such consequences deserve mention.

First, the slowing down of metropolitan growth in terms of population and employment increase during the late 1960s resulted in a relatively faster improvement of housing conditions within the core areas, compared to the remaining parts of metropolitan regions; the same was true of public services. Second, control over employment growth brought about a measurable increase in labor productivity within metropolitan areas. Third, the limiting of in-migration and its rather high selectivity became reflected in changing age and sex composition of the population as well as in natural increase rates. This produced a long-run feedback effect on manpower resources and a shorter-run effect with respect to the demand for public services. Fourth, it was clearly shown that control over employment constitutes a very effective tool of urban growth limitation policy, compared, for example, with population in-migration control—the latter policy had been used in Warsaw since 1954, with less pronounced results.

These developments may be of certain interest for the North American experience, despite the difference in the nature of deconcentration phenomena, that is, planned versus self-generating deconcentration. It is often emphasized, however, that the widespread deconcentration of metropolitan areas in America to a certain degree has been stimulated, if not induced, by institutional factors; in particular by federal and state policies for housing, transportation, and organization of metropolitan government. They demonstrate stability or decline in terms of quality and overall development level. They also indicate that a slow-growth process may carry in itself the roots of a trend reversal. This latter aspect has been demonstrated by the growth experience of Poland's metropolitan areas in the 1970s.

Although past performance of metropolitan areas in terms of population and economic trends cannot provide a fully reliable basis for predicting trend reversal, it is instructive to recall some theory and policy statements referring to earlier phases of metropolitan growth. Forty years ago the authors of a widely quoted report had this to say about metropolitan problems in the United States:

Because cities do not reproduce their population (in 1930 only three cities of over 100,000 had a reproduction index above 1.0) if the largest cities are to grow or even maintain themselves, their population must ... [come from rural areas]. But since ... the rural birth rate is also declining rapidly, a marked slowing down of city growth is impeding. [These prospects] presage a number of important changes in the economic and social life of cities.... These enterprises ..., the growth of which depends upon and responds to increase in population, should become more stable. Thus we may look forward to a lessening need for the expansion and to an increased need and opportunity for improving the quality of public utilities, of welfare and educational institutions, and to more gradual changes in land values.[15]

Two decades later another well-known statement by the Committee for Economic Development documented substantial changes in metropolitan development patterns as compared to the 1930s.[16] It pointed to the increasing concentration of population, employment, and investment in metropolitan areas, and to the likely continuation of such trends. At the same time, intrametropolitan problems, especially the need for urban renewal and for more comprehensive metropolitan governments, were strongly emphasized. Substantial population and employment deconcentration within metropolitan areas (from central cities to ring) was predicted for the 1960-75 period, but the overall picture was one of further growth and expansion.

By the mid-1960s, along with falling birthrates, the growing concern about environmental quality, and the mounting problems of central cities, new tones appeared in urban literature. In an influential article on urban fields, Friedmann and Miller predicted a reversal of the established core-periphery proportions, and displayed a picture of "an utmost dispersal" for the United States in the year 2000: the evidence for 1970-74 seems in accordance with this line of thinking.[17]

Nonetheless, in light of earlier arguments, it seems equally safe to predict a trend reversal as to assume a trend continuation for the United States. This would involve an upturn of spatial concentration, following after the present phase of deconcentration. Such a sequence would depend on a multitude of factors, some exogenous, others endogenous to metropolitan growth itself. Among the former, it is customary to allude to energy and environmental problems, while the latter seem to include primarily forces shaping intrametropolitan patterns and the evolution of proportions between regionally and nonregionally oriented segments of the metropolitan economic base.[18]

Finally, a key factor determining future metropolitan trends is that of population growth. As argued in this chapter as well as in Chapter 2, the nature of this factor is both external and internal to the trends under discussion; but so far a comprehensive theory of demographic structure and change within metropolitan areas remains to be developed.

Notes

1. A. Pred., "The Growth and Development of Systems of Cities in Advanced Economies," in *Systems of Cities and Information Flows: Two Essays,* Lund Studies in Geography, Ser. B, 38, 1973; and "The Interurban Transmission of Growth in Advanced Economies: Empirical Findings versus Regional Planning Assumptions," International Institute for Applied Systems Analysis, 1976, Report RR-76-4.

2. K. Dziewoński, "The Place of Urban Agglomerations in the Settlement System of Poland," *Geographia Polonica,* vol. 30, 1975, pp. 9-20.

3. See L.S. Bourne, *Urban Systems: Strategies for Regulation,* Oxford: Clarendon Press, 1975; B.J.L. Berry and E.E. Horton, eds., *Geographic Perspectives on Urban Systems,* Englewood Cliffs, N.J.: Prentice-Hall 1970; and G.M. Lappo, "Basic Characteristics and Problems of the Development of Urban Agglomerations," *Georgraphica Polonica,* vol. 37, 1976.

4. P. Hall, "International Urban Systems: Outline of a Research Project,"

in H. Swain and R.D. MacKinnon, eds., *Issues in the Management of Urban Systems,* International Institute for Applied Systems Analysis, 1975, Report CP-75-4; and N. Hansen, "Systems Approaches to Human Settlements," Laxenburg: International Institute for Applied Analysis, 1976, Report RM-76-3.

5. P. Korcelli, "An Approach to the Study of Functional Urban Regions," Laxenburg: International Institute for Applied Systems Analysis, 1977.

6. K. Dziewoński et al., Rozmieszczenie i migracje ludności a system osadniczy Polski Ludowej (Distribution, Migrations of Population and Settlement System of People's Poland), Prace Geograficzne, 117, Ossolineum, Wrocław, 1977.

7. A. Jagielski, Struktury społeczno-ekologiczne miast polskich (Sociological Structure of Polish Cities), paper presented at the Conference on Urbanization Concepts in Poland, Kazimierz, Poland, 1975; and G. Weclawowicz, Struktura prezestrzeni społecznogospodarczej Warszawy a latach 1931 i 1970 w świetle analizy czynnikowej (The Structure of Socioeconomic Space of Warsaw, 1931 and 1970, in the Light of Factor Analysis), Prace Geograficzne, 116, Ossolineum, Wrocław, 1975.

8. K. Dziewoński, "Population Problems in the Polish Regional Planning," paper presented at the Conference on Demography and Urbanization in Eastern Europe, University of California at Los Angeles, 1975, (unpublished).

9. S. Leszczycki, "Long-term Planning and Spatial Structure of Poland's National Economy," Ossolineum, Wrocław: P.Ac.Sc., 1971.

10. B. Malisz, Ekonomika kształowania miast (Economics of City Formation), Studia, 4, Committee for Space Economy and Regional Planning, Warszawa, P.Ac.Sc., 1963. For a criticism, see Kozlowski, Analiza progowa za granica (Threshold Analysis Abroad), Studia, 34, Committee for Space Economy and Regional Planning, Warszawa, P.Ac.Sc., 1973.

11. M. Ciechocińska, Deglomeracja Warszawy, 1965-70 (Growth Limitation Policies for Warsaw, 1965-70), Biuletyn 80, Committee for Space Economy and Regional Planning, P.Ac.Sc., Warszawa, 1973.

12. K. Dziewoński, Hipoteza przekształceń sieci osadniczej w Polsce do roku 2000 (A Hypothesis on the Transformation of Settlement Network in Poland until 2000), in Prognozy rozwoju sieci osadniczej (Committee "Poland 2000"), P.Ac.Sc., Ossolineum, Warszawa, 1971, p. 28.

13. K. Fiedorowicz, System osadniczy w planie przestrzennego zagospodarowania kraju do 1990 r (Settlement System in the National Plan of Physical Development until 1990), Warszawa, Miasto, 9, 1-5, 1976, p. 29.

14. J. Friedmann and R. Wulff, "The Urban Transition," *Comparative Studies of Newly Industrializing Societies, Progress in Geography,* London: Edward Arnold, 8, 1976, pp. 1-93.

15. National Resource Committee, "Our Cities: Their Role in the National Economy," Washington: Government Printing Office, 1937.

16. B.J.L. Berry, "The Geography of the United States in the Year 2000," *Transactions,* Institute of British Geographers 51, 21-53, 1970, p. 27.

17. Committee for Economic Development, "Guiding Metropolitan Growth," New York, 1960.

18. J.T. Little and C.L. Leven, "Internal Migration in the Mature American City," in A. Brown and E. Neuberger (eds.), *Internal Migration; A Comparative Perspective,* New York: Academic Press, 1977; and H. Richardson, *Regional Growth Theory,* London: MacMillan, 1974.

Part IV
Functions of the Mature Metropolis

6

The Central City in the Postindustrial Age

Harvey S. Perloff

Some of the major economic trends—particularly the continuing growth of the service industries—would seem to favor large central cities. Services provide many jobs of the kind that fit the characteristics of the segment of the labor force that is most unemployment-prone: unskilled or semiskilled work, often part-time, frequently calling for interests and talents found among groups living in the central cities. But there is a *Catch 22* situation here. Public service jobs have a definite ceiling imposed by fiscal restraints; in fact, resistance to increased public outlays is growing. Private service jobs are in an underdeveloped state. And therein lies a tale, a tale which is all tied up with the socioeconomic transformation on which we are embarked.[a]

Socioeconomic Changes Under Way

There is broad agreement that the United States is going through a major transformation, entering on a postindustrial age. As the vagueness of the term "postindustrial" suggests, there is not the same agreement as to what the nature of the new era is, but two features of the postindustrial era emerge as particularly significant and are widely accepted as central to the concept. One is the growing importance of the service industries, as contrasted to the goods-producing industries. The other is the importance of information, or knowledge, technology and of a technical and professional class, or what Daniel Bell calls a "knowledge class."

It is interesting to note that the centrality of these notions was identified as early as 1935 by Allan G.B. Fisher, a British economist.

The transfers (to service employments) are being made, but they are not being made with sufficient speed, and they are made in the face of widespread feeling that the new types of work are wasteful and unproductive. If our argument is sound, poetry and philosophy are significant not only on account of their own intrinsic value, but also because their organization on an economic base is an essential condition for stability in a progressive economy.... It is essential that steadily increasing attention should be paid to the production of the amenities of life, of things which poorer communities have been in the habit of regarding as luxuries....

---

[a]Leland Burns, Richard Kirwan, Peter Marris, Donald Shoup, and Martin Wachs made valuable suggestions on an earlier version of this "tale" and Lee Lashway assisted in a literature review and data collection for this chapter.

When we reach a level of wealth where the provision of personal services become economically important, the importance of the limitations of physical natural resources in the narrow sense steadily diminishes. We are then much more concerned with the exploitation of human capacity (which is also perfectly "natural"), and the maintenance of a moving equilibrium in a progressive economy comes to depend more and more upon the effective organization and education of human capacity.[1]

In 1940 Colin Clark established the fact of the shifting importance of the primary, secondary, and tertiary (service) sectors as an economy develops and incomes grow.[2] Both Clark and Fisher stressed sector differences in income elasticity of demand and changes in productivity as responsible for the growth of services. People want just so many things and, above certain income levels, buy more and more services. At the same time, goods-producing industries enjoy higher productivity than service industries, thus releasing workers for nongoods production.

In the United States, in the decades since these writings by Fisher and Clark, agricultural and manufacturing employment have indeed decreased in relative importance and service employment has grown steadily, until today about two out of every three workers in the country are engaged in service industries.[b] At the same time, knowledge technology has achieved ever-greater importance, and professional and technical employment (normally, jobs that require relatively high levels of education) has grown tremendously: from 3.9 million in 1940 to 11 million in 1970, making it one of the largest of the census occupational categories, second only to the 13.5 million in clerical and kindred workers.

The impact on the central cities of these and related changes has, not unexpectedly, been enormous. The related changes are themselves of no small significance. These include the flood of migrants (mostly poor and relatively uneducated) from the countryside and small towns to the central cities as agricultural jobs disappeared and the location of manufacturing changed. They also include the increasing footlooseness of manufacturing industries as mechanization and automation progressed and as communication technology reduced the importance of face-to-face contacts and permitted the separation of various processes in manufacturing.

Actually, the rapid growth of manufacturing which characterized the period between the Civil War and World War II, and which accompanied the decline in resources industries, continued past the midpoint of the twentieth century, stimulated to no small degree by the military demands of World War II and the

[b]Here the figures for employment in services are based on the census concept of nongoods-producing industries. A different figure would be appropriate if "service jobs" are related to occupations, so that managers and clerks in manufacturing, agriculture, and other goods-producing industries were encompassed. The concept of services is still a very fuzzy one, but this is not the place to try to put the concept on a sturdy foundation. That remains for later research, but here it should be noted that the conventional definitions we are using, if anything, understate the shift to services.

Korean war and by postwar filling of delayed consumer demand. But it soon became apparent that manufacturing employment was declining in relative terms. Manufacturing employees as a percentage of employees in nonagricultural establishments fell from 34 percent in 1950 to 26 percent in 1974, while service employment rose from 59 percent to 69 percent.[3] In the not-too-distant future even absolute numbers in manufacturing might flatten out or decline, leaving all employment expansions to be filled by service activities.

The first major impact of the changes under way was felt in the older cities of the Northeast in which manufactures had long been important. Boston, New York, Detroit, Pittsburgh, Cleveland, St. Louis, and other giants of the Northeast and Midwest manufacturing belt found themselves facing problems of economic decline and resultant fiscal difficulties in the public sector. Important insights into what was going on were provided by large in-depth studies of New York and Pittsburgh at the end of the 1950s and the early 1960s as well as by a number of detailed national studies.[4] It was noted that the flattening out of overall industrial employment, as in the earlier cases of agriculture and mining, were accompanied by large interregional and interindustry shifts. Some industries and regions were hard-hit while others were experiencing expansion. Manufacturing industries, particularly where production processes had become routinized, as in textiles, were beginning to move away from the older high-cost areas and were locating in areas that had cheaper labor or pleasant climate and other amenities. The so-called Sunbelt was increasingly becoming a favored section of the country.

In addition, the various studies noted, economic activities were becoming more footloose, and this helped not only to explain the differential growth of employment and population among the various regions of the country but also their location in outlying parts of the large metropolitan regions. With flexible truck and automobile transportation, a firm could locate anywhere within the metropolitan region or beyond, and still take advantage of agglomeration economies and economies of scale in the specialized services and labor skills provided by a large metropolis, yet achieve the desired amenities for its managers and workers in the pleasanter, more protected outlying sections of the metropolis.

Whatever hopefulness was to be found in the situation of the central city was associated with the services industries. The studies of the 1950s and early 1960s stressed the fact that while the cities had grown as they did in order to accommodate the industrial expansion of the earlier years, and were in fact the products of the industrial age, they were also the natural habitat of the rapidly expanding service sectors of the economy. The service sectors were in fact more subject to economies of agglomeration through clustering than were the manufacturing industries, as verified by Robert Healy, based on the 1963 national input-output table.[5]

Also, these various studies suggested that services growth in the cities might well be bolstered by the growth of *new* manufacturing and service industries since the large cities were the source of much of the invention and innovation which were key to an expanding economy, so that while some industries were being lost, other industries were germinating in the cities and providing new sources of employment. Jane Jacobs argued that the decline and growth of cities are directly tied to the relative vigor of their innovative activities.[6] Economic expansion, she suggested, results from the unpredictable growth of innumerable offshoots that break away from established businesses. Interestingly enough, almost all the examples she gave referred to manufacturing activities.

Is a Turnaround Likely?

Now, as we review the figures of population decreases in such a high proportion of the larger central cities in the recent past, and employment decreases in some of them, we have to cope with the question of whether we are merely seeing a temporary phenomenon, and can expect future continued growth of the central cities by way of expansion of existing industries, or are we observing a long-term change in urban structure, despite the fact that over half of the large central cities (those with a population of a half million or more) lost population between 1960 and 1975.

My own view is that we can eliminate the possibilities of a substantial turnabout in the forces that have brought about a leveling off in manufacturing employment nationally and that are encouraging the move of manufacturing firms away from the central city. Automation continues unabated and is likely to have the same impact in the future as in the past, in the face of increasing labor costs and of improved techniques of quality control. Increased manufacturing footlooseness also seems assured with the continued automation of production, the greater possibilities for separation of the different manufacturing processes, increasing miniaturization, and the improvements in communications. Manufacturing firms can be expected to continue to seek out locations where wages are lower and unionization limited, or the appropriate labor force is available.

So strong are these forces that one can assume that even if the city was to continue to be an important source of invention and innovation in manufacturing, actual production and employment in the manufacturing realm resulting from this entrepreneurship would still take place largely in the outlying areas of the metropolis and in communities beyond the metropolis.[7] Thus, the economic future of the central city would seem to depend on the growth of service activities within the city. What can we anticipate, then, in the critically important services realm?

First, we should note that the service sector is merely a convenient catchall category for the many kinds of activities other than goods production. It is made up of wholesale and retail trade, business services, consumer services, and government, and each of these is composed of a wide variety of activities which can be classified in many different ways, depending on the purpose of the classification. A useful way of looking at this sector, in trying to get at the dynamics affecting the future of the central city, is in terms of, first, locational propensities and, second, organizational characteristics.

By looking at locational propensities of the various traditional services, we can see readily that the play of agglomeration economies does *not* serve to cluster these different services *together*, except in limited instances, but rather tends to relate the services to people and to manufacturing industry.

In the trade category, retail trade is, of course, associated with household numbers and income, and both of these factors have dictated, and will continue to dictate, a continued move to the suburbs and beyond. Wholesale trade has also been moving outward: (1) because the new technologies (such as mechanized and automatic loading) generally call for substantially increased space which can more easily be had in outlying areas, (2) because of wholesaling's close association to manufacturing, and (3) because the flexibility of trucking makes outlying locations attractive and feasible. The trend is clearly outward, without any reason to expect a turnabout.

In the business service category, such as transportation and repairs, a substantial proportion of the activities are related to manufacturing and wholesaling, so that further decentralization can be expected. The development of major activity centers throughout the metropolitan region and beyond is of significance, since the needed amount of clustering (for example, to be sure of nearby financial and legal services) can be achieved in many centers rather than necessarily downtown. Only where the services are provided over a very wide area and substantial face-to-face contacts are involved does the hold of the central city continue to be strong. This has been the situation in the case of the so-called FIRE (finance, insurance, and real estate) group, but even here it is not at all certain that decentralization may not be found attractive and feasible in the future.

In general, the agglomeration that was traditionally associated with the downtown area, and which gave the central city as a whole its economic vitality, can now be achieved in a variety of activity, or employment, centers spotted around the metropolitan field, over a very large area.[c] It is difficult to conceive any strong reasons why the present forces behind the trend lines would change

---

[c]In 1960, 413 of the 500 largest industrial corporations had their corporate head offices—activities which are information intensive and are supported by agglomeration economies—in central cities. That number had declined by twenty-two by 1970. An even larger relative change was registered for the home offices of retail firms, where 10 percent suburbanized between 1960 and 1970. However, there was virtually no change in the concentration in central cities of corporate home offices of commercial banks and life insurance companies. Leland S. Burns, "The Location of the Headquarters of Industrial Companies," *Urban Studies,* June 1977

and create conditions for a return of the various services discussed so far—which have been the dominant services of the past industrial era—to the central city.

Among the services, the most substantial employment growth in the central cities, aside from FIRE, has been in government and in the medical and education services, private as well as public. Here the locational propensity is different in nature than in the case of most of the other service categories. Agglomeration economies play only a limited role. The services tend to be subject to political pressures and to the evolving situation which categorizes the new era we are entering. This is particularly so in the case of public employment; a number of factors seem to be at work here. One is the generally higher demands for the services supplied by city governments in both quantity and quality.[8] A second is the service requirements imposed on the central city by the concentration of poor persons and the continued in-migration of poor families, particularly in welfare, health, education, and police protection. A third, and critically important, feature is the political pressure for the absorption of otherwise unemployed individuals into government employment. As poor and minority persons become an increasing proportion of the total population in the central city, the provision of jobs in government for these groups becomes a political imperative. This, however, is a self-limiting solution to the problems of employment in the central city, since a brake is inevitably applied by the increasingly serious fiscal difficulties the city faces as private jobs and higher-income taxpayers leave the city.

The picture that emerges from this view of service employment is quite different from one where the focus is limited to the relatively high growth of the service category *as a whole* and when the phenomenon of agglomeration economies is interpreted in terms of the situation that characterized the services *in the past*.

Are New Services in the Offing?

Some insight into the new and the more rapidly evolving services is provided through a review of the census occupation statistics (the service and nonservice categories are not as clearly differentiated as would have been desired). For the two decades between 1950 and 1970, the largest increase by far has been in the professional and technical category: an increase of 121 percent as against a total labor force growth of 37 percent for the two decades. Most striking is the increase in the "knowledge class" categories, a substantial proportion of which were not even listed in the 1950 census (e.g., computer specialists, mathematical specialists, operations and systems researchers and analysts, and vocational and educational counselors). Also striking is the increase in the number of "technologists and technicians," many of a paraprofessional character. Thus, while physicians, dentists, and related practitioners increased 31 percent in numbers, registered nurses, dietitians, and therapists increased by 125 percent, and health technologists and technicians grew by 238 percent. Also impressive is the growth of engineering and science technicians, a category not listed in 1950, to a total of 828,000.

Less recognized is the fact that there has been a relatively small increase in the managers and administrative category. The only substantial increases were in health administrators, public officials, school administrators, and in the FIRE group, particularly bank officers and financial managers. There has been a major decrease in the self-employed category, from 2,248,000 in 1950 to 913,000 in 1970.

In the large clerical category, the greatest increases (not shown in Table 6-1 to keep it to reasonable size) were in the following well-established groups: bank tellers, bookkeepers, cashiers, secretaries, library attendants, and office machine operators; the last of these grew from 146,000 in 1950 to 572,000 in 1970, up 292 percent. More interesting are the new categories not separately identified in 1950: teacher aides, enumerators and interviewers, estimators and investigators, and expediters and production controllers. In the "service worker" category the largest increases and the new groups are in health services (particularly nursing aides, orderlies and attendants, and other health aides), cleaning service workers (outside the household), protective service workers, and in such new categories as child care workers (outside the household).[d]

What Is New About the New Age?

The question about *new* services raises the basic question of what might be new about the emerging postindustrial period and what services might be particularly appropriate to this period. Further, can such new services develop on their own to help overcome the problems of the declining large central cities, or will they need special assistance to come into being or to expand. The discussion in this chapter will make the case that, to an important degree, the future economic viability of the large central city can be expected to depend on a special kind of invention and innovation—the development of *organizational capacity and skill* for encouraging the emergence and growth of those services which are particularly fitting to the future central city. The traditional kinds of invention and innovation—those associated with private R&D (research and development) activities and private business risk taking—by themselves, may well not be adequate to the evolving new situation. In an oft-quoted comment, Wilbur Thompson has noted:

---

[d]A confusion in terminology could result because of the different meanings attached to the word service. Here it covers cleaning service workers, food service workers, health service workers, personal service workers (barbers and hairdressers, child care workers, etc.), and protective service workers (guards, firemen, policemen, etc.).

Table 6-1
Occupation of Experienced Civilian Labor Force,[a] 1950 and 1970

	1970	1950	% Increase
Professional, technical, and kindred			
Accountants	712,703	383,676	85.8
Architects	56,878	25,000	127.5
Computer specialists	258,279	Not listed	
Engineers	1,230,652	534,424	130.3
Foresters and conservationists	41,687	27,052	54.1
Lawyers and judges	273,536	181,226	50.9
Librarians, archivists, and curators[b]	123,885	55,750	122.2
Life and physical scientists	205,501	116,445	76.5
Mathematical specialists	35,795	Not listed	
Operations & systems researchers, analysts	81,168	Not listed	
Personnel and labor relations workers	296,214	52,858	460.4
Physicians, dentists, and related practitioners[c]	540,934	414,166	30.6
Registered nurses, dietitians, and therapists	959,525	426,619	124.9
Health technologists & technicians	263,964	78,033	238.3
Religious workers	255,061	210,117	21.4
Social scientists	110,026	35,893	206.5
Social workers	221,125	76,467	189.2
Recreation workers	53,596	16,799	219.0
Teachers, college & university	490,877	125,583	290.9
Teachers, except college & university	2,779,046	1,127,845	146.4
Engineering and science technicians	827,519	Not listed	
Vocational and educational counselors	107,764	Not listed	
Writers, artists, and entertainers	794,598	570,976	39.2
Research workers, not specified[d]	118,185	76,962	53.6
All others	179,917	452,121	
Total	11,018,435	4,988,012	120.9
Managers and administrators, except farm			
Health administrators	64,966	Not listed	
Inspectors, public admin. (incl. construction inspection)	100,172	56,807	76.3
Officials and administrators, public admin., n.e.c.	248,210	155,303	59.8
School administrators	210,279	Not listed	

Table 6-1 (cont.)

	1970	1950	% Increase
Managers and administrators, n.e.c.	3,756,299	4,352,493	(−13.7)
Construction	397,130	291,251	36.4
Manufacturing	751,977	655,581	14.7
Transportation	164,459	148,609	10.7
Communications[e]	114,771	67,346	70.4
Wholesale trade	309,598	338,153	(−8.4)
Retail trade	1,119,077	1,949,689	(−42.6)
Finance, insurance, & real estate[f]	523,616	256,707	104.0
Personal services	223,014	212,068	5.2
Others	464,564	435,089	6.8
Other	1,531,804	511,830	
Total	6,223,637	5,076,436	22.6
Sales workers	5,432,633	4,044,143	34.3
Clerical and kindred workers	13,456,637	7,070,023	90.3
Service workers, except private household	8,448,671	4,511,996	87.2
Private household workers	1,142,598	1,487,574	(−23.2)
Transportation equipment operators	2,888,180	3,063,110	(−5.7)
Total, mainly service occupations	31,368,719	20,176,846	55.5
Craftsmen and kindred workers	10,435,084	8,152,743	27.9
Operatives, except transport	10,517,417	8,652,496	21.5
Laborers, except farm	3,515,336	3,750,990	(−6.3)
Farmers and farm workers	2,345,198	6,835,356	(−65.7)
Total nonservice and mixed occupations	26,813,035	27,391,585	(−2.1)
Occupation not reported	5,179,626	1,366.064	
Total Labor Force	80,603,453	58,998,943	36.6

Sources: 1950: U.S. Bureau of the Census, *U.S. Census of the Population: 1950,* Vol. II, *Characteristics of the Population,* Part I, U.S. Summary, table 124; 1970: U.S. Bureau of the Census, *Census of Population: 1970,* Vol. I, *Characteristics of the Population,* Part I, U.S. Summary–Section 2, table 221.

[a]Fourteen years old and over.

[b]Includes librarians only, because curators and archivists were not listed for 1950.

[c]Includes chiropractors, dentists, optometrists, pharmacists, physicians (medical and osteopathic), podiatrists, veterinarians, health practitioners.

[d]The 1950 figure is "Technicians, testing"; 1950 census listed nothing comparable to "research workers, not specified."

[e]Includes utilities and sanitary services.

[f]In 1970 a separate category of "bank officers and financial managers" was established, but here the two categories are combined to make the 1950 and 1970 figures comparable.

n.e.c. not elsewhere classified

The long-range viability of any area must rest ultimately on its capacity to invent and/or innovate or otherwise acquire new export bases.

The economic base of the larger metropolitan area is, then, the creativity of its universities and research parks, the sophistication of its engineering firms and financial institutions, the persuasiveness of its public relations and advertising agencies, the flexibility of its transportation network and utility systems, and all the other dimensions of infrastructure that facilitate the quick and orderly transfer from old dying bases to new growing ones.[9]

The new postindustrial era may well call for invention and innovation of a kind not contemplated by Thompson.

Against this background, what services *are* appropriate to the emerging period? To arrive at some notion of what such services might be, we cannot avoid conjecture on the characteristics of the age we are anticipating. Daniel Bell, who has written extensively on the postindustrial concept, puts the major emphasis on the centrality of theoretical knowledge, involving increasing dependence on science as the means of innovating and organizing technological change. "Most of the industrial societies," he has written, "are highly sensitive to the need for access to scientific knowledge, the organization of research, and the increasing importance of information as the strategic resource in the society."[10]

The importance of knowledge and information certainly seems key to everything else. But there are other forces at work as well which are likely to have a profound impact on the nature of future society in the United States. These include:

1. Increasing importance of transnational and international economic (and other) activities: There are many forces making for increasing interdependence among nations and for investment, production, and sales of resources, goods, and services and transmission of information across national boundaries.

2. Increasing leisure and leisure-time activities: Both actual events—such as the emphasis on vacations and other free time and of early retirement in Gallup, Harris, and other polls suggest that activities related to leisure can be expected to gain in significance in the future, even though some of us may be uncomfortable with this idea in a period when "lowered expectations" are asked for.

3. Increasing emphasis on the arts and on culture in all aspects of American life: This may be associated with rising incomes and greater leisure time, but may also be related to a reaction or resistance to the increasing role of science and technology in our lives.

4. Increasing concern with self (self-awareness and mental and physical health) and with quality of life: Again, probably associated at least in part with rising incomes and greater leisure time and with the creation of a counterforce to the powerful technological and economic developments under way and to the power of the organizations directing these developments.

These tendencies are not easy to pin down (certainly not in traditional measurement and conceptual terms), and it is difficult to judge whether they are likely to be basic long-term forces or are temporary (fashionable?) features of current life. For the time being, at least, they seem very real and quite powerful and are likely to have a significant impact on the middle-term future, say, the next two decades or to the magic year 2000.

For our purposes, these tendencies, taken with the two central features—growth of service industries and of knowledge technology—provide a suggestive base for thinking about the service activities that could conceivably evolve as important employment outlets in a postindustrial era. Thus, there are a number of candidate services that should be considered as potentially significant in the future life of the city.

Head Office and Knowledge-Technology Activities

The management and administration of economic and other societal activities are often organized into separate offices, removed from the operations they direct. Hoover and Vernon stress the importance to central offices of being near a host of specialized services. "Face-to-face interchange is the only adequate means of communication for much of the executives' work.... Delicate negotiations and subtle, complex ideas are not easily entrusted to the telephone or the letter." They suggest that the other factors that favor central-city location are mass transit, the better opportunities for after-hours recreation, lunch-hour shopping (or window-shopping), and "the greater opportunities for husband hunting," on the part of the young women who make up the largest part of the office workers.[11] These "headquarter" activities have grown rapidly in recent decades and are expected to continue to expand. Substantial numbers of them have located in central cities because of the advantages of face-to-face contacts both with others in the same industry and with persons and groups performing a wide variety of specialized services.[12] Increasingly, headquarter services employ knowledge technology to substantial degrees. It is interesting in this connection to note that computer specialists increased from some 12,000 in 1960 to 258,000 in 1970; there was no such census category in 1950.

Certain trends in these activities are likely to have a major influence on their future location, particularly the fact that they are increasingly national and international in scope. Thus, convenience in regard to transportation, particularly air transport, and movement between suburbs and central city, already significant, will be even more important in the future. The effectiveness with which transportation is organized in central cities will undoubtedly play a large role in the location of these activities.

The growing international scope of central-office activities is particularly intriguing. The likelihood of large foreign investments in the United States suggests the counterpart of foreign office employment here and substantial back-and-forth movement of foreign business and government officials. The existence of ethnic enclaves in many of our major cities could conceivably turn out to be an advantage in locational terms with regard to some countries (such as Japan) *if* these enclaves are themselves satisfying places for visiting, work, living, and recreation. In a more general sense, the relative attractiveness of the city as a place in which to live and work will probably have a more substantial impact on the location of this set of activities than any of the other service categories.

Recreation and Tourism

While these are already significant in present-day cities, if we look ahead to the likely pattern of life in the postindustrial era, we can begin to appreciate the tremendous scope for enlargement and elaboration of recreation and tourism into major service industries. Reasonable projections of family expenditures for recreation in the future suggest a large demand for such services *overall,* but the form of these outlays will be determining of the share that will provide employment opportunities in central cities. While there is a temptation to assume that if there is demand for a service, supply will be forthcoming, the fact is that there have been very few creative, imaginative private investments in recreation in the cities. The concentrated urban form of Disneyland and Disneyworld have yet to be invented; and Disneyland, it should be noted, attracts 20 million paying customers a year. Nor have any U.S. cities yet developed an attraction to match Tivoli Gardens in Copenhagen.

Sports are only now being organized as sizable businesses, but most recreation is still in the horse-and-buggy stage. In the public realm, "parks and recreation" activities in most places provide a primitive attempt to cope with the new demands. It seems likely that quite new kinds of agencies, sponsored and supported by local governments but possibly private or mixed in form, will have to go into the recreation-development business if the necessary physical facilities are to be created which fit the scale of recreation and leisure-time activities appropriate to the postindustrial period. Such agencies will have to stop being squeamish about charging for the use of recreational facilities if they are to be built at the scale and with the quality and imagination to make them economically successful.

Tourism is already a major central-city industry, but it, too, has a long way to go. Certain trends are particularly suggestive. Thus, tourism tends to be combined with conferencing and other activities as there is a greater tendency to combine work and play. Also, the "package deal" is becoming the heart of the tourism industry and this means that expert marketing is key to tourist dollars. To date, there has been remarkably little imaginative planning in cities of this key service and the facilities required, though private groups have invested large sums in the business end of the services (in hotels particularly), and governments have lent a hand in a limited way through the building of convention centers and other facilities. While outlying areas have advantages in the space available for tourism activities, cities also have certain advantages which come with clustering and urbanity. However, both the facility and service elements have not been planned and developed as yet in a form fully to exploit these advantages.

Arts and Cultural Services

As outlets for employment and income generation, the performing, graphic, and other arts present even more of a problem in the organizational realm than do recreation and tourism; and the latter are difficult enough. One can readily see the arts and cultural activities as a dominant feature of the future urban scene, if appropriate organizational (including financing) forms and techniques can be developed.

Certain of the "popular" performing arts are just now beginning to be organized as major business activities (e.g., rock and jazz concerts and the giant record industry), but the employment and income-generating potentials are hardly being scratched. Also, a revival of the crafts that seems to be under way may have some potential. Substantial numbers of potters, leather workers, stained glass workers, photographers, furniture makers, and other craftsmen and artists appear in large numbers at street fairs in major cities around the country. It is intriguing to speculate whether American cities, in the most advanced industrial nation, might begin to develop the kind of "informal" sector which accounts for so much of urban employment in the Third World, as suggested by Peter Marris in discussion with the author. This development could be encouraged by relaxing zoning restrictions and by a willingness to preserve old, cheap, small-scale facilities suitable for craft workshops rather than redevelop them out of existence. This is a counterpart to the plea made by Raymond Vernon in his New York study twenty-five years ago not to destroy the old lofts which are important for small businesses just getting started.

Aside from their direct contribution to employment, the arts in various forms may turn out to be as much an element in the future infrastructure of the city to support its economic base as is transportation or other traditional infrastructure elements. But its potential contribution to the economic base should not be underestimated; the backward linkages in the arts, particularly the performing arts, are substantial, with backstage employment opportunities providing semiskilled and low-skilled persons over and above the front-stage professionals. Special efforts in training paraprofessionals can help expand the role of such workers.

A city flourishing in the arts can be expected to attract tourism, office employment, and other activities. Providing appropriate public facilities, sensitivity in the preservation of old buildings and facilities that can be useful for the arts, provision of tax breaks for performing groups, adjusting regulations building by building rather than zoning in large blocks in certain sections of the city, sponsorship of art fairs and changing those regulations that hinder them, and many other kinds of assistance can help meet the special needs of the arts if they are to comprise a substantial service component in the city of the future.

Health, Learning, and Other Personal Services

There are at least three considerations in this area of services. First, a major expansion of the more-or-less traditional medical and educational services in the cities will depend on new forms of national financing and organization, such as the creation of a national health service, adoption of national health insurance, or substantial national support of community and junior college education. For example, as the medical care for local people is more and more often paid from state or national governments, health insurance plans, or other sources external to local communities, the health industry takes on the character of an export activity contributing to the local economic base. Traditionally, manufacturing generated the "foreign" income which triggered the local employment multiplier; now services which are paid for externally do the same. Hence, a regional hospital may stimulate local economic growth, through generating "foreign exchange" just as a manufacturer of, say, optical goods did in the past. The possibilities involved in this type of development have been so widely discussed in recent years that no further elaboration is needed here.

Less widely discussed have been the newly developing health and learning services, as contrasted with conventional medical and educational services. These may be of special interest to the central city. On the health side, there has been a proliferation of health-related activities, such as the health spas and clubs, exercise studios, yoga centers, body-beautifying salons, hair care centers, reducing parlors and other nutrition-related activities, and a wide variety of similar activities. Particularly profuse—and intriguing—are the activities broadly related to mental health and emotional stability, for a fee. Somewhat associated are psychological types of activities, including self-awareness and consciousness-raising activities. Some religious types of activities relate to these various elements.

On the learning side, new services—both private and public—are being created which extend beyond traditional schooling, for example, which offer to help parents in the development of their children in the supposedly critical early years of life, which train skills of every conceivable type from the martial arts to rapid reading, and which offer child-sitting service in a supposedly educational environment.

Related to both health and learning services are activities associated with child care, care of the aged, and the care of others who need continuing attention. While some of these services are already well established (e.g., nursing homes), it seems evident that personal care is at an early stage of development and has a long way to go, including the probable development of such features as interage care and the creation of various forms of communal living which involve extended family characteristics.

All of these developing activities are of interest here because they involve employment and income-generation features of potential importance for central cities as well, of course, as for suburbs and outlying communities. Unless there is something quite special about our own period which has given birth to many new activities noted above, so that they can be expected to peter out over time, we can expect a substantial growth of such activities and their development as regular service *industries*. Substantial portions of the employment and income generation from these services could conceivably be in the central cities.

A third consideration is the fact that the future scope for these services will depend in no small part on how the delivery of the services is organized. It is in this light that the reorganization of these services to permit the use of less-skilled and more readily available labor achieves importance for the future. An indication of the potentialities here is the development of paraprofessionals in the medical field that has taken place in recent years, which permits the use of semiskilled labor and the conserving of the rarer and more expensive skills of the doctor and specialist. There has been some interesting work on the portion of a physician's tasks judged by physicians to be appropriate for delegation. It turns out that even physicians think that substantial portions can be turned over to "physician extenders."[13]

Another useful and appropriate response to the needs in the medical field has been the development of emergency services, particularly associated with fire departments. This is clearly only a beginning and in the future many paraprofessionals and nonprofessionals will have to be employed and many nonhospital facilities used for medical and public health purposes if medicine is to achieve its full service potential.

The same holds for education. Experiments have been carried out to encourage the use of less-skilled and lower-cost personnel in education as well, but there has been substantial resistance among educators because of the fear that trained teachers will lose their jobs or suffer a decrease in salary levels. Given the tremendous needs for education in the future, to enable urbanites to live and work well in the highly complex and interdependent environment of the postindustrial era, there is clearly need for a vast array of paraprofessionals and nonprofessionals in the educational field as well as in medicine. As pointed out long age, however,

Barriers are maintained or raised to limit entry into the professions and similar "tertiary" types of work. In a poor community few people can be spared for work of these kinds. In a wealthy community it is inevitable and desirable that the number of workers in these departments should increase, but fearful lest the quasi-monopolistic privileges which they have been in the habit of enjoying should be destroyed, those who are already at work there raise the cry that "the professions are overcrowded."[14]

Thus, our ability to make appropriate use of such personnel and thereby enlarge the job as well as service-delivery possibilities of these important services in the postindustrial period will depend on organizational inventiveness, involving, in many cases, a major departure from present practices.

Neighborhood, Preservation, and Rehabilitation Services

Preservation and rehabilitation to maintain, modernize, and enrich the tremendous social overhead in our cities have only just begun; the scope for the service components of these activities has been severely limited. But they fit evolving tendencies and have characteristics which suggest that they *could* achieve importance in a future period. These activities are closely related to the construction industry, but they have been a construction "step child," moving along in a disorganized, isolated, sporadic fashion, which, of course, means a highly costly fashion. If they were to proceed on an economically viable scale, there would be need for substantial innovation in learning how to do the job, the support of craftsmanship related to these activities, and a greatly improved legal and fiscal framework to encourage such efforts.

Similar considerations hold for what might in total be referred to as *neighborhood services,* ranging from the encouragement of "sweat equity" (individuals gaining assets through their own work) and of tenants furnishing housing services as a way of paying rent to the *collective* provision of security services, education services, rehabilitation activities, and the like. While such services might involve less money exchange than in the traditional patterns of providing services, they could add substantially to *real* local income and product, make life in the postindustrial era more community oriented than in the past, or reduce the high cost of living in cities. The further development of neighborhood cooperative food stores, lending operations, and related cooperative activities is in the same category.

There are other services that may well play a significant role in the life of the city in the future. There may be substantial employment possibilities in the many newer types of communication services that are already beginning to develop, for example, as well as in newer types of privately organized and community-organized protective services; there were almost a million protective service workers in 1970, reflecting the widespread concern for safety in response to growing crime rates. And, of course, there will be other opportunities, but they are likely to have many of the same basic characteristics as those described above.

How Is a Proper Fit to Be Achieved?

Central cities, as indicated earlier, are facing severe economic problems arising from the clustering of the poorer families and the unemployed and the mismatch of jobs and low-income people in metropolitan areas. Some 90 percent of the labor force in central-city poverty areas and an equal percentage of the long-term unemployed are in occupational categories other than high-skilled professional and managerial workers. Yet 100 percent of the net new male-held jobs created in central cities in the 1960s were professional and managerial jobs, not at all suited to the skill level of central-city poor and unemployed. Even in the best of times economically, the unemployment rate for minority youths ran as high as 15 to 20 percent; during the recession in the mid-1970s it was over 50 percent in some areas. The fact that many persons cannot get jobs when they want to, and particularly those first entering the labor market, is a personal and social tragedy of the greatest dimension.

As we review the economic activities that *can* be expected to grow in volume and in the provision of job opportunities that *might* be located in the central city in the future, we find that they have certain special characteristics in almost every case which pose serious problems from the standpoint of providing needed central city employment:

1. Many of them, *as now organized*—the arts and cultural activities, recreation, and preservation and rehabilitation activities, for example—are likely to require large amounts of public financial support and sponsorship if they are to expand substantially.
2. Many of them, *as now organized,* call for a relatively high level of skills.
3. Many of them provide a high proportion of part-time jobs and relatively low wages and salaries.
4. Most of them, to achieve much greater economic importance and service-industry status (i.e., a highly organized, sustained, exchange and employment-provision system) would need provision of substantial social overhead—for example, improved transportation, appropriate facilities, various public supports, helpful legal arrangements, and improvements in residential quality.

In general, a close look at the most promising services for the postindustrial age suggests that if they are to become important features of central-city life, they will require *substantial reorganization* in the forms in which they are provided and financed and will require a very close public-private partnership as well as sophisticated planning and provision of appropriate infrastructure.

At this point, a pessimist would say that the population and job decreases of the recent past, the fiscal difficulties, and the planning inadequacies of the large central city signal not only a culmination of the environmental and organizational mess left by the retreating industrial age but also signal an inadequate preparation for the coming postindustrial age, with its unique and different requirements and possibilities. In fact, he might say that what has emerged here is a perfect *Catch-22* situation. The only way the city can achieve rejuvenation, in the face of the powerful, well-established trends, is by a very substantial reorganization of service activities by governments and other institutions that today are unprepared and ill-equipped to lead such reorganization. Thus, we can expect the continuing decline of the central city for some time to come, with increasing social tensions and increased reliance on inadequate welfare solutions, the "city as sandbox," as George Sternlieb has called it.[15]

On the opposite side, an optimist might point to the fact that it took a very long period of time before private industry organized itself for the industrial era, and at least as long for the necessary infrastructure and other public supports for industry to be forthcoming; the adjustment to the postindustrial era, at worst, is likely to be much shorter. What is now most needed is the development of a new outlook that can enable us better to cope with the requirements of the new era, together with intensive and sustained study about these requirements and social experiments to learn to deal with them effectively. Taking this optimistic view as reflecting, at a minimum, a possible socially beneficial speeding up of what can be expected to happen anyway over time, we can draw on what has been described above to outline the kind of approach that seems to be called for.

First, decision makers and the general public will have to be convinced of the probability that, in the middle-term future, the present economic system will have difficulty in providing the number and kinds of jobs needed and that a conscious effort to develop and encourage the kind of new era services discussed here will have to be made. The price system should, supposedly, be able to guide the necessary adjustments if there is indeed greater and greater demand for services as compared to goods. But we have powerful institutional barriers. The minimum wage law, particularly as it impacts the employment of young persons in services, is one of them. The governmental requirements for preservation and building reconstruction and the controls with regard to construction crafts employment are another. The economic system is still largely geared to goods production, distribution, and consumption, and that extends from lending practices to the character of sales outlets.

Second, in-depth studies of the locational propensities of the various service industries are needed, so that cities can gear themselves to attract the most promising ones—that is, those that can conceivably gain from being located in the central cities. Trying to attract manufacturing firms seems to me to be misplaced. The cities must try to adjust to the economics of the evolving new era.

Third, given the nature of present unemployment in central cities, particular efforts will have to be made in promoting the new services to extend the scope for employing substantial numbers of workers from the poverty and minority communities as well as others who have found it difficult to enter the employment mainstream. What has been done to develop paramedical personnel and other paraprofessionals is in the right direction, but a very small drop in the bucket so far. Special efforts will have to be made to open up the scope for many new talents and skills as well as many jobs that are essentially unskilled. Some of the services, as in the case of neighborhood and rehabilitation services, are community oriented (or they can be) and can be geared specifically to help workers from within specific communities. Even the services that demand certain advanced skills, as in the case of most of the personal services, would, if appropriately organized, provide many jobs for workers in presently disadvantaged communities.

Fourth, many of the jobs in service industries today are part-time in nature and often poorly paid relative to the average wages and salaries in the nonservice industries.[16] It is quite possible that these characteristics will be as important in service occupations in the future, and maybe even more so. This is a two-edged proposition, however. While the disadvantages are obvious, there are also some advantages in terms of many women and young persons who are already in the labor force or who would like to enter it. A 1977 Labor Department survey showed that while only 15.6 million families continued to rely on one breadwinner, some 26.9 million families had two or more wage earners—nearly 22.3 million with both husbands and wives working, but with many of the wives working on a part-time basis only. Moonlighting, part-time jobs, and multiple family earners may well characterize the postindustrial age. Again, our laws and regulations may well have to be adjusted to make this a positive force in people's lives rather than largely a negative one.

Fifth, it seems inconceivable that there can be a "grand strategy" for promoting postindustrial era services, a strategy that can fit all the many different kinds of services, the various needs for physical infrastructure and other social overhead, and the wide variety of situations in which the different central cities find themselves. A variety of approaches will undoubtedly have to be worked out and all sorts of special situations provided for. Here is where the next phase of invention and innovation is needed; we cannot rely on the traditional sources of invention and innovation in this regard. We will need more public R&D than we have had in the past, including central-city organizations that can initiate and carry out social experiments. We need experiments on how to make services more *self-supporting,* when traditionally they have been publicly supported. Given the anticipated growth in service demands, public funds will otherwise be stretched thinner and thinner. We need experiments on the development of neighborhood services and preservation and rehabilitation services, on the extension of recreational and cultural services, on child care and care of the aged and on interage care services, on enhancing the attraction of ethnic enclaves, and similar developmental possibilities. Also, R&D approaches need to be applied to the development of central-city transportation and other infrastructure geared to the requirements of the new era. And we will need a much more flexible and sophisticated type of central-city planning than we have had to date. Such planning will have to be much more concerned with economic, social, and fiscal considerations than has been true to date, as well as with the new physical requirements of the emerging postindustrial age. However, while a grand strategy of the type envisaged in the national urban renewal, model cities, or poverty-program efforts in the past, seems inappropriate, that is not to say that central cities can meet future requirements entirely on their own. They will need federal financial support, given their own fiscal limitations. Central-city governments will also have to find ways to relate to sources of income and organizational strength in the remainder of the metropolitan region, so that the move-out of persons and industries is not as economically and fiscally damaging as in the past.

Finally, at least some of the older large cities will have to learn how to adjust to a situation of population and job decrease (or steady state) and how to grow old gracefully. Here, there is much to be learned from the experience of European cities, as suggested in Chapters 4 and 5. The difficulties, however, should not be underestimated. Most of our institutions and our thinking are adjusted to expectation of continuing growth. We have never learned the art of diminution. Now that art has to be learned, and quickly. That seems essential if population and job decreases are to be levers in achieving a higher quality of life rather than the kind of unhelpful decline and abandonment that older sections of the older cities are now experiencing.

Notes

1. A.G.B. Fisher, *The Clash of Progress and Security*, London: Macmillan & Co., 1935.

2. Colin Clark, *The Conditions of Economic Progress*, London: Macmillan & Co., 1940, pp. 31 and 38.

3. *The Statistical Abstract of the U.S., 1975*, Washington: Government Printing Office, 1975, Table No. 563, p. 345.

4. See particularly Raymond Vernon, *Metropolis 1985: An Interpretation of the Findings of the New York Metropolitan Region Study*, Cambridge, Mass.: Harvard University Press, 1960; and Pittsburgh Regional Planning Association, Economic Study of the Pittsburgh Region, vol. 3, *Region with a Future*, Pittsburgh: University of Pittsburgh Press, 1963.

5. Robert Healy, *Agglomeration and Footlooseness: The Distribution of Economic Activities among Metropolitan Areas*, Ph.D. dissertation, UCLA, 1972 (unpublished).

6. Jane Jacobs, *The Economy of Cities*, New York: Random House, 1969.

7. See several articles in Parts I and II of George Sternlieb and James W.

Hughes, ed., *Post-Industrial America: Metropolitan Decline and Inter-Regional Job Shifts,* New Brunswick, N.J.: Center for Urban Policy Research, Rutgers, 1975.

8. See George E. Peterson, "Finance," in William Gorham and Nathan Glazer, eds., *The Urban Predicament,* Washington, D.C.: Urban Institute, 1976.

9. Wilbur R. Thompson, "Internal and External Factors in the Development of Urban Economies," in Harvey S. Perloff and Lowdon Wingo, Jr., eds., *Issues in Urban Economics,* Baltimore: Johns Hopkins Press, 1968, p. 53.

10. Foreword to the 1976 edition of *The Coming of Post-Industrial Society,* New York: Basic Books, 1976, p. xix.

11. E. Hoover and R. Vernon, *Anatomy of Metropolis,* Cambridge, Mass.: Harvard University Press, 1960, p. 102.

12. For a useful analysis of the location of headquarter offices of large firms, see Leland Burns and Wing Ning Pang, "Big Business in the Big City: Corporate Headquarters in the CBD," *Urban Affairs Quarterly,* September 1977.

13. See Gary L. Appel and Aaron Lowin, *Appendices to Physician Extenders: An Evaluation of Policy-Related Research,* Final Report, January 1975, Interstudy, 123 East Grant Street, Minneapolis, Minnesota 55403.

14. A.G.B. Fisher, *Progress and Security,* p. 64.

15. George Sternlieb, "The City as Sandbox," Part I, in George Sternlieb and Norton Long, "Is the Inner City Doomed?," *The Public Interest,* Fall 1971.

16. See discussion in Victor R. Fuchs, *The Growing Importance of the Service Industries,* Occasional Paper 96, New York: National Bureau of Economic Research, 1965.

7

Tomorrow's Agglomeration Economies

Norman Macrae

People live in cities either because the job they want can most economically be located there, or because they are induced by a mixture of very good and very bad reasons to live snuggled or huddled up there, even when they are not actively seeking city jobs or the satisfactions that a city can most economically provide. This chapter will discuss the possible future trend of agglomeration economies or diseconomies, that seem likely in the medium term to affect the supply of city jobs and the number of willing or stranded city dwellers among the unemployed, the latter including the voluntarily unemployed and the increasing number of people who will not need to live near their jobs. This calls for definitions of "agglomeration economies" and of "medium term."

Here, agglomeration economies mean an extended version of what economists have long called "external economies": namely, the advantages for making particular things, for enjoying particular life-styles, or of having a lot of like-minded people close at hand. A major, but not always recognized, problem of the past forty years is that agglomeration economies and diseconomies have been passing through a period of erratic change; this is an important reason why so many work places and people are stranded in the wrong areas. During the next thirty years it is logical to expect that agglomeration economies and diseconomies will pass through another period of erratic change, often in the opposite direction from what conventional opinion today supposes.

"Medium term" is defined as "the period after present fashions of thinking and acting about city affairs will have worked themselves out." Perhaps the most important reform for city management may be to shift thinking about policy into the medium term as thus defined. This is because of the operation of what I call today's economic "law of opposites."[1] Quite seriously, I believe that it is nowadays rather easy to make one sort of correct medium-term economic forecast, and to become immensely unpopular thereby. The correct medium-term microeconomic forecast today is usually the opposite of whatever is at that moment the most frenetically fashionable forecast.

The reason for the law of opposites is quite logical and rather technical. In modern conditions where advancing technology has created high elasticities of both supply and substitution, we will generally produce a temporary but large surplus of whatever the majority of decision-making people a certain number of years earlier believed was going to be in the most desperately short supply. This is because the well-advertised views of the decision influencers tend to be believed, both by rather too many profit-seeking private producers and by far too many concensus-following arms of government. These two, then, combine to cause excessive production of precisely the things that the decision influencers had been saying would be most obviously needed.

Planners so Prone

The law of opposites works most violently when (1) there is a long time lag between the start and completion of investment, and (2) when things are produced otherwise than in day-to-day obedience to free market demand. It was therefore probably inevitable that it should ravage the field of urban planning, which largely consists of attempts to produce things that somebody in a position of elected or bureaucratic authority (or of academic or media influence) judges, usually wrongly, are not going to be adequately produced in day-to-day obedience to free market demand.

Planners tend to look out on what are regarded as obvious ills (sprawling urban slums, traffic jams, "obscene profits" from property development for big businesses' offices instead of housing for the poor), and then rush as in Gadarene to what are regarded as the obvious but nonmarket-obedient remedies. Good examples of the latter are demolition of slums and their replacement by subsidized, but soon deserted, high-rise apartment buildings, with lots of lovely mugger-infested open spaces between them; urban motorways and pedestrian malls instead of marginal cost pricing for the use of roads, per unit of extra congestion created at different hours, by both private automobiles and freely competing public transport vehicles; discriminatory tax or control measures that drive "obscenely" profit-making office-builders spectacularly bust, so that they are then subsidized by public authorities, even while rent controls continue to render unprofitable market-oriented house building or house conversion for rent.

In my home city of London in England we have in the past thirty years provided a classical example of creating policies and institutions to do the ongoing opposite of what is actually required. In the 1930s Britain set up a Royal Commission on the Geographical Distribution of the Industrial Population. It reported rather late, in 1940, when London had other things on its mind.

The main finding of the report was that the growth of manufacturing industry in the preceding decades had been strikingly concentrated around London, to the detriment of older industrial areas which were declining. One of the last pieces of legislation passed by Winston Churchill's coalition government in 1945 was therefore the Distribution of Industry Act, which laid down that any new industrial plant or factory extension above a minimum size, must have an Industrial Development Certificate from the Board of Trade. This control has been used ever since to steer new manufacturing jobs away from London, just as the Office Development Permit has been used to steer new office jobs away from it.

When the results of the middecade 1966 sample census were analyzed in 1968, it was suddenly discovered that, as in cities all over the world, the departure of manufacturing jobs from London had reached calamitous proportions. An attempt has therefore been made to reverse exoduses, but when a bureaucracy is dug in to fire at invading hordes, it is difficult to tell it to start firing in the opposite direction in order to blast down all impediments in their way. The Greater London Council is nowadays very cross that the obligation on firms to apply for Industrial Development Certificates still inhibits the growth, or hastens the demise, of manufacturing industry in London. The government replies that 90 percent of all applications are nowadays granted. The council rightly responds that the mere delays caused by having to apply under a process which is 90 percent unproductive turns some investment away. But the discouragement of office development has gone on even longer, because there has been an even longer period during which discouragement of what is now urgently needed has been regarded as progressive.

Homes before Offices?

If the top 10 percent of income receivers are called the tenth decile and the bottom 10 percent the first decile, then the history of cities in rich countries across the world in the past half century is broadly that much of the ninth and tenth deciles moved out to suburbia in the 1920s and some of the 1930s; then in the 1940s to 1960s some of the sixth to eighth decile moved out too; but thereafter the suburbanization of the first to the fifth decile was impeded by (1) the increased cost of suburbanization, including high-interest rates, and the mere fact that suburbia was becoming filled up and thus more expensive in land values; (2) the fact that the lower deciles included a large number of nonwhites or foreigners whose entry suburbia resisted; and (3) policies which obliged the rent of poorer houses in cities to stay below the sum of housing's capital-related costs plus (as a much more important factor) its service and maintenance costs.[2] And so poorer people could live most cheaply in accommodations in inner rings round cities that were becoming more and more quickly dilapidated. The people who lived in this sort of accommodation were the least suitable people to be filling the white-collar jobs in offices which were the cities' main growth occupation in the 1950s and 1960s. Thus, white-collar workers commute in from suburbia, daily burrowing under the problem territories in subway trains or driving through without noticing, intent on their destinations.

The poorer people in the old first to fourth deciles, in those rotting inner rings, make up most of the electorate for the city governments. Those city governments, at least in Europe, are therefore mostly left-wing inclined, and regard office development as in some way competing with housing rather than providing jobs. From 1950 to 1970, an antioffice-development policy was therefore followed in London, and most present guesses of the effect of this will prove to be underestimated. The 1976 middecade sample census was canceled as one of Britain's central government's expenditure cuts. If this 1976 census had been held, and if it had been analyzed by 1978, then it would probably have revealed a downturn in office employment in London as dramatically as the 1966-68 census revealed the collapse of manufacturing employment. There are the beginnings of an understanding of this, so that the expensive institutions which have helped to create this particular operation of the law of opposites are now having some counterinstitutions set in being against them.

As a ratepayer and taxpayer in London, I have to read each day on my subway train journey to work, amusingly copywritten advertisements from one taxpayer-supported body (the Location of Offices Bureau) which seeks to dispense office jobs from London, while also as a taxpayer, compulsorily supporting various public authorities' efforts to keep businesses in London and office buildings occupied there.

These kinds of errors in urban and regional planning in the last thirty years may be about to bring an excessive swing of opinion against the whole concept. This will be as mistaken as the surge the other way during the period 1948-68, the two decades that led to urban crisis. The arguments advanced throughout this volume will be most helpful if some decision influencers see at the end, that the need for planners is to keep a sense of balance on a seesaw.

This means that all policies put into effect should include mechanisms for self-adjustment in accord with the future day-to-day dictates of the market, even when those dictates are (as they eventually will be) the precise opposite of the ones now expected. Further, insofar as forward planning has a place, planners should peer into the medium term, when present fashions and trends will have brought some features of the law of opposites into effect.

Jobs in Four Categories

As we peer into the medium term, however, we are most likely to see that erratic changes are liable to occur in the agglomeration economies affecting city jobs. These jobs can conveniently be summarized under two broad heads, each with two subgroups. The two heads are (1) export-oriented jobs (i.e., those producing services or goods purchased by people outside the city) and (2) internally-oriented jobs (i.e., jobs in which the citizens take in each other's washing). Group (1) can then be subdivided into (*a*) manufacturing and wholesaling jobs and (*b*) the production of services, especially in what I am going to call the widely defined information industry. Group (2) can be subdivided into (*a*) government payroll jobs and (*b*) market-oriented inside-the-city jobs.

Manufacturing and Wholesaling Jobs

In manufacturing during 1952-77 there has been a temporary switch of external economies of accustomed area into being actual external diseconomies at least as revealed by experience in London. Agglomeration economies have turned into agglomeration disasters. The worst place in which to make widgets is now often any area "with a long tradition of making widgets already." Manufacturing plants are temporarily worst built as cathedrals in already built-up areas, with large site-clearing costs; log-jammed access roads; trade union traditions; local government officials, whose self-importance depends on being authorized to delay development with long planning inquiries; and articulate aesthetes who safeguard every Victorian relic. In other words, they are least efficiently built in existing industrial towns. They are most frequently built as one-story buildings stretching across many green fields.[3]

In consequence of these new external diseconomies, while total jobs in London between 1961-74 fell by 400,000 (9 percent) to 4 million, manufacturing jobs actually fell by 490,000 (34 percent) to 940,000. This 34 percent rate of decline in manufacturing jobs in London was seven times the rate of decline in England and Wales as a whole, as already indicated in Chapter 4.

It is conventional to suppose that this "seven times ratio" will go on expanding. To an extent, though, one could be optimistic here, because we may be coming to the end of some delayed seesaw effects from the period when planners were trying to get manufacturing jobs out of cities. If this is so, then the drop in manufacturing jobs in cities will be smaller soon, though the drop in manufacturing jobs in the other areas of rich countries may be even greater.

The reasons for some optimism for manufacturing jobs in cities spring from the usual operation of the law of opposites, and the usual tendency for agglomeration economies (like everything else in microeconomics) themselves to be affected by market forces. The seesaw effect applies to all the factors that have hitherto driven manufacturing jobs out of cities—congested land, technology, excessively trade-unionized labor, and local government prejudices.

Rays of Hope

In most old cities surpluses of development land and usable industrial facilities are now becoming available. One factory or warehouse in every five within twenty miles of Marble Arch (the geographical center of London) is now empty. This is not yet providing enough of the large, uncongested sites on which construction can go forward efficiently. Labor costs in the construction industry in London are about 14 percent higher than in the rest of the country, and building a two-story local authority house costs 29 percent more than elsewhere. But this differential seems no longer to be rising, and it well may fall.

Technology will probably make most new factories less land intensive than now. Until the 1960s industrialists worked to schedules which led them to believe that a certain optimum (often large) size could be designated for each factory, and that any factory smaller than that optimum would suffer in productivity. Now—in Britain at least—there is clear evidence that the larger the work place in any particular business, the worse and more frequent the industrial disputes, and the higher the absenteeism, including that for obviously bogus sickness. This shows itself in "idealistic" social services as well as in unidealistic British Leylands. In British hospitals those with under 100 beds have shown between one-half and two-thirds the sickness rates among nurses as those with over 100 beds.

Very high technology will probably make new factories less land intensive. This is even true of what are grandiloquently called "industrial robots," but are much better called "general-purpose jigs." Present manufacturing plants contain a lot of machine tools, which are special-purpose jigs that temporarily have to be constructed in many shapes and sizes, mainly because a human being cannot hold work against a cutter with the required accuracy and strength. When there is a general-purpose jig that can be programmed to keep repositioning work against a cutter, with the same nous as a human would show if he were quickly reacting and strong and accurate enough, then many present machine tools will be unnecessary. Once this general-purpose jig, or industrial robot, is mass manufacturable, it should allow manufacturing industry to have a very small number of types of machine tools flexibly deployable in small factories, instead of a very large number of types of machines used in ones or twos in larger factories. Other technical developments—especially the integrated circuit revolution—will speed microminiaturization.

Manufacturing firms in cities have traditionally been small, competitive businesses in areas where homes, work places, cafes, and shops have all been jumbled up together. Because most of these buildings have been very old and grimy, it became the fashion to say that this was an appalling way to live. It is now becoming the new fashion to say that it is the natural way to live. There will probably be a shift back to this mode of living, and away from industrial parks or estates (which have some of the disadvantages of high-rise apartment buildings, and spring from some of the same fashionable mistakes).

Manufacturers will also flock back to cities to get away from trade unions. A city like New York was originally created by the "virtually unbridled exploitation of the laboring classes." Newcomers off the boat in the nineteenth century had little difficulty finding jobs, but at the marginal wages that the market would bear. By the 1960s the older-established industrial centers, like New York, were the most heavily unionized. Black newcomers to the city, surging up from the South as agriculture there became more mechanized, were, in those 1960s, less able to get new city jobs at marginal wages, because the old heavy-employment manufacturing industries (e.g., apparel and food processing) were moving down to the less-trade-unionized South, to take advantage of the labor that had been released there by the mechanization of agriculture. My guess is that—now labor in the cities has become more anonymous, more footloose, more young, and more unemployed—the degree of trade unionization will be looser in new industries in the declining cities than it may become in the expanded outer areas of SMSAs. I also expect new styles of entrepreneurship to start to flourish more luxuriously in the day-before-yesterday's cities rather than yesterday's industrial estates. This manifestation of the seesaw tendency, or law of opposites, could be a potent factor in bringing new industries to the cities.

Similarly, both local authorities and environmental pressure groups may become less restrictive toward industry in cities, and more restrictive toward it in expanding areas.

Three Barriers

There are, probably, three main barriers in the way of the return of some manufacturing jobs to cities like London, Tokyo, or New York. They are not usually talked about. The first misfortune is that a market-oriented system is not used to relieve congestion. When 100 extra vehicles join a traffic jam on London's roads, the extra jam they cause (and thus the cost to everybody else by slowing their progress) can be precisely measured. But at present the extra cost is not put on the drivers of these 100 extra vehicles, at the moment when they join the jam and intensify it.

There is a logical way of dealing with the agglomeration diseconomies of traffic congestion, and eventually cities will have to come round to something like it. Various bodies (including professionally competing commercial concerns) could run for local election, with proffers of a choice of performance contracts. A contract would promise that at any time of the day a traveler would be able to travel by some mode from one point in the city to another within some particular number of minutes; and similar performance contracts could be promised for freight. Then, these "urban transport performance contractors" should have the right to charge all vehicles, including private cars, for the use of the roads, by some meter system, according to the extra costs they imposed on the rest of the community by driving their cars on to congested streets. The changing meter charge for crossing each strip on the road would be flashed up on signs by the roadway, so that motorists would know what costs they were running up. Something like this may also be the only way in which new traffic modes can sensibly be introduced. Japanese companies, among others, have ready for development an interesting range of new vehicles that could help to solve urban transit problems—computer-assisted hybrids between a minibus and a taxi, part-monorail-part-road vehicles, and so forth. But there will be no market for them until the body which has to invest in the infrastructure is also a body which is rewarded according to its achievement of the economic speed of traffic flows.

The agglomeration diseconomies of traffic congestion will not disappear so long as a market system is not set up to deal with congestion. This delay could have serious effects in depleting city jobs, especially as warehousing is likely to become both a more efficient industry (because of the development of more automated and computer-controlled warehouses) and an industry which will sprout new and quite labor-intensive ancillary industries (trade marts at terminals, etc.). But these will prosper only in areas with sensibly congestion-free approach roads.

The next barrier in the way of the return of manufacturing jobs to the cities may be racial or class antagonism. When earlier generations of immigrants came to the cities, they could get jobs at marginal wages. Today's underclass are prevented from doing that by trade union restrictions which keep wages high, and so the younger members of the underclass (particularly black teenagers) suffer from longer unemployment. Government efforts to counter these misfortunes are then usually antimarket initiatives, and thus tend to make them worse. Minimum wage legislation drives still more youngsters into unemployment. And there is evidence that employers in London are steering clear of areas with large numbers of blacks, because they are afraid that those who enforce the legislation against racial discrimination might force them to employ workers whom they do not want.

The third reason why manufacturing jobs may not come back in flood to poor people in the cities is that jobs may emigrate in flood to still poorer people in the underdeveloped two-thirds of the world. In the next two decades, 1000 million kids in Asia alone will pass the age of eighteen, and enter into the most productive age groups of their working life. An actual majority of these kids will be literate. They will be by far the biggest sudden upsurge in a potentially productive labor force that the world has ever seen.

If technology is put behind these youngsters in Asia, much of the world's manufacturing industry may move there. Earlier this year I was in a heavy machinery factory in South Korea. Its method of operation is to look round the world for the most advanced technological ways of making anything, and import those ways on license from Japan, America, Europe, or elsewhere. One of the shops in this factory was "old," having been built in 1969. A brand new one has been built next door. From the very first day of operation their productivity is expected to rise threefold and the old shop will be stripped down and go over to producing something else. One set of machines was British; they were being operated at three times the productivity at which they are operated back home in Teesside, at one-fourth the wages.

It is possible that some manufacturing jobs within America and Europe will return to the cities. But is is probable that many more manufacturing jobs will move out of these rich continents altogether, as the rich one-third of the world enters the postmanufacturing age.

Exportable Services

During the first stage of the postmanufacturing age, the biggest boom industry has been a temporarily labor-intensive provider of rather toffee-nosed city jobs, suitable for daily commuting suburbanites but not for many of the older inhabitants and newer migrants in the poor areas of the inner cities.

This boom industry can be called the "broad information industry," though Emanuel Tobier, who has called it the "elite sector," perhaps defined it best. He said that the elite sector in New York included industries such as finance, insurance, communications, advertising, foreign trade, corporate legal services, non-profit organizations, the headquarters offices of the largest manufacturing firms.[4] The key individuals are concerned with the production of answers to unstandardized problems: problems that change frequently and unpredictably.... Because speed in decision-making is vital, even the swiftest means of travel may be too slow while the complex (and intangible) source of the matter often precludes the use of the telephone. Considerations such as these dictate that these offices, for efficiency's sake, cluster very close to each other and to those who service them." During the early stage of the growth of the broad information industry, the elite workers in it have required an extensive retinue made up of more moderately recompensed workers, like clerks and doormen. They have clustered in cities' central business districts.

I am afraid that I believe that the jobs provided in cities by the recently booming information industry will stop rising, and start precipitately to fall.

Productivity is going to rise most sharply in precisely the fields where for decades face-to-face contact has wrongly been supposed to be most important. Once people are used to it, computer-augmented confravision across continents will be seen to be a more sensible way of getting twenty people to make a decision than ordinary face-to-face meetings: because views can be entered in the printout at each person's own convenience instead of everybody having to speak immediately after somebody else has spoken; because a usual process will be to leave a printout and videotape for executives not at the conference to see, so they can enter their own views within a strict timetable before a decision is taken; because votes and sometimes inputs can be anonymous, so that all options can be considered without fears of offending superiors; and because there is a "whispering" capability in computer conferences, which allows subgroups to enter separate negotiations without other conferees being aware that those are taking place.[5] Importantly, all these will be at the chairman's volition.

Wise chairmen will, however, realize that there are great advantages in this sort of conference, compared with the ordinary committee meeting. The fashionable thought will suddenly dawn that there is a positive agglomeration diseconomy in having all executives together in the same building.

Simultaneously, the need for retinues of lower white-collar staff will decline, as clerkdom becomes automated. Data will be fed into the computers from ongoing conferences, and can be drawn on by an executive anywhere. The dash to the "paperless office" will probably become a fetish in the 1980s. Most of the 80 percent of America's first-class mail which consists of business items is likely to be sent digitally by the 1990s, so there will be no point in having offices in central cities "where there is a better mail delivery service." Anyway, even in cities there will not be a good mail delivery service because mail delivery is going to go bust.

During the first stage of postmanufacturing revolution, there has been little success in sending head offices out of cities to suburbia, mainly because a fair proportion of head office men think that a central location gives them greater opportunities for advancing their own careers. But when one meets people more meaningfully on confravision than face to face, there will be less resistance to the second wave of attempted exile of the information industry out of the central business areas, especially as this exile will be rather pleasant. It will be an exile into telecommuting.

Telecommuting Is Coming

Brain-workers could already more easily dispatch their work to their offices than dispatch themselves. It would be economic for many workers, for example, in insurance companies, to work from home, even now.[6]

Some of the nonmetro areas now sprouting in population in the United States are rich men's outer exurbia—for example, fishing villages filled on weekdays by fishermen and top bankers' wives, but at weekends also by the bankers themselves, because New York is too far for hubby to commute every day. Telecommuting will start spreading from there, provided the rich like their wives.

It is possible that telecommuting will start originally from the "neighborhood work centers" foreseen by many in the communications industry: centers from which you can buy season tickets to have contact at will by telex and videoscreen, with all the interesting colleagues and noninteresting computers with whom you work. But these neighborhood work centers may be quite short-lived, with telecommuting spreading rather quickly to the home, aided by two technical developments.

One is that computer terminals, which by some time in the 1980s will be a principal business tool, should at a later stage become a household mass durable:

possibly sweeping through homes in a single decade, like television did in the decade ending in the mid-1950s. Household demand for computer terminals will grow as an entertainment device, as a device for education, data retrieval for shopping and health care, and with the accelerating agglomeration advantage that they will be a durable necessary for keeping up with both the elder and the younger Joneses.

Since telecommunications will greatly increase mobility, it will probably be right eventually to finance them as roads have been financed, or rather as roads will eventually be financed, with people paying for the use of them only insofar as their marginal use increases congestion. Once satellites are bused into space, the marginal cost of using them does not vary greatly with distance of message sent, so it should eventually become as cheap to telecommute daily into one's office in New York while living in Tahiti, as while living next door. People will then go to live in and work from the places they like. Instead of voting for governments in the places where they live, they will often move into the areas ruled by the sorts of governments (or nongovernments) which provide the life-style they choose. This is what our parents did during the march to suburbia, and what our grandchildren will do internationally in the Tahiti-telecommuter age.

By early in the next century people will be living in cities only if cities are nice or cheap places in which to live. Which brings us to the future agglomeration economies or diseconomies of jobs that are internally oriented within the city itself.

Within-the-city Jobs

Cities cannot live by their citizens agreeing to take in each others' washing. But between 1950-73 the second boom industry in cities, next only to the broad information industry, was inefficient, labor intensive, and internally oriented. It was called local government.

In a properly functioning economic system, people flock into the industries where their marginal productivity is highest, and is rising most rapidly, relative to other occupations. In the boom industry of local government services in 1950-73 marginal productivity was falling relative to other occupations, as discussed in Chapter 12. In some fields it was actually negative (e.g., in British hospitals in 1963-76 there was a large increase in hospital administratoi ; during a period when bed occupancy went down).

A main reason for this absurdity is that local government service is not ruled by day-to-day obedience to free market forces. A record is that bureaucracy was becoming a less efficient mechanism for production during 1950-73 because the technological revolution meant that an efficient producer had to keep asking all the time, What is the best and quickly changing and labor-saving technology I should use in order to accomplish this task? In a bureaucracy anybody who keeps asking these questions all the time is regarded as a bad colleague who is constantly rocking the boat. The new tradition that even bankrupt local governments do not go bankrupt has naturally led to greater trade unionization of local bureaucracies. Until recent decades, many American cities were run by corrupt political machines, which could be turned out when the citizens became resentful of them. Now the top political leadership in American cities is honest and rather liberal, but the trade-unionized permanent bureaucracy (with early pension rights, etc.), which electorate finds it cannot turn out, costs far more in total money from the citizenry (though not, of course, nearly as much per finger in the pie) as the less egalitarian Boss Tweeds ever did.

Another accelerating agglomeration diseconomy has, as usual, been a Gadarene operation of the law of opposites. When Professor J.K. Galbraith raised the cry in the late 1950s about mounting "public squalor amid private affluence," he speeded the switch from private to public spending which pre-Galbraith (despite his slogan) was already taking place. As resources were switched from the private to the public sector, they moved from the sector with higher marginal productivity to the one with lower marginal productivity. As this throwing of money at every problem did not solve the "crisis" of the cities and did restrain real income compared with what would otherwise have occurred, the usual (probably excessive) backlash has set it. During the current world recession even lefter-wing democratic governments have regarded it as a vote winner to say that they will slash government spending even at the bottom of a slump.

The problem can be solved best by a rise in productivity in the public sector. I belong to a small minority of people who think this will eventually come mainly through reprivatization and recompetitioning of some present local government services—including in some places decisions by local communities to hire competitive private enterprise companies to run the administration of their local governments on performance contracts.

In any event, within-the-city services are bound to become less labor intensive as they turn from being mere services into becoming service industries (see discussion in Chapter 6). The growth and industrialization of some service industries (the internationalization of hotel chains, supermarkets, and hypermarkets, etc.) has been one of the remarkable and efficient developments of the past three decades. The same sort of development is likely to bring a new efficiency to within-the-community services over the next few decades, both in present public services (neighborhood services, protective services, health and learning services, etc.) and in private enterprise (recreation, etc.) services. Many of these new service industries will benefit from agglomeration economies, and take root first in the cities.

Who Likes to Live in Cities?

If people are going to have a much wider choice of where they want to live, including being able to telecommute to their offices, then the future of cities will depend on whether people want to live in them.

The urban crisis has been built up during a period when market incentives have not been allowed to operate to bring cities in line with the needs of the new age: as witness the way in which the rotting tenements of Harlem coexisted even during the office boom a few blocks up from the most expensive office sites on earth.

The years of urban crisis also saw a swelling in many big cities of welfare recipients, including especially (1) families with lots of children (particularly one-parent families) and (2) the old. For group (1) there are huge agglomeration diseconomies in living in cities. The worst places for welfare teenagers to live are where there are lots of other welfare teenagers. Welfare systems need to be reorganized so that existing welfare recipients would be able to keep their present higher city benefits if they moved out to rural areas in which it is cheaper to live. This is another reason why the "welfare state" functions of city governments need increasingly to be taken over by central government with some such system as a negative income tax, which I believe will be internationalized by the middle of the next century (i.e., there will be harmonization of welfare systems via a negative income tax in the European Economic Community, then there will be a harmonization treaty with the United States and Japan, and then there will be pressure for some extension to poorer countries in a reform which will in practice end the old-style nation state). Meanwhile, the administrative functions of local government need to be put up for competitive tender.

For old people, by contrast, there is an interesting mixture of agglomeration advantages and disadvantages in living in cities, but mostly the former. With the mobility advantage of being able to live "right on the bus route," an increasing number of the old might want to live in a city if a city can again be made a nice place. It is quite possible, though unfashionable to say this, that the nucleus of inhabitants of big cities by around 2020 will be old people and a new wave of sophisticated refugees from what Karl Marx 100 years ago called "the idiocy of village life."

In the last three decades, television has wrought a temporary and egalitarian revolution in leisure habits. For several hours this evening, Manhattan's millionaires and its welfare mothers will be doing exactly the same thing, namely, watching the same television programs.

It is probable that television-watching will eventually start to decline, as people choose new ways of expressing themselves in their leisure hours.

Self-expression usually means some hobby in which one manages to become more than averagely proficient or interested (and interesting). If only one per thousand of the population is as adept as you at épée fencing, then you need to live in a community with 20,000 males of the same age group as yourself if you are to enjoy twenty interesting companions in your sport. True, telecommuting will play a part in the pursuit of hobbies by the 1990s; you will be able to leave a message in the computer terminal "anybody of such and such a standard for bridge?" Also, people will telecommute from areas which they have chosen because some favorite recreation (golf, sailing, etc.) is available there. But the man with varied and civilized tastes, for example, the man who is both an épée fencer and an amateur literary critic and a connoisseur of fine wines should gravitate most to the city, once the city escapes from its recent bleak years.

In the urban crisis of recent years there has been an analogy with America's Wild West a hundred years ago. In the last third of the nineteenth century there was one decade when the per capita murder rate in cow towns and mining settlements was between ten and twenty times that in New York today, and in the next decade these were the towns of the Bible Belt. In the last third of the twentieth century there has been one decade—broadly 1964-74—in which the big cities across much of the rich one-fifth of the world have become cowboy settlements. How now to make thrive the homesteaders?

The main recommendations and judgments in this paper have been: all policies put into effect should include mechanisms for self-adjustment in accord with future day-to-day dictates of the market, which will likely be in the opposite direction from what is at present most trendily believed. Some manufacturing jobs may come back to the towns. Office employment will begin to disappear from the towns as the telecommuting revolution starts.

Many local government services need to be reprivatized, and policies for affecting the redistribution of incomes need to be controlled by central government, not local government. Other within-the-city services will turn into service industries. Cities will reexpand only when people again begin to regard cities as a pleasant place in which to live. The telecommuting age, and the gradual need not to work so many months a year, are going to allow people a wide choice of life-styles. This is what freedom in the future will mainly mean.

Notes

1. See Norman Macrae, *The Next 40 Years,* The Economist Brief Books, London: *The Economist,* 1972, for a fuller discussion of this.

2. See the Urban Institute, "A Report—1968-71," Washington, D.C.: Urban Institute, 1972.

3. See Norman Macrae, "The Coming Entrepreneurial Revolution," *The Economist,* December 25, 1976.

4. Institute for Public Administration, "Agenda for a City," New York: Institute of Public Administration, 1970.

5. See the section written by Laurence H. Day and Peter Goldmarks, in *World Future Society,* Report of the Second General Assembly, 1975; and Murray Turoff, "Potential Applications of Computer Conferences in Developing Countries," presented at the 1974 Rome Conference on Future Research (unpublished).

6. Norman Macrae, *America's Third Century,* New York: Harcourt Brace Jovanovich, 1976.

**Part V
Physical Organization of
the Mature Metropolis**

8

Transportation and Land Use in the Mature Metropolis

Alex Anas and
Leon N. Moses

This chapter deals with the urbanized areas that grew to large size under the influence of nineteenth and early twentieth century technologies of production, transportation, and communication. These areas—New York, Philadelphia, Boston, Chicago, Detroit, and St. Louis are examples—are viewed as mature today because their populations and levels of economic activity are either stable or somewhat declining. At one time, the core areas of these cities were the most dynamic growth centers of the nation. They absorbed huge numbers of immigrant laborers and immense amounts of capital to develop the nation's great manufacturing and service industries. Here, we explain some of the factors that contributed to this growth and the decline that has taken place, and we provide insight into how current social and economic forces are likely to condition future growth, transportation networks, and land-use patterns in the emerging metropolis.

Production, Transport, Communications, and Growth and Decline of the Great Cities

We tend to think of cities as centers of finance, insurance, advertising, education, and cultural activities. However, the cities that developed rapidly during the last century were products of the industrial revolution. Their growth was driven by the rapid development of textiles; iron and steel and related foundry products; animal slaughtering, rendering, and meat and leather production; milling, and so forth. Coal production expanded tremendously to provide electric power for factories, for lighting cities, and for their transportation systems. Banking, finance, and insurance were essential to the expansion of manufacturing. In addition, the growth of cities would not have been possible without electric power, clean water, sewage disposal, and such cheap means of transportation as trains and trolleys. But up until World War I, the main driving force in economic development was manufacturing.

The Period 1850 to World War I

The CBDs of the great nineteenth-century cities tended to be compact; as much as 90 percent of total employment would be found one to three miles from the center. Downtown areas often had subdistricts relatively specialized in finance, retailing, and legal and other services. Land values were high in the core but they quickly declined with distance from the center and from the main routes of passenger transportation; so did population densities. Why did manufacturing establishments become concentrated in relatively few places, thereby contributing to the huge agglomerations of population and economic activity that characterized cities like New York, Chicago, and St. Louis? One reason was that there were scale economies in the production of goods. As a result, there were relatively few plants in many industries. Given that there would be some concentration in production, why did most of it locate in cities rather than spread out over the countryside? The main reason was the scale economies in transportation.

Manufacturing firms tended to be material intensive, requiring more tons of raw materials per ton of finished product than do comparable products today. Immense quantities of raw materials and finished products had to be moved to and from cities and, in the main, these shipments went by water or rail. Areas with natural water tributaries of sufficient depth and width had tremendous economic advantages. Both canal and railway transport are characterized by scale economies, in both line haul and terminal operations. Their rights-of-way were expensive to construct, but once in place, could accommodate large quantities of freight at very low cost. The larger the flotilla of barges, or the longer the trains, the lower was the cost per ton-mile shipped. In addition, because of the high frequency of in-bound and out-bound service, producers who were located near a major terminal area could operate with smaller inventories of raw materials and finished products than could those who were located in outlying areas. These influences channelized shipments along relatively few but expensive-to-construct routes; even some quite large cities were served by only one or two railroads.

Terminal operations of ports and rail yards also exhibited scale economies and there were, therefore, relatively few of them in a city. Firms tended to locate near these terminals, though there were several reasons why they could have achieved certain economies had they chosen to locate away from them and from the central areas of cities. The price of land was much cheaper away from the core. In addition, there were potential savings in wage rates for firms that chose to locate in outlying areas and employ labor domiciled there. These savings would have arisen because such workers could have reduced their money and time costs of travel, and thus have been willing to accept wages lower than those paid at the core.[1] However, such firms would still have had to assemble the raw materials they needed, and arrange for the export of their finished products through the warehousing and transportation facilities of the core area.

Thus, outlying locations would have raised total firm costs by more than the savings in land and labor costs they would have brought. The explanation is that the cost of moving goods inside cities was very high relative to the per ton-mile cost of interregional shipments. More important, it was also high relative to the cost of moving people inside cities. Within cities, freight was transported by a mode that had remained essentially unchanged for hundreds of years, the horse and wagon moving on unpaved city streets: a high-cost, low-scale, undependable operation. On the other hand, people were transported quite early by horse-driven rail lines, and later by electric trolley, both of which were more efficient and less costly than the horse and wagon. As a result of the differential between the cost of transporting people and freight within cities, the savings in space and labor costs associated with outlying locations were less than the increased costs of freight movements they entailed.

Three other influences reinforced these tendencies for dense core development. First, urban firms had to ship goods to each other due to interindustrial linkages; the cost of transporting these goods caused firms to cluster closely. Second, a communications gap existed in the transmission of information within cities. Interregionally, this was done via the telegraph, but the telegraph could not handle efficiently the heavy demands of intraurban communication since it was not adaptable to switchboard-type operations. The principal method of communication between manufacturing firms and between them and banks, insurance companies, and other business services firms, was either through messengers or face-to-face meetings. Inefficient and high-cost communication added to the clustering tendencies of service as well as manufacturing within the compact core area. The high cost of communications was a major factor in the agglomerative tendencies of business services. Third, the incremental cost of providing such municipal or public utility services as water, waste collection, treatment and disposal, and electric power, fell over a considerable range with increases in output, particularly when that output was distributed in a compact, densely settled area. As a result of these three kinds of economies, urban growth increased central-city tax revenues rather than tax rates.

The great overall growth in urban economic activity, and its concentration in the center, caused the core to expand and intrude into the surrounding ring of low-income, poorly maintained housing. As the core expanded, more poor laborers were accommodated by converting single family, middle-income housing into multiple-family units and to boarding houses. Higher-income population groups lived outside this inner area and commuted to the center via horse-driven carriages or rail-guided horse and wagon.[2] Only shortly before World War I did motorized transportation begin to influence the internal structure of cities.

The Truck, Telephone, and Interwar Period

Earlier, we argued that the compact form of the nineteenth-century city was in very substantial measure due to the high cost of carrying out the functions of intraurban freight movement and transfer of information; these costs were radically altered in the interwar period. The reduction in the cost of intraurban goods movement was the result of the substitution of the truck for the horse and wagon, and a very significant improvement in the quality of urban roads. These changes permitted still more manufacturing to be accommodated inside central cities, because it was no longer necessary for industry to cluster as closely to the terminals of the interregional routes as it had been when freight within cities moved by horse and wagon. The introduction of the truck also led to an expansion of the warehousing districts of major cities, and firms did spread out somewhat. The average distance between firms and between firms and ports and rail terminals increased. However, most firms did not leave the central areas of cities. Thus, the truck increased the economic vitality of the core by increasing the supply of lower-priced land for industry.[3]

The expansion of the economic core into residential areas led middle-income households to move further out, and their housing to filter down to the large numbers of low-wage immigrant workers. Thus, though somewhat decentralized, the expanding manufacturing sector continued to rely on the central-area's terminals for interregional shipments. The continued growth of manufacturing also created a base for expansion in central-city finance, insurance, and other business services.

The telephone and the radio did similar things for the efficiency of intraurban communication. The telephone did not eliminate the need for face-to-face meetings, but business was no longer bound by such communication. Information of a relatively straightforward variety could be transmitted by telephone. It also played a crucial role in improving the efficiency of those face-to-face meetings that were required for strategic, educational, and other purposes through prior staff communication. Through the telephone, information was exchanged much more cheaply than before, and much faster over longer distances. Through the radio, public information of all sorts became available at a much lower cost than before.

The interwar period was essentially replicative of the 1850-1920 era; large cities continued to grow in size and economic power. Except for the Great Depression (whose effects on cities was temporary in terms of the long-run historic dynamics view of this discussion), the population of cities increased, their land values rose, and their areas of settlement widened, pushing agriculture further out. Core areas continued to develop as centers of finance, entertainment, medicine, and education as well as manufacturing. The tax bases of the largest cities grew, and they were able to provide municipal services of high quality. Annexation of surrounding suburbs continued in many cases, and the jurisdictional size of cities increased.

Suburbanization and Decline of Central Cities

The years since World War II, and particularly since the early 1950s, have seen the decline of the large nineteenth-century city and the growth and development of highly dispersed metro areas such as Los Angeles, Phoenix, Dallas, and Houston. To understand the decline of the older cities, we must look to the factors that caused their manufacturing firms and then a variety of their business service industries to move beyond their political boundaries, as discussed further in Chapters 6 and 13. This movement caused core areas and their fiscal bases to decline. It became difficult for them to maintain municipal services such as police protection and education, which reinforced the tendency of firms and households to move to politically independent suburban areas.

The conventionally accepted explanations for central-city decay do not adequately emphasize the primary role of manufacturing decentralization. Rather, they focus on the growth of personal automobile transportation and the federal home-financing policies. Still another explanation attributes the decline to the movement into central cities of blacks as well as poor whites from areas such as Appalachia. The claim is that in-migration of these groups caused the central city middle-income and upper-income groups to suburbanize, which reduced the tax bases of central cities while increasing the need for and cost of many social services. A spiraling process was set up which led to a further out-migration of middle-income and upper-income households. Though there are elements of truth in the above arguments—they are discussed in more detail in Chapter 12—they do not explain the massive suburbanization of basic manufacturing employment in the post-World War II period.

There is no doubt that increased car ownership and greatly improved urban roads drastically reduced the overall cost (including time) of passenger transport from many outlying areas to centers of employment. Effectively, this change increased the supply of residential land. As the car became the major means of shopping and recreational trips, large suburban shopping centers developed, which contributed to the decline of central-city retail activity. *However, the important question is what impact the automobile and the improvement in urban roads would have had on the location pattern of industry if everything else, but especially the cost of transporting goods in cities, had remained unchanged.*

Each previous innovation that had reduced the cost of personal travel—the horse rail, the electric trolley, or the elevated and subway train—caused population to move out to new areas served by the new systems; retail activity followed. With the automobile, a similar but more ubiquitous spreading out of population occurred, but this suburban expansion could not, by itself, have caused the massive outward shift of manufacturing and business services. *In fact, a reduction in the cost of personal travel would have increased the relative attractiveness of the central city and its core areas as a location for commerce and industry.*

Taken by itself, a reduction in personal travel cost would have caused workers to require a higher wage for working close to home, as an alternative to core area employment, than they did before. In addition, such a reduction in costs would have increased the price of land in the outer, relative to land in the inner, portions of the city. This also would have increased the relative attractiveness of core as a location for economic activity. Finally, an opposite effect on which we will have further comments should be mentioned. High-quality suburban roads and low-cost personal transportation did greatly increase the area from which a suburban firm could draw labor at reasonable wage rates.

To understand the suburbanization of manufacturing activity, we must turn to the reduction in the costs of shipping goods by truck between cities and between cities and their supply areas in the post-1950 period. The immense expansion in interstate highways, the building of outer-circumferential routes, and the increase in the size and efficiency of the long-distance truck, all contributed to a radical decentralization of manufacturing. These changes gave firms the freedom to build new efficient plants on lower-priced land, without incurring increased costs of assembling raw materials and shipping finished products. The intercity truck and interstate highway gave firms an efficient and highly dependable form of transportation that did not involve the older congested terminal areas of the core. To compete for the shipment of intercity freight, railroads established modern suburban rail terminals. This contributed still further to the decline of central cities, since even rail-oriented firms could then shift to suburban locations.

Let us now consider the decentralization of those business services—such as banking, insurance, and advertising—that many urban specialists believed must be located downtown and near one another because of their need for face-to-face contact. First, we observe that service sector decentralization often takes the form of a *relative* shift in activity levels. In other words, such activities as banking have expanded in satellite areas, while the industry has expanded relatively little or remained stable in downtown areas. This is different from manufacturing, where many central cities experienced absolute declines while suburban areas were expanding. The expansion of the service industries in suburban areas is partially explained by the fact that some of their functions are really retail in nature and oriented to the household, rather than the business establishment. Thus, savings and loan associations should be expected to evolve in much the same geographic pattern as retailing; the same applies to personal and home insurance offices. Finally, while the large, nationally known firm can borrow funds from a downtown bank, or a bank in any other city for that matter, a bank probably needs a certain amount of personal contact with a small firm before it will grant a loan. It is therefore not surprising that the great growth of smaller manufacturing and other establishments in suburban areas has been accompanied by a growth of commercial banking. Among the things this chapter is emphasizing, is the importance of improved communications on the form and development of urbanized areas, as was emphasized in Chapter 7.

But why, then, could not business services, such as banking, have expanded in downtown areas and relied on modern communications to maintain contact with manufacturing and other firms growing up in satellite areas? This question has several answers. First, land values and construction costs are very high in core areas. Where branch banking was permitted, it was therefore much cheaper to expand by building a branch in a suburban area, depending on intrafirm communications to make certain that all records needed for central evaluation of performance were readily available within the firm. The suburban branch location also gave the bank closer contact with and more knowledge about smaller customers. Thus, suburban branches gave banks a low cost and efficient way of expanding while bringing the side benefit of closer contact with smaller customers. A third reason for the relative decentralization of the business service sector is that improved communications permitted many firms to separate functions geographically, and perform some of them from less centrally located, and less costly, land and buildings. For example, the keeping of insurance records, the maintenance of information on claims, the mailing of insurance bills and settlement checks do not require a downtown location. Here, the typical contact between company and customer is by mail or telephone, and modern communications and computers provide relevant parts of the firm with almost instant access to the central data file no matter where they are located.

The outflow of all this activity caused a deterioration in the quality of public services and secondary waves of decentralization. The concentration of poor and minorities in the central cities, on the other hand, pushed up the demands for services, and revenue-expenditure imbalances became aggravated, as will be indicated in Chapter 12. This led to increased incentive for middle-income groups to leave central cities.

Some Empirical Observations

U.S. census data for six mature metropolitan areas—New York, Boston, Philadelphia, Chicago, Detroit, and St. Louis—illustrate the basic dimensions and extent of central-city decay and suburban development.[a] The number of manufacturing establishments in the New York SMSA has been declining since 1963 and more recently—from 1967 to 1972—at a rate of 11 percent. Boston and Philadelphia show a similar, but much less pronounced trend, while Midwestern cities show gains in metropolitan manufacturing between 1947 and 1972. Central cities in the six SMSAs we are looking at show a consistent decline in number of manufacturing establishments and suburban areas, a marked increase. In 1967-72 the average rate of decline for the six central cities is 18 percent, while all except New York suburbs show an average growth rate of 21 percent. In New York the suburban growth rate was 2 percent but there was a slight decline between 1958 and 1967. All six areas except New York and Boston have tripled or at least doubled suburban establishments since 1947. Only in the New York and Chicago metro areas does the central city still contain a larger number of establishments

---

[a]The data discussed in this section has been compiled from U.S. Census of Manufacturing and Population publications.

than is found in the suburbs. Data on manufacturing employment are not comparable by date to data on establishments, but do show the same overall trends of suburban expansion and city decline. Rough calculations also show that "mean firm size" is, in most cases, significantly larger for suburban firms and increasing over time. Somewhat surprisingly, it is not increasing much more rapidly than central-city mean firm size.

Of the cities examined, only New York still had more population in the center city in 1970 than did the suburbs, and by a factor of close to two. In the remaining five areas, suburban population is up to several times central-city population, with Chicago having the narrowest difference of only 4 percent, but a suburban growth rate of 35 percent; central-city populations have been declining. The data also show that the nonwhite population has been growing in both suburbs and central cities, but at a faster rate in all six central cities.

With the exception of New York and Philadelphia, all six cities experienced declines in the number of owner-occupied and tenant-occupied housing units between 1960 and 1970. This trend is especially strong in St. Louis where the number of owner-occupied units in 1970 was 8 percent less than in 1960 and the number of tenant-occupied, 17 percent less. This reflects the attrition and abandonment of the central-city stock as well as the gradual accumulation of central-city vacant land. In New York City both owner-occupied and tenant-occupied units increased by 16 and 4 percent, respectively, between 1960 and 1970, probably reflecting the fact that the number of households increased, even though population fell. Some might argue that the increase in occupied units in New York also reflects the continuing cultural-recreational attractiveness of the area. The data also show that although the number of tenant-occupied units in the suburbs of our six cities is smaller (usually about a third of the suburban stock), they are increasing at rates up to two to three times greater than owner-occupied units, reflecting a boom in suburban apartment construction.

Data on retail trade for mature areas reveal that establishments in suburban areas have been increasing, while the number in central cities and CBDs has been declining; within cities, the number of establishments in CBDs has been falling less rapidly than in the rest of the central city. Surprisingly, Chicago was an exception; the decline in the number of establishments in the CBD in the 1967-72 period was greater than in the remainder of the central city. Overall, there has been an increase in the average numbers of employees per retail establishment. This is especially true in suburban areas, where the number of establishments and their size, as measured by employment, have both increased very significantly.

A comparison of the various work-trip categories shows that the mature cities are still significantly centralized, with the number of commuters from the suburbs to the city still being more numerous than the number of reverse commuters from city to suburbs. However, the number of traditional suburban commuters is increasing at low rates of up to 13 percent (down by 6 percent in

Detroit) while the number of reverse commuters is increasing much faster, more than doubling in Chicago between 1960 and 1970, almost doubling in St. Louis, up by more than half in Detroit and Philadelphia, and up 20 percent in New York and 14 percent in Boston. At the same time, the number of work trips within central city is strongly declining in each case, down by up to 34 percent in St. Louis and by 12 percent in New York City. On the other hand, the number commuting from one suburb to another shows a strong increase in each case. Strikingly, the number of trips from both the cities and the SMSA to exurban locations outside the SMSA also is increasing rapidly except in St. Louis, where there has been a strong decline in both; for details see Table 8-1.

These strong trends in reverse commuting patterns are explained by the rapid suburbanization of jobs to suburban and exurban areas. One can safely conjecture that many of the reverse commuters are low-income and minority residents constrained to live in affordable central-city housing, but with a strong motivation to move out closer to their suburban jobs and to better suburban schools and public services. Whether they can do so or not, depends in part on how vigorously the federal government pursues a policy of low-cost suburban housing construction. It also depends on filtering, particularly in the inner suburbs where the housing stock is older. The rise in reverse commuting could therefore be a temporary, short-run adjustment phenomenon. However, some of the reverse commuters may be middle-income and upper-income households, without children, who are attracted to central-city cultural-recreational amenities and work in the suburbs. The number of such reverse commuters might well increase over time.

Data on central-city public employment trends show increases for all cases, except Detroit. Moreover, the rate of increase is generally greater than that for total SMSA population for 1960-70, with the exception of St. Louis, where SMSA population increased more than central-city public employment. The data must be interpreted with care since the underlying process is quite complex and political. However, others have shown that changes in the composition of population caused central-city public employment to rise despite the lessening dependence of suburbanites on center-city services and declines in central-city populations.[4]

Energy, Public Policy, and the Future Metropolis

The rest of the chapter will deal with three forces we believe will have a strong influence on the distribution of population and economic activity, between as well as within, metropolitan areas. These are (1) changes in the rate of growth of population and its composition, (2) change in the relative importance of international trade for the United States and the impact it will have on the competitive position of various areas of the country, and (3) changes in the cost

Table 8-1
Changes in Work Trip Patterns in Six Mature SMSAs

Residence	Place of Work	1960	1970	% Change
New York				
City	City	2,885,038	2,549,609	−11.6
City	Suburbs	82,865	99,087	+19.5
City	Outside SMSA	63,530	119,690	+88.3
Suburb	City	307,827	335,715	+9.0
Suburb	Suburb	670,314	891,118	+132.9
Suburb	Outside SMSA	20,379	68,548	+336.4
Boston				
City	City	215,994	177,644	−17.8
City	Suburbs	43,596	49,690	+14.0
City	Outside SMSA	6,055	6,365	+5.1
Suburb	City	193,384	196,094	+1.4
Suburb	Suburb	467,224	564,451	+20.8
Suburb	Outside SMSA	28,561	45,410	+58.9
Philadelphia				
City	City	670,761	559,771	−16.5
City	Suburbs	51,960	80,359	+54.7
City	Outside SMSA	7,946	16,361	+105.9
Suburb	City	198,987	212,553	+6.8
Suburb	Suburb	594,542	743,957	+25.1
Suburb	Outside SMSA	45,772	81,753	+78.0
Chicago				
City	City	1,249,641	994,277	−20.5
City	Suburbs	88,855	206,467	+132.4
City	Outside SMSA	11,490	17,614	+53.3
Suburb	City	328,395	355,135	+8.1
Suburb	Suburb	615,896	992,777	+61.2
Suburb	Outside SMSA	25,255	37,639	+49.0
Detroit				
City	City	461,430	320,668	−31.5
City	Suburbs	96,779	161,095	+66.5
City	Outside SMSA	5,741	7,249	+26.3
Suburbs	City	231,274	216,705	−6.3
Suburbs	Suburbs	433,241	694,206	+60.2
Suburbs	Outside SMSA	17,629	28,445	+61.3
St. Louis				
City	City	240,962	158,068	−34.4
City	Suburbs	21,742	42,234	+94.3
City	Outside SMSA	1,546	1,355	−12.4
Suburbs	City	160,017	181,850	+13.6
Suburbs	Suburbs	238,703	426,762	+78.7
Suburbs	Outside SMSA	43,176	10,884	−25.2

of personal and freight transport due to rising energy prices or energy conserving regulatory measures. Since aspects of the first two factors are discussed elsewhere in this volume—mainly in Chapters 2 and 7—we deal with them rather briefly. Most of the discussion here will be concerned with the implications of rising energy prices and costs of travel on long-run trends in land use. A number of issues related to job suburbanization, minority housing, and mass transit policies also will be discussed.

Population Growth and Composition

Changes in the composition of population will have an important impact on the spatial structure of the United States. Population growth is likely to continue to be lower in the next twenty years than it has been in the past. Both rural migration and foreign immigration (with the exception of illegal immigration) have declined in importance in recent years, and most of the large, older cities have not drawn much population in the last fifteen years or so. Though overall population growth is likely to be quite modest in the next two decades, there is likely to be a continuation of existing trends in the composition and distribution of the population. Population and employment are likely to continue to be attracted to selected cities in the South and West. Such limited out-migration of population from rural areas as does occur will probably take the form of a movement to these newer growing regions. In addition, low-income and minority households from the central cities of older regions will probably migrate to the smaller, growing cities of the newer regions (and to some extent, smaller cities of older regions) because of their more favorable employment opportunities.

The size composition of households will probably change, the average number of children per family falling; the trend will not be as great for the poor and minority groups as for the middle-income and upper-income groups so that the former will comprise an increasing percentage of the labor force. Marriages will probably continue to take place later in life, which will contribute to the decline in the average size of household. The above trends have a number of important implications for the mature metropolis. Though the overall population of most of the mature areas will decrease, they will need more housing to accommodate changing household formation patterns. The larger number of smaller households will require more multiple-family dwellings. A very important question concerns where this housing will be constructed. This question is tied to the issue of rising energy prices, increased costs of personal transport, and the effect these are likely to have on the geographic distribution of population and industry in metropolitan areas. These questions are taken up after a brief consideration of the impact of foreign trade on regional growth.

Foreign Trade and Regional Growth

Throughout most of its history, the United States was not very dependent on foreign trade. Most of the nation's capacity was devoted to producing goods and services for domestic consumption; foreign trade was a small percentage of GNP. The nation did absorb huge amounts of capital and labor from the rest of the world but the expansion in plant and equipment these factor increases permitted, were largely devoted to the production of goods for domestic consumption. The situation has changed in recent years; we are dependent on foreign nations for supplies of many raw materials besides petroleum. However, raw material imports do not by any means comprise the full picture. Many nations compete effectively with us in the production of a wide variety of manufactured goods, including those that entail high technology. Foreign sources of supply and foreign markets are likely to have much more influence on domestic locational choices in the future than they have had in the past. Foreign markets will tend to become much more important to U.S. producers than they were in the past. Firms that depend on raw material from abroad or wish to sell in those markets may be expected to be drawn to those coastal areas that provide the best access to them.

These trends will be reinforced by increases in the cost of shipping goods due to rising energy prices and general cost increases as well. Internal areas that enjoy good inland navigation will not suffer from as great a disadvantage as those that are landlocked. However, even the former will probably suffer some reduction in their capacity to attract industry because there is a very good chance that a system of user charges will be imposed on the waterways. When such charges are imposed, it is hoped that they will take the form of tolls at locks rather than fuel taxes. Tolls are to be preferred because there is congestion at locks and especially if they are adjusted for peaks, they would add to the efficiency with which these resources are utilized.

This discussion has suggested that increased reliance on foreign raw materials, balance-of-payments problems, and a much greater need for American firms to compete in foreign markets, will convey a locational advantage on coastal areas. A number of the mature metropolitan areas are in such locations. Cities like New York are likely to receive some benefit from the above forces but the effect is unlikely to be strong enough to reverse the negative trend of recent years.

Energy, Travel Cost, and Future Patterns of Land Use

As we saw in the first part of this chapter, the costs of personal and freight transport act directly on the internal fabric of the metropolis. This is unlike the influences of population growth and foreign trade which have their primary influence on the overall level of activity; their influence on the internal structure of cities is indirect. In this section we consider how changes in energy prices, but especially motor fuel prices, are likely to influence the long-run demand for urban transportation and land and buildings in different parts of metropolitan regions.

Three alternative patterns of long-run development in metropolitan land use and transportation can be identified. One entails a continuation of the trend toward dispersal of population and jobs within metropolitan areas. Some urban specialists have seen this as quite likely, drawing on the recently observed population increases in exurban areas as evidence of the continued strength of the tendency toward a more uniform distribution of population and employment within metropolitan regions. A second alternative is the drawing back of population and jobs into a more centralized pattern that resembles the spatial structure of the nineteenth and traditional twentieth century city. There are public officials and others who see in the rising price of energy a powerful force that will increase the demand for public transportation in the short run, and draw households back to areas that are well located with respect to the main corridors of public transportation in the long run. A third alternative is for increased multinucleation: the formation of distinct and quite dense suburban and exurban centers. This alternative entails the development of relatively few major employment centers in suburban and exurban areas. It implies a greater degree of centralization of jobs and household locations within suburban areas than has been true in the past. It also implies significant increases in public bus transportation and in the number of multifamily dwellings in the vicinity of major suburban nuclei. In this scenario, no single employment center would have as much employment as the CBD of a mature metropolitan area, but together, suburban areas are seen as having two or three times as much employment as the CBD.

We view the last of these three land-use patterns as the most likely. In part, this conclusion is based on an assumption, the same assumption employed by those who believe that jobs and population will return to the traditional employment areas and corridors of travel. The assumption is that the energy crisis is a long-run economic reality and that there will be very large increases in the real price of petroleum and in the real cost of personal transportation in the future. These increases will either be achieved by allowing market prices to approach the true costs entailed in expanding petroleum output or by a variety of public policy devices, such as gasoline taxes or rationing, that work mostly to reduce demand.[5] The long epoch of low-cost energy probably is over. The actual output of petroleum and other forms of energy in all likelihood will increase, but the increases will entail much more costly forms of production, such as offshore drilling at greater and greater depths, and solar energy at high-capital cost, for example.

Our conclusion concerning the development of multinucleated metropolitan areas, is based also on a belief that people will respond to increases in the cost of personal transportation by buying smaller, lighter cars, and reducing miles traveled to and from work. The view of the elasticity of demand for travel implicit in this conclusion conflicts with the popularly held belief that the demand for transportation, and the demand for personal travel in particular, is highly price inelastic. It is quite common to hear the opinion expressed that gasoline prices have risen very considerably, but reliance on the car for work and other trips is essentially unchanged. We disagree with this conclusion on two grounds. First, the real price of personal transportation has not risen very much and, second, it does not properly distinguish between the short-run and long-run elasticity of demand for travel.

As to the former of these objections, Table 8-2 shows that the real price of motor fuel increased only slightly between 1967 and 1977. The increase was only 4.1 percent in real terms. In addition, a number of durable transportation items such as tires and autos fell in real terms. Overall, the cost of personal transportation either fell or rose very slightly in recent years. The evidence from Europe is similar. A recent study reported that the real price of motor fuel reached an all-time low in England in the period 1971-73; it was cheaper in 1976 than it was in 1953, the overall reduction in the postwar years being about 15 percent.[6] The fact that the public has not yet acted to reduce miles traveled and

Table 8-2
Real Percent Change in Components of Travel Cost (1967-April 1977)

	Consumer Price Index April 1977	Real Change 1967-April 1977
All items (1967 = 100)	179.6	—
Transportation	176.8	−1.6%
Private	176.3	−1.8%
Automobile, new	140.6	−21.7%
Automobile, used	187.8	+4.6%
Gasoline	187.0	+4.1%
Motor oil	164.7	−8.3%
Tires	137.2	−23.6%
Auto repair and maintenance	201.3	+12.1%
Auto insurance	210.1	+17.0%
Auto registration	142.2	−20.8%
Parking fees	191.6	+6.7%
Public	180.4	+0.4%
Local transit	177.4	−1.2%
Taxi cab fares	187.7	+4.5%
Railroad fares	173.6	−3.3%
Airplane fares	180.7	+0.6%
Intercity bus fares	211.2	+17.6%

Sources: Handbook of Labor Statistics 1976; CPI Detailed Reports, July 1976; CPI Detailed Reports, April 1977. U.S. Department of Labor, Bureau of Labor Statistics.

gasoline consumption, also is due to significant differences between the short-run and long-run elasticities of demand for travel.

It is difficult to quantify all aspects of the cost of personal travel; it is particularly difficult to measure the impact of changes in the quality of service, comfort, or convenience. Nevertheless, econometricians have attempted to measure the elasticity of consumer demand for motor fuel, automobiles, and travel mileage. These studies are severely constrained by the form in which aggregate data are available and by the relative unavailability of disaggregate data. It is possible to draw some inferences about aggregate and per capita consumption. However, the data do not permit drawing strong conclusions about long-run elasticities because these depend on changes in the locational distribution of jobs and homesites as well as on car ownership, and the cost, quality, and availability of alternatives to private transport.

There have been a number of studies in which attempts were made to measure price elasticities of motor fuel demand for both the short and long run. Of particular interest are those by Houthakker and Taylor, Verleger and Sheehan, Houthakker and Verleger, McGillivray, Chase Econometric Associates, and Burright and Enns.[7] Though the studies differ in the data they use, in the assumptions they make, and in the models they employ, their results are remarkably similar. These results are summarized by Burright and Enns who report that the short-run elasticity of demand for motor fuel in the United States is between −0.1 and −0.3, but that the long-run elasticity of demand ranges between −0.65 and −0.85. These differences between the short-run and long-run elasticities are similar to those reported for West Yorkshire, Great Britain, by Bonsall and Champernowne.[8] They report values of −0.5 and −1.4.[b]

Both sets of findings suggest that increases in the real price of personal travel tend to have much more pronounced effects on gasoline consumption in the long than in the short run. However, the studies do not really take account of the possibility that households will in time tend to choose homesites and job locations that reduce the average length of the work trip. It can be argued that most of the models used to estimate long-run elasticities do not provide insight into the impact of changes in the cost of travel on household location patterns. This purpose is better suited by a full urban simulation model. Bonsall and Champernowne have performed such a simulation for West Yorkshire.[c] They state:

It is interesting to note that the elasticity of mean trip length by car is higher than that of modal choice suggesting that in the long term the population would change their destination rather than desert their cars.[9]

---

[b]While it is tempting to argue the transferability of elasticities across the Atlantic, it should be recalled there is a hidden income effect. Verleger and Sheehan, for example, compute the income elasticity of the demand for gasoline at about +1. If the mean income in England is lower than that in the United States, then the difference between the two long-run elasticities ought to be discounted.

[c]The authors also find via simulation that a sixfold increase in the price of gasoline is needed to achieve a state where virtually no one chooses to travel by car.

Clearly, if such a response can be expected from the British consumer, the effect should be much stronger in the United States, particularly in cities that do not have public transportation services comparable to those of England.

While Americans are unlikely to abandon their cars, they will almost certainly shift to smaller, lighter cars. These do not lend themselves to one-way work trips of thirty and more miles because they are uncomfortable, and the comfort and convenience part of personal travel cost is likely to increase markedly in the future. The capacity and quality of much of the nation's urban network is very likely to decline in the years ahead. The cost of maintaining roads has risen dramatically in recent years and will probably continue to do so in the future. The funds needed to maintain the quality and capacity of the network are simply not available, and reductions in travel probably mean that still less will be available in the future, at least via conventional sources of revenue, such as motor fuel taxes. Much of the secondary and tertiary road system of the nation is already in poor condition; this condition is now spreading to cities. New York is surely an example of a city which has less highway capacity, and where that capacity is lower in quality than it was ten years ago. The passage of time and weather, the movement of more heavily loaded trucks and the damage they do to pavements, the increased cost of road repairs, and the reduced availability of funds for such repairs, mean that reductions in the quality and capacity of urban streets and highways will become quite common. The real cost of trips will rise because they will be less comfortable and more time consuming. The cost will also rise because of the effect that poor roads have on automobile life and repair expenditures.

If, as we believe, the real price (including comfort, convenience, etc.) of personal travel is going to increase greatly over the next twenty years or so, then the first of the land-use patterns mentioned earlier—a continuation of the trend toward decentralization and increases in the average length of work trip—is the most costly, and therefore the least likely, of the three alternatives. However, acceptance of the argument that the price of personal travel will increase, of itself does not permit judging which of the other two alternatives is most likely. Multinucleation would reduce energy consumption and travel expenditure by reducing average miles traveled, especially for the work trip. A return of households to the principal corridors of public transit might seem to have an equal potential for reducing travel expenditure by substituting public for private transportation, but we do not believe that a significant number of households will responds in this way.

A rise in the price of personal transportation can be expected to bring some segments of the population back to the central city. Enough of the retired, the young, households without children, and those attracted to cultural and recreational activities may return to the central city to contribute to a revitalization of some of its older neighborhoods, though at much lower densities than before. More widespread recentralization in the mature central cities cannot be expected because their infrastructure, and particularly their school systems, are of poor quality, and could not be brought up to the standards of suburban schools without public expenditure of billions of dollars. Widespread recentralization of population in central cities is not possible unless significant numbers of manufacturing and other establishments return to the central city, a shift that is highly improbable.

Elimination of slum housing, clearing of land, and building of industrial parks and commercial malls might well bring some manufacturing and other establishments to central cities, but it is unlikely to bring any significant increase in the number of central-city jobs. An increase in the price of personal transportation and the clearing away of a certain amount of slum housing to make way for industry will certainly not be enough to bring about a rebirth of the economically dominant, nineteenth-century central city. Access to the Interstate Highway System will probably be even more important in the future than in the past because it is the one part of the road network that is likely to be maintained at its current level of quality. Firms that ship and receive goods by truck will still find it advantageous to have a suburban location. Increases in fuel prices may lead to an increase in the cost of shipping goods by truck, relative to rail, and to some diversion of low-value freight to rail. However, this does not argue for a return of manufacturing establishments to central cities, since the most modern rail handling facilities now are in suburban locations. Finally, there is the question of access to the highly skilled and educated part of the labor force. Most of this labor is located in the suburbs and, given the low quality of central-city schools and other infrastructure, it is almost certain to remain there.

Thus, we conclude that reconcentration of jobs and population within suburban areas, and the development of a truly multinucleated metropolitan region within which there are important employment centers and densely settled areas, is the most likely of the three relevant land-use alternatives. Suburban areas will change; there has already been a very significant increase in the number of high-rise apartment houses built in them; this trend will undoubtedly continue; the rate may even increase; whether or not it does, will depend on public policy decisions on transport, housing, and employment. The distribution of commercial and retail establishments in suburban areas probably also will change. Increases in the cost of personal travel may bring the decline of those shopping centers that must draw customers from a very large area in order to be economically viable. There may well be something of a return to a community pattern of shopping much like the pattern of neighborhood shopping of an earlier era.

The conclusions we have reached on central-city recentralization have implications for some issues in public policy that involve mass transit. In many metropolitan areas, Chicago is an example, local and some federal officials feel that it is important to improve and extend fixed-rail systems. However, the construction cost experiences of BART and METRO are a severe deterrent to such plans. The great expense of constructing rail systems has led some federal government officials to search for new ways to finance them; one such scheme is known as value capture.[10] It is based on the assumption that the building of new fixed-rail facilities, or the improvement of old ones, will draw population to transit stations, and lead to the construction of new multifamily dwellings and to substantial increases in land and property values in their vicinity. The idea behind value capture is that such increases can then be taxed to pay for the transit system. The reasoning is not new; highway planners long ago argued that increased land values in the vicinity of highways proved the existence of significant nonuser benefits, and that such benefits should be counted, along with savings in travel time, in project evaluations. The fact that savings in travel time explain a major part of the property value changes and that the inclusion of nonuser benefits in project evaluations involved double counting was often ignored by highway planners. They also ignored possible negative benefits on areas bypassed by a new road, which have relevance for value capture.

Whatever the political and legal obstacles in its way, certain conditions must hold before value capture policy can make economic sense. If transit extensions and improvements do not result in a net increase in central-city employment and population, it is unlikely that there will be any net overall increase in the value of land and buildings, and we have already argued that business is unlikely to expand in central cities to any significant degree. Thus, if the population that is drawn to a transit line comes from within the area, it is almost certain that any increases in land values around transit lines will be matched by decreases elsewhere in the city. If owners of property whose value falls as a result of the building of a transit line and the population readjustments it causes were compensated, there would be little, if anything, left with which to finance the transit system.

There is a role for expanded public transportation. If we are correct in our conclusion that there will be very large increases in the size and number of multifamily dwellings in the vicinity of suburban employment centers, it should be possible to have economically viable bus systems that transport workers from areas of dense settlement to nearby jobs. It may even be possible to design self-financing bus systems that link some of the major suburban employment centers and their satellite settlement areas.

Housing and employment policy for minority and low-income groups, which is discussed in Chapter 14, also is relevant to the kind of spatial pattern that will evolve in metropolitan areas. Earlier, we indicated that there has been a very large increase in the number of reverse commuters. We reasoned that many of these workers are from low-income and minority groups that are constrained to live in the central city by discriminatory housing practices, and because that is where the stock of low-price housing is found. Increases in the cost of personal travel will work a severe hardship on these groups. If a forecast that the number of jobs in suburban areas will continue to increase is correct, the number of such low-income reverse commuters also will increase. The demands of the low-income population for suburban locations will be very strong, not simply because such locations reduce travel time and cost but because they appear to promise access to higher-quality schools and other suburban amenities. If governments cannot act to increase the supply of low-income subsidized housing near major suburban employment centers, there will be a strong tendency for minority and low-income workers to concentrate in inner, older suburbs that have stocks of older housing ready for filtering. The result will be new suburban ghettos, with many of the same old problems such as poor schools, inadequate street maintenance, infrequent garbage collection, and poor hospitals. The development of bus systems that link low-income neighborhoods and important suburban employment centers might reduce the demand for suburban housing somewhat. However, the time and inconvenience of reverse commuting by bus are likely to be very great. The demand for suburban housing by low-income and minority households, therefore, can be expected to increase despite expanded and even subsidized bus transit.

Notes

1. For the basics of spatial wage theory, see Leon N. Moses, "Towards a Theory of Intra-urban Wage Differentials and Their Influence on Travel Patterns," *Papers and Proceedings Regional Science Association*, vol. 9, 1962.

2. Observation of these concentric ring patterns in cities led to an extension of von Thünen concepts in order to explain urban land use. See R.L. Fales and Leon N. Moses, "Land-use Theory and the Spatial Structure of the Nineteenth Century City," *Papers and Proceedings Regional Science Association*, vol. 28, 1972.

3. See L.N. Moses and H.F. Williamson, "The Location of Economic Activity in Cities," *American Economic Review*, May 1967, for a detailed study of industrial decentralization in this period, and the emergence of the truck between 1910 and 1920.

4. R.B. Pettengil and J.S. Uppal, *Can Cities Survive?: The Fiscal Plight of American Cities*, New York: St. Martin's Press, 1974.

5. See, for example, C. Kenneth Orski, "The Potential for Fuel Conservation: The Case of the Automobile," *Transportation Research*, vol. 8, no. 415, 1974.

6. See P.W. Bonsall and A.F. Champernowne, "Some Findings on the Elasticities of Demand for Petrol," *Traffic Engineering and Control*, October 1976.

7. Of particular interest are H.S. Houthakker and L.D. Taylor, *Consumer Demand in the United States: Analysis and Projections,* Cambridge, Mass.: Harvard University Press, 1970; H.S. Houthakker and P.K. Verleger, Jr., "The

Demand for Gasoline: A Mixed Cross Sectional and Time Series Analysis," Report to the Energy Policy Project, 1973 (unpublished); R. McGillivray, "Gasoline Use by Automobiles," *Highway Research Record*, 1975; Chase Econometric Associates, "The Effect of Tax and Regulatory Alternatives on Car Sales and Gasoline Consumption," Report for the Council on Environmental Quality, May 1974 (unpublished); P.K. Verleger and D. Sheehan, "A Study of the Demand for Gasoline," Report prepared for Council on Environmental Quality, 1974 (unpublished); and B.K. Burright and J.H. Enns, "Econometric Models of the Demand for Motor Fuel," Santa Monica: The Rand Corporation, April 1975.

    8. Bonsall and Champernowne, "Elasticities of Demand for Petrol."

    9. Bonsall and Champernowne, "Elasticities of Demand for Petrol."

    10. Carl Sharpe, "A Value Capture Policy," *U.S. Department of Transportation Research Studies*, vols. 1-4, 1974.

9

Environmental Problems in the Mature Metropolis

*Edwin S. Mills,
Daniel Feenberg,* and
Randall Zisler

Environmental problems have probably been as well studied by economists as any microeconomic problem for the last decade or so. Many books and hundreds of scholarly articles have appeared. Environmental economics is now a thriving subspecialty, with several scholarly journals, research conferences among specialists, and numerous undergraduate and graduate courses.

There are basically two reasons for the outpouring of environmental economic research. First, and most obvious, environmental problems have been high on the list of public concerns during the late 1960s and early 1970s, and economists are much influenced in their choice of research projects by topics that figure prominently in public concern. During the postwar period, substantial amounts of economic research have focused successively on problems of defense, poverty, environment, cities, and energy as public attention has shifted its focus. It would surely be undesirable if a large part of the economic profession rushed from the study of one problem to another as public attention shifted, but it is surely desirable that groups of economists are willing to devote their energies to issues of current public concern.

Second, and equally important, economists are convinced that they have a set of analytical tools that can provide deep insights into environmental problems. There is a strong consensus in the profession that pollution results in straightforward and comprehensible fashion from basic characteristics of production and consumption, and that explicit government intervention is needed to prevent excessive environmental deterioration. Furthermore, there is a strong consensus about the form that government intervention should take. There are few, perhaps no, practical problems about which economists have as strong a professional consensus as they have about the causes and cures of pollution. It is important to mention this because laymen frequently believe that economists rarely agree on anything.[1]

Writers define the environment and environmental problems in various ways. The tendency, especially among popular writers, is to define the terms broadly to include many influences on well-being that are beyond the control of individuals or of small groups of individuals. We have no quarrel with such broad definitions, but it is difficult to be precise about broadly defined subjects. In this chapter, we discuss a special, but important, class of environmental problems, those that arise from the discharge of wastes to air, water, and land. It is to the special class of environmental problems that the consensus referred to above applies.

Here, we will survey and analyze likely environmental problems in mature and declining metropolitan areas. It is worthwhile at the outset to point out that the situation is not one of unrelieved gloom and doom. In the years surrounding 1970 it was common to claim that the environment was deteriorating rapidly and that the important causes were the growth and concentration of production and waste disposal in large metropolitan areas. Though the argument was frequently overstated, it is basically correct. Pollution results when discharges are large in relationship to the air or water medium receiving them. Large, dense metropolitan areas result in large volumes of waste discharges to the air over them and to streams and estuaries in and near them. Receiving media are thus overburdened and deteriorate in quality.

Some people even advocated explicit government programs to disperse economic activity away from large metropolitan areas as a pollution control program. Such dispersal programs are certainly poor government policy. But trends since about 1970 represent private actions with exactly the same effect. As indicated in Chapter 2, there has been a dramatic deceleration in metropolitan growth during the 1970s; the deceleration is especially strong in large metropolitan areas. The most dramatic measure is the fact that all of the five largest metropolitan areas have grown more slowly than others in recent years. Finally, metropolitan areas have decentralized for decades. Average population and employment densities of metropolitan areas of given size have declined. This trend has continued unabated in the 1970s.

These facts mean that production, consumption, and waste discharges to the environment have dispersed both within and among metropolitan areas in the recent past. In large degree, private decision making is accomplishing precisely the dispersion that will reduce the polluting effects on the environment. Effects during short periods of time, which may nevertheless be measured in decades, may be less favorable. Short-run effects are the main subject of this paper. The purpose of these introductory remarks is simply to indicate that the situation is not one of unrelieved gloom. We do not advocate metropolitan dispersal by government action as a means of improving the environment. Nor do we believe that environmental deterioration has been an important reason for out-migration from large metropolitan areas or from their central cores. We merely suggest that reduced environmental stress is a beneficial long-run side effect of trends occurring for other reasons.

Why Is There a Pollution Problem?

An industrialized economy extracts massive amounts of materials from the environment to make products that satisfy the needs and wants of people. In the United States about 4.3 billion tons of materials are extracted from the environment each year, which implies that materials with about the weight of the entire population are extracted each day. With relatively minor qualifications regarding imports, exports, and capital accumulation, the weight of materials extracted equals the weight of materials returned to the environment each year. Much of the massive tonnage of materials extracted is returned to the environment without being processed into products, in such forms as mine tailings, slag, and agricultural wastes. But large volumes of materials are processed to make products and fuels. Perhaps 80 percent of the materials processed into products and fuels are consumed in metropolitan areas. Consumption entails the burning of fuels, eating of food, and use of products in various ways. Neither production nor consumption of products creates or destroys matter. Therefore, all the materials withdrawn and incorporated in products remain after use and must be returned to the environment.[a]

Most of the materials consumed in metropolitan areas are returned to the environment within the metropolitan area. Fuels burned are mostly discharged to the air, much organic waste is discharged to nearby water bodies through the sewage system, and most durable household products are discharged as solid wastes in local landfills and dumps. There are no comprehensive data on waste discharges in metropolitan areas, but rough magnitudes can be established. By volume, most waterborne discharges are of organic materials. Manufacturing industry and domestic sewage generate some 40 billion pounds of organic wastes per year. Perhaps three-fourths, or one pound per day per metropolitan resident, is discharged to watercourses in metropolitan areas. Remarkably, airborne discharges, about half of them carbon monoxide, are many times greater than waterborne discharges, perhaps seven pounds per day per resident in metropolitan areas. Solid waste discharges are the largest component of the three. Total solid wastes generated in metropolitan areas are probably about 300 million tons per year, about twelve pounds per metropolitan resident per day. Some two-thirds, or eight pounds per metropolitan resident per day, is collected from homes, commercial facilities, and institutions. These figures suggest that perhaps twenty pounds of solid, liquid, and airborne wastes per person per day are returned to the environment in U.S. metropolitan areas. By any standards, it is a massive waste disposal system.[2]

Why does this waste disposal system represent a government policy problem? In fact, it represents two quite different kinds of problems for governments. The more subtle will be referred to as a property rights problem; the other will be referred to as a management problem. Each will be discussed in turn.

The fundamental concept of law in the United States and elsewhere is that people have rights to do what they want unless it is more or less specifically prohibited by law. The essence of private property is that owners have the right

---
[a]Reuse of materials does not affect the equality between withdrawals and discharges. If materials are reused, it reduces both withdrawals and discharges by the same amount. Thus, withdrawals equal discharges, regardless of the amount of materials reuse.

to determine the use and disposition of their property. In particular, you cannot dispose of wastes on my property without my permission. To the extent that waste disposal is on private property, no issue of government policy is raised. If I dispose of waste on my property, it is presumably because I have determined that it is the best use of my property. If I contract to dispose of wastes on someone else's property, presumably the contract represents his determination of the best use of his property. Thus, only mutually beneficial waste disposal uses are made of private property. *Provided there are no effects of waste disposal off the property*, no third parties are affected by waste disposal on private property. Parties to any waste disposal contract are made better off by it or they would not agree to it, and no third parties are affected. Therefore, waste disposal on private property makes the parties involved better off and no one worse off. This is the economist's criterion for a desirable use of a valuable resource.

The above explains why solid waste disposal is a less fundamental environmental problem than air and water pollution. By definition, solid waste disposal is that which takes place on land. Property rights are relatively easy to define and enforce regarding land. Therefore, the system of efficient resource use described above, which depends on carefully defined property rights, works reasonably well with solid waste disposal. The most important example of failure to prevent excessive waste disposal on land is, not accidentally, illegal "litter" in public places such as streets or beaches. Land that is kept in the "public domain" is treated like air and water are in the public domain, and excess waste disposal results.

The property rights system breaks down altogether regarding airborne and waterborne discharges. Navigable waterways and the air above metropolitan areas are part of the public domain, which means that everyone has the right of free access and use. Of course, every society places some restrictions on use of public domain, at least to the extent of antinuisance laws or traditions. But in the absence of specific environmental protection laws, people can use the ambient air and water environments for waste disposal more or less freely.

Discharges to the air and water environments are cheap to the discharger precisely because these media are part of the public domain. Wastes tend to be discharged on private property only to the extent that use of the property for waste discharge is more valuable than alternative uses of the property. A high-quality environment is valuable in that it protects health, property, recreational opportunities, and aesthetic values. Furthermore, waste discharges to air and water impair those valuable uses of a high-quality environment. But being part of the public domain, the air and water environments are not protected by the institution of private property. Thus, dischargers do not pay a price representing the value of foregone uses for the privilege of discharging wastes to the air and water environments.

The foregoing is an abstract statement of a very practical and widely appreciated notion. Suppose there were no property rights in land and anyone had the right to grow or harvest crops anywhere. Then no one would plant crops because, at the first sign of ripening, hungry people would harvest them without rewarding the grower for his efforts. That is precisely the problem with the air and water environments. No one has an incentive to protect them because no one can prevent others from damaging them; everyone discharges wastes to them to everyone's disadvantage. There are no villains regarding pollution, only a failure to assign property rights. The failure to assign property rights to the air and water environments, is not because of the perfidy of the political system. It is that property rights are technically difficult to define for fugitive substances such as air and water in their natural domains.

The second environmental problem is a management problem. Mainly for historical reasons, local governments have undertaken to collect and dispose of certain kinds of wastes. By far the most important examples are commercial and residential sewage and refuse in metropolitan areas. These activities of local governments do involve property rights issues because, at best, local governments represent the interests of people in small jurisdictions. Frequently, local government waste disposal activities impair the environment of people outside their jurisdiction. In that situation, local governments are in the same position regarding the property rights issue as is a private discharger.

Otherwise, local governments have the same problems in disposing of wastes for which they take responsibility as does any business; they strive to achieve high-quality waste disposal as inexpensively as possible. Everyone who studies local government sewage and solid waste disposal operations concludes that they do a poor job. Presumably, the basic reason is that economic incentives are less effective in the political system than in profit-making firms, but that subject is beyond the scope of this discussion.

Government Environmental Programs

There is a remarkable dichotomy regarding government policies to correct for imperfections in property rights. For half a century, economists, following Pigou, have argued as follows:[3] environmental property rights are ill-defined with the consequence that users, that is, those who discharge wastes to the media, do not pay the opportunity cost of their actions. For technical reasons, the ambient environment cannot be bought and sold privately. But the government can simulate a private market by charging appropriate fees for use of the environment; here, such fees would be referred to as effluent fees. Government must estimate the dollar value of damages from polluting discharges at the margin and charge all identifiable dischargers an effluent fee of that amount. Then, the beneficial effects of private markets would be realized: each source would abate discharges until the marginal cost of abatement equaled the fee, thus minimizing the cost of the abatement achieved; and dischargers continuously would seek economical means of further abatement as long as any discharges remained. Effluent fees would extend to the environment the advantages that the market system provides for privately owned productive resources. This bare-bone statement has been worked out in painstakingly practical detail by environmental economists during the last two decades.

Economists' thinking has had no effect whatsoever on government policy. U.S. environmental protection programs, dating back to the 1950s and currently embodied in air and water legislation from the early 1970s, have relied entirely on a moral and police power concept. The attitude in the Congress, the executive, and environmental groups, is that pollution is sinful and should be prohibited with civil and criminal penalties. Like many kinds of sin, pollution has been found to be ineradicable by the authorities. The result has been an accretion of rules and regulations, court cases, and legislation that would literally fill a large room and is by now incomprehensible to any mind.

The U.S. pollution control program now costs about $15 billion per year, about 1 percent of GNP, including both government and private funds.[b] It is impossible to spend such vast sums without accomplishing something. In fact, one of the worst indictments of government programs is that after two decades of effort, we still lack an environmental monitoring system that permits us to measure progress in pollution control.

Water pollution data are the worst. We know there has been substantial reduction in organic discharges to water bodies, mainly the result of massive federal government investment in municipal sewage treatment plants. Some rivers have higher-dissolved oxygen levels than a few years ago and game fish have reappeared upstream in some. Otherwise, there is little evidence of pervasive improvement in water quality of lakes, rivers, and estuaries.

Air-quality data are somewhat better. National data show that total airborne discharges have decreased 1 or 2 percent per year since about 1970. Most of this improvement is the result of substitution of clean for dirty fuels and of effectively modest controls on motor vehicle emissions.

It is unfortunate that the federal government does not publish indexes of environmental quality by metropolitan areas. We should have average ambient concentrations of the four or five most important air pollutants published each year by metropolitan area and representing the Environmental Protection Agency's best judgment as to the appropriate average. In addition, we should have similar averages of dissolved oxygen content in major water bodies in metropolitan areas, and indexes of a few other water pollutants. In a later section of this chapter, we will present our estimates of average air quality for a sample of metropolitan areas, but we are hampered by lack of knowledge of exact locations of metering stations, of reliability of measurements, and of appropriate averaging procedures.

---

[b]This is annualized cost, including only interest and depreciation costs of pollution control capital. Actual annual outlays are twice as great, about $30 billion per year, because capital investment for pollution control is large.

Environmental Problems of Mature Metropolises

Are pollution problems worse in stagnant and declining metropolitan areas? The answer is not obvious. This section is devoted to an analysis of characteristics that might plausibly be thought to make environmental problems worse in mature metropolitan areas than elsewhere. Subsequent sections present attempts to test these theoretical ideas against some data.

Each environmental medium can absorb limited amounts of wastes without significant degradation. A flowing stream can degrade organic wastes and purify itself by natural processes. Likewise, modest amounts of each important air pollutant can be absorbed by the atmosphere without measurable damage to people or property. Limited waste discharges are a legitimate use of each environmental medium.

As discharges become large, the environment becomes overloaded and damages increase at a rapid rate. Thus, the relevant measure of pollution is the rate of discharge relative to the capacity of the environment to degrade, dilute, disperse, and otherwise dispose of wastes. The capacity of the environment to absorb wastes is a complex concept. A flowing stream can degrade organic wastes, whereas it can merely dilute acid that drains from abandoned coal mines. And a rapidly flowing and churning stream can absorb much more waste per gallon of water than can a slow-moving tranquil stream. Lakes are the most vulnerable of all water bodies, because they are relatively still. The air mantle over a metropolitan area can absorb more wastes the better it circulates. Inversions that inhibit vertical circulation limit the capacity of the air mantle to absorb wastes. Sunlight enables smog to be formed from air pollutants; rain washes pollutants out of the air.

Interaction effects are also important. A thermal electric plant's heat discharges reduce the capacity of a stream to degrade organic wastes without polluting the water. And hydrocarbon and nitrogen oxide discharges interact in the air to form smog. Thus a first conclusion of this section is that natural conditions affect pollution levels. Other things equal, a metropolitan area with good air circulation has less air pollution than one with stagnant air, and a metropolitan area on a turbulent stream has less water pollution than one on a still lake. However, it is difficult to specify precisely the natural conditions likely to lead to good or bad environmental quality.

The second conclusion is that high density of population and production leads to a poorer environment. A high-density metropolitan area discharges more wastes per unit volume of the receiving media than does a low-density metropolitan area. The most important reason that large metropolitan areas tend to have more pollution problems than others is that large metropolitan areas tend to have higher population and production densities than others.

A third consideration is that pollution levels depend on the mix of production and consumption in a metropolitan area. A metropolitan area that produces or consumes large volumes of manufactured goods is likely to have more pollution problems than one that concentrates on services. For that reason, Washington, D.C., has fewer pollution problems than Detroit.

The final consideration is that pollution depends not only on the kinds and amounts of production and consumption but also on how wastes are handled. Wastes may be reused in greater or lesser extent instead of being discharged. Reuse varies enormously by kind of waste, by time, and by place. A recent trend has been reuse of organic wastes as fuel in thermal electric plants, an activity pioneered in St. Louis. All wastes can be treated or modified before discharge, at some cost, to make them less polluting. Liquid organic wastes can be treated in sewage treatment plants, automobile exhaust can be converted to innocuous gases by careful engine design and by catalysts, and so on. In the United States, pollution control is a national program which, by legislation, administration, and judicial interpretation, has permitted relatively few local options as to environmental quality. There is thus a presumption that preferences of the local population have little effect on environmental protection programs in metropolitan areas; but it is no more than a presumption.

There are two basic answers to the question of why might mature metropolitan areas have more serious environmental problems than others. First, mature metropolitan areas tend to have higher densities of population and production than others. It is a statistical fact that stagnant or declining metropolitan areas tend to be large metropolitan areas. It has already been mentioned that all five of the largest metropolitan areas in 1970 lost population by 1974. And the tendency for large metropolitan areas to shrink or grow less rapidly than others goes back much further than 1970, as pointed out in Chapter 2. Also, it was pointed out earlier in this section that large metropolitan areas tend to be high-density metropolitan areas and that high-density metropolitan areas inevitably have more serious environmental problems than others. Thus, if mature metropolitan areas tend to be large, and if large metropolitan areas tend to be high density and therefore to have poor environmental quality, it follows that mature metropolitan areas tend to have poor environmental quality. As a qualitative matter, this relationship is almost inevitable. But it is unclear how important it is or even if the relationship between mature metropolitan areas and environmental quality may not be swamped by other relationships and by the poor quality of environmental data. At sizes below the largest, the relationship between growth and size of metropolitan areas is not strong. And it is likley that the relationship between size and environmental quality of metropolitan areas is also somewhat weak. Thus, whether the correlation between slow growth or shrinkage of metropolitan areas and environmental quality is substantial, needs to be tested against the facts.

Second, mature metropolitan areas tend to have relatively poor environmental quality because they tend to have relatively old capital equipment. Other things equal, a rapidly growing population tends to be a young population, and a slowly growing population tends to be an old population. For the same reason, a metropolitan area whose population, and therefore its stock of structures and machinery, is growing rapidly tends to have a young capital stock. If the average capital item lasts ten years, a metropolitan area whose capital stock has been constant for some time has a capital stock whose average age is five years. The average age of its capital is less than five years if its capital stock is growing, and more than five years if it is shrinking. Other things equal, old capital stock is more polluting than new capital stock. Just because of the way technology progresses, wastes discharged per unit of output decrease as time passes and technology improves.

For the economy as a whole, material inputs have grown less rapidly than material output in a secular sense. Technical progress enables production gradually to make more effective use of materials. In addition to the pervasive effect of technical change, since the early 1970s pollution control laws have required construction of capital that was much less polluting than capital constructed earlier. A larger proportion of the capital in rapidly growing metropolitan areas was built since the strict pollution control laws came into effect than in slow-growing or shrinking metropolitan areas. Thus, both the pervasive effect of technical progress and the specific effect of the pollution control laws mean that newer capital is less polluting than older capital. For both reasons, the relatively new capital in rapidly growing metropolitan areas should make them have higher-quality environments than do mature metropolitan areas.

Once again, it is not clear how important this matter is. Recent years have witnessed a pervasive decline in population growth rates and in urban growth rates. In this situation, differences in the age of capital stock between more and less rapidly growing metropolitan areas are probably not great. In addition, the new pollution control requirements have been applied with considerable severity to existing as well as to new facilities. Thus, environmental quality effects of differences among metropolitan areas in the age of the capital stock may be small relative to other effects in the data.

The last two paragraphs have discussed basic differences in environmental quality between mature metropolitan areas and others. In addition to these differences, there is another correlate of mature metropolitan areas that may affect environmental quality. Many presently mature metropolitan areas, especially in the Northeast, had their most rapid growth during the period preceding about 1925, when manufacturing growth was most closely related to urban growth. The argument is frequently made that presently mature metropolitan areas had growth based on growth of the manufacturing sector, whereas metropolitan areas that have recently grown rapidly have had growth based on growth of the service sector. If so, presently mature metropolitan areas may have a larger share of their labor force in manufacturing than do other metropolitan areas. Manufacturing is presumably more polluting than the service sector and the result may be a poorer-quality environment in mature metropolitan areas.

Whether mature metropolitan areas have a larger share of their labor force in manufacturing is easily testable by available data.

The next consideration to be mentioned in this section works in the opposite direction. To the extent that mature metropolitan areas are concentrated in the Northeast, they probably have more favorable climates than other parts of the country. Hot parts of the country are likely to have poor environments for several reasons. Warm water has less capacity to degrade wastes without pollution than cool water. Bright, sunny weather causes smog more than cloudy weather. To the extent that a metropolitan area is both hot and dry, as in the Southwest, it has a double disadvantage. Dry regions have little water to dilute and degrade wastes. And precipitation filters pollutants out of the air. Thus, the parts of the country that contain most of the mature metropolitan areas have moderate temperatures and adequate precipitation, both of which enable the environment to cleanse itself.

The final theoretical issue to be mentioned is that causation may run from environmental quality to urban growth as well as vice versa. People dislike living and working in polluted metropolitan areas, and some studies have suggested that a poor environment is a deterrent to growth. The importance of this consideration is more dubious than the causation discussed in previous paragraphs. There is grave doubt how well people can perceive differences in environmental quality and whether they take such differences into account in choosing among metropolitan areas in which to live and produce.

Evidence on Environmental Problems in Mature Metropolitan Areas

The last section presented some speculations about the relationship between environmental problems and population growth in metropolitan areas.[4] It was concluded that there are some reasons to expect mature metropolitan areas to have severe environmental problems, but that it is uncertain how strong the reasons are; this can be answered by a look at some facts.

Looking at the facts is never easy with environmental problems. Environmental data still are not plentiful. More important, there is conceptual uncertainty concerning the appropriate environmental variables. Should one take annual averages, peak readings, or some other measure of environmental quality? Should one use measures taken at the dirtiest places or averaged over the environmental medium in a metropolitan area? What kinds of averages should be used? These questions stem mainly from uncertainty as to what characteristics of environmental quality are most relevant to health and property damage.

We have been able to assemble data useful for our purposes only for air pollution. For two air pollutants, sulfur oxides and particulates, ambient air quality data are collected at a large set of measuring stations all over the country. For each of the two pollutants, we compiled an air quality index for a sample of metropolitan areas. For each metropolitan area, annual averages of pollutant concentrations are published for each measuring station. Our index is the median of these averages for all stations in the central city of the metropolitan areas.

Air quality data were obtained from Environmental Protection Agency (EPA) reports.[5] As the EPA prepares no summary statistics for average air quality in any geographic region, the following procedure was adopted. Within each SMSA, suburban monitoring stations not designated as "population oriented" were excluded. This left from one to twenty-four reporting stations per city during the two-year sample period. The EPA reports the annual arithmetic mean atmospheric concentration (micrograms per cubic meter) for SO_x and the geometric mean for particulates (same units) at each station. The median of these values for each city was taken as a more robust measure of central tendency than the mean for such a sample. Sources for the other data used in the regression were wind,[6] rain,[7] population,[8] and production workers by employment sector.[9]

Our sample of metropolitan areas consists of a randomly chosen set of thirty-eight metropolitan areas, stratified to ensure inclusion of metropolitan areas in the country's major regions, a variety of metropolitan area sizes, and both growing and shrinking metropolitan areas; St. Louis was included on a nonsampling basis.

As was shown in the last section, ambient air quality depends on both economic and meteorological variables. The economic variables determine volumes of pollutants discharged and the climatic variables determine the pollution level resulting from given discharges. The two climatic variables most likely to affect ambient concentration of sulfur oxides and particulates are wind speeds and precipitation, both of which are available for large cities. Temperature variables that would reflect the need for heating and cooling might also be appropriate, but we have not included them. Relevant economic variables should measure both discharge quantities and the area over which pollutants are discharged. The most natural measure of the latter is population density, which is included in the regressions reported below. We also tried total metropolitan area population and land area, but they gave predictably less satisfactory results. The best measure of polluting discharges is, of course, the discharge quantities themselves. Discharge data are mostly unavailable by metropolitan area but, in any case, what is wanted here are broad measures that are readily available and will help predict ambient pollutant concentrations in other metropolitan areas. For this purpose, we experimented with total manufacturing employment and with employment in six generally polluting two-digit manufacturing industries. Employment variables in the regression equations reported below are those that gave the best results.

The discussion so far in this section indicates that regressions to explain polluting levels should include as independent variables wind speed, precipitation, population density, and employment in polluting industries. But our main concern is whether declining metropolitan areas have more serious pollution problems than others. For this purpose, we need a measure of metropolitan growth or decline among the independent variables. The simplest such measure is the percent change in metropolitan population during a recent period.

The latest environmental data available refer to 1974, so our regressions are for that year. The above discussion had indicated variables that common sense indicates should be used to explain ambient air pollution levels. Our concern is with the question whether, other things equal, mature metropolitan areas have worse environmental problems than others. This question can be answered by including in the regressions a variable that measures the extent to which the metropolitan area is mature. Several variables have been used for this purpose in other studies. Perhaps the most common is a variable equal to the number of years since the metropolitan area reached half its present population. The kind of stagnation that is the concern of this volume is in good part of very recent origin. We have therefore used as our measure of mature metropolitan areas the percentage growth of the metropolitan area's population between 1970 and 1974. About 20 percent of all SMSAs lost population during that period, but our sample has been stratified to overrepresent them. The hypothesis that mature metropolitan areas have worse environmental problems than others is supported by a negative sign of the growth rate variable in the regression. Our estimated linear regressions are:

$$\text{Particulates} = 122 - 3.90 \text{ Wind} - 0.843 \text{ Rain} + 0.00127 \text{ Density}$$
$$(7.44) \quad (-2.53) \quad (-3.40) \quad (1.10)$$

$$+ 2.25 \text{ Chem. Emp.} + 2.70 \text{ Stone Emp.} - 0.075\% \text{ Growth}$$
$$(3.63) \quad (2.93) \quad (-.158)$$

$$R^2 = 0.608 \tag{9.1}$$

$$SO_x = 11.1 + 1.99 \text{ Wind} - 0.230 \text{ Rain} + 0.00217 \text{ Density}$$
$$(.67) \quad (1.30) \quad (-.94) \quad (1.90)$$

$$+ 1.11 \text{ Prim. Met. Emp.} - 0.719\% \text{ Growth}$$
$$(5.49) \quad (-1.49)$$

$$R^2 = 0.596 \tag{9.2}$$

where the dependent variables are medians of annual average concentrations of the pollutants recorded at central-city metering stations; wind is average annual wind speed; rain is annual average inches of precipitation; density is population per square mile; chem. emp. is production workers in the (two-digit) chemical industry; stone emp. is production workers in the (two-digit) stone, clay, and glass industry; prim. met. emp. is production workers in the (two-digit) primary metal industry; and % growth is percent population change between 1970 and 1974. Sample size is thirty-eight for each regression.

The only coefficient that has an implausible sign in the two regressions is that of wind in the SO_x regression. Windy cities should have low pollutant concentrations. It is not known why the perverse result was obtained. Otherwise, all coefficients have the expected signs. Employment in the included industries has strong effects on pollution, though it must be remembered that the employment variable was retained in the final regressions in only those industries that showed strong effects. Other things equal, high-density metropolitan areas have slightly dirtier air than others.

The growth coefficients both have the signs predicted by theoretical considerations in the previous section. Other things equal, high-growth metropolitan areas have cleaner air than low-growth or shrinking metropolitan areas. The effects, however, are not strong. Indeed, the growth coefficient is not significantly different from zero at any conventional significance level in the particulate equation. It is significantly different from zero at only about the 90 percent significance level in the sulfur oxide regression. Although the best guess is that declining metropolitan areas have somewhat worse environmental problems than other metropolitan areas, the evidence we have presented is much too weak to serve as a basis for recommendations for action.

The final comment on the two regressions in that the R^2s are surprisingly large for cross-sectional regressions, especially considering likely errors in the pollution variables. These regressions are not the end result of large-scale experimentation with the data. Various combinations of employment in six apparently polluting industries were tried, and alternatives to the density measure were tried; and some regressions were estimated omitting certain variables.

Pollution as a Deterrent to Growth

The previous section analyzed whether rapid metropolitan growth implies, other things equal, that pollution problems are less serious than otherwise. The reasons for this relationship, discussed in an earlier section, are presumed to be that rapidly growing metropolitan areas are smaller and have newer capital stock and less dependence on manufacturing industries than other metropolitan areas. But the causation might conceivably go the other way. That is, high pollution levels may deter growth by making the metropolitan area an unattractive place to live and do business. Indeed, some studies on the economics of the quality of life have presented evidence that, other things equal, workers must be paid higher wages to induce them to live in metropolitan areas with poor environments.

We are thus left with the possibility that causation between environmental quality and metropolitan growth may go both ways: pollution deters growth and growth deters pollution. Resolution of this issue requires formulation and estimation of a simultaneous equation model. The complete model should consist, in addition to equations (9.1) and (9.2), of an equation showing how metropolitan growth depends on pollution levels and on other things. Unfortunately, there exists no theory of the determinants of urban growth that can be used for the purpose. The best we can do is to list variables that can plausibly be thought to be determinants of urban growth.

The most important variable to include is income. High-income metropolitan areas attract migrants. If size is a deterrent to growth, it suggests including either total population or density; we have chosen the latter, but the two variables are strongly correlated. Other studies have shown that urban areas with a high concentration of manufacturing employment have grown only slowly in recent years, so we included manufacturing employment per capita as an independent variable. The final two independent variables are the pollutant concentration variables that are dependent variables in equations (9.1) and (9.2).

We now have a system of three simultaneous equations consisting of equations (9.1), (9.2), and the equation just described. Together the three equations are intended to explain urban growth and concentration of the two pollutants. The three equations were estimated by two-stage least squares for the sample of thirty-eight metropolitan areas. The estimated equations are:

$$\text{Particulates} = 122 - 3.90 \text{ Wind} - 0.840 \text{ Rain} + 0.00128 \text{ Density}$$
$$(6.06) \quad (-2.52) \quad\quad (-2.46) \quad\quad (1.06)$$

$$+ \; 2.25 \text{ Chem. Emp.} + 2.70 \text{ Stone Emp.} - 0.062\% \text{ Growth}$$
$$(3.60) \quad\quad\quad (2.93) \quad\quad\quad (-0.067)$$

$$R^2 = 0.608 \quad\quad\quad\quad\quad\quad\quad\quad\quad\quad (9.3)$$

$$SO_x = 14.1 + 1.981 \text{ Wind} - 0.290 \text{ Rain} + 0.00209 \text{ Density}$$
$$(0.69) \; (1.29) \quad\quad (0.84) \quad\quad (1.76)$$

$$+ \; 1.089 \text{ Prim. Met. Emp.} - 0.928\% \text{ Growth}$$
$$(5.11) \quad\quad\quad\quad (0.96)$$

$$R^2 = 0.593 \quad\quad\quad\quad\quad\quad\quad\quad\quad\quad (9.4)$$

$$\% \text{ Growth} = -10.3 + 0.00456 \text{ Income} + 0.108 \text{ Particulates}$$
$$(-1.07) \quad (1.43) \quad\quad\quad\quad (1.85)$$

$$- \; 0.0967 \; SO_x - 273.19 \text{ Manu. Emp./Pop.} - 0.000315 \text{ Density}$$
$$(-1.50) \quad\quad (-2.92) \quad\quad\quad\quad (-0.708)$$

$$R^2 = 0.364 \quad\quad\quad\quad\quad\quad\quad\quad\quad\quad (9.5)$$

The coefficients in equations (9.3) and (9.4) are remarkably similar to those in equations (9.1) and (9.2). All variables have the same signs in corresponding equations and their magnitudes are similar. In the growth equation, (9.5), all coefficients have the expected signs, except particulates. Both pollutants should have negative coefficients. As expected, high income leads to growth and high density and manufacturing employment deter growth. The R^2 in equation (9.5) is considerably smaller than in equations (9.3) and (9.4), and significance levels of the coefficients are not reassuring.

The equation system (9.3)-(9.5) provides stronger evidence that growth deters pollution than that pollution deters growth. The growth coefficients have the anticipated signs in equations (9.3) and (9.4), whereas only one of the two pollution coefficients has the anticipated sign in equation (9.5). Thus, the estimated simultaneous equation system provides weak confirmation of the theoretical analysis.

National Environmental Policy in Mature Metropolitan Areas

In this chapter we have presented theoretical reasons why rapidly growing metropolitan areas may have less severe pollution problems than others, and we have presented evidence that suggests a somewhat weak cause-and-effect relationship. Other things equal, mature metropolitan areas appear to have somewhat dirtier environments than other metropolitan areas. The remaining question to be raised is what, if anything, governments should do about it through environmental protection programs.

At present, the national environmental program aims to achieve roughly the same environmental goals in all metropolitan areas. It makes no distinction between growing and shrinking metropolitan areas. The primary ambient air quality standards are chosen to protect against adverse health effects from air pollution. Dirty air has as much effect on health in a shrinking as in a growing metropolitan area; therefore, the same ambient standards are set for both.

In setting discharge standards from industrial facilities, an important concession is made. Facilities designed after the environmental laws were passed are required to meet more stringent discharge standards than facilities designed before the laws were passed. This reflects the simple fact that it may be much more expensive to retrofit a facility to meet a stringent discharge standard than it is to design a new facility to meet the same standard. In a mature metropolitan area, a larger fraction of the industrial plant was designed before the environmental laws came into effect than in a rapidly growing metropolitan area. Thus, a mature metropolitan area may, in effect, be permitted to meet a less stringent environmental standard than a rapidly growing metropolitan area. But the effect is temporary; capital must eventually be replaced. When it is, it must meet discharge standards for new facilities. By the time the entire capital stock in a metropolitan area has been replaced after the environmental laws came into effect, a mature metropolitan area should meet the same ambient environmental standards as any other metropolitan area. A mature metropolitan area might require a decade or so longer to meet ambient standards than would other metropolitan areas.

Exactly the same consideration holds for discharge standards from mobile sources. Cars made since about 1974 have had to meet much higher standards than those made before them. Undoubtedly, a larger fraction of cars in mature metropolitan areas were made before 1974 than in growing metropolitan areas. For that reason, air quality is presumably worse in mature metropolitan areas. But by the early 1980s, nearly all cars will be post-1973 models and the effect will become unimportant.

It seems certain that governments should permit old facilities to take longer than new facilities to meet stringent discharge standards. It would be prohibitively expensive to equip all the nation's industrial facilities and vehicles to meet the most stringent discharge standards within a year or two. But if the government does not require retrofitting, mature metropolitan areas will inevitably take longer than others to reach a high ambient air standard. In this respect, the national environmental program has already made special provisions for mature metropolitan areas.

Should mature metropolitan areas receive special attention from the national environmental program in other respects? The most common claim is that certain metropolitan areas should receive special subsidies for one reason or another. Once again, a minor concession is made to mature metropolitan areas in existing federal practice. These days, construction costs of local government sewage treatment plants are mostly paid by federal and, to a lesser extent, by state grants. Theoretically, federal subsidies are given where they are most needed. It is likely that mature metropolitan areas have a relatively large percentage of water polluting industries just as they have a relatively large percentage of air polluting industries, as noted earlier. In addition, they are concentrated in the most densely settled regions of the country. Both reasons may cause them to have more severe water pollution problems than other metropolitan areas. This should qualify them for a relatively large share of federal sewage treatment plant construction subsidies. In practice, federal subsidies appear to be allocated among states mainly according to population, so any special advantage to mature metropolitan areas is probably small.

Many reasons are given in popular discussions as to why some or all mature metropolitan areas should receive special federal subsidies; New Yorkers are certainly the most skillful participants in this game. Only some of the arguments made for federal subsidies have to do with environmental problems. We cannot go through the catalog of arguments for subsidies here. But careful thought has left us unpersuaded that slow growth or decline should be a component of a formula to determine federal subsidies based on environmental problems.

Our conclusions can be stated simply. Americans have plenty of environmental problems, some serious, some not. Some problems are at least marginally worse in mature metropolitan areas. There are marginal concessions in the existing federal environmental protection programs for mature metropolitan areas; these concessions are justified. There are plenty of things wrong with our national environmental programs. But we are not persuaded that they should pay any more special attention to environmental problems of mature metropolitan areas than they do.

Notes

1. A fine statement of this consensus, in a government policy context, is found in A. Kneese and Charles Schultze, *Pollution, Prices, and Public Policy*, Washington, D.C.: The Brookings Institution, 1975.

2. Figures in this paragraph are calculated from estimates in Allen Kneese et al., *Economics and the Environment*, Washington, D.C.: Resources for the Future, 1970.

3. A.C. Pigou, *The Economics of Welfare*, London: Macmillan, 1921.

4. The only previous high-quality study of air pollution by metropolitan area we have found is by Brian J. Berry, et al., *Land Use, Urban Form, and Environmental Quality*, Department of Geography Research Paper No. 155, Chicago: University of Chicago, 1974.

5. U.S. Environmental Protection Agency, *Air Quality Data*, Research Triangle Park, N.C., 1973; and *Monitoring and Air Quality Trends Report*, Research Triangle Park, N.C., 1974.

6. U.S. Bureau of the Census, *Statistical Abstract of the United States*, Washington, D.C.: Government Printing Office, 1975.

7. U.S. Department of Commerce, *Climates of the States*, Washington, D.C.: Government Printing Office, various years.

8. U.S. Bureau of the Census, *Population Estimates and Projections*, Current Population Reports, Series P-25, No. 618, January 1976.

9. U.S. Bureau of the Census, *Census of Manufactures*, Washington, D.C.: Government Printing Office, 1967, 1972.

Part VI
Governmental Organization of the Mature Metropolis

10 Metropolitan Governance and the Mature Metropolis

Alan K. Campbell

It is commonly assumed that there is some correlation between governmental structure and solutions to the major public sector problems of the day. This at least is the underpinning of many previous efforts to reorganize local government, and certainly reflects much of the basis for the current reorganizational activity in Washington. The president ran on a platform of national government reorganization, presumably because of his success in the State of Georgia with relating state problems to structure, through reform. Reorganization is not new to the federal bureaucracy, and it demonstratively ranks as one of the favorite activities of local and state officials and civic leaders.

The reasons for governmental restructuring are many, ranging from strictly political power considerations to accomplishing technical efficiency. Such justifications come into play whether the discussion is at the highest federal level or in the smallest local community. For some years now, students of urban America have debated just what should be the optimal structural form of local government in metropolitan areas. The resolution of this debate has generally pointed toward the centralization of some functions across an SMSA and the decentralization of others; but, as in all reorganization, such arguments may overlook the political likelihood of accomplishing such changes. The term political is not meant here to denote those tensions that arise between elected officials whose power lies in the current structure, and those professional elites who wish to form new coalitions. It is meant to cover the whole gamut of incentives—economic, demographic, social—which lead a community to align itself, or not, with another community for the provision of services or the redistribution of resources.

Relating Governmental Structure to Public Issues

Once we recognize that the pattern of influences on governmental reform decisions is complex, that the groupings of incentives and disincentives are not homogeneous from place to place, we should account for how these different types of metropolitan areas will respond to efforts at reorganization. The discussion in this chapter will distinguish between three kinds of metropolitan areas.

Declining Metropolitan Areas

The first kind of metro area is one in which both the central city (or county) and the metropolitan area are declining in population or economic base. These metropolitan areas, among them New York and Cleveland, are recipients of what might be called the "double whammy": they are experiencing the national slowdown in population and economic growth as well as an out-migration of their resident population and economic base.

At the national level the demographics are clear, as indicated in Chapter 2. The almost consistent decline in birthrates since the 1950s has resulted in considerably reduced family size. The number of children of elementary school age has declined by a fifth; secondary and postsecondary age cohorts will soon follow. The reduced birthrate is neither temporary nor confined to the white middle class, according to a survey of women in the childbearing age. It will be almost the end of the decade before age groups under twenty-five will experience any absolute growth.

While only Pittsburgh lost population during the 1960s, from 1970 to 1975 a number of the largest SMSAs were losing population, as indicated in Chapters 1 and 2. In fact, a total of thirty-seven SMSAs have lost population from 1970 just up to 1974; as a group, the SMSAs with over two million population experienced no growth at all during that period.

At the local level, much of the loss can be attributed to out-migration. Population decline, of course, is not necessarily a serious problem, as the Urban Institute's study of the City of Pittsburgh demonstrates.[1] The key is in identifying *who* are the leavers and the stayers. But the evidence of the recent past is conclusive: persons exiting, first to the suburbs and then to other metro areas of the country or to rural environs, are those with families, with mobile skills, and with income levels on which the financing of city services depend.

We all hear stories that are the reverse of this trend; young marrieds and singles are supposedly returning to the city to reclaim declining neighborhoods. Their incentives range from the absence of parental responsibilities to the availability of less socially restricted life-styles to savings in energy costs associated with less need for transportation. In Washington, D.C., the evidence, while still rather anecdotal, seems convincing. Housing restoration is no longer confined to Georgetown and Capitol Hill. Similar stories come from Philadelphia, Boston, Baltimore, and even New York City. Every few weeks the *New York Times* and the *Washington Post* report that such trends are growing. But if this is true, the data suggest that the *mix* of residents must be changing—not just people returning to the city—because none of the central cities mentioned showed a positive net migration during the 1970-74 period. One columnist recently suggested that the trend toward "saving" our cities would be accompanied by suburban slums.[2] If both the data and conventional wisdom are true, such a conclusion may be warranted.

However, there is no empirical evidence, as yet, that affluent suburbanites are exchanging their present housing for inner-city dwellings. Robert Embry, Assistant Secretary for Community Development at HUD, recently testified before a Senate Committee that "about 70% of the home buyers are current city residents"—blacks investing in their own neighborhoods and young whites who are not yet affluent, but have great earning potential.[3] All in all, it seems premature to depend, for the salvation of cities, on a massive return of suburbanites to old urban areas. While such a return to the city would bode well for the central-city tax base, it might not alter in any way the configuration for the metropolitan area as a whole. And for an overall declining metropolis, such positive signs may have little real substance.

Metropolitan Areas with Suburban or Central-city Growth

The second category of metropolitan areas is characterized by declining central cities, surrounded by stable or moderate growth suburbs. If the former category was largely the province of the Northeast and North Central regions, this category is most represented in the Midwest and Far West. In many ways, these metropolitan areas pose the most difficult case for governmental change; expanding and economically sound suburbs have historically shown little inclination to rescue declining central cities. There seems to be every incentive for accelerated exodus from the central city, countered only by the undocumented trends hinted at earlier.

The third category of metropolitan areas are those with stable or moderate-growth central cities (or counties) and a growing metropolitan area. These occur in regions of the country where the economy is expanding—the South and the Southwest—the so-called Sunbelt, a movement primarily from the Northeastern and North Central regions. The 1970 census hinted at this change, and census estimates since then have documented it. Further, this migration is much different than the 1950 to 1970 movement of people from countryside to city, a movement of people with less education and lower incomes than that of the people already living in the communities to which they moved. According to the analysis in Chapter 2, just the opposite is true of those moving from the Northeast and North Central regions to the South and Southwest. They possess, on average, higher incomes, more education, and are younger than those who are remaining in the areas from which they are moving, and by the same measures exceed the averages in the region to which they are moving. This movement, therefore, weakens economically and socially the areas being abandoned and strengthens the receiving areas.[4]

Recent census data support this interpretation.[5] Between 1970 and 1974 the central cities of U.S. metropolitan areas, in the aggregate, experienced a population decline of 4.9 percent compared to a growth in suburban population of slightly over 20 percent. The greatest declines (−9.6 percent) were in central cities of metro areas of over 1 million and the greatest gains (28.7 percent) were in the suburbs of metro areas with less than 1 million population. The second greatest gain between 1970 and 1974 was in counties designated metropolitan since 1970 (26.0 percent). Using nationwide data, the decline in central-city size has been consistent since the 1950s, though suburban growth has been uneven: in large metropolitan areas, suburban growth has been at a declining rate; in smaller areas, growth fluctuates; and in nonmetropolitan areas the rate appears to be increasing.

When this information is disaggregated by region—one of our chief concerns here—we see that population declines are explained by the large central cities in the Northeast and North Central states (−14.9 and −17.8 percent, respectively, between 1970 and 1974). In these areas of the country, even counties recently designated as metropolitan have declined (dramatically in the Northeast). In the Northeast and the North Central states, only counties with largest towns of under 25,000 population experienced high growth; 47.7 percent in the Northeast. In sharp contrast is the experience of the South and West, where central cities are either declining more slowly (3 percent for large central cities in the South) or still growing (4.3 percent for similar cities in the West).

Most dramatic, however, in these two regions is the growth of the new metropolitan areas: 59.6 percent in the South and 71.2 percent in the West. The base numbers in new metropolitan areas are generally small, but the trend is one that bears watching. Furthermore, out of forty-one major central cities, only three that could not be classified as Southern or Western had positive employment level shifts in 1972 relative to 1958; these were Cincinnati, St. Paul, and Kansas City. Of these three, moreover, Cincinnati did not have a gain in manufacturing, though most Southern and many Western metropolitan areas did.

A Brief History of Governmental Reform

The three distinct types indicated above seem a more useful way of viewing urban issues than past frameworks. For some time, the major analytical device was a sort of monolithic central city—outside central-city analysis, emphasizing disparities in socioeconomic characteristics, in fiscal effort, in the distribution of resources between education and municipal services, and in rates of economic and population growth. It was believed these characteristics were sufficiently similar for all metropolitan areas to justify generalizations about metropolitanism and to base public policy recommendations on them.[6]

For many metropolitan areas, particularly the larger ones, and especially in the Northeastern and North Central regions, these generalizations were accurate enough. Migration from countryside to city and from city to suburb, and the movement of economic activity, particularly manufacturing and services, from city to suburb, all contributed to a central-city tax base unable to keep pace with increased service needs of cities; and this was accompanied by increased political strength of the suburbs. Although these characteristics and resulting problems were never true for all metropolitan areas of all sizes and in all sections of the country, it required considerable effort, largely at the hands of economists, to disaggregate the issues.

While our categories for thinking have improved, the question that loomed so large in the earlier analytical framework is still the major issue for governmental reform at the metropolitan level: that is, Does the maturing of a city alter in any way the usefulness of metropolitan government to its well-being, or to the likelihood of such a governance system being adopted?

When we treated all cities alike, the answer to that question seemed far simpler. And many students of urban affairs championed metropolitan government unreservedly. But with the recognition that cities differ in significant ways, the answers to these questions become contingent on such considerations as (1) the nature of the problems which beset the mature city, (2) the distribution of population and economic activity within the metropolitan area in which the city is located, (3) the assignment of fiscal responsibilities within the statewide governmental system of which the city is a part, (4) interregional and intraregional rates of economic growth, and (5) the political culture of the city, its metropolitan area, and its state.

While we may not have the conceptual framework and the methodology to address adequately all of the above considerations at the present time, our sophistication about the problem certainly exceeds that of previous reformers. Reform of local government has long been a favorite undertaking of American civic leadership. From the late-nineteenth century to World War II, emphasis was primarily on reorganization of the internal structure. As indicated in Chapter 3, muckrakers at the turn of the century were outraged by bosses and by corruption. "Too many governments," though not the central issue of that period, was perceived by a few reformers in the 1920s as a bad condition. Inefficient and undemocratic local government was a prime concern of academicians and good governmentphiles alongside these first two targets.

Bosses thrived on inefficiency, but so did nonbossed governments. The economy and efficiency drive was to wax strong in the 1920s and peak in the 1930s. Administrative concepts developed at the local level were applied to the national government by the Brownlow Committee before World War II and the Hoover Commissions in the 1940s and 1950s.[7] The research bureaus and their studies were the major resource for reform at the local level, beginning with the New York Bureau founded in 1906. While reformers perceived crises, the answers they provided were, first of all, mechanical in nature. The antidotes for bossism and for inefficiency were the council-manager plan, the merit system, a neat hierarchical structure with responsibility pinpointed. If these could be installed, then the recommended follow-up strategy was twofold: elect *good men* to office and organize a research bureau to serve as a gadfly.

This diagnosis of the maladies of the local intrajurisdictional system and the prescriptions for its cure have been developing since at least the 1870s. A new ingredient, however, was added after World War I. The 1920 census documented for scholars and other reformers what only a few of them had suspected before that time. Since 1910 the suburbs in the fifty-eight metropolitan districts had been growing faster than the central cities; and these fifty-eight districts accounted for 28.6 percent of the total U.S. population.[a] More important, the increase in the total U.S. population had been only 14.9 percent in the previous decade as compared with 26.4 percent in the fifty-eight metro districts.[8]

With these data, the academics found a new justification for reform. Maxey wrote, "The great problems which demand governmental action in metropolitan communities—public health, recreation, public utilities, crime, and the like—hold political boundaries in contempt."[9] Harvard's W.B. Munro wrote in his college textbook, "Out of all this is sure to rise, in due course, some movement for unification, complete or partial, such as will ensure the broad treatment of metropolitan problems by a centralized authority."[10] Out there in the real world, a few campaigns were mounted to establish metropolitan government, as in Pittsburgh-Allegheny County and Oakland-San Mateo. The syndrome of "too many governments" had been identified and the battle against it begun.

The reform emphasis in the 1950s and 1960s on adequate jursidictional scope represented a substantial shift from the concern in the 1920s and 1930s with the internal structure of urban governments. The earlier emphasis on "boss politics" and on the need for greater professionalism was virtually ignored in local campaigns to establish some form of metropolitanwide government. Many critics of recent efforts argue as if the justifications for metropolitan reform were the same as those offered for the internal structural reforms of the 1920s. For instance, "economy and efficiency" are still invoked in reform campaigns, but rarely has corruption or inefficiency been seen as the chief motivation for establishing a broader jurisdiction. The call for reform of the local government system was encouraged by the movement of people and economic activity. *The logic was simple: as the metropolitan area was economically and socially interrelated, it seemd to follow that the governance system should reflect this interdependence.* The specific response was to suggest a metropolitanwide jurisdiction.

As the population of the United States grew and people were attracted to cities, municipalities used a number of adaptive responses to ensure that city boundaries kept current with city growth. Annexation was the most widely used tool for Eastern and Midwestern cities prior to 1900. Annexation continued to be used by Southern and Western cities during the 1950s and 1960s, especially

---

[a]Metropolitan districts were defined as cities of 100,000 or more in 1920 together with the suburban territory within ten miles of their city limits.

in places like Kansas City, Houston, and Oklahoma City. Residents outside of central cities often welcomed annexation, since it was one of the few ways that they could obtain municipal services; it was relatively easy to annex as referendums were seldom required, and the passage of an ordinance by the city council was sometimes all that was needed.

With the advent of the commuter railroad in the 1920s, urban growth occurred not only on the city fringes but also in freestanding commuting communities located along the railroad line. These independent urban centers grew up around the railroad station and mostly attracted higher-income residents who could easily commute by rail to their central-city office. The central city could not annex these urban areas since they were not adjacent territory, and their residents were already receiving services from existing towns or villages. Thus, after 1920, the annexation tool was relied upon less and less by Eastern cities, basically for three reasons: (1) state legislatures began to restrict the ease of its use; (2) areas adjoining the city began to incorporate themselves into towns and villages, often for defensive reasons; and (3) many local jurisdictions other than cities—counties, towns, and special districts—began delivering traditional municipal services.

Around the turn of the century, structural responses such as city-county consolidation or city-county separation were applied extensively by a number of major U.S. municipalities. In 1898 the City of New York merged with the surrounding counties of Brooklyn, Queens, and Richmond to create the present "supercity" with five boroughs. Merger of city and county had occurred earlier in other major U.S. cities: Boston in 1821, Philadelphia in 1854, and San Francisco in 1856. In 1876 the city of St. Louis separated from its surrounding county to resolve the dual issues of representation and taxation.

In the few cases where consolidations occurred (Nashville-Davidson and Jacksonville-Duval, for example), the resulting government had more functions and was more tightly organized than the county government before reorganization. Consolidation advocates stressed the need for greater economy and efficiency in government, but also argued that eliminating overlapping governments would result in a system easier for the citizen to understand and to control.

Another, less noticed, adaptive response has been the transfer of functional responsibilities, such as health or welfare, from a lower level of government to a higher level. Functional shifts often are easier to implement than structural reform or boundary changes, and are less disruptive to existing systems of political power. Functional consolidations have been used effectively in such New York counties as Westchester, Nassau, and Monroe. While such transfers as health and welfare have provided some fiscal relief to declining core cities, this approach has seldom affected the fundamental economic problems of central cities. The reason is simply that shifting functions and financial responsibility for functions to a higher level relieves municipal expenditures, but does not affect a city's economic base or the social problems existing within its boundaries.

Nevertheless, the notion that governmental functions have an appropriate level proved to be a powerful idea on two fronts. First, champions of technical efficiency in government could argue that economies of scale and fairer distribution of services would accrue from consolidation of those functions that were inappropriately spread across numerous smaller governmental units. Second, those wishing to exercise greater political control over governmental functions could reverse the argument and call for greater decentralization on the grounds that some functions are appropriately managed by smaller, not larger, units of government. Decentralization was especially important in the reform movements of the 1960s, since consolidated government or areawide jurisdiction did not always guarantee equity in the provision of services to all parts of a single jurisdiction; numerous studies have documented the higher level of certain services provided within large cities, to middle-income and higher-income communities, as compared with services provided to the low-income portions of the same cities. Further, it is quite possible that the particular services provided do not reflect the needs and aspirations of all parts of a community, even though there may be equity in distribution.

The lack of a fit between services provided and services needed, characterized many large city governments in the middle and late 1960s, and led to the demand for an increase in community or neighborhood control, normally related to the provision of education services, but gradually spreading to include other services. Experiments with different modes of decentralization, from little city halls to actual control by neighborhoods of parts of some services, such as education, are going on in dozens of localities today. The justification for these decentralization demands usually stems from perception of a lack of responsiveness on the part of the central-city government.

Such efforts to overcome the inequities in service delivery have undoubtedly produced an adjustment in services in some cities. In many cities today, more resources are devoted to education in low-income areas than in other parts of the city; federal antipoverty efforts also often have concentrated resources in low-income areas. The institutional response, however, has been slow, and it is interesting to note the argument that this is a fortunate situation for people in the low-income areas. If, indeed, decentralization and community control were carried to the logical conclusion of neighborhoods becoming dependent upon their own resources, the disparities in resource bases among jurisdictions that now exist in all metropolitan areas would be accentuated (this conflict is discussed in Chapter 9).

Ambivalent Federal Policies

The federal government responded to the problems created by the movement of economic activities and people in two general ways. First, by requiring areawide planning and interlocal cooperation as conditions for the receipt of such functional aid programs as airports, urban renewal, transportation, water supply, and waste disposal; second, by targeting federal dollars to specific social problems such as manpower, housing, and education. The first approach was aimed at reducing friction and duplication between local governments and encouraging metropolitanwide planning. The latter approach sought to meet individual human needs rather than to improve the state-local jurisdictional system.

During the liberal administration of the 1960s, the maldistribution of wealth and opportunity was clearly recognized and explicit, and national goals were set to deal with the gulf between rich and poor, black and white. Federal initiatives were launched under the Great Society to assist the disadvantaged populations living in both rural and urban ghettos. The main effort was focused on the central city because that was where many needing assistance were concentrated. The social programs which comprised the War on Poverty were targeted toward individuals—the aim was not to help cities but rather to help the people who lived within them. The programs, in fact, often exacerbated the fiscal consequences of the movement of people and economic activities out of central cities by forcing the cities to meet the matching requirements from local taxes in order to receive the aid. Further, and even more devastating, as the federal programs were cut back or eliminated, the city became heir to them with their citizens expecting or, better said, demanding their continuation.

The Kennedy-Johnson policy of an active, dominant national role in domestic, social issues was rejected by the Nixon Presidency in favor of a radically different philosophy of government which came to be known as the "New Federalism." Key to this new view of American government was the devolution of responsibility to state and local jurisdictions—decisions were to be made at the level closest to the people. The manifold social problems which the Great Society attempted to solve were now to be the province of state and local politics. Accompanying the New Federalism was increased federal support for the establishment of councils of government (COGs). Depending on one's views of these organizations, they can be seen either as supportive of the current local jurisdictional system or as a step toward genuine metropolitan grievance.[11]

COGs are viewed by many of their supporters as a device for local officials to cope with regional issues and to coordinate federal grants which flow into their region. The growth of regional planning agencies or councils of government has been a very recent phenomenon. In 1960 only fifty-six regional councils were in operation; by 1970 the number had risen to 476. Most COGs are voluntary associations of elected officials, created ostensibly to increase coordination and communication among units of local government. Federal policy toward COGs is stated positively through the Office of Management and Budget Circular A-95 which requires that over 100 federal grant programs be subjected to review by a regional agency and by HUD's Section 701 planning assistance program, which has been the mainstay of financial support for regional planning staffs. While both continue, they have received only lukewarm support, as evidenced by the failure of federal agency heads to pursue compliance with the A-95 review process, and by attempts to reduce the 701 annual funding level from $75 to $25 million. This federal ambivalence is seen further in the continued reliance on and promotion of single-purpose areawide agencies for economic development, mass transit, and health planning.

This condition worries many of today's reformers, including particularly the Advisory Commission on Intergovernmental Relations (ACIR). A-95 arrangements thus far have not been effective, even as a review process for project applications. Since the first issuance of Circular A-95 in 1968, the state governments have been encouraged to attain coterminality of all their administrative areas. Forty states are said to be working on this today, but the going is slow.[12] Neither states nor the federal government have been able to adopt a consistent approach to the impact that they would like to have on local government organization. Block grants and revenue sharing tend to strengthen the fragmented system, while demands for regional planning and for clearance of local grant requests by a regional body will have the opposite impact. In general, it can be demonstrated that the federal thrust has created a large number of regional jurisdictions, some of them functional, some of them general, but has simultaneously often provided the hard cash necessary for otherwise economically nonviable local jurisdictions to survive.

Local and State Politics

Despite the mixed signals from the federal level, it remains doubtful whether voluntary regional agencies composed of elected officials who represent local units can pursue policies which will advance regional goals, especially when those policies may undercut the short-term advantage of individual localities. One of the most distinctive characteristics of the Minneapolis Metropolitan Regional Council, for example, is that the members of its government board do not represent jurisdictions but are appointed by the governor. Not being required to represent a local jurisdiction, as is the case with those on COG boards, they are more likely to view issues on a regional basis.

Perhaps the major example of reorganization at the substate level, the consolidation of school districts, was not really voluntary. The carrot of state aid largely can be credited with this success. But unlike the situation for school districts, it cannot be expected that many states will move in a direction like Minnesota's on local government reform, so long as political parties see the preservation of local governments as key to their well-being. Recall, for example, that federal poverty programs often were designed consciously to work around established local political units. Community action and Model Cities agencies were created as paragovernments on the premise that status-quo-oriented local officials would undermine or stall the accomplishment of higher goals. Since 1949 fifty proposals for city-county consolidation have gone to referendum. During that period thirty-eight were defeated at the polls and only twelve were adopted by the voters. The rate of success has been very low; there have been only three city-county consolidations approved by the voters since 1970. Five were attempted in 1974; all of them failed.[13]

Today, the same local elites as in the 1920s take the lead in individual city, county, and metropolitan reform campaigns. Nor does it seem that opponents of consolidation have changed; in several cases, though, they have been joined by black leadership in opposing metro ideas. This tendency for black opposition is not unlike the attachment of European ethnic groups to central-city political machines during the 1920s. Politics, sports, and entertainment have been about the only avenues of improved mobility for these groups.

The Role of Theory in Reorganization

Most of the discussion to this point has dealt with the practical world of reorganization: the reform movements of the past sixty years, the federal response to (or perhaps interference in) those reforms, and the limits imposed on reform by state and local politics. Fortunately, there exist some social science theories that *aid* us in sorting out the merits of these reform efforts and in charting future directions.

Theory, of course, is a little like faith: you cannot do a lot with it, but you can do virtually nothing without it. In fact, there is no internally consistent theory which can be used to guide either the placement of governmental functions or the design of a system in which to place those functions. Nor at a more general level do theories of federalism offer much help. Over the past several decades politicians have provided at least three different slogans to describe American federalism—cooperative, creative, and new—but the differences in the content of each was never very clear. In fact, there is little evidence that federalism as a system necessarily dictates functional assignment or subnational boundary systems any different from those in a unitary system in terms of a need to develop an efficient, effective, and responsive distribution of functions.

Political scientists have generally accepted the proposition that the closer government is to the people, the more likely it is to be responsive to their demands and needs. From this proposition has grown a set of ideas which favor so-called grass roots democracy. When extended to certain economic concepts, one has the premise on which is built "public choice theory."

Public choice advocates argue that the nearer the public sector can approach the alternatives permitted by the private market, the better. This private market analogy is, of course, appropriate, if the public sector is simply perceived as a set of services citizens may purchase on the basis of their ability to pay, a view of the public sector as having the same purposes as the private sector.

Public choice advocates use the concept of economic rather than technical efficiency to attempt to relate choice of public services to personal preferences. Accordingly, consumers of public services should be able to select public services as they select private services, thereby maximizing their utility. As preference patterns differ from individual to individual, the logical outcome would be a government for every individual or a common government for individuals who have exactly the same preference patterns. Obviously, this theoretical construct for determining the best governmental system omits any role of government in overcoming jurisdictional externalities, or any role for using government services to redistribute income. This difference comprises the heart of the argument between public choice advocates, who defend the fragmented governmental system, and reformers, who believe government has a role to play in overcoming externalities and in redistributing income.

The externality issue is one the public choice people may attempt to sidestep too lightly. The "spill ins" and "spill outs" of benefits and costs of governmental activities are well-known phenomena, though very difficult to measure. The pollution which flows from one jurisdiction to another, be it water or air, is perhaps the most obvious. But equally important are those resulting from different benefits derived by different services; for example, young people educated in one jurisdiction who, when moving to another, carry with them the advantages or disadvantages of the education they received in their home jurisdiction.

The ability of small governmental units to use their zoning power to zone in desirable activities, and zone out undesirable ones, creates another kind of externality. To the extent that the flow of externalities is to be minimized, the greater the number of activities which must be assigned to larger jurisdictions—to metropolitan units of government, to states, and frequently to the national government. An alternative, of course, would be a system of charges back to the jurisdiction which produces negative externalities; the impracticality of such a system is self-evident.

Regardless of where one falls on the self-interest/social-interest continuum of public goods theory, there are several measures other than externalities that must be accommodated. According to ACIR, which since 1963 has been publishing research on criteria to measure the success or failure of government institutions, there are four basic yardsticks to judge the "goodness" of governmental systems, all of which it is argued are more readily met by metropolitan forms of government. The four main criteria are economic efficiency, fiscal equity, administrative effectiveness, and political accountability.[14] In the following, though, we will distinguish between economic and technical efficiency.

Economic Efficiency

Economic efficiency in this instance relates to the possibility of the individual optimizing the satisfaction he receives from his consumption of public services. The appropriate analogy is the private market, for there the individual may purchase that combination of goods and services which maximizes his satisfaction. The larger the population of a governmental jurisdiction, the more likely that people within that jurisdiction will be heterogeneous in taste. The particular package of services provided by such a jurisdiction is unlikely, therefore, to fit the desired package for any but a very few residents. This is the underpinning of the public choice analysis. It is important, however, to note that this analysis assumes people value public goods in the same way that they value private goods. While we must concede that people probably weigh public against private goods in their calculus of wants, and that private goods are not available in every variety possible, it is not clear that the logic of choosing is the same for both kinds of goods. These suspicions would seem to be reinforced by what little we know about "free-rider" effects in the selection of public goods.

Technical Efficiency

Here, the term technical efficiency is meant to stand loosely for the achievement of "economies of scale." For every activity of government there is an optimum scale, and we note "activity" advisedly, since a *function*—police, fire, education, for example—is normally made up of quite disparate activities, and each has its own optimum scale. Therefore, it is activities to which the concept of economies of scale must be related, not functions. A system based upon making best use of possible economies of scale would produce different geographical areas for each activity of government. Therefore, this doctrine, instead of suggesting a government for every person as might economic efficiency in the extreme, suggests a government for every activity of government.

Thus, public choice theory suggests small units of local government, each encompassing a relatively homogeneous population, with authority over a wide range of services. Competing political science concerns for general government and simplicity in structure and economic concerns for the control of externalities, both suggest large units of local government, combined with assignment of substantial responsibility to higher levels of government. The economy of scale criteria leads to functional fragmentation with a government for each activity measured at such size as to minimize cost.

Fiscal Equity

Many would argue that of the good government criteria, the equity criterion deserves highest priority. This selection is not scientific, though the measurement of whether a system is, in fact, equitable can be objectively measured, assuming agreement can be reached on definitions.

One area of research, fiscal disparities, does ask one version of the equity question. It is a field which has been well plowed by ACIR and many public finance scholars. Their findings, though differing in detail, have generally argued that the current system abounds with disparities—disparities in both tax burdens and services as measured by differences in expenditures: disparities between central cities and suburbs, between low-income and high-income suburbs, between metropolitan and rural areas, and between regions.

The prescriptions which have emerged from disparities analyses call for larger-scale local government in order to incorporate in such governmental areas an economic base which captures both the growing and declining portions of that base. It further suggests a distribution of expenditures which relates services to needs. Also emerging from the disparities literature have been suggestions about the flow of governmental aid, suggesting that the flow should be in the direction of governmental jurisdictions with weak tax bases and containing populations with substantial need. If the equity criterion is accepted as the one which ought to be dominant, then the other criteria can be used to the degree they are not inconsistent with it.

Effectiveness and Accountability

Administrative effectiveness addresses the need for professionalism, comprehensive planning, and sophisticated management, especially in the development of complex transportation systems, environmental pollution control efforts, and other large-scale public activities. "Effectiveness," a word intended to avoid the narrowness of "economy and efficiency," is much more tentatively defined and understood. It aims to relate outputs or "impacts" to agency goals. Effectiveness represents the effort to bring together, efficiency and quality, with possibly equal emphasis on quality and costs. Impact or "outcome" of a program is more nebulous still. It must take account of public perceptions of the service, and thus hinges on interrelatedness and feedback. Impact and "responsiveness" are extraordinarily hard to disentangle.

The political accountability criterion contradicts the previous standards by highlighting the need for governmental responsiveness and citizen control as against the overbureaucratization of government agencies. Accountability supposedly would relate service delivery to what people or consumers, in fact, want or demand. Some fairly good work is now being done in an attempt to measure attitudes about services.[15] If so-called objective measures of service outputs are ultimately developed, it will be interesting and useful to contrast these objective outputs with the effect they have on consumer attitudes, that is, subjective outcomes.

Taken together, the criteria drawn from political science and economics provide little consistent guidance for either the drawing of governmental boundaries or the assignment of function among the levels of government. Since the criteria themselves often point in contrary directions, it is only through trade-offs of advantages and disadvantages that they can be combined in a way which will provide direction for the placement of functions, or the structuring of the governmental system. If regional institutions are better able to meet most of these good government criteria, as the ACIR suggests, one must ask why this country has so few examples of fully developed and effective regional or metropolitan forms of government. The answer lies, in part, in the history of urbanization and the accompanying local government response during the last three-quarters of a century.

Although public choice advocates do not suggest a system to increase equity, they provide an explanation for the difficulty in accomplishing metropolitan reform. Since such reforms might result in a redistribution of resources and services, persons satisfied with their current situations, already having voted with their feet, will oppose the reforms. The history of the failure of metropolitan reorganization amply demonstrates, in their eyes, the satisfaction with the current system that most people within metropolitan areas allegedly feel. We have tried to show here that this position is neither necessarily empirically accurate nor theoretically defensible.

Earlier in this chapter a question was posed, Does the maturing of a city alter in any way the usefulness of metropolitan government to its well-being? What followed has been a somewhat circuitous way of saying "yes"; circuitous because we do not have any empirical basis for answering that question head-on. Most metropolitan reorganization in this country has been concerned with such issues as fiscal equity between jurisdictions within a region, technical efficiency in the allocation of governmental functions, and the quality-of-life gains afforded by centralized planning and zoning. But all these concerns are related to the internal affairs of a single region. Some of the mature (we might say, simply, older) cities in this country face a problem of an entirely different dimension: the region taken as a whole is in decline—in some cases an accelerated decline—and there seems to be no strong empirical basis for saying that metropolitan government will impede this trend. But there are some impressionistic bases for suggesting that reorganization can make a difference.

Those metropolitan areas with total stability and just central-city decline, confront an eroding tax base. The forces that lead to the relocation of industries from one region to another include the nature of markets and the factor costs of production. Metropolitan government will probably not alter these forces in any direct way. One can only speculate that governmental reform—meaning greater efficiency and effectiveness in the provision of services—will make an area somewhat more attractive to industries. But the marginal importance of this variable in determining job mix must be stressed.

The fact that Minneapolis, Indianapolis, and Jacksonville have weathered fiscal difficulties better than those cities which have not utilized metropolitan government is, I believe, reinforcing of the impression that good government—in the ACIR sense—does make a difference in stemming the economic erosion of a region. This is probably because metropolitan government is better able to cater to some of the interests of private development, for example, in transportation, zoning, and water resource policy. Still, metropolitanization of a structural character will offer small relief for those areas where decline has spread from city to suburb and affects the entire region; their salvation must come from the state and federal levels. Even so, those salvation efforts could be more rationally designed, if they were designed on a regional basis rather than on the basis of the current jurisdictional system.

To the extent that there has been effective reorganization and change, it has occurred primarily in communities that have had a viable third sector: the volunteer or nonprofit sector. Certainly, the Citizens League in Minneapolis and St. Paul made a very substantial difference there. But we do not know why some communities tend to develop this kind of third sector much more effectively than others. Through the Metropolitan Fund, citizens in the Detroit area have tried very hard and with some success to create a regional approach to metropolitanism, but it seems clear that those efforts have not been as successful as in Minneapolis—St. Paul. But there is at least the suggestion of a rising business sector interest in these problems, and a readiness to make common cause with the public sector in relationship particularly to central-cities problems. The very fact that CED, as one of the leading business organizations in the country, is now undertaking a project in the area of revitalizing central cities is evidence of a concern which goes beyond what has been true before, and which is further indicated in Chapter 15. This could suggest that reordering the structure in metropolitan areas will probably only happen when a viable third sector exists and is willing to turn its attention to it.

In those SMSAs which still are within the traditional pattern of central-city decline, with modest suburban growth, increasing regional responsibility for service financing and delivery would greatly benefit core-city residents; but such assistance, if the past is a sufficient guide, will be bitterly opposed by suburban residents. Such a change, however, might contribute to the continuing economic and political viability of entire metropolitan areas. Again, if Indianapolis and Jacksonville had not regionalized their governments, their central cities would today be experiencing severe financial problems.

In metropolitan areas, mostly in the South and Southwest, where the entire region enjoys economic health and fiscal vitality, the issue of reform is not likely to be high on the public agenda for two reasons. With both city and suburbs experiencing economic growth, fiscal problems are not likely to be severe and, more important, disparities are not likely to be great, because many of these cities have captured a substantial portion of their suburbs through annexation.

However, there is still likely to be some interest in reform, and metropolitan reorganization may be easier to achieve in these areas than elsewhere. Memphis and Tucson are good examples; both are growing regions with dominant and healthy central cities. Memphis has recently attempted consolidation and failed, but civic and public leaders continue to work for a metro government. A study commission in Tucson is now completing a final report, which recommends the creation of a consolidated city-county with strong decentralization built in. The motivation for reform in areas such as these may not be fiscal survival, but rather a desire to eliminate duplication and inefficiencies, a throwback to the motivation of earlier reform movements.

Leadership for change must come in part from outside the local government system. There would not have been reform of government in Canada had it not been for the central role played by the Ontario Provincial government, nor would there have been local government reform in Great Britain without the leadership of the national government. And one might well doubt if there would have been reform in Indianapolis or Minneapolis-St. Paul witout state leadership.

Nor is it undemocratic to suggest that higher levels of government participate in the reforming of local government. The evidence is strong that had the reorganization of either Toronto or London been put to referendum in those communities, it would have been defeated. It is now equally clear that if the current systems were to be placed on referendum in those same communities today, they would be upheld by the local citizenry. Democracy does not imply that leadership should be abdicated by those who have moral, legal, and constitutional responsibilities for maximizing the effectiveness and the equity of the system.

Notes

1. M.J. Flax, *A Study in Comparative Urban Indicators: Conditions in 18 Large Metropolitan Areas*, Washington, D.C.: Urban Institute, April 1972.

2. Neil Peirce, "Will 'Saved' Cities Mean Suburban Slums?" *Washington Post*, July 30, 1977, p. A15.

3. U.S. Senate Committee on Banking, Housing, and Urban Affairs, July 7, 1977.

4. Thomas Muller, *Growing and Declining Urban Areas: A Fiscal Comparison*, Urban Institute, Washington, D.C., 1975; see also George Sternlieb and James W. Hughes, eds., *Post Industrial America: Metropolitan Decline and Inter-Regional Shifts*, Center for Urban Policy Research, New Brunswick, N.J.: Rutgers University, 1975; for a journalistic summary of the shift of population and economic activities to the South and Southwest see six-part series, "Sunbelt Region Leads Nation in Growth of Population," *New York Times*, February 8-13, 1976.

5. U.S. Department of Commerce, Bureau of the Census, *Estimates of the Pay of Met Areas, 1973 & 1974 and Components of Change Since 1970*, Current Population Reports, Series P-25, No. 618, January 1976; (also, U.S. Census of Manufacturing).

6. Numerous volumes have based their analyses on this metropolitan model. For an examination of the current state of knowledge see Amos H. Hawley and Vincent P. Rock, eds., *Metropolitan America in Contemporary Perspective*, New York: Halsted Press Division, John Wiley and Sons, 1975.

7. Frederick C. Mosher, ed., *American Public Administration: Past, Present, Future*, Florence, Alabama: University of Alabama Press, 1975.

8. U.S. Bureau of the Census, vol. 1, *Population*, 1920 Washington, 1921; see especially pp. 62 ff. and tables 40 and 41.

9. *National Municipal Review*, vol. 11, 1922, p. 229.

10. *Municipal Government and Administration*, New York: Macmillan, 1923, p. 437.

11. M.M. Mogulof, *Governing Metropolitan Areas*, Washington, D.C., Urban Institute, 1971; also by the same author, "Federally Encouraged Multi-Jurisdictional Agencies in Three Metropolitan Areas," chapter 5, ACIR, vol. 2, *Substate Regionalism and the Federal System*, pp. 141-197.

12. David B. Walker and Carl W. Stenberg, "A Substate Districting Strategy," *National Civic Review*, vol. 63, January 1974, p. 5.

13. Vincent L. Marando, "The Politics of City County Consolidation," *National Civic Review*, vol. 63, February 1975, p. 76.

14. Advisory Commission on Intergovernmental Relations, *Alternative Approaches to Governmental Reorganization in Metropolitan Areas*, 1966, and *Substate Regionalism and the Federal System*, vol. 4, *Governmental Functions and Process*, 1974, Washington: Government Printing Office.

15. Urban Institute and International City Management Association, *Measuring the Effectiveness of Basic Municipal Services: Initial Report*, Washington, D.C.: Urban Institute, 1974, pp. 99-112.

11 The Role of Neighborhoods in the Mature Metropolis

M. Leanne Lachman
and *Anthony Downs*

The *idea* of urban neighborhoods as key parts of American cities appears to be increasing in vogue at the same time that their *reality* is declining in importance. There is even a new Assistant Secretary for Neighborhoods in the U.S. Department of Housing and Urban Development—a possible sign that they have passed their zenith. In spite of the recent ascendancy of the idea of neighborhoods, that term has no single widely accepted definition. Nor is there any clear agreement among urban experts or officials about what functions neighborhoods do, can, or should perform in the lives of mature American metropolitan areas. In fact, the immense diversity of neighborhood conditions and roles across the nation seems to preclude generalizations about either what they are or what they should do.

Nevertheless, our recent experience analyzing neighborhood conditions in many large cities has convinced us that certain important principles about them can be validly derived from reality. Therefore, we will examine the *concept* of neighborhood as related to American metropolitan areas. We will discuss what people mean by it, what functions neighborhoods actually perform, and what roles they are likely to perform in the future. We will also indicate how we believe city officials can most effectively increase their emphasis upon neighborhoods in city planning and program implementation.

Different Concepts of Neighborhood

Certain words like *love, truth,* and *justice* denote fundamental and commonly encountered realities; hence they assume a tremendous diversity of meanings in practice, because they are used by many different people for widely varying purposes. Neighborhood is such a word. Our analysis of the literature and of common usage concerning this word in the field of urban affairs reveals at least the following meanings—each associated with a specific perception of the function of a neighborhood.

Neighborhood as a Focal Point

One way of looking at a neighborhood is as a local area serving as a focal point for personal interactions among its residents. "Back in the neighborhood" means where the speaker grew up as a child and adolescent and experienced the socialization process that made him or her an adult. Children naturally tend to interact most intensively with the people residing closest to them because they have limited mobility. But neighborhoods can serve as "organizing space" for the daily interactions of adults, too. This is true in their patronage of local institutions like churches and stores, and in their leisure-time use of taverns, theaters, clubs, parks, or street corners.

Recent analyses of social interactions indicate that the urban neighborhood—that is, the close vicinity of one's residence—is more likely to serve as the source and location for intensive adult social interaction in working-class or lower-income residential areas than in middle-income or upper-income residential areas. This is partly because residents of the former have less mobility than those of the latter. Also, they are less likely to organize their social lives around contacts with fellow workers, associates in special-interest groups, or those in related professional or vocational fields, who are likely to be somewhat scattered in residence. But this concept of neighborhood as a social community has an *ideological* as well as a *descriptive* dimension. Many urban philosophers would like to see neighborhoods become the focal points for far more intensive interactions among their residents than actually occur, even in closely knit enclaves.

Neighborhood as a Social Unity

A neighborhood can be seen as a social unity of persons who share a common relationship with some institution important to them. This is a quasi-religious concept of neighborhood, derived from the Old Testament idea of the "people of God." God's word goes forth and calls together a group of formerly disparate persons who become a unified community because of their mutual relationship to Him. The shared relationship creates a common bond that serves as the basis for a many-faceted set of social interactions among them. This theological concept underlies the Catholic idea of the neighborhood parish—a fundamental building block in many American cities during the late-nineteenth and early-twentieth centuries. It is a combined spatial and religious community built upon shared faith and interaction of a group of people who worship at the same church and send their children to the same Catholic school; in some cities, neighborhoods even took on the names of specific churches. Most of the people in such a neighborhood were often from the same European ethnic group, or from one or two such groups, in contrast to the people from very different ethnic groups who lived in adjoining parishes. Similar quasi-religious neighborhoods developed in Jewish and Buddhist communities where religious schooling and shared value systems also contributed to social solidarity.

More recent secular versions of social unity based upon a shared relationship with an important institution are found in areas served by a single public school, or ancillary to a major urban university. Examples are the multijurisdictional "neighborhood" served by New Trier High School north of Chicago, the Morningside Heights areas around Columbia University, or the Hyde Park-Kentwood area around the University of Chicago. These secular manifestations of the "unified people" idea tend to involve far less comprehensive forms of social interaction among the participants than did the old Roman Catholic parishes or other religious neighborhoods. The latter's institutional activities permeated many different aspects of daily life, including worship, education, adult social events, local politics, and welfare activities. An idealized vision of neighborhoods based upon urban parish experience probably underlies the approach of many of the Catholic priests now involved in neighborhood organizing. Whether such a comprehensive form of unifying experience can be created in future metropolitan-area neighborhoods remains to be seen.

Neighborhood as a Real Estate Entity

A neighborhood often is perceived as a discrete entity in the urban residential real estate market. It serves as the basic unit through which the larger community experiences social and physical changes in market conditions. This is a rather complex definition that could be restated more simply as, "A neighborhood is what real estate brokers perceive as the smallest housing market unit beyond the individual house and block." The two key ideas in this definition are *community perception* and *market unit*. Community perception is crucial because it both determines boundaries and shapes certain types of behavior that have decisive impacts upon what happens to the locality concerned. For example, consider a single urban block bounded by four streets. Just north of this block is an area perceived by the community as a whole—and the real estate profession in particular—to be in excellent condition with good prospects for continued future prosperity. But just south of this block is another area perceived by the community and the real estate profession to be a different neighborhood from the first one, and one which is now declining with far less favorable future prospects. In which neighborhood does this sample block lie? The answer is not determined by the objective characteristics of the block in relation to those of the two contiguous areas, or even its precise spatial relationship to them. Rather, the answer is wholly dependent upon how the community and the real estate profession perceive the situation. Moreover, their perception has vital implications for the future of this block. If they believe the block is really part of the neighborhood with favorable prospects, then owners in that block will be encouraged to maintain their property well, lenders will provide outside capital for rehabilitation and mortgage financing, and brokers will steer affluent buyers into the area. Those actions will help ensure that the block in fact has an excellent future. But if the community and the real estate profession perceive the exact same block, with the same present conditions prevalent in it, to be part of the neighborhood with an unfavorable future, that perception will lead to opposite types of behavior. And those opposite actions will help drive the neighborhood into worse physical condition and lower socioeconomic status, as is discussed later.

Thus, community perceptions not only define the boundaries of specific neighborhoods but also tend to become self-fulfilling prophecies influencing future conditions in those neighborhoods. In this sense, neighborhoods are what the local real estate profession says they are. True, its perceptions are certainly infuenced by objective conditions, and by the actual behavior of both buyers and sellers in the market. Therefore, neighborhoods as perceived and defined by the real estate profession tend to exhibit some degrees of internal homogeneity concerning physical structure types, land use, maintenance levels, ethnic composition, socioeconomic status, or other variables; that is why they are seen as discrete entities. Most people in the real estate profession are extremely conservative in their evaluations of neighborhood conditions, and they usually anticipate decline far in advance of reality. Thus, their self-fulfilling prophecies can weaken neighborhood stability. Watchful community organizations and city staff can pinpoint signs of negative real estate sector behavior. If such signs are detected early enough, they can be counteracted.

There are often sufficient ambiguities in local conditions so that the exact boundaries of each neighborhood become matters of professional self-definition, unless precise legal jurisdictional lines (such as municipal borders) are highly correlated with differences in objective conditions. If the community perceives of a certain territory as all part of one neighborhood, and therefore treats all parts of that territory in the same way, that treatment may itself help create a homogeneity of results within the territory that reinforces the original perception that it should be considered a single neighborhood.

In the rest of this chapter, we will assume that neighborhoods as defined by the real estate market are in fact the key units for physical and social change within all parts of a metropolitan area. This particular concept of neighborhood, which is the central one employed in our analysis, is not necessarily inconsistent with the others set forth here. In fact, the specific boundaries perceived by the real estate profession as appropriate for a certain neighborhood may be decisively influenced by one or more of the other conceptions of a neighborhood, such as local school attendance area boundaries, or parish boundaries.

Neighborhood as a Political Entity

Even on a small scale, a neighborhood can be a political entity through which local residents attempt to exercise some control over conditions in their area, and to exert influence upon larger government organizations. Several diverse urban philosophers have advanced this political view of neighborhoods. It is consistent with the traditional belief that the most genuinely democratic form of government is that closest to the governed. Such truly local governments are administered in units small enough so that each resident seems to have an opportunity to influence the governing officials personally. Many suburbs and suburban school districts are small enough to be almost neighborhood size so they come under this category. In this case, support for neighborhoods as effective political units reinforces the legitimacy of existing governmental arrangements. In contrast, within large cities, support for more political power at the neighborhood level is usually a protest against the existing governmental "establishment." The latter is considered to be too highly centralized at city hall and therefore too insensitive to local neighborhood interests. It is sometimes accused of being unduly dominated by sinister "downtown interests." Some advocates of legalized decentralization of governmental powers to small neighborhood units even view existing centralized local government as a form of neocolonialism. Since the protestors often represent low-income, minority-group neighborhoods, their analogy to neocolonialism has more than metaphorical similarities to earlier forms of exploitation.

A somewhat less radical and more pragmatic form of political protest has been adopted by many neighborhood organizations seeking to increase the influence of local residents over citywide governmental agencies. In the Saul Alinsky tradition, they have used particular local grievances to coalesce local residents into pressure groups that capture more political power at the neighborhood level. Some sociologists see the transfer of more political power to neighborhoods as a potentially effective way of reducing the alienation and feelings of powerlessness felt by many urban residents concerning their government. This concept has even been endorsed by a national business group, the Committee for Economic Development, as part of its proposal for "two-tier" governmental reform. One tier is at the neighborhood level, and the other is at the metropolitan level.

Although some elected local officials have expressed sympathy for such decentralization, nearly all citywide bureaucratic organizations have resisted it vehemently, and usually successfully. These include public school administrators and unions, and most other citywide administrative departments. Their leaders fear loss of power if the hegemony of such organizations is threatened by breaking them up into smaller units, each under some "outside" authority from a group of local neighborhood residents. Thus, the movement for more political authority at the neighborhood level within large cities has become a struggle between local residents and organizers on the one hand, and citywide administrators and union leaders on the other. Some decentralization of administrative offices has occurred, and sensitivity to local concerns has significantly increased because of greater citizen participation; but little movement toward legalized decentralization of political powers within large city governments has occurred anywhere. On the other hand, within the suburbs, many residents are satisfied that such legalized decentralization is already embodied in the fragmented nature of suburban jurisdictions.

Neighborhood as an Instrument for Exclusion

A neighborhood as a geographic entity can be used by its residents to protect their environment from "undesirable outside elements" through various forms of exclusionary arrangements, even though the residents have limited commitments to it as a vehicle for positive personal interactions. This is the view of most middle-income and upper-income and most suburban neighborhoods adopted by the Social Science Panel of the National Academy of Sciences Advisory Committee to HUD in its study of the significance of community in the metropolitan environment.[1] The panel concluded that "community" was more a negative than a positive concept in such areas. That is, the communality producing some cooperative action among residents was their shared desire to protect the local area from a perceived "external threat," such as a new highway passing through it or a low-income housing project. It was not prompted by any positive desire to engage in direct personal interaction in normal social life or by a shared relation to some "internal" institution such as a church or school. Most of the residents in such areas were quite conscious of the likelihood of their moving somewhere else in the near future. Hence they had "limited liability" commitments to the local area based mainly upon protecting their short-term investment in property values. They tended to ignore the neighborhood except when a potential threat to its economic prosperity appeared on their horizon.

Some Implications of Concepts of Neighborhood

Do these five different concepts of neighborhood have anything in common that could be considered part of a generic definition? Yes, but not much. For one thing, they all consider a neighborhood as a relatively limited geographic territory, all parts of which are close to and contiguous with all others and share about the same basic location within the entire metropolitan area. Second, every neighborhood is perceived as a definite entity by the community at large and treated as a whole (or all parts of it treated quite alike) by at least certain key actors within the community. However, it is true that the specific sizes of neighborhoods so perceived vary tremendously from one city to another. In Milwaukee, for example, the entire South Side, which contains almost half of the city's nearly 670,000 residents, is widely considered to be a single neighborhood. In Cincinnati, on the other hand, the total population of 450,000 is divided into forty-four well-defined neighborhoods: an average of just over 10,000 persons per neighborhood.

Each neighborhood also supposedly embodies some type of internal homogeneity that differentiates it from surrounding territories. However, there is no widely shared agreement about either what variables must exhibit such homogeneity or how much homogeneity they must exhibit. Among the homogeneity variables included under different concepts of neighborhood are the ethnic composition of the residents, their relationship to certain key institutions (especially schools, churches, and shopping districts), types of land use, types of residential structures, and age and condition of structures. A neighborhood can also have many different forms of internal organization and many diverse community organizations within it. Consequently, neighborhoods can differ immensely in almost all characteristics from one city to another, or even within a single city.

There seems to be one important cross-cutting trait among these diverse views of a neighborhood, namely, that neighborhoods in lower-income and working-class residential areas appear to have more positive social-interaction-related functions than those in middle-income and upper-income residential areas. The former may also be more important as political organizing entities, enabling local residents to seek greater influence over their environments than the official government structure provides them. Middle-income and upper-income residents are not as likely to use neighborhoods as political levers for change because they are more satisfied with the power their official governments already provide for them. This is especially true in suburban areas marked by relatively small and fragmented local governments. Insofar as lower-income and working-class residential areas are found mainly in the suburbs, the future roles of neighborhoods in the life of each metropolis will be determined by the degree to which power there shifts from their large cities to their suburbs, or vice versa. In recent years, large cities have experienced major losses of population and of relative power compared to surrounding suburbs. If that continues, neighborhoods will be of less and less importance as organizing entities in the overall life of the metropolis, except insofar as they coincide with small suburban jurisdictions. If large cities succeed in halting or reversing the outflow of jobs and residents to surrounding suburbs, however, neighborhoods may take on increasing importance in the life of the metropolis.

Another implication of the concepts of neighborhood set forth above is important for those city officials or other persons who want to make more effective use of neighborhoods as active units in their city planning and development process. This implication is that the more of these different concepts of neighborhood that can be combined in dealing with a specific area, the more effective that neighborhood can be made as an instrument of local action. Many cities already use the real estate market concept of neighborhood in carrying out their community development and revitalization planning. This involves dividing each city into separate territorial areas for purposes of analysis, interaction with local residents, and program administration. This approach can be enhanced if at least some of those areas also exhibit traits associated with the other concepts of neighborhood mentioned above. Then they are likely to prove far more viable entities for carrying out public policies. For example, consider a neighborhood defined along real estate market lines that also happens to coincide spatially with a strong local Catholic parish, to contain a well-established local neighborhood organization of homeowners, and to serve as a focal point for a great deal of social interaction among its residents—most of whom are of a single ethnic group. That neighborhood would draw its identity not only from the real estate market but also from the common relationship of many of its members to a local religious institution, from their common ethnic heritage, from a strong community organization, and from the sentimental attachment to the area generated by constant social interactions among many of its residents. Such a neighborhood could become a far more important and potent force in local planning and program activity, and in the overall life of the city, than a neighborhood that embodied fewer of these internally coalescing traits. Therefore, city officials who want to use neighborhoods to revitalize their cities should set their boundaries so as to encompass as many of these concepts as possible as significant dimensions of each neighborhood.

Dynamics of Neighborhood Change

For any analysis involving more than a one-time snapshot of conditions, urban neighborhoods must be viewed as *dynamic* and *changing*. They are not static places but instead are constantly experiencing both inflows and outflows of people and money. The composition of the population changes as people are born, grow older, and die, and as households form, expand, contract, and break up. Furthermore, in the average neighborhood, one-fifth of the households move every year, so there is continuous turnover of residents. Household mobility rates differ by type of tenure and by region. For instance, about 38 percent of all renters move each year, whereas the turnover rate for homeowners is 10 percent per year. Despite these facts, large fractions of residents in all but the newest neighborhoods have not moved for five years or more. According to the 1975 Annual Housing Survey, slightly less than half the households in the United States had lived in the same dwelling units for at least five years. The figure was much higher for owner-occupants (62 percent) than for renters (24 percent).[2]

Paradoxically, therefore, a neighborhood can have a very high annual rate of movement—35 percent to 50 percent is not uncommon in urban rental areas—but also have a significant proportion of long-term residents. The latter often become the stable core population that imparts continuity to an area's internal life and external identity. By the same token, though, high turnover rates can lead to rapid change in the socioeconomic characteristics of a neighborhood, and the population can change almost totally in three to five years.

The buildings and infrastructure of a neighborhood also have their dynamic aspects. On the positive side, they are repaired, modernized, rehabilitated, or replaced with new construction. On the negative side, they become obsolete, deteriorate, or are removed. Neighborhood stability is dependent upon property maintenance and a healthy, active real estate market. These in turn require constant reinvestment and in-flow of capital and goods—in other words, ongoing commitment to the area by households, investor-owners, lending institutions, and the local government.

Within any city, it is possible to identify different stages of residential quality, or neighborhood condition, using a real estate market definition. In a study published by the U.S. Department of Housing and Urban Development titled *The Dynamics of Neighborhood Change*, Real Estate Research Corporation developed a five-stage model that can be used to classify residential areas along a continuum.[3] As depicted in Figure 11-1, it extends from healthy, viable stage 1 neighborhoods where the private real estate market is functioning well to extremely blighted stage 5 neighborhoods with heavy abandonment and no in-migration. Through field testing in neighborhoods where preservation programs were underway in over sixty cities, the model proved to be a widely applicable descriptive device.[4] It has since been used as an analytical and program planning tool in several diverse cities.[5]

Although the wording in the description in Figure 11-1 suggests that neighborhoods can only move downward once decline begins, movement can actually occur in either direction. There are abundant examples of areas across the country that have improved through rehabilitation and preservation efforts. Spontaneous rehabilitation has caused sections of the South End in Boston and Capitol Hill in Washington, D.C., for example, to rise from stage 3 to stage 1. Federally assisted code enforcement programs resulted in many neighborhoods moving up from stage 2 to stage 1 or from stage 3 to stage 2. The Hough area of Cleveland improved from stage 5 to stage 4 through extensive demolition that created open spaces where there had been rows of vacant and abandoned buildings, thus leading to an increase in residents' perceptions of personal security, which were shown to be so important in the discussion in Chapter 3. Improvement is easier and less expensive in the early stages of decline, and that is where more and more cities are now focusing their neighborhood preservation efforts.

Only a small number of cities contain stages 4 and 5 neighborhoods. In Milwaukee, for instance, well over 50 percent of all residential areas are in stage 1, and its most deteriorated neighborhoods are between stage 3 and stage 4. No neighborhoods in Anaheim, California, are below stage 2, and stage 3 is the

Stage 1: Stable and Viable. These are healthy neighborhoods that are either relatively new and thriving or relatively old and stable. No symptoms of decline have yet appeared, and property values are rising. Some neighborhoods remain in this stage for decades, if they have attractive locations near major amenities and/or if they continue to attract residents able and willing to perform high-quality maintenance.

Stage 2: Incipient Decline. These are generally older areas experiencing some functional obsolescence. As older families with grown children move out, younger ones with fewer economic resources move in. Minor physical deficiencies in housing units, plus some rising density, begin to appear. Property values are stable or only increasing slightly, and a high proportion of mortgages are federally insured because many buyers have not yet accumulated substantial equity. The level of public services and the social status of the neighborhood often decline somewhat.

Stage 3: Clear Decline. If the Stage 2 instability is not corrected, the changes that began then can become more definite. Renters become more and more dominant, and tenant-landlord relations deteriorate with rising absentee ownership. Social shifts to lower-status groups occur. Minor physical deficiencies multiply until visible everywhere. Conversions to higher-density use increase, and overall confidence in the area slackens. Some housing abandonment may begin.

Stage 4: Heavy Decline. By the fourth stage, housing becomes very deteriorated and even dilapidated, requiring major repairs for most structures. Properties are now marketable only to the lowest socioeconomic groups through contract sales. Profitability of rental units declines and cash flows wane. More and more subsistence-level households move into and dominate the area. Pessimism about its future becomes widespread and is accompanied by abandonment.

Stage 5: Unhealthy and Nonviable. Neighborhoods of this type have reached a terminal point at which massive abandonment occurs. Expectations about the area's future are nil. Residents are those with the lowest social status and lowest incomes in the region, and the neighborhood is considered an area to move out of, not into.

Source: Donald S. Cannon, M. Leanne Lachman, and Arlyne St. Bernhard, "Identifying Neighborhoods for Preservation and Renewal," *Growth and Change*, VIII, 1 (January, 1977), 36.

Figure 11-1. Neighborhood Change Continuum.

lowest category in Rochester, New York. Thus, there are many variations in the number of stages present in particular cities. Moreover, neighborhoods at the same stage can be stable or improving or declining. In addition, the sizes and physical characteristics of neighborhoods vary tremendously, even within a single city. Nonetheless, in any given city, the process of change can be identified, the geographic boundaries of areas at different stages can be delimited, and generic intervention programs can be matched with household, structural, and real estate market characteristics. Taking into account the unique attributes of individual neighborhoods means fine-tuning program packages for each area; that is why neighborhood preservation is both so complex and so challenging.

The overall process of urban development in the United States provides the framework for understanding the dynamics of change in neighborhoods at different stages. Basically, the growth pattern of American metropolitan areas has been a series of concentric rings expanding outward from the downtown core. Pior to World War II, new construction generally followed public transit corridors, and densities stayed quite high. With the mushrooming growth in automobile ownership and usage after World War II, however, new construction densities dropped and metropolitan areas expanded rapidly in geographic size as builders accommodated the pent-up demand that accumulated during the depression and war years; this was discussed more fully in Chapter 8.

Beginning with the earliest urban construction, each wave of new development has represented the latest styles in housing—in design, size, construction materials, and appliances. Each wave has also reflected contemporary needs in community facility planning for transportation, recreation, education, shopping, and so forth. The newest housing is generally at the top of the price range in the metropolitan area. It attracts relatively affluent households, or those with expectations of rapidly rising incomes who feel they can temporarily overspend on housing in order to live in a modern unit in a new neighborhood. The somewhat older houses and apartments vacated by the people moving into new housing units are purchased or rented by slightly less affluent households. They are in turn improving their housing conditions by moving into well-established neighborhoods with sound but older housing. Many households in this second wave of movers vacate even older housing—usually closer to downtown—that then becomes available to households with still lower incomes. On average in the United States, construction of each new house occasions from 2.0 to 3.5 household moves, even though some of the units accommodate newly formed households that are not vacating other houses or apartments.

This "trickle-down" or filtering process of urban development has worked relatively well for most people. However, it has led to a concentration of the poorest people in the oldest and cheapest housing, most of which is located in the central core of metropolitan areas. In the 1950s, when a housing shortage still remained from the prewar years and poor inmigrants were flowing from rural areas to cities, serious overcrowding existed in physically substandard buildings in inner-city neighborhoods. Inmigration slowed down in the 1960s, but new construction continued at the edges of metropolitan areas, so that the trickle-down process enabled population densities to drop in the oldest neighborhoods. The worst housing was removed, much of it through urban renewal clearance, but now, in the 1970s, we are passing the equilibrium point and *are building excess housing in many metropolitan areas.* As indicated by high vacancy rates and spreading abandonment in the oldest, poorest sections of more and more metropolitan areas, we simply have too many housing units. This is an inevitable result of continuing to construct large quantities of new units while household formation and population growth rates are low. The excess eventually filters down to the oldest housing, even though the new development occurs in outlying parts of each metropolitan area. We have reached the point where a large proportion of the cast-off units are in habitable structures in livable neighborhoods.

This brings us to a complementary process of change that has emerged in many urban areas in the last ten years. The urban development or filtering process described above matches houses and apartments of differing ages and costs with households' ability to pay for them. The complementary effect is that new construction on the fringes of the urban area *pulls* households outward from the center of the city into better houses or apartments in newer neighborhoods that are geographically further removed from the inner city. The more recent secondary process involves people purposefully moving out of neighborhoods that they perceive as undesirable. This movement is associated with neighborhood conditions rather than the condition of housing units. In cities where this is occurring, the worst neighborhoods have become stigmatized, especially by high crime rates. They are viewed by residents as places to move out of, even if the housing itself is adequate for the residents' needs. This desire to upgrade by moving to a better neighborhood creates an outward *push* of households wanting to leave inner-city areas. It begins in the oldest and poorest neighborhoods but, through a chain reaction, it extends successively to adjacent area after adjacent area. In well-maintained areas that are in the path of change, residents are often afraid that approaching socioeconomic or racial changes are going to cause their property values to drop. They become anxious to move before this happens. Then the push of households moving away from deterioration accelerates the process of neighborhood decline.

When the "pull" of the filtering process is combined with the "push" of residents wanting to escape from their current neighborhoods, there can be rapid change and widespread neighborhood deterioration. Residents lose confidence in the future stability of their areas and are unwilling to invest in home improvements, assuming that property values are not going to rise as rapidly as in the past. When this kind of attitude is prevalent in a neighborhood, the houses become shabby and values actually stabilize or decline.

Postwar national housing and urban development programs focused on the lowest-income, most deteriorated geographic areas. The Urban Renewal, Neighborhood Development Program, Model Cities, and even Federally-Assisted Code Enforcement and Section 312 Rehabilitation efforts all concentrated on the worst neighborhoods in the communities participating in the programs. Consequently, little attention was paid to the transitional areas between the healthy stage 1 neighborhoods and the least healthy ones. Yet these are the areas where change is occurring, often at a rapid rate, and where blight is spreading. By intervening earlier in the process of decline, change can be slowed down and a much larger proportion of the existing housing stock and established social fabric can be preserved.

Some Lessons for Neighborhood Policy

Four key conclusions emerge from the foregoing analysis of the role of neighborhoods in the mature metropolis; each of these will be summarized in turn.

Neighborhood Interaction

The orientation toward neighborhood-based social interaction is strongest among working-class and lower-income people. A high proportion of the urban population falling into these two groups is located in central cities, though many older suburbs and more and more newer, middle-income suburbs also contain sizable working-class populations. Middle-income and upper-income households reside predominantly in newer or healthy, well-maintained older suburbs. In recent years, adult higher-income households have been attracted to architecturally or aesthetically distinctive rehabilitation areas in older central cities. Although these inner-city enthusiasts represent only a tiny fraction of all middle-income and upper-income households, they tend to be people who exhibit a neighborhood spirit and strong commitment to the social and physical vitality of their residential areas.

By and large, then, residents' neighborhood orientation is most pronounced in the central cities, where there are also the greatest needs for physical, financial, and social assistance. This combination of circumstances strengthens the likelihood of effectively carrying out neighborhood-based preservation or revitalization programs.

As discussed earlier, many suburbs behave as neighborhoods, especially when the residents coalesce in opposition to a perceived threat. Furthermore, these suburban jurisdictions often have political powers that well-organized inner-city neighborhoods would like to replicate. As the suburban areas age, these powers will become increasingly important, though the small jurisdictions will find, as older central cities already have found, that they cannot control as much of their destinies as they might like.

If national, categorical, neighborhood-based programs were to be undertaken (which we do not recommend), it would be politically advisable to include suburban jurisdictions as eligible for whatever aids were provided. This is happening now with state rehabilitation loan programs. The majority of the declining areas are concentrated in central cities and older, inner-ring suburbs, however, and that is where most of the funds for corrective action should be focused.

Categorical Programs for Neighborhoods

Generic or categorical program approaches can be developed that will lead to appropriate neighborhood intervention at specific stages in the process of neighborhood change. In application, however, such program approaches would have to be tailored sensitively to mesh with the strengths and needs of each specific neighborhood. Generic approaches will differ somewhat from city to city, depending upon the age of the city, the number of neighborhood stages present, the recent rate of upward and downward change, and local housing market conditions. Nonetheless, the match up of types of programs and specific stages should generally be as follows:

Stage 1: Stable and Viable—Because the private real estate market is, by definition, operating fairly efficiently in these neighborhoods, little needs to be done in the way of special programming. Provision of normal city services is all that is required.

Stage 2: Incipient Decline—City public works programs in these areas will demonstrate public commitment to the neighborhoods and will bolster residents' confidence and encourage reinvestment. This is where redlining has historically begun, so it is important to assure availability of mortgage and rehabilitation financing. Shallow interest-rate subsidies for rehabilitation loans can serve as incentives for structural improvement, especially if code enforcement is undertaken.

Stage 3: Clear Decline—Job retention and job creation are usually the most important concerns in these areas. City services may have to be increased if population densities are relatively high. Rehabilitation will require deep subsidies and, in many cases, outright grants. Also, in most of these neighborhoods, a comprehensive approach to revitalization will have to include programs to assist absentee property owners, with code enforcement used as the stick to spur action. If the neighborhoods at this stage are the most deteriorated in the city, demolition may be necessary to remove the worst blight. Then, if the cleared land is not readily marketable, it should be landscaped and maintained so that it does not become a blighting influence in and of itself.

Stage 4: Heavy Decline—Jobs and social services are far more important in these neighborhoods than physical programs. However, aggressive demolition is essential to remove blight and stabilize such areas for remaining residents. This can be expensive, especially if it is followed by landscaping and maintenance of open spaces.

Stage 5: Unhealthy and Nonviable—Fortunately, there are not many neighborhoods in the United States at this stage. Because new residents do not move into these areas, the only feasible program approach is demolition and landbanking of the vacant properties for future redevelopment. In such cases, the most promising foreseeable reuse is subsidized economic development.

As is clear from the above descriptions, in each successive stage, program costs increase and the likelihood of stabilizing or improving the neighborhood decreases. In stages 2 and 3, public expenditures can be leveraged so that program dollars generate private spending by property owners, businesses, and financial institutions. Leverage is seldom possible in stages 4 and 5.

Though these generic approaches can be used as guidelines for program planning, successful implementation requires careful adaptation to the conditions of particular neighborhoods. If there is a great deal of diversity within a neighborhood, this will include block-by-block analysis. It will also include evaluation of household composition. For example, high numbers of elderly households on fixed incomes in stage 2 or stage 3 areas may suggest the need for rehabilitation grants in the form of lifetime liens on the residences.

Administering Neighborhood Preservation

Successful neighborhood preservation is dependent upon highly sensitive program administration. This is not a mode of operation to which city staff are readily adaptable. As Richard Harris observed in a *New Yorker* article on the South Village in New York City, "The bureaucrat cannot approach life, and especially the immense and seemingly intractable problems besetting our society, without thinking in systematic terms."[6] True, matching generic programs with neighborhood stages requires systematic thinking. But actual preservation of neighborhoods can only be accomplished through awareness and appropriate treatment of individual destabilizing forces. Such forces can be as various as one or two absentee landlords who are milking their buildings, elderly homeowners on fixed incomes, high traffic volumes on residential streets, unnecessarily rigid lenders, inadequate parking space, blighting concentrations of bars and pornographic bookstores, broken sidewalks, lack of recreation space for teenagers, conversion of large old houses to rooming houses, and so forth. A planner or program administrator dealing with a specific neighborhood must be able to both identify and address a combination of discrete physical and social problems.

New forms of organization are needed to administer neighborhood preservation and revitalization programs. Community development staff members in most cities are not sufficiently attuned to the diverse issues in enough neighborhoods to be effective in comprehensive programming. Simply focusing on the few geographic areas that staff members know a lot about will not be adequate to slow or reverse the spread of deterioration. Instead, more efforts must be made to tap the organizational networks that already exist in many neighborhoods, and to create such networks where they do not exist.

City staff can draw upon the strengths of established religious institutions, ethnic organizations, issue-oriented coalitions, political subdivisions, and block groups. In New York City, for example, there are over 10,000 block associations that can be used in varying degrees to provide local knowledge, to disseminate information, or to participate in such programs as surveillance, self-help code enforcement, youth clean-up campaigns, or bulk ordering of materials for home repairs. All of the other types of organizations mentioned above could provide similar assistance in program development, coordination, and implementation.

Clearly, cities will have to pay more attention to two questions: (1) how to identify or create representative neighborhood organizations oriented toward coordinated preservation action, and (2) how to establish effective working relationships between those organizations and city staff. Many such alliances have been formed across the country, and ideas are being shared informally. More formal mechanisms are needed for monitoring and disseminating information on a national basis. There is no one form of administrative organization that is going to work in every city or in every neighborhood within a single city. So as many organizational arrangements as possible should be tried to expand the pool of workable methods.

One example of public/community relationships is Neighborhood Housing Services (NHS), a residential revitalization program that began in Pittsburgh in 1968 and is being replicated by the Urban Reinvestment Task Force. There are about thirty operational programs, and development efforts are under way in sixteen additional cities. Each NHS is a private nonprofit corporation with an executive director and a board consisting of community members and representatives of local lending institutions. The board is primarily concerned with making rehabilitation and mortgage money available in the neighborhood, but many counseling, clean-up, weatherizing, and other activities are also undertaken. The local government agrees to perform appropriate code inspections and complementary public works programs in the NHS area. Development of most NHSs takes at least a year of delicate persuasion and negotiation, and the strength of the initial leaders is crucial in getting the program underway.

Another example of effective organization is in Lincoln, Nebraska, where the city established a *Neighborhood Assistance Bureau* in 1974 to help residents in neighborhoods of all types identify key issues or concerns, and then work with city departments to meet local needs and goals. The city assists neighborhood groups in preparing plans and provides funding for attitude surveys designed by the University of Nebraska. Once this initial planning and surveying is done, neighborhoods can choose to begin a comprehensive Neighborhood Assistance program, which can include such elements as rehabilitation loans, land-use changes, commercial revitalization, subsidized street improvements, and home repair assistance.

A third example of what can be done is in Rochester, New York, where a *Neighborhood Planning* approach for noncentral business district community development is being employed. One or two planners work in specific inner-city neighborhoods, coordinating their activities closely with resident organizations. If general city guidelines are established for community development activities, a neighborhood-based structure can meet small area as well as citywide needs.

A final organizational example that we cite is in Baltimore, which has a tradition of innovative community development programming, and is a city with extensive, long-term community organizational activity. No preservation programs are undertaken in Baltimore now unless there has been a *request for assistance from a neighborhood organization*. This is not because the city has a "hands-off" policy. Rather, it is because the staff recognizes that such programs rely heavily on resident participation. More city governments need to adopt a similar attitude. Ample illustrations like these exist in other cities, and the number is steadily growing.

Block Grants and Neighborhoods

Community Development Block Grants provide cities with the latitude to develop new alliances with community organizations and to tailor their programs to the unique needs of their own neighborhoods. Thus, it is extremely important that this form of funding continue. The Community Development Block Grant program has fared well in Congress so far. In fact, the funds have risen each year. Within HUD, however, there have been efforts to make the program more categorical: in essence, to limit the eligible activities more strictly to low-income and very-low-income areas. These efforts have met with intense resistance from city administrators, and well they might. The bulk of the neighborhood preservation efforts would have to be discontinued, and we would once again be ignoring transitional areas.

Although some large and medium-sized cities have had difficulty functioning in the relative freedom of the Block Grant approach, far more have devised innovative programs in which public funds are leveraged with private capital and very specific neighborhood problems are addressed. Cities need this opportunity for innovation and diversity in program planning, administration, and implementation, if they are to intervene effectively in the process of neighborhood change.

We began this chapter by saying, "The *idea* of urban neighborhoods as key parts of American cities appears to be increasing in vogue at the same time that their *reality* is declining in importance." Yet, as the above conclusions point out, there is considerable potential for drawing effectively upon the strengths inherent in the concept of neighborhood. Those strengths can be used for working toward rehabilitation and preservation of physical structures and social networks in our mature cities. This potential is enhanced by the fact that central cities contain high proportions of the working-class and lower-income households that are most likely to exhibit neighborhood-oriented social interaction.

Out-migration from central cities will undoubtedly continue, but the pace could be slowed. A reduction in suburban new construction would have the greatest impact on reducing the population flow out of large cities. However, intervention in the process of neighborhood change within such cities can also affect residents' perceptions of the stability and ongoing vitality of their communities. In some cities, successful preservation of existing neighborhoods will only mean enabling population and household loss to occur without serious disruption of established areas. In other cities, successful preservation will mean reversal of early decline and reestablishment of healthy neighborhood conditions. In both instances, sensitive intervention will be required. Given that approach, the attributes of neighborhoods—under any definition—offer potential strengths that can be built upon to preserve and revitalize older residential areas.

Notes

1. National Research Council, *Toward an Understanding of Metropolitan America*, San Francisco: Canfield Press, 1974.

2. U.S. Bureau of the Census, "Urban and Rural Housing Characteristics," *Annual Housing Survey: 1975*, Current Housing Reports Series H-150-75E.

3. Real Estate Research Corporation, *The Dynamics of Neighborhood Change*, Washington: U.S. Department of Housing and Urban Development, December 1975.

4. Real Estate Research Corporation, *Analysis of Data on Neighborhood Preservation Program Areas*, report prepared for U.S. Department of Housing and Urban Development, June 1976 (unpublished).

5. For a similar, independently conceived classification method that has been applied in Boston, see Rolf Goetze, *Building Neighborhood Confidence: A Humanistic Strategy for Urban Housing*, Cambridge, Mass.: Ballinger Publishing Company, 1976, pp. 23-38.

6. Richard Harris, "A Nice Place to Live," *The New Yorker*, April 25, 1977, p. 59.

Part VII
Public, Private, and Human Investment in the Mature Metropolis

12 Public Sector Investment Strategies in the Mature Metropolis

Dick Netzer

Just as hard cases make bad law, spectacular and idiosyncratic events in public affairs often cloud the analysis of underlying trends and public policy alternatives. The New York City fiscal crisis that emerged in early 1975 was just such an event. Initially at least, it obscured rather than clarified the problems associated with the behavior and financing of the public sector in the older metropolitan areas of the country. The powers, responsibilities, and political circumstances of New York's municipal government have always been quite unlike those of any other American local government, and the first reaction to the New York crisis was to seek explanations in the realm of political behavior rather than economic characteristics. After all, there were other cities that appeared to be in even worse economic straits, but had not been going through anything like the New York melodrama. More recently, analysts have been focusing on the economic explanations for New York itself and on the fiscal consequences of a weakened economic base in other large older cities as well.[1] The common expectation is that the end of rapid economic growth will result in increasing fiscal stress for the mature metropolis, in the absence of federal intervention to forestall it.

Memories are short, however. With few exceptions, the mature metropolises experienced fairly substantial economic growth during the 1950s and 1960s, particularly in suburban areas but in most cases in the central cities as well. During *that* period, the conventional wisdom was that rapid urban growth was the cause of overwhelming fiscal stress. There were enormous needs for publicly financed urban infrastructure and huge increases in requirements for operating the new infrastructure, facilities, and services. State-local government purchases of goods and services increased in real terms by 5.2 percent annually during the 1950s and 1960s, a rate of increase about half again as great as real GNP. In current dollars, the pressures were even greater, because the state-local government sector was bidding resources away from other sectors and necessarily experiencing differentially high increases in input costs in so doing.

In retrospect, it is clear that rapid urban growth was good, not bad, for the fiscal system of urban areas. It is surely true that the combination of rapid growth in urban populations and rapid growth in real per capita income or product in urban areas dissolved some fiscal problems, in the sense of making it easier to raise more revenue from taxes and increasing the revenue base for the issuance of debt. In 1974-75 state and local government tax revenue was just under nine times as great as it had been twenty-five years earlier, 1950. I estimate that, had the tax systems in effect in the earlier year continued unchanged to 1974-75, state-local tax revenue in 1974-75 would have been roughly 5.4 times the 1950 level. That is, economic growth, both real and inflationary, accounted for about 60 percent of the huge increase in tax revenue.

Beyond this, economic growth must have made it politically easier to increase tax rates and adopt new forms of taxation, regardless of whether we explain this as showing diminishing marginal utility of private consumption expenditure or high income elasticity of demand for public services. Pragmatically, rapid economic growth rates combined with the buoyancy of the federal government's revenue system underlie an important structural change in our fiscal system, the eighteenfold increase in federal aid to state and local governments between 1950 and 1974-75, which increased federal aid from 12 to nearly 21 percent of state-local general revenue in this period.

Why then did rapid growth appear to be so troublesome in fiscal terms during the era of rapid growth? Some years ago, in a broader appraisal of the economics of growth in two very large suburban counties in the New York area, the conclusion was that some of the apparent fiscal difficulties were transitory ones, stemming from the sudden change from preurban to urbanized environments.[2] Some of the difficulties, though, were the result of unsuitable, but correctable, institutional arrangements, and some were the consequence of interjurisdictional and interpersonal differences in economic and social circumstances within a single metropolitan area, partly but not completely amenable to institutional reform. And some of the problems were illusory, in that they resulted from the entirely unwarranted expectation that a high level of urban public services could be provided without correspondingly high-tax levels or that someone else can be made to pay for the benefits I receive. In short, the fiscal problems associated with rapid urban growth were not very serious ones, however contentious they seemed to be at the time.

Slow Growth and Urban Public Finances

In the 1970s, of course, everything has slowed down, for the country as a whole as well as for the mature metropolis: the rates of growth in population, GNP, and state-local purchases of goods and services all have been well below the levels of the preceding decades. Nonetheless, state-local spending has continued to rise more rapidly than GNP. In fact, the increase in real per capita state-local expenditure in the 1970s has been only slightly below the rate experienced in the 1950s. There are two major problems of financing associated with these differential rates of change that apply to the state-local sector as a whole; these problems are far more serious for the mature metropolis.

The first is the prospect that the increase in federal aid to state and local governments as a percentage of total receipts of the state-local sector will be far smaller over the next decade than it has been over the twenty years from 1956 to 1976. It seems paradoxical to put forth such a statement early in the term of office of a federal administration that is widely characterized as an activist one that is especially sensitive to the well-being of the country outside Washington, D.C. But as successive reviews of the federal budgetary outlook by the Brookings Institution and congressional committee staffs for the past few years have consistently indicated, the budgetary leeway for major new departures in federal programs—of the type necessary if the federal role in the financing of the state-local sector is to expand relatively—will be quite modest for the intermediate-term future. Leeway for new departures will be small partly because of inexorably rising expenditure for existing direct federal programs, notably the Social Security and federal employee retirement "entitlement" programs. If the rate of national economic growth is not high, federal revenues will not be buoyant, to look at the other side of the budget. Moreover, there is some evidence that the income elasticity of the federal revenue system is lower now than it was in the 1960s.

If there are few major new federal departures, the mature metropolis is likely to suffer disproportionately. This is because, by and large, existing federal grant programs—for reasons that are entirely understandable and often entirely appropriate—aim at universality and do not focus on the mature metropolis. Also, some of the reforms of the early 1970s, notably the replacement of categorical grants by block grants are just now becoming fully effective and will actually reduce certain types of federal grants to older cities in absolute dollars. It will take major new programs, specially designed for the mature metropolis, if federal financing is to assume a substantially larger role in these kinds of places.[a]

A second unfavorable factor for the financing of the state-local sector as a whole has to do with the change in the economy's product mix, away from the production of physical things destined for private consumption and toward the production of privately consumed services on the one hand, and goods and services purchased by governments on the other. This structural transformation has gone much further in the mature metropolis than for the economy as a whole. But state and local tax systems depend heavily upon the output and private consumption of goods. The property tax is a case in point: it is overwhelmingly a tax on the value of privately owned reproducible physical capital. State sales taxes, both general and selective, fall largely on the sale of tangible personal property. At least two-thirds of state-local tax revenue

---

[a]This is *not* to suggest that it is necessarily efficient or equitable to enact new federal programs to provide aid to the subnational governments serving the large old central cities (as distinct, say, from federal programs designed to assist groups of *people* within those cities). Few people would advocate massive federal grants to finance the salaries of policemen, fire fighters, and refuse collectors, but such grants would have a stronger impact on the finances of big-city governments in the Northeast and Midwest than any other conceivable federal grants.

currently is generated by the production and consumption of material things. Generally speaking, state-local tax systems are reasonably effective in reaching things like privately owned structures, privately purchased durable goods (other than exports), personal consumption expenditures for nondurable goods, and personal consumption expenditures for housing, household operations, and transportation. In combination, these comprise a declining share of GNP.

The revenue implications of changing economic composition were explored in some detail in the course of a large-scale study of New York City finances conducted by the Maxwell School of Syracuse University a few years ago.[3] The investigators allocated collections of all the major city taxes (other than the residential property tax) to major industry groups and related these calculations to employment, for the 1960-70 period. Although the specific results are very much a product of the specific features of New York's tax system and economic base, the general conclusions are widely applicable. Indeed, in some respects New York City suffered, in revenue terms, much less from changes in employment compensation than must have been true for a more "typical" mature central city. The finding was that the change in industrial composition over the decade *by itself* reduced 1970 revenue from the major taxes examined by 1.5 percent. More to the point, to replace the revenue lost by reductions in jobs in manufacturing and wholesale and retail trade required substantially larger increases in jobs in services and government. In revenue terms in 1970, one manufacturing job was equivalent to 1.1 service jobs or 1.6 government jobs; one job in trade was equivalent to 1.6 service jobs and 2.3 government jobs.

By and large, the two problems explored in the above paragraphs must be viewed as constraints—or threats—for the future rather than as unfavorable trends that have shaped the public finances of the mature metropolis in the recent past. Although the large central cities of the Northeast and North Central states have faced a variety of social ills associated with maturity for a long time, in most cases for two decades or more, serious fiscal problems are a relatively new phenomenon. For one thing, booms or boomlets in the 1950s and 1960s had favorable effects on the finances of the local governments serving these central cities. It is only in the past few years that economic weakness has produced a generalized deterioration in the fiscal position, essentially since the end of the 1961-69 national prosperity. To place the fiscal problems in some quantitative perspective, some comparative data for eleven large Northeastern and Midwestern central cities have been assembled. These eleven cities include all those places with slow-growth characteristics in the northeast quadrant of the country, that had populations of 500,000 or more in 1970 and were located in metropolitan areas with populations of 1.4 million or more in that year. All eleven central cities experienced population declines between 1970 and 1973 and only three were in metropolitan areas with population growth of more than 1 percent between 1970 and 1975 (in seven of the other eight, the SMSA population declined by percentages ranging between 0.6 and 4.3 percent).

The fiscal data presented here apply to the finances of the local government units serving the central city, like the municipal government itself, the county, the city school district, and the transit authority, for which Census Bureau releases provide data for both 1969-70 and 1974-75.[b] State governments are important direct providers of public services, but they are not covered here except as grantors of funds to local governments. It should be noted, however, that the role of the state government as a direct provider of service is smaller in the Northeast and North Central regions than it is in the South and West (with the notable exception of California), and that this is especially true in the larger cities of these regions.

These local governments have per capita expenditures that are about two-thirds above the level for all U.S. local governments. That is, they accounted for 14.5 percent of total local government expenditure in 1974-75, but the eleven cities had only 8.7 percent of the U.S. population in 1973. In part, the high level of per capita expenditure reflects the substitution of local for state government as a direct service provider, but the main reason for the disparity is the notorious tendency of per capita expenditure to increase with city size, even if the special case of New York City is excluded.

Table 12-1 shows the rate of increase in local government finance in the first half of the decade of the 1970s. Expenditure for the ten mature cities other than New York increased appreciably less rapidly than was the case for other U.S. local governments, especially expenditure for capital outlay and personal services. Even for New York, the increases were slightly less than for other local governments, aside from the ten cities.

Between the fourth-quarter of 1969 and the fourth-quarter of 1974, the implicit price deflator for state-local government purchases of goods and services rose by 47.5 percent. Thus, there were real increases in local government expenditure only in the cases where the recorded dollar increase exceeded that percentage. By that measure, real increases in capital outlays occurred in only five of the eleven cities. There were declines or zero increases in actual dollar capital outlays in four cities. Also, in four of the eleven cities, outlays for personal services did not rise in real terms. Between October 1970 and October 1975, local government employment declined in New York, Detroit, and Pittsburgh; it was essentially stable in Chicago, Boston, Cleveland, and St. Louis. It rose appreciably only in one city, Minneapolis, in our group. This was a sharp contrast with the pre-1970 experience, when local government employment was rising sharply even—or, sometimes, especially—in large central cities with declining populations.

---

[b]Some large local government units serving the central city are omitted, notably for Chicago, Minneapolis, Pittsburgh, and St. Louis. On the other hand, there has been no effort to adjust the data for units extending beyond the central-city boundaries, notably the counties in six of the eleven cases. Rough estimates suggest that the omissions just about balance the overly broad coverage of county governments, in terms of local government expenditure in 1974-75.

Table 12-1
Percent Increase in Selected Local Government Finance Variables, 1969-70 to 1974-75, Eleven Mature Cities versus Other U.S. Local Governments[a]

	\multicolumn{3}{c}{Selected Units of Local Government Overlying the Central City}	All Other U.S. Local Governments
Variables	New York	Ten Other Cities[b]	Eleven Cities	All Other U.S. Local Governments
Total general and utility expenditure[c]	75	60	68	77
Capital outlay[d]	129	38	78	70
Other	69	64	67	79
Personal services[e]	61	50	56	69
General and utility revenue[c]				
Federal government sources	330	208	249	334
State government sources	112	115	113	85
Property taxes	44	27	35	54
Other local taxes	86	52	73	101
User charges[f]	54	28	41	74
Debt outstanding	70	27	51	46

[a]Adapted from U.S. Census Bureau Governments Division releases.
[b]Baltimore, Boston, Chicago, Cleveland, Detroit, Milwaukee, Minneapolis, Philadelphia, Pittsburgh, and St. Louis. See text for discussion of the units of local government included in the coverage.
[c]The principal exclusion is the finances of local government employee retirement systems.
[d]New York City classifies as capital outlay very large amounts of expenditure generally considered current operating costs in other jurisdictions. Thus, the capital outlay figures in columns (1) and (3) are not truly comparable to those in columns (2) and (4).
[e]Compensation of employees before payroll deductions, does not include fringe benefits.
[f]Includes the census categories of "current charges" and "utility revenue." In census definitions, utilities include *only* water supply, electric, gas, and transit operations. For the eleven mature cities, utility data are dominated by the figures for transit operations.

On the revenue side, all the mature cities, including New York, recorded increases in own-source revenue that were less than those recorded by other U.S. local governments. This was to be expected, given the economic characteristics of our mature cities. In real terms, property tax revenue declined in all the cities except Minneapolis, nonproperty tax revenue declined in three of the eight cities that employ such taxes at more than trivial levels, and user charge revenue declined in eight of the eleven cities. All experienced substantial increases in revenue from federal and state sources, and our large cities did significantly better in regard to state aid than did other U.S. local governments.

In fact, this relatively large rise in state aid appears to reflect a basic structural change. For decades, it has been an article of faith among elected officials of big cities that they were "shortchanged." Before one-man, one-vote, the metropolis typically was underrepresented in the state legislatures. Equally important, until relatively recently, the big cities *were* the center of income, wealth, and economic activity; they *were* significantly richer than the rest of their states, and it was entirely fitting, legislative malapportionment aside, that state taxes collected in the big cities should be spent elsewhere in the state. Of course, the big cities no longer represent peaks of income and wealth, and it is therefore fitting that the pattern of state government financial flows should shift in their favor. The surprising thing is that precisely this has occurred, despite the fact that, with losses in population, one-man, one-vote often means that the big cities have less representation in the state legislatures than they did twenty years ago, prior to *Baker vs. Carr.*

One example of this transformation is found in state school finance reforms. A large number of states have adopted school aid schemes that provide exceptionally large amounts per pupil to big-city school systems, amounts substantially in excess of the aid that would have been provided by the basic formula applicable to all the states' school districts. The school aid arrangements in Detroit, Cleveland, and Philadelphia are striking cases in point. What is especially worth noting is the fact that the rationalizations offered to justify favoring the big cities are so shaky in their logic and, often, contradictory; nonetheless, the cities have been favored. Similarly, state legislatures have been departing from ancient traditions to provide aid to urban-area local governments for the performance of functions that do not exist, in local governments, outside urban areas. The tradition had been to aid only those local government functions that were ubiquitous: public schools, roads, and health and welfare activities. Recently, however, the states have been aiding such city-only activities as housing and urban renewal, parks, sewers, mass transit, and airports.[4] The result is the large relative increase in state aid shown in Table 12-1, and the emergence of the state governments as the preeminent source of funds for mature city local government, as shown in Table 12-2. If these cities are shortchanged today, the data do not reveal it.

The top panel of Table 12-2 shows another structural difference between our eleven cities and all other U.S. local governments: the lesser relative importance of expenditure for capital purposes. In one sense, this is not surprising; the large old central city with a declining population should have most of its needed public capital in place, in contrast with the expanding Sunbelt city or suburb. However, much of the old city's public capital is very old and physically or functionally obsolete. To some extent at least, the low share of expenditure devoted to capital outlay is a sign of fiscal stringency (capital outlays are easier to cut back on than are current operations), not capital adequacy. This is a point to which we will return subsequently.

The last line in Table 12-2 suggests a major aspect of "New York City

Table 12-2
The Structure of Local Government Finance, 1974-75, Eleven Mature Cities versus Other U.S. Local Governments[a]

	\multicolumn{3}{c}{Selected Units of Local Government Overlying the Central Unit[b]}			All Other U.S. Local Governments[b]
Variables	New York	Ten Other Cities	Eleven Cities	All Other U.S. Local Governments[b]
Total general and utility expenditure	100	100	100	100
Capital outlay	14	14	14	18
Other	86	86	86	82
Personal services	45	55	49	47
General and utility revenue[c]				
Federal government sources	5	10	7	7
State government sources	46	35	41	31
Property taxes	20	28	24	33
Other local taxes	17	11	14	6
User charges	12	14	13	17
Debt outstanding	113	88	102	93

[a]The notes to table 12-1 also apply to this table.
[b]Expressed as percentages of total general and utility expenditure in each geographic grouping.
[c]The revenue sources listed should approach but not equal 100% of total general and utility expenditure because some miscellaneous revenue sources are ignored, as are borrowing in excess of debt redemption and the finance of employee retirement systems.

exceptionalism," the very high level of its indebtedness. Aside from New York, our mature cities have low, not high, indebtedness, by the standards of other U.S. local governments. As Table 12-1 shows, New York City is also exceptional in the rapidity of its increase in debt during the 1970s. In a sense, the New York City fiscal crisis was less a result of high and rising expenditure than of high and rising indebtedness, above and beyond the indebtedness that would have been proportionate to the city's spending levels and trends.

Service Needs and Spending Pressures

A decade ago, there was a more-or-less standard list of service needs and reasons for rising public expenditure within the mature central city. The list was headed by the governmental response to racially and ethnically bounded poverty: what local and state governments should do, with their own money and with money provided by the federal government, in response to the growth of low-income ghettos in the midst of generally prosperous metropolitan areas. The components of the response included new activities under the aegis of the federal antipoverty program; higher payment levels and increased eligibility under cash assistance welfare programs; great expansion of personal social services, like day care; the enactment of Medicaid; broadened scope of urban renewal and housing programs; extensive manpower training programs; and compensatory education activities and money in inner-city schools. The standard list also included, but at a far lesser level of importance, upgrading of environmental protection efforts by urban governments; the completion of the urban expressway systems; in most cities, grandiose plans (or hopes) for expansion of mass transit systems; and, at the bottom of the list, upgrading of both operations and capital in the ordinary municipal "housekeeping" services, like public safety, refuse collection, street maintenance, and central administration.

Meeting Basic Service Needs

Those were the service needs identified. At least as important—and well recognized—were the cost pressures that were independent of specific service needs, notably the rapid rise in personnel costs. That rise could be explained by a number of factors, such as the rising militancy of public employee unions; the unwillingness or inability of elected officials, for one reason or another, to resist that militancy strenuously; and, as noted earlier, the simple economic necessity to bid labor away from other sectors if the scope of the local public sector were to expand more rapidly than other sectors. This necessity that could be obviated only if labor productivity were increasing more rapidly in government than elsewhere, which was hardly the case.

An illustration of the relative importance of unit cost increases can be found in Table 12-3, which decomposes increases in current operating expenditure for the public schools for the 1962-72 decade, using Census of Governments data for the nation as a whole. The data are nationwide and schools are not a distinctly urban function. However, the illustration is a convenient one and, if anything, big-city school finance has been even more marked by increases in input costs pure and simple. In any event, the table shows that the bulk of the expenditure increase cannot be explained by either increases in work load (the number of pupils) or program enrichment in the form of expanded staffing ratios (if indeed such expansion does enrich programs). Fully half of the increase represented increases in average salaries.

No one would expect productivity increases to make a major dent in school costs, but we would expect such results in some of the overhead services of government which are far more amenable to applications of capital. Take, for example, financial administration which has been heavily computerized during

Table 12-3
Sources of Increase in Local Government Current Operating Expenditure for Local Schools, 1962-72[a]

Factor	Percent Increase in Factor	Contribution to Total Increase in Expenditure (%)
Total expenditure	184	100.0
Number of pupils	24	13.0
Expenditure per pupil	129	87.0
Staff per pupil		
Teachers	17	8.2
Other	45	4.8
Average staff salaries	71	50.2
Nonpersonnel costs per pupil	144	23.8

[a]Adapted from data in the 1962 and 1972 Census of Governments.

the past fifteen years. Census of Governments data once again were used to examine expenditure for and employment in financial administration by state and local governments for the same decade, 1962-72. Expenditure for this function increased by about 135 percent during the period; we estimate that the number of transactions handled increased by no more than 75-80 percent.[c] Thus, the cost per transaction rose by about one-third, as the reduction in employees per 1000 transactions (perhaps 35-40 percent) failed to offset average salary increases in this potentially extremely capital-intensive governmental activity.

It is highly unlikely that big-city governments will need to cope with input cost increases anywhere nearly as great as those in the 1960s. Table 12-1 shows that personal service costs have been increasing relatively slowly in the selected mature cities in the 1970s. It has been noted that local government employment has been stable or declining, in the main, in these cities, which suggests that the rate of increase in average employee compensation has been modest, typically well below the rate of inflation during this period. Clearly, this is not a result of a sudden inclination to be mean-spirited on the part of elected officials, but instead is a consequence of the severe budget constraints many of them confront now. Moreover, if employment is being allowed to decline, there is no good reason to match market bids for labor. Matching the market will produce large

[c]The gross financial magnitudes, like own-source revenue collected, increased by about 160 percent during the decade. But GNP more than doubled. Therefore, it is likely that at least half of the increased financial volume represented increases in the dollar size of transaction rather than more transactions.

numbers of applicants for few openings and will discourage voluntary quits by public employees. Just as it was economically rational for relative wages to rise when local government was a growth industry in the 1950s and 1960s, it is rational for relative wages to decline now that local government in the mature metropolis no longer has that characteristic.

So the standard list of spending pressures in the public sector of the mature metropolis differs from that of a decade ago in the very important respect of a lower degree of cost pressures. But the standard list differs with regard to the perception of service needs, too. Most sensible and humane people will agree with the proposition that the need for public intervention to cope with urban poverty concentrations is at least as great in 1977 as it was in 1967, the year in which, in response to riots, President Johnson appointed the celebrated Kerner Commission (the National Commission on Urban Problems). But most sensible and humane people also are convinced that local and state governments do not have the financial capacity to finance, themselves, the provision of costly income-redistributive public services, that in some respects they lack the capacity to manage such programs, and that our collective ability to design efficacious public responses to health, education, and welfare programs is too limited to warrant grandiose new departures. Thus, the list of service needs that urban governments are now addressing, and likely to address in future years, gives a high priority to the more mundane and traditional responsibilities of municipal government.

The combination of budget constraints and more realistic aspirations makes the number one job of the public sector in the mature metropolis the assurance that minimum maintenance needs are satisfied, referring here to the maintenance of the entire urban fabric, not just publicly owned physical facilities. This involves spending a lot of money for current operations and for public safety, to assure against further deterioration in the quality of inner-city schools and to provide at least minimal levels of those social services for which urban governments necessarily must be responsible.

It also involves coping with a relatively new phenomenon, quite unexpected ten or fifteen years ago, namely, the emergence of large deficits in the operating budgets of enterprises that were established with large capital subsidies, but then expected to be self-sufficient from user-charge revenue. Good examples are mass transit systems and public housing. In 1974-75 local governments recorded operating deficits of well over $1 billion on transit systems and operating deficits of $700-800 million for housing and urban renewal ventures. Ten years earlier, in the aggregate there were no operating deficits for housing and less than $100 million for transit. It seems quite likely that the scale of public investment in transit and housing over the past decade would have been far smaller had deficits of the current magnitude been anticipated.

But perhaps the most troublesome of the financial responsibilities involved in meeting "minimum maintenance needs" has to do with slowing the rate of disinvestment in the public capital of the mature city. It is, of course, entirely appropriate that, over time, there be *some* disinvestment in real terms in central cities that have become substantially smaller in population size. Population is a determinant of capacity requirements for most types of public capital and, while marginal declines in population can be reflected in marginal increases in standby capacity, major declines in population—like 25 percent and more over two decades—surely permit some contraction in capacity. Moreover, the efficiency of public capital has tended to increase, just as the efficiency of private capital has increased.

However, there is no sign that the very considerable disinvestment that is occurring has any coherent relation to the population declines experienced. Instead, the standard governmental response to budgetary constraint is to defer maintenance generally, and to refrain from replacing anything that is even tolerably serviceable. This strategy leads to generalized deterioration and disinvestment in the plant and equipment that may be needed, even by a much smaller population. In pursuing this strategy, urban governments are not doing anything new, for governments in the United States have never operated with systematic replacement planning and usually have tended to skimp on routine maintenance.

In the past, rapid urban growth combined with changing technology and improvements in the standards for public services called for a fairly high rate of investment in entirely new public structures and infrastructure. In such an environment, it made little sense to maintain, like new, plants that soon would be discarded entirely, or superseded in some other fashion. For example, why worry about a high level of maintenance for a street that is likely to be obliterated for a new expressway within a few years? Obsolete plant *was* being replaced, not as part of a coherent strategy, but existentially as a consequence of the rush of new projects. In essence in most cities, the needs of growth were accommodated by building marginally more new capacity than actually was required; this permitted retirement of some old capacity typically after the fact.

In the mature metropolis it will no longer be possible to replace old public capital by accident, as a by-product of handling growth. Instead, cities will need to fashion a deliberate replacement strategy, and in the older of the cities this may prove terribly expensive, in part because the new capacity may be required on the site of the old, in part because so much of the work must be done in heavily built-up areas. For example, century-old water and sewer mains in the central parts of some of the cities surely must be nearing the end of their life expectancy. Of course, wholesale, all-at-once replacement will not be necessary in many cases, but minimizing the number of such cases will require considerably improved, and more costly, regular maintenance practices.

Developmental Services for the Central City

The list of service needs discussed so far deals with public expenditure necessary to keep the mature metropolis going at a fairly minimal level. It does not provide for a developmental posture, that is, for public sector intervention to try to dramatically improve the competitive position of the mature city as a location for residents and economic activity. For such a posture, the expenditure requirements are much larger and the risks of making bad investment decisions are much greater, in part because we really cannot speak with assurance about the impact of local public services and facilities on economic development in the context of urban America in the late-twentieth century. In developing regions, it is easy to devise public investments that radically improve accessibility and lower transport costs or provide a water supply previously unavailable. In the mature metropolis, almost any public effort is likely to make only a marginal change in any of the variables relevant to the competition with other places, but even that marginal change may involve a very large application of public funds.

Three types of conceivable effort illustrate the point. First, it is hard to dispute the proposition that the mature city would be a lot more attractive place if we could improve substantially the output of the public education and criminal justice systems, that is, turn out truly proficient high school graduates and reduce the incidence of violent crime. But it is by no means clear that we know how to increase the output of these systems and it is a reasonable guess that any effective way to do so will be expensive.

Second, most of the mature cities have extensive "bombed-out," largely depopulated areas, often areas with high accessibility. It is obvious that 1950s-type urban renewal projects are wholly irrelevant to this situation. If such areas are to be reused, the intervention will have to be on so large a scale that the program should be described as "urban reclamation" (like reclaiming square kilometers, not hectares, from the Zuider Zee), not "urban renewal." Moreover, there is little demand for the high-density residential or commercial redevelopment that characterized the old urban renewal program. So any effective intervention is likely to be costly because it would be on a very grand scale, and it is by no means clear what the appropriate new land uses are.[d] Yet, it *is* clear that large-scale reclamation of the bombed-out sections, even for very-low-density uses, would have strongly positive effects, both real and symbolic, on the economy of the city.

Third, historically the large central city provided the technologically most advanced public services and facilities available, like the highest-quality water supply and the newest in short-distance transport facilities. In the late-nineteenth century, the big cities of the Northeast and Midwest were hothouses for prodigies of civil engineering genius, much of it generated by the public sector. This is hardly the case today. But it is surely true that if the mature city could offer the most advanced forms of waste disposal, energy supply, transport, and the like, it would have significant competitive advantages. The trouble is that we do not really know how to restore this type of competitive edge, and we suspect that to do so would require a great deal of scarce public money.

---

[d]Very probably, the appropriate uses are low-density ones that require low investments in structures per acre reclaimed and that can readily be replaced by higher-density uses in later years if and when such replacement is economic. The only land uses (aside from parks) that meet this description are things like single-story plants and single-family houses built at, say, early post-World War II densities.

Squaring the Fiscal Circle

To recapitulate, public expenditures in the mature cities have been growing relatively slowly in the 1970s and are not likely to grow nearly as rapidly as in earlier years, partly because the revenue growth to sustain rapid increases in spending will not be available, and partly because aspirations are less grandiose and hopes more modest. However, even a relatively modest rate of change in public spending, one that provides for minimal maintenance needs and makes some small contribution to a developmental posture, is likely to cause considerable fiscal difficulty. This is because of the weakness of the economic base of so many of the mature cities and the weakness of the larger regional economic base in the Northeast and Midwest.

Of course, there would be no real fiscal problem if one had any confidence in the success of the strategy pursued by local government officials during the 1960s. Essentially, that strategy amounted to wringing one's hands, pleading poverty, and threatening riots, in the hope of generating a rain of manna from heaven in the form of large infusions of federal money. That strategy worked only fitfully in the 1960s and almost surely will not work at all in the 1970s and 1980s. What then are some conceivably acceptable approaches that might, singly or in combination, resolve the prospective fiscal problems of the mature city?

First, there are a number of grounds for seeking additional funds from higher levels of government, particularly the federal government, grounds in which the cities are not mendicants begging for alms from a presumably softhearted and muddleheaded federal government but rather are lobbying for specific help for cogent reasons. These could include:

1. Federal help in the form of budget relief (either by federal assumption of additional direct program responsibilties or additional grants-in-aid) for the costs of income-redistributing expenditures now borne from local and state government funds
2. Continuance and expansion of federal countercyclical grants
3. Federal assistance for research and development, to improve the effectiveness of conventional activities and to find and implement new technologies
4. Additional federal help to cover operating deficits in transit and public housing, at least in part on the argument that federal capital grants induced cities to invest in ventures that proved, unexpectedly, to be deficit-prone
5. Reforms in school finance, especially at the state level, that more generously assist big-city school systems

Also, there are things which local governments themselves could do which would improve the utilization of local government revenue instruments and more frugally and productively applying local revenues, such approaches as:

1. Greater regionalization, within metropolitan areas, of both tax bases and operations where costs or benefits spill heavily over existing city lines
2. Converting revenue systems from their dependence on the private production and consumption of physical things to systems that more accurately reflect the changing economic character of the mature city
3. Aggressively seeking out possibilities for technological innovation in program operations and other opportunities for reducing unit costs in real terms
4. Learning how to be far more ruthless in setting priorities among public programs, services, and activities than either the public or the private sector has been for more than a generation

Rescue from Without

Close to 40 percent of all civilian public expenditure in the United States is, by now, for explicitly income-redistributing activities, notably income maintenance programs of all kinds, the provision of health care services to the low-income population, and in-kind subsidies for housing (conservatively excluding the income-redistribution element in the provision of public education, on the grounds that the income-redistribution objective cannot be separated from the other goals of public education). The great bulk of this expenditure, about 80 percent, is financed by the federal government either directly, as in Social Security, or indirectly, close to 20 percent of the revenues state governments themselves raise, and about 10 percent of own-source local government revenue is absorbed by explicitly income-redistributing programs. These percentages are somewhat higher in the urbanized states of the Northeast and Midwest.

Lobbying for federal assumption of substantial portions of these costs is a promising strategy for the mature metropolis. By now, the philosophic argument for this has gained very wide acceptance; it is difficult to find reasonable people who argue that the redistribution of income is a sensible role for state or local governments, in principle. Most agree with both the equity component of the argument—in an open society characterized by much geographic mobility of persons, the public sector costs associated with concentrations of low-income people ought to be borne nationally, not locally—and the efficiency component—local efforts to depart from the national consensus on the proper degree of income redistribution will generate inefficient shifts in the location of people and economic activity.

Moreover, the dollar amounts involved are large. For example, in 1974-75 state-local expenditure for public welfare net of federal aid amounted to 10 percent of state-local tax revenue in the twenty-one states of the Northeast and North Central regions and about 8 percent of state-local tax revenue in the twenty-nine other states. Thus, had the federal government absorbed half of the state-local financed welfare expenditures in the Northeast and North Central states, raising the federal share from 50 to 75 percent of total costs, this would have been equivalent to increasing total state-local tax revenue by a little more than 5 percent, which is hardly a trivial amount.

Nonetheless, it would be unwise to expect this kind of federal rescue at an early date. The problem is not one of principle, but rather of program design. As the efforts to enact a comprehensive reform of welfare and national health insurance in the past few years have demonstrated, it is extraordinarily difficult to design national programs that reconcile all the important objectives. Any revised program must provide benefits that are comprehensive and uniform, make few or no present beneficiaries worse off, restrain increases in aggregate program costs, provide appropriate incentives (for work, in the case of welfare, and for efficiency in service provision, in the case of health), all of this besides relieving state and local government budgets. To date, our collective wisdom has been inadequate to the task of such reconciliation, and it is clear that the welfare reform at the federal level now under discussion would, at best, require a lead time of several years for full implementation. Therefore, the most we can expect in the near-term is a shift of some part of the costs—ideally, a large part—to the federal treasury.

The case for generous federal countercyclical aid also is strong in principle. An open economy vulnerable to cyclical fluctuations will generate pronounced local and regional fluctuations and those fluctuations will differ in intensity among places; state and local governments should be afforded some insulation from such shocks.[e] We now have legislation that embodies the principle. There are, however, two practical difficulties in the way of large-scale expansion of the program. First, it is clearly very hard to cut back the federally financed expenditure when local unemployment declines below the specified thresholds. This leads to pressure to set the thresholds fairly low, making the program less countercyclical and more a permanent increment to general revenue sharing but one distributed on the basis of criteria that are, to say the least, less than self-evidently appropriate. This in turn suggests a second practical difficulty. While it makes obvious sense to utilize high thresholds that concentrate the amounts appropriated on those places in the most serious economic straits, federal programs that significantly assist only a very few places have very limited political attractiveness. Thus, it seems unlikely to expect countercyclical federal aid to provide large amounts of help to the mature metropolis over the long run.

Although the short-run dollar consequences of federal R&D assistance to state and local governments are small, pursuit of this approach has much to

---

[e]This proposition was advanced first by Alvin Hansen and Harvey Perloff in the 1940s. After some early discussion in connection with concern about the post-World War II economy, the idea disappeared from view (for no good reason). Walter Heller revived the proposal in the late 1950s, but his efforts received little attention, even among academics, at that time.

commend it. Here, too, the principle is an accepted one. R&D efforts are inherently risky ventures. Because the nation as a whole profits from both successes and failures, it is proper that the federal government should assume a good deal of the risk. The subnational public sector is not distinguished by its technological precocity; indeed, the sector is rather poor at the application of the latest in currently available technology, not to mention its use of state-of-the-art technology. Thus, the potential payoff from greatly increased R&D efforts is considerable and probably greater in the mature metropolis—where the superficial obstacles to technological change are most disabling—than elsewhere in the country.

The problem of large operating deficits in federally assisted transit and housing ventures is not a universal one, but it is widespread enough to suspect that pleas for additional federal operating assistance will be at least partly successful. This may not be a policy that ranks high on grounds of economic efficiency. The best that can be said for it on this score is that greater federal responsibility for operating deficits may lead to more caution in financing new capital investment and more federal effort to encourage rational pricing and cost control policies.

Earlier in this chapter, it was noted that state governments have been doing well by the big cities in recent years, notably in connection with school finance reforms. Traditionally, big-city school systems received amounts of state school aid per pupil that were quite low relative to the rest of the state. This was a consequence of the interaction of two factors: the heavy concentrations of taxable wealth, and the relatively small size of the public school population in the large central cities, which together meant that taxable property values per pupil tended to be very high in the central cities. Despite the economic decline of the central cities, this situation continued in a good many places. Thus, the initial impact of the great wave of school finance reform—toward more equalization of disparities in the per pupil tax base—of the last several years would have been to worsen, not improve, the finances of big-city school systems in most states, had the state legislatures not chosen to insert into the school finance laws special provisions for the big cities.

These provisions differ; in some states there are "density corrections," typically justified on the grounds that unit costs are inherently higher in high-density urban school districts. In others there are adjustments for the costs of "compensatory education," that is, the presumably higher costs of proper schooling for low-achieving children from low-income households. Sometimes there are simple corrections based on the proportion of children from low-income or welfare families, labeled "urban aid." And in a few cases there are adjustments for "municipal overburden," the high nonschool expenditures of big-city governments. The logic behind all of these features can be criticized, especially the municipal overburden argument.[5] Nevertheless, the features exist and seem to be expanding.

There is another way of looking at all this, however. It is a reasonable presumption that the taxable wealth of the mature central city will continue to decline over time relative to the statewide averages and that, in a relatively short time, the per pupil taxable wealth of the large central city will fall below the statewide average in most places. If that occurs, a vigorous state school finance equalization plan—even full state government finance of the schools—will benefit the large central-city school system, whether or not there are special urban features. This argument suggests that the cities should be ardent supporters of all-out equalization, in a rather pure form, and not oppose it, as many now do, for all-out equalization provides a very real fiscal safety net for the future.[6]

Changes at the Local Level

If the United States were devising a brand new system of government responsibilities and finances appropriate for the last quarter of the twentieth century and wholly ignoring the existing institutional arrangements, the structure of subnational government would look very unlike the one we live with. As noted earlier, the income-redistributive responsibilities of government would be highly centralized. The remaining responsibilities for the provision and financing of public services in urban areas would be assigned to "metropolitan states," units of government encompassing whole metropolitan areas, with some degree of decentralization designed to enhance public choice within the metropolitan state. Such a system would reflect the reality that the income and wealth of the country is centralized within metropolitan areas and that, despite regional differences in economic growth rates, whole metropolitan areas are viable fiscal entities that could be self-financing for nearly all nonincome-redistributive public services. Few would think it proper or necessary to tax residents of freestanding small towns or rural areas in order to raise central government funds that are then transferred to the metropolitan states to finance urban-type public services.

The fiscal transfers that are generally considered appropriate under existing arrangements very largely amount to transfers from suburbs to central cities, that is, within metropolitan areas. The state governments and the federal government are utilized as vehicles for such transfers because we do not have metropolitan states, but highly fragmented structures of government within metropolitan areas. For at least a generation, scholars and reformers have been attracted to the notion of greater regionalization as either partial solution or panacea. The relative or absolute economic decline of the mature central cities makes the argument more, not less, cogent, at least in principle, as indicated in the discussion in Chapter 10.

Moreover, by and large, the extent of local government fragmentation is greatest in the older regions of the country. In particular, the central cities tend to be small relative to the size of the metropolitan area. For example, Northeastern central cities (excluding New York) house only about one-third of the region's SMSA population while Southern central cities include just over half the SMSA population. New York aside, none of the eleven mature cities listed in Tables 12-1 and 12-2 contained as much as half of the population of its SMSA in 1973; and seven of the ten had a third or less of the SMSA population.

In general, the smaller the relative size of the central city, the worse its fiscal position should be. The central city that is small relative to its SMSA is likely to be characterized by relatively low per capita income, retail sales, and housing values. It may also contain a relatively small share of nonresidential property values, though this need not be the case; it is true for Detroit and Cleveland but not for Minneapolis and Pittsburgh. Among the twenty largest central cities in the Northeast and North Central regions, there is a positive and statistically significant relationship between the size of the central city relative to the SMSA that includes it, on the one hand, and both the growth rate of taxable property values from 1966 to 1975 and the central city/SMSA ratio of per capita property values, on the other.

Regionalization to overcome these intra-SMSA fiscal disparities, via the creation of outright metropolitan governments, extending the boundaries of central cities, city-county consolidation, expanding the responsibilities of urban counties that include both central cities and suburban territory or other tax-base-sharing devices, is highly attractive to reformers, but it has proved rather unattractive to those being reformed because the pecuniary self-interests of suburban majorities are so obviously involved. Thus, there are only two places outside the South and West in which there has been any major move to "fiscal regionalization," Minneapolis and Indianapolis, both of them areas that are atypical of Northeastern and Midwestern metropolitan areas in numerous respects. There is no good reason to believe that continued relative decline in the central cities will make this strategy more, rather than less, popular in coming years.

There is an alternative form of regionalization in which the self-interest of suburbanites and central-city people can coincide, namely, regional organization and financing of public services that obviously spill over narrow jurisdictional boundaries, for example, transportation, water supply, and the protection of environmental quality. This is widely recognized and accepted. However, the dollar amount of fiscal relief this affords the central city is relatively modest. And even here, the politics can be awkward, so much so that in a good many cases the regional solution has been intervention by the state government as financier or service provider rather than the creation of self-financing metropolitan entities. Thus, the "self-help" fiscal solution of metropolitan regionalization is not a promising one and it would seem that in the United States, the state government is the best form of metropolitan government we have or are likely to get.

To acknowledge the economic weaknesses of the mature city is not to deny the possibilities for improving its local government revenue system, for revenue instruments differ considerably in their economic consequences. Even in a place like New York where the level of local taxes in the aggregate is extremely high, it is possible to conceive of ways of generating additional revenue without adding to the adverse economic effects of the present system. Even more, there are ways of raising the same revenue total with a good deal less economic damage.

Moreover, as noted earlier in this chapter, most present local revenue systems are badly conceived in the light of prospective economic change. Take what may be the most extreme example, the taxation of business inventories under the property tax, still done in a majority of the states. Because the old central city is at a competitive disadvantage for most goods-handling activities, inventories have been and will continue to be a declining base for central-city taxation, whatever happens to business inventories in the economy at large. But it seems inevitable that inventories also will decline relative to GNP over the long run, as sophisticated computerized inventory control systems diffuse throughout the economy, to small as well as large enterprises. Thus, the central cities are likely to house a declining share of a relatively declining magnitude.

The ideal revenue system for the mature metropolis is one that reaches the aspects of the local economy most likely to be expanding, without choking off the expansion. But the mature city needs to emphasize damage-minimizing tactics, where there is a conflict between taxing growth and not impeding that growth. Concretely, the appropriate policies should include the following:

1. General taxes on property, sales, and business income should be revised to reduce the impact on manufacturing and other goods-handling activities, because they are declining activities in the mature central cities and because they appear to be especially sensitive to tax increases and tax differentials, which is a consequence of the central city's lack of attractiveness as a location for such activities. A recent analysis of New York City's business tax reform in 1966 suggests that the reform cost 65,000 manufacturing jobs. The study estimates the elasticity of manufacturing employment or output with respect to the change in tax rates after a four-to-five-year lag at −0.35, and suggests that the increase in business taxes may well have resulted in a decline in aggregate state-local revenue from all taxes combined.[7]

2. For other types of economic activity, a given central city may maintain substantial locational attractiveness and thus it may be able to tax such activities more heavily without damage. However, it is difficult to be wildly optimistic on this score for the long run. A cautious policy would be one that refrains from heavier taxation of such activities per se, but does not extend to them the benefits of the de-emphasis urged in paragraph 1 above.

3. The central-city retail sales tax on goods is a loser, as ample experience in those places with large sales tax rate differentials suggests. The only economically safe central-city sales taxes are those on services.

4. There is much evidence that land values in mature cities have been declining in real terms, if not in current dollars. Nonetheless, land value taxation imposes no economic damage whatever and a shift from other forms of taxation—those which *are* economically harmful—to land value taxation will be economically beneficial. Virtually all American cities tax land values at very low rates—usually far below the rates that apply to reproducible capital—so that substantial increases in the taxation of land values have merit on equity grounds as well. However, it appears impossible to overstate the universal unpopularity of higher taxation of land values or to exaggerate the lack of understanding of the economic principles involved.

5. Alfred Marshall, the great British economist, divided taxes into "beneficial" and "onerous" taxes. Beneficial taxes are those that finance benefits the specific taxpayers receive and perceive as at least equal in value to the taxes paid. Onerous taxes are those that finance benefits to others, or benefits that are of low value. No rational taxpayer would shift the location of his activities in response to beneficial taxation. Income-redistributive public services must be financed by taxes that appear onerous to taxpayers. But there is no obvious reason why this need be true of other public services, including the bulk of the services that local governments should be financing from their own fiscal resources.

The foregoing argues for making the link between the financing of local public services and their benefits explicit wherever possible. In small homogeneous suburban communities, the link is fairly clear, even when a general tax like the property tax is the instrument employed. In large central cities, however, the link can be made clear only by employing suitable financing instruments, which typically requires the utilization of explicit charges for the use of specific public services. All American cities underemploy user charges and nearly all of them are extremely inept in the application of the user charges they do employ. The local financing of the street and road system by the typical combination of property taxes, vehicle license fees, and parking meter receipts illustrates the point. None of these sources has a direct relation to the benefits received, the public costs incurred, or efficient resource use.

In fact, there are only two really efficient and economically safe local revenue instruments: land value taxation and well-designed user charges. This has been true for some years for the large central city, though the truth has been disguised by economists' inability in earlier years to provide convincing empirical evidence of the harm done by other revenue instruments and by the political attractiveness of levying taxes whose burden can be exported to others in the short run. This truth will be increasingly evident, but acceptance of it, in a fair number of large cities, will require abandonment of the notion that the local revenue system can successfully include major elements of income redistribution. Therein lies a major difficulty, for ours is an age in which there is a great focus on equality of results and the demand for equality probably is greater in the large cities than elsewhere. In essence, this is an argument for urging on the cities a very "capitalist" revenue system, at a time when and in places where the virtues and values of capitalism are not in great favor.

Limited Local Public Spending

The damage that even a poorly designed local revenue system does will be minor if the total amount of money that system must yield is small. The prospects for outside aid, outlined earlier, are that the mature city will receive more external fiscal help, in one way or another, but the additional help will be neither huge in amount nor overnight in arrival. Over the ten years from 1974-75 to 1984-85, federal and state government aid, in one form or another, to the eleven mature cities shown in Tables 12-1 and 12-2 might rise from 48 percent to, say for example, 55 percent of expenditure, growing at moderate rates.

It was noted earlier that the expenditures of the mature cities recently have been growing at rates more moderate than those of the past, but that significant pressures and needs continue. If expenditures increase in real terms in the near future at the 1970-75 rate of about 2.5 percent a year, the forecast of external aid in the preceding paragraph implies an increase in local taxes and charges in real terms over the decade, in contrast to the decline in real terms in the 1970-75 period. But is there any possibility of cutting the rate of expenditure increase to obviate the pressure on the local revenue system of the mature city?

Perhaps alone among serious analysts of urban public finance, I believe that there is. This belief is founded upon the observations that, crisis or no, urban governments are profoundly conventional in management styles and priority determination as well as profoundly backward technologically. Urban governments are not unique in this respect. Most large organizations, in both the private and public sectors, live by incremental budgeting and luxuriate in their rigidities and familiar modes of operation. Only half-facetiously, I argue that virtually all organizational units with 100 or more people not engaged exclusively in physical production are grossly overstaffed and that the overstaffing ratio rises with unit size. But most large organizations do not confront the difficult economic prospects of the governments of the mature city, or if they do confront such prospects, they can confidently anticipate some type of rescue from without that obviates the need to truly revolutionize their conventional modes of operation.

If urban governments are not rescued from without and do *not* make major changes in their conventional modes of operation, the prospects for the mature city are indeed dismal. Public expenditure will be reduced in the manner it has been in the cities hit by fiscal crises, like New York, Detroit, Cleveland, and Newark, more or less across the board, with all conventional activities continued by marginally smaller but considerably more superannuated work forces doing the same old things, only much more inadequately.

But the fact is that *none* of the major services provided by local governments are performed in ways that differ significantly from the methods and approaches used fifty years ago. Police patrol, refuse collection and disposal, schooling, health services, street repair, park maintenance, library operations, and transit operations have actually changed a lot less in the past fifty years than they did in the previous half century. Take as an example the operation of public libraries, which continue as if there were only two possible ways for people to gain access to the knowledge and culture stored in books—to buy hardcover books or to borrow them from libraries; the existence of paperback books, not to mention nonprint media, has largely passed the libraries by. A few years ago, it was observed in New York that library book circulation had declined sharply and that the free distribution of paperbacks would be substantially cheaper than the continued operation of branch library circulation departments. The observation was treated as a call for a return to barbarism, not a goad to change.

Obviously, if things have changed so little in fifty years, change must be difficult indeed. And so it is, so much so that I conclude that the approach often urged on local governments, the application of "modern management methods" to ordinary operations, is a fruitless one. Instead, what is necessary is the stripping away of functions and activities of marginal value, leaving them to private entrepreneurial initiatives or leaving them entirely undone. It is foolish to expensively sweep city streets if the result is to reduce street litter by less than 5 percent; it is preposterous to deploy fire fighters to rescue cats from trees; it is pointless to maintain hospital clinics to treat the common cold; it is wasteful in the extreme to use municipal government money to subsidize commercial sports.

In short, governments in the mature metropolis must learn to combine tightfistedness and an unwillingness to do all sorts of "good things" with an eye for the main chance, that is, the spending of public money on things that actually, *not allegedly*, foster the competitive position of the area, things that range from the prosaic (like replacement of essential elements of infrastructure) to the way-out (like becoming the locus for large-scale experiments in new waste management technologies). And governments must also learn how to stay out of the way of the entrepreneurial energies and initiatives of residents, firms, and nonprofit institutions; the potential supply of these energies and initiatives in the mature city remains very large.

Notes

1. See, for example, George E. Peterson, "Finance," in Gorham and Glazer, eds., *The Urban Predicament*, Washington: Urban Institute, 1976; Richard P. Nathan, "Is There a National Urban Crisis?" *New York Affairs*, vol. 3, No. 4 (Summer/Fall 1976); and the recent General Accounting Office Study of the economic and fiscal prospects for New York.

2. See Dick Netzer, "Financing Suburban Development," in Dieter K. Zschock, ed., *Economic Aspects of Suburban Growth*, Stony Brook, N.Y.: State University of New York at Stony Brook, 1968.

3. Roy W. Bahl, Alan K. Campbell, and David Greytak, *Taxes, Expenditure and the Economic Base: Case Study of New City*, New York: Praeger, 1974, chapter 2.

4. For a summary of state aid for municipal-urban programs in 1972, see Advisory Commission on Intergovernmental Relations, *The States and Intergovernmental Aids* (February 1977), pp. 32-37.

5. See essay by D. Netzer, in U.S. Office of Education, *Selected Papers in School Finance, 1974*, Washington: Government Printing Office, 1974.

6. This position has been developed by George E. Peterson; see his chapter in Gorham and Glazer, *Urban Predicament*.

7. See R.E. Grieson, W. Hamovitch, A.M. Levenson, and R.D. Morganstern, "The Effect of Business Taxation on the Location of Industry," *Journal of Urban Economics*, vol. 4 (April 1977), pp. 170-185.

13 "Basic" Economic Activities in Metropolis

Harry W. Richardson

In recent years, the nation's large cities, especially those in the Northeast and the Midwest, have been buffeted by spatial forces that have dampened their growth and weakened their economic bases. The nature of these forces is well known: the shift in population to the West and the South, partly in response to the pull of amenities; the twin processes of industrial decentralization and household suburbanization out of the central cities into the suburbs and beyond; and, most recently, the growth of population and employment in nonmetropolitan areas.

Some of the implications of these trends are apparent in the data of Tables 13-1 and 13-2. Population growth in the United States has been decelerating for decades. The growth of the million-plus SMSAs has slowed down more, growing more than 40 percent above the national average in the 1950s but less than one-half the national average today. In the 1950s and 1960s, the big-city population increased a little faster than that of the smaller SMSAs, but in the 1970s its rate of expansion has plummeted to one-third that of smaller cities. Moreover, the nonmetropolitan areas that formerly grew much more slowly than the national average have, since 1970, exhibited slightly above-average growth. However, since much of this growth has occurred in areas just beyond metropolitan boundaries rather than in traditional rural areas, this trend should be regarded as an extension of rather than a revulsion against metropolitanization. A recent study has demonstrated the critical importance of proximity to a high-ranked metropolis as the key determinant of the rate of population change, income growth, and the location of economic activities in nonmetropolitan areas.[1]

Regional deviations from this national average picture are quite striking. The North Central and Northeast regions have shared a similar experience, particularly since 1970 when their rate of population growth has slowed to a snail's pace, and in the million-plus cities has even declined. However, only in the Northeast have the nonmetropolitan areas surged, perhaps a reflection of the higher densities of development in the region. The South has followed its own peculiar course; growth rates have remained much the same overall, but there has been convergence in growth by type of areas as growth decelerated in the large cities and accelerated in the nonmetropolitan areas. Even so, the SMSAs of the South are still growing faster than the nonmetropolitan areas, with little difference in growth rates between the large and the small cities. Although growth in the West has also decelerated since 1950, it remains the fastest-growing region. Also, there has been a striking switch in the pattern of growth. In the 1950s the million-plus

Table 13-1
Population Changes by Size of SMSA and Region, 1950-60, 1960-70, and 1970-74 (%)

	United States			North Central			North East			South			West		
	1950-60	1960-70	1970-74[a]	1950-60	1960-70	1970-74[a]	1950-60	1960-70	1970-74[a]	1950-60	1960-70	1970-74[a]	1950-60	1960-70	1970-74[a]
Total	18.5	13.4	10.2	16.1	9.6	3.3	13.2	9.8	2.9	16.5	14.3	16.7	39.0	24.2	20.1
SMSAs > 1 million	26.7	16.8	4.9	23.5	12.5	-0.4	13.8	7.8	-1.1	43.1	31.2	18.7	47.9	27.5	11.2
SMSAs < 1 million	26.1	16.3	14.8	24.2	13.5	5.8	12.1	10.7	6.8	30.7	16.9	19.4	48.9	30.2	32.1
Nonmetropolitan areas	5.3	7.0	12.5	4.1	3.5	4.6	13.0	14.3	12.7	1.3	5.8	13.5	16.0	11.0	29.0

Source: U.S. Department of Commerce, Bureau of the Census, *Census of Population*.
[a]Rate per decade.

Table 13-2
Covered Employment Changes in the United States, Excluding New England, 1970-73 by Type of Area (%)

	Total	Construction	Manufacturing	Transportation and Public Utilities	Wholesale and Retail Trade	FIRE	Services
Total	8.0	19.2	0.3	5.8	11.1	14.0	14.7
SMSAs > 1 million	6.3	15.4	−3.6	−4.8	11.1	12.8	12.7
SMSAs < 1 million	5.2	13.7	0.0	−0.4	7.1	9.7	11.5
Nonmetropolitan areas	17.0	36.2	6.7	73.0	16.4	27.0	25.3

Source: U.S. Department of Commerce, Bureau of the Census, *County Business Patterns*.
Note: Employment is only that covered by U.S. social security taxation.

metros grew at three times the rate of the nonmetropolitan areas, but in the 1970s the growth rate differential has been virtually reversed. The smaller metros, however, have remained vigorous throughout.

The national employment data of Table 13-2 show that the post-1970 employment changes replicate the trends in population to some degree, especially with respect to the growth of nonmetropolitan areas. However, a surprising difference is that the larger SMSAs experienced a healthier employment growth than the smaller SMSAs. There are several complementary explanations. The large cities retain considerable pull as employment centers, especially for distribution and FIRE, though not for manufacturing and transportation and public utilities, and especially in the South and the West. Also, to the extent that nonmetropolitan growth has occurred close to large metropolitan areas, this has not been incompatible with continued metropolitan employment growth, particularly when connected with the provision of nodal services. The nexus between migration and employment has weakened (e.g., the migration of retirees), and this may be a contributory factor in the more vigorous growth of population than of jobs in the smaller SMSAs. The strong growth of employment in the nonmetropolitan areas, particularly in transportation and public utilities, construction, and services, suggests that their expansion is not merely a short-term aberration but the beginning of a secular trend, since the new jobs should have repercussionary effects on the rate of population growth.

The sectoral employment changes show little variation among types of area, since the differentials noted in total employment are more or less repeated for the individual sectors. The stagnation in manufacturing employment, with a marked decline in the large cities, is consistent with generalizations about the shift from manufacturing to services and about the impact of productivity gains in dampening employment growth in manufacturing. The rapid expansion in construction jobs, on the other hand, is more a reflection of a temporary construction boom than a long-run permanent trend.

Basic Employment in the Large Metros

Table 13-3 shows the sectoral distribution of employment in thirty-two large cities. Although basic industries are found outside manufacturing (e.g., the tiny mining contribution and parts of the FIRE and government sector), most of the variation among cities is due to the relative size of their manufacturing sectors.[a] For instance, with very few exceptions (e.g., San Jose, Anaheim) the cities of the West and South have small manufacturing bases. The older cities of the

---

[a]"Basic" industries here imply any activities serving markets beyond the metropolitan area boundaries. Thus, nonlocal business services, tourism, and state (and federal) government are as basic as manufacturing.

Northeast and the Midwest, on the other hand, have large manufacturing sectors, and many of them merit the label of million-plus "factory towns."[2]

The crude correspondence between fast growth in the West and the South with a generally low dependence on manufacturing and slow growth or stagnation in the Northeast coupled with a large manufacturing base is, in part, a reflection of the secular trend for service employment to expand faster than manufacturing. On the other hand, rates of industrial growth are now far higher in the West and the South. The manufacturing bases of the larger cities in these areas have been expanding, but much more important have been the spillover effects on their service and nodal functions of manufacturing growth in nearby smaller cities and towns. This is a growth-pole, spread effect in reverse, in that it is traditionally assumed that "trickling-down" effects diffuse hierarchically downward rather than upward.

It is noticeable, and perhaps a little surprising, that the employment structures of these large metropolises are so heterogeneous. Of course, some of the cases are quite obvious: government in Washington, D.C., and San Diego; transportation and public utilities in New Orleans and San Francisco (but also in Miami, Atlanta, and Kansas); the manufacturing bias of Detroit, Milwaukee, and San Jose; FIRE in New York City; mining (i.e., oil fields) in Houston. But below the surface, there are other differences and contrasts. For example, compare Tampa and Newark in wholesale and retail trade, Detroit and New Orleans in manufacturing, New York City and San Jose in FIRE, Washington, D.C., and Milwaukee in government. The diversity of employment structures warns against universal diagnosis and a standard prescription. Sectoral composition will affect metropolitan economic performance because difference sectors have grown at different rates and because sectors vary in their pace of decentralization. Thus, the manufacturing cities have been more vulnerable, partly because productivity growth has dampened the creation of jobs, partly because in the past the economic incentives to decentralization have been stronger in the case of manufacturing than in other sectors due to central city-suburban differentials in land prices, labor supply, transportation costs, and so on. However, a comparison of the personal income growth rates of Table 13-4 (column 3) with the manufacturing employment shares of Table 13-3 (column 3) suggests that the equation of manufacturing dominance with slow growth is too facile. Of course, there are the slow growers such as Buffalo, Pittsburgh, Chicago, Newark, St. Louis, Cincinnati, and Milwaukee. But there are high fliers too; San Jose and Anaheim have above-average manufacturing shares and high income growth rates.

The employment performance of individual large cities for the 1967-76 period should be evaluated against the 20 percent increase in national total employment and 1.2 percent decline in national manufacturing employment; see Table 13-5. In all cases save one (New York), total employment continued to expand. However, the differentials were very wide, with employment in eight

Table 13-3
Sectoral Distribution of Employment in Thirty-two Large Cities, September 1976 (%)

City	Mining	Construction	Manufacturing	Transportation and Public Utilities	Trade	FIRE	Services	Government
Phoenix	0.1	5.2	16.8	5.2	26.4	7.5	19.2	19.5
Anaheim	0.4	4.5	26.0	3.1	25.9	5.8	19.4	15.0
Los Angeles	0.4	2.9	25.4	5.9	23.1	6.2	21.0	15.0
San Diego	0.1	4.4	14.7	4.8	23.6	5.6	20.9	25.9
San Francisco	0.1	4.4	14.5	9.1	21.9	8.6	20.3	21.0
San Jose	*	3.6	33.4	3.7	19.4	3.9	20.6	15.1
Denver	1.3	6.2	15.3	6.6	24.9	7.2	20.4	18.2
Washington, D.C.	—	5.7	3.5	4.8	19.3	5.8	23.3	37.8
Miami	—	5.7	14.5	10.1	25.4	7.6	23.9	14.8
Tampa	—	5.8	13.3	6.4	28.6	7.0	21.6	17.3
Atlanta	—	4.4	16.4	9.2	27.4	7.7	18.0	16.8
Chicago	0.1	4.5	28.2	6.5	22.7	6.1	18.8	13.0
Indianapolis	—	3.1	26.8	6.0	23.5	7.1	15.1	18.3
New Orleans	3.8	6.2	11.7	9.8	25.2	6.1	20.4	16.4
Baltimore	*	5.5	19.3	6.5	22.9	5.6	19.0	21.3
Boston	—	3.4	20.5	5.4	22.7	7.2	26.0	15.0
Detroit	0.1	2.7	35.0	4.8	19.8	6.0	17.6	15.4
Minneapolis	—	4.3	22.4	6.8	25.4	6.2	20.3	14.5
Kansas City	0.1	4.6	20.4	9.1	25.6	6.6	19.2	14.5
St. Louis	0.3	4.4	27.3	7.0	22.3	5.4	19.2	14.1
Newark	0.1	3.3	28.1	7.6	18.8	7.0	18.7	16.2
Buffalo	—	3.5	29.8	5.7	22.2	4.1	18.3	16.5

New York-NE New Jersey	*	2.8	21.1	7.3	21.5	9.5	21.6	16.2
New York City	0.1	2.3	16.8	8.3	19.8	13.2	24.0	15.6
Cincinnati	0.1	4.1	28.9	5.5	22.4	5.2	20.0	13.8
Cleveland	0.2	3.4	30.4	5.4	23.0	5.2	19.1	13.2
Portland	–	4.5	21.0	6.8	25.3	7.0	19.3	16.0
Philadelphia	0.1	3.9	25.5	5.4	21.7	6.1	21.4	16.0
Pittsburgh	1.3	4.5	28.4	6.4	21.6	4.9	20.5	12.4
Dallas	1.1	4.1	22.6	6.8	26.8	7.8	17.6	13.0
Houston	4.4	9.2	17.0	7.4	24.0	2.4	19.4	12.4
Seattle	–	4.5	20.4	7.2	24.5	7.1	18.8	17.5
Milwaukee	–	3.3	33.1	4.9	21.6	5.5	19.3	12.3
United States	1.0	4.5	24.3	5.7	22.1	5.4	18.5	18.5

Source: U.S. Department of Labor, Bureau of Labor Statistics, *Employment and Earnings* (December 1976), vol. 23, no. 6, table B.8, pp. 66-75.
*Less than 0.05.

Table 13-4
Performance Indicators in Thirty-two Large Cities

City	Per Capita Income % of National Average 1950	Per Capita Income % of National Average 1970	Rate of Growth in Personal Income 1950-72 (%)	Rate of Increase in Prices	Rate of Growth in Real Personal Income	Unemployment Rates (%) 1976
Phoenix	91	104	11.42	—	—	6.5
Anaheim	126	103	13.82	—	—	8.7
Los Angeles	130	121	7.28	3.29	3.99	8.7
San Diego	113	105	9.39	—	—	10.7
San Francisco	140	131	6.60	3.48	3.12	10.5
San Jose	110	107	11.66	—	—	6.8
Denver	120	115	8.60	—	—	6.6
Washington, D.C.	138	130	8.12	3.20	4.92	5.2
Miami	111	116	10.15	—	—	10.6
Tampa	85	94	10.55	—	—	10.2
Atlanta	97	107	8.81	3.25	5.56	6.7
Chicago	140	124	6.04	3.16	2.88	7.0
Indianapolis	123	107	6.55	—	—	3.7
New Orleans	102	94	6.72	—	—	8.2
Baltimore	113	102	6.44	3.41	3.03	6.7
Boston	110	113	7.28	3.45	3.83	6.7
Detroit	132	121	6.36	3.19	3.17	9.6
Minneapolis	118	112	7.11	3.27	3.84	5.4
Kansas City	110	109	7.05	3.28	3.77	5.5
St. Louis	119	107	6.02	3.21	2.81	6.3
Newark	126	122	6.32	—	—	7.9

Buffalo	118	104	5.53	—	9.1
New York	140	136	5.37	3.46	9.4
Cleveland	133	116	5.84	3.21	5.7
Cincinnati	113	102	6.11	3.14	6.8
Portland	115	108	6.66	3.21	7.8
Philadelphia	117	110	6.18	3.39	8.2
Pittsburgh	112	103	5.12	3.23	6.9
Dallas	115	103	7.93	—	4.5
Houston	123	102	8.09	3.21	5.6
Seattle	124	108	6.88	3.23	8.4
Milwaukee	131	112	6.00	—	4.7
United States	—	—	6.67	—	7.8
SMSAs total	114	107	6.82	—	—

Sources: Columns 1-3: U.S. Department of Commerce, *Survey of Current Business*, vol. 54, No. 5 (1974), Part II; column 4: Economic Statistics Bureau, *Handbook of Basic Economic Statistics*, vol. 30, No. 10, 1976; column 5: column (3)-column (4); column 6: U.S. Department of Labor, Bureau of Labor Statistics, *Employment and Earnings*; the rates are for the month of September.

Table 13-5
Changes in Manufacturing and Total Employment in Thirty-two Large Cities, 1967-76 (%)

City	Manufacturing	Total
Phoenix	20.2	68.2
Anaheim	23.6	70.1
Los Angeles	−8.6	13.9
San Diego	22.1	51.6
San Francisco	−8.5	12.6
San Jose	28.4	44.9
Denver	26.1	48.7
Washington, D.C.	12.1	33.2
Miami	34.3	47.2
Tampa	14.5	60.1
Atlanta	7.7	45.4
Chicago	−4.2	12.6
Indianapolis	−7.6	13.0
New Orleans	−14.7	17.5
Baltimore	−19.2	15.4
Boston	−14.8	2.1
Detroit	5.1	18.4
Minneapolis	3.0	26.3
Kansas City	−11.9	13.8
St. Louis	−15.3	2.7
Newark	−8.8	9.8
Buffalo	−17.6	0.6
New York-NE New Jersey	−27.4	−3.9
New York City	−40.1	−14.5
Cincinnati	−3.1	15.0
Cleveland	−11.6	6.9
Portland	16.5	31.7
Philadelphia	−21.1	4.6
Pittsburgh	−13.4	4.2
Dallas	73.8	100.1
Houston	37.5	61.5
Seattle	−30.5	9.2
Milwaukee	−2.0	12.1
United States	−1.2	20.0

Source: U.S. Department of Labor, Bureau of Labor Statistics, *Employment and Earnings*.

cities (Buffalo, Boston, St. Louis, Pittsburgh, Philadelphia, Cleveland, Seattle, and Newark) growing by less than 10 percent. The geographical concentration of these cities, with the exception of Seattle where the overall job market suffered as a result of the catastrophic decline in employment at Boeing, is consistent with the regional stagnation thesis. Conversely, all the cities experiencing an employment increase in excess of 40 percent were located either in the South—Dallas, Houston, Tampa, Miami, Atlanta—or the West—Anaheim, Phoenix, San Diego, Denver, San Jose.

These regional generalizations may be carried over to an analysis of manufacturing employment. The greatest declines occurred in New York City, Seattle (the exception, again, due to the collapse of aircraft production), Philadelphia, Baltimore, Buffalo, and St. Louis, while the cities with the largest increases in manufacturing jobs were Dallas, Houston, Miami, Denver, San Jose, Anaheim, San Diego, and Phoenix. Even apart from Seattle, the regional dichotomy does not apply universally, however. Los Angeles and San Francisco both experienced a modest growth in total employment and had significant manufacturing job losses. Washington, D.C., Minneapolis, and Detroit are examples of cities outside the favored South and West which performed better than the national average in manufacturing and, except Detroit, in total employment.

The most general inference from the data assembled in Table 13-5 is that manufacturing, the prototypical basic industry, is no longer the pacemaker in metropolitan employment growth. There is no case where manufacturing jobs increased at a faster rate than total jobs, and no case where manufacturing jobs declined less than total jobs. Tampa is the striking example of a city where a rapid growth in total jobs has been associated with a modest expansion in manufacturing. In general, the gap between manufacturing and overall employment growth widened the faster the rate of overall employment growth.

Nationwide Prospects for Basic Industries

To the extent that the future of the large metropolises is dependent upon what happens to their basic industries, it is clear that there are severe constraints on the opportunities open to the individual city. First, interurban competition is very tough, not only among the large metropolitan areas but also because of the improved competitiveness of smaller cities, especially for manufacturing industry. Second, and more important, the performance of the national economy sets limits on the achievements of the individual metropolis. Changes in the sectoral composition of output at the national level alter the set of opportunities facing particular subareas. For example, increasing international competition in basic manufacturing industries (e.g., steel, textiles, transportation equipment) impacts adversely on mature industrial nations, such as the United States, and on their industrial cities. Similarly, the growth in emphasis of energy resources on the one hand dampens growth via its balance-of-payments effects and on the other increases the development potential of isolated, underdeveloped towns in regions with abundant energy resources. There is no deus ex machina kit to save the ailing city. If the city is to be saved by patching up its economic structure or by injecting new industries, an examination of national sectoral trends should reveal what scope, if any, exists.

Table 13-6 displays sectoral changes in employment at the national level between 1967 and 1976. Over this period, the national growth in jobs has been very acceptable, but manufacturing has not shared in this expansion. Instead, jobs in the manufacturing sector (now smaller than one-quarter of the work force) have declined, at much the same rate in durables as in nondurables. Although the decline was small, it does not augur well for the future. Of course, as Table 13-6 shows, some industries expanded while others declined. But the evidence that the large cities have a comparative advantage in those industries with an expanding labor force such as instruments, furniture, machinery, and petroleum and coal products is inconclusive. Studies by several authors have found evidence of urbanization economies in manufacturing industries such as petroleum products, food, electrical machinery, transportation equipment, timber products, and apparel.[3] However, what is interesting is that there are many industries that have very small urbanization economies indexes, so that their location is insensitive to urban size. These include textiles, rubber and plastics products, chemicals, scientific instruments, and leather products. These two-digit results can be disaggregated via a three-digit analysis. The results confirm that the locational pull of large cities for many manufacturing industries is weak. Of course, this crude generalization really needs to be made more specific via a dynamic analysis. Two questions worth testing are: Are the nonagglomeration economy industries fast-growing or stagnant? Is the force of urbanization economies for agglomeration-economy industries diminishing over time?

This bleak diagnosis is somewhat relieved if basic industries are defined more broadly to include the nonresidentiary service sectors. Several sectors provided at least a third more jobs in 1976 than in 1967, such as medical services, hotels, state and local government, and FIRE. These sectors serve regional or national markets as well as local markets, and in many of them, such as medical services, insurance and finance, and hotels, the large metropolises are very well represented. However, it may be unwise to extrapolate past performance into the future. It is dubious whether medical services can expand over the next few years as rapidly as in the past, the growth of state government has been checked (the most optimistic description of the next phase is one of consolidation), and the FIRE sector is just beginning to be revolutionized by

Table 13-6
U.S. Employment by Industry, October 1976 and Change, 1967-76

	1976 (thousands)	1967-76 (percent)
Total employment	79,467	20.0
Mining	800	34.2
Construction	3,340	3.2
Transportation and public utilities	4,506	5.9
Trade	17,610	27.9
Wholesale	4,292	20.1
Retail	13,318	30.6
FIRE	4,359	33.4
Services	14,781	44.9
Hotels	1,031	45.8
Personal	814	−20.7
Medical	4,519	80.8
Education	1,283	18.8
Government	15,130	28.8
Federal	2,730	0.7
State and local	12,400	37.2
Manufacturing	18,941	−1.2
Durables	11,018	−1.1
Ordnance	155	−42.2
Lumber	613	3.7
Furniture	491	7.9
Stone, clay, glass	630	0.5
Primary metals	1,194	−5.8
Fabricated metals	1,387	4.4
Machinery	2,078	7.4
Electrical equipment	1,849	−2.4
Transportation equipment	1,645	−8.9
Instruments	511	12.6
Miscellaneous manufacturing	415	−2.4
Nondurables	7,923	−1.3
Food	1,706	−4.4
Tobacco	76	−7.3
Textiles	961	0.7
Clothing	1,273	−7.9
Paper	677	−1.0
Printing and publishing	1,087	2.1
Chemicals	1,032	3.2
Petroleum and coal products	202	5.2
Rubber and plastics	645	21.9
Leather	264	−24.8

Source: U.S. Department of Labor, Bureau of Labor Statistics, *Employment and Earnings*.

computer and data processing automation. Also, service employment growth rates probably will be lower in the future than in the recent past. Combining this belief with the assumption that decentralization trends will continue, the prospects of reviving the older metropolises of the Northeast and the Midwest via job creation seem dim.

The Incubator and Filtering Hypothesis

Among the many stimulating ideas thrown out by Wilbur Thompson, the incubator and filtering hypothesis is one of the most interesting.[4] The economic strength of the large metropolis is based on its capacity to innovate and to nurture new firms in new industries. The agglomeration economies of urban scale provide the right climate and environment for incubation to take place. Moreover, this process not only continuously regenerates the economy of the large city, it is also a source of growth for the national economy because the newer industries subsequently filter down into smaller cities and into other regions. Thus, the national metropolises play a crucial systemic role in the development of the economy as a whole.

It is probably easy to exaggerate the force of this argument. To the extent that the major research and development laboratories and the great universities tend to be located there, the large cities are inevitably the fount of much innovative activity. But the total volume of such activity is constrained by national parameters that change over time for complex reasons that are difficult to unravel. It is possible that American society is less inventive than in the past; in any event, not all inventive activity results in more industrial output, while the conditions for successful industrial development embrace a much broader set of variables than innovation, and indeed innovation may not even be one of the preconditions. Even where innovative activity leads to industrial production, the results in terms of output, employment, and income may be almost negligible relative to the total volume of metropolitan activity. Relying on casual empiricism, the spurts in the growth of the major metropolitan economies in the United States have relied much more on increased demand for the products of their basic industries than on the proliferation of new industries. Of course, these basic industries benefit from innovation which transforms their products and occasionally reduces their relative prices; but this is a different point from the incubator hypothesis.

Another serious problem with the hypothesis is that it is very difficult to test. Evidence such as the deceleration of employment growth in large cities is hardly support for the weakening of the incubator function because there are numerous alternative explanations. To identify and trace the emergence of new industries would require a degree of industrial disaggregation far finer than the four-digit level. If it could be assumed that each firm embodied a slightly different technology, a comparison of the numbers of entry firms and exit firms might shed some light on the problem. However, since incubator firms would in most cases be small, at least initially, while larger firms are the most likely to decentralize because they rely less on core agglomeration economies, the discovery of a net increase in firms is insufficient support for the incubator thesis; nor would a decrease be adequate basis for rejecting it.

The filtering component of the hypothesis also raises nagging problems. What exactly it means relies on inference since its implications have never been precisely spelled out. Most descriptions draw upon the concept of hierarchical diffusion in which the industries filter down from the largest cities to smaller urban areas. This might take place either by relocation or by the creation of new branch plants in the smaller cities. The former case would weaken the metropolis of the origin, while the latter might even strengthen it because of the expansion of ancillary headquarter functions. However, the concept of hierarchical filtering has recently been challenged by Pred.[5] If information linkages are becoming relatively more important than physical input-output linkages, it may be necessary to revise the orthodox argument that emphasizes the intimate connection between agglomeration economies and urban scale. As the core of basic industries changes from manufacturing toward nonlocal services, this revision becomes plausible. A major corporate headquarters controlling jobs in many cities, and even in foreign countries, may no longer need to locate in a New York or a Chicago. An example is Boise, Idaho, which is the home of four major corporations employing more than 70,000 workers. Unless the headquarters locate in the major metropolises, it is possible that filtering might bypass the large cities altogether.

Decentralization and Dispersion

The decentralization of economic activities out of their central cities has undoubtedly been a factor undermining the economic base of the large metropolitan areas. This decentralization has been associated with the suburbanization of population, though in a simultaneous fashion rather than via a simple cause-and-effect sequence. The projected rates of population growth for the million-plus metropolitan areas is less than 5 percent per decade for the 1970s, but this masks a 9.6 percent fall in the central cities and a 16 percent increase in the suburbs. Already only two out of five of the residents of these large metropolitan areas continue to live in the central cities. However, the demographic instability of the large cities of the East and the Midwest is not due to suburbanization, but metropolitanwide stagnation (see Table 13-1). Several of them are now experiencing an absolute decline in population at the *metropolitan* not the central-city level. Moreover, though the generalization of a net decline in central-city jobs accompanied by substantial gains in the suburbs holds, it is important to note that as far as the traditional basic industry, the manufacturing sector, is concerned, employment in the large metropolitan areas is now falling in *both* the suburbs and the central cities. This is not so much a comment on the economic vulnerability of the large cities as a reflection of the fact that the manufacturing sector has ceased to be a source of net employment growth in the United States as a whole, even though locational shifts may permit manufacturing jobs to expand in selected areas, including a few of the larger cities of the South and the Southwest.

The upshot of this last critical point is that an evaluation of the comparative advantages of decentralized versus core sites for manufacturing activities is not going to shed much light on the future prospects of the large cities. Much more relevant is the determinant of the rate of decentralization for basic service sectors such as corporate headquarters, FIRE establishments, medical and educational facilities, and even nonmunicipal government agencies. Thus, the decentralizing forces for manufacturing such as the costs of loading and unloading trucks at core sites,[6] the role of trucking costs in reducing the input price gradient relative to the land price gradient, as discussed in Chapter 8 and elsewhere,[7] and the shifts in manufacturing technology in favor of single-story production lines,[8] are less important than the factors increasing the relative attractiveness of the suburbs for offices and other service activities. This has not been analyzed in as much detail as manufacturing. However, the critical forces include a continued differential in net and gross (i.e., including utility charges and local taxes) rentals between the CBD and suburban subcenters; the possibility that agglomeration economies are really economies of concentration rather than of centralization; and the pull of suburban labor pools.

The decentralization of service industries should not be exaggerated. There are many examples where core locations have been reinforced by a cluster of high-level service activities, such as the construction of new headquarter banks. Even if the relative growth rates favor the suburbs, the absolute increase in the number of jobs in many service industries remains higher in the central city. Also, the big cities have suffered because job growth failed to keep pace with the increase in the value of service output. The automation of routine business services, the substitution of communication for transportation, the shift in emphasis from indoor to outdoor recreation, and the internalization of external economies (such as business services) in large-scale manufacturing plants not infrequently located in smaller cities have all dampened the growth in service jobs that had been expected to replace the lost jobs in manufacturing; for further comment see Chapter 7.

Nevertheless, trends in manufacturing location have weakened the big-city economies. Even apart from the national decline in manufacturing employment, the large metropolitan areas in the traditional manufacturing belt have been losing jobs very rapidly (see Table 13-5) because of competitive weaknesses relative to other locations. In this case, however, the key struggle has not been between the central cities and the suburbs but between the large metropolitan areas, long specializing in manufacturing, and newer manufacturing cities, both large and small, in other regions. Thus, in the case of manufacturing industries the "problem" for the large cities is interregional dispersion not intraregional decentralization.[b] In particular, the improved competitive power of the South has hurt the traditional manufacturing metropolises of the Northeast and Midwest. This has been due to a myriad of influences: the development of interregional truck transportation and its relatively low costs have opened up many small Southern towns without rail lines to manufacturing plants; wages remain much lower, and unionization is far from complete; educational and skill levels have been rising; house prices and living costs are low; the spread of air-conditioning has increased the attractiveness of the South as a year-round region; and Southern labor pools are easily expandable via return migration from the North. Two notable characteristics of the Southern renaissance are the increasing importance of chemicals, machinery, metals, paper, and printing relative to the traditional industries of textiles and clothing and the spatial concentration of the new manufacturing plants in areas in the white South, such as northern Mississippi, the hill country, and northwest Arkansas.

The Case of New York

The experience of New York City with basic industries, both manufacturing and nonlocal office establishments, presents a dilemma for interpretation. One point of view is to treat it as a unique case with no inferences for the future of other large metropolitan areas. The other is to hold up New York as a harbinger and a warning, characterized by trends that will be replicated in many other large cities of the country, especially those in the East and Midwest. It is not easy to decide between these alternatives. In many respects, New York City is singular. The tradition of heavy involvement in small-scale "external economy" industries and its dominance as a corporation headquarters city are far ahead of any other metropolitan area. Its size alone places New York in a category of its own, at least in North America. On the other hand, some of its recent experiences have been shared with other large Northeastern cities, such as Boston, Buffalo, Newark, Philadelphia, and Pittsburgh. These cities led the way from manufacturing to government and private white-collar industries. All of them, with the possible exception of a revitalized Boston, now suffer from a weak competitive position in the sense that they failed to attract a proportionate share of new activities. In the early 1970s manufacturing job losses were substantial in all cases, while the growth of service jobs stagnated.[9] Given this perspective, it

---

[b]A qualification is that about 30 percent of the smaller SMSAs (less than 350,000 population) of the Northeast and Midwest have grown faster than the national average rate since 1970.

might be reasonable to describe the problems of New York as part of a wider regional problem.

In any event, the severity of New York's problems, from the economic not to mention the fiscal point of view, is beyond dispute. The stable population of the two decades 1950-70 dived abruptly after 1970, losing 2.3 percent between 1970 and 1973 at a time when the U.S. population as a whole rose by 3.3 percent. Suburbanization was the dominant factor since the regional population has grown substantially over the last quarter-century; but New York City's share fell from more than 60 to less than 50 percent. Suburbanization was the mirror image of the decentralization of economic activity. Between 1969 and 1974 New York City lost an average of 43,000 manufacturing jobs a year, including a cataclysmic decline in its traditional apparel industry, and 30,000 jobs a year in the service industries. Part of the slack was taken up by growth in state and local government employment—the federal job sector actually declined in New York City—but at a much slower rate than in the 1960s.

The reasons for the fall in employment are complex and need a deeper examination than is possible here. However, some of the strands of an explanation are evident. New York has suffered from a shift in the center of national power to Washington, D.C., an obvious reflection of the growth of the federal sector, but one which has rubbed off in the attraction of national and regional offices and service industries. The decline in manufacturing and expansion of service activities predicted by Hoover and Vernon has occurred, of course, but the automation of information and routine office functions has led to such an increase in labor productivity that the compensating growth in service output was not matched by an equivalent increase in jobs. The large metropolis' key role as an incubator of new industries has not been performed recently by New York City, perhaps because new firms are repelled by high costs, such as the very high cost of living and much larger utility bills. The growth of municipal employment has contributed to higher taxes and fiscal instability, and this has weakened New York's competitive pull for mobile industry.

The dramatic decline in manufacturing jobs, by more than 38 percent in the period 1953-73, was not totally unexpected. Core cities have long lost their attraction for manufacturing for a variety of reasons, including changes in production technology toward greater land intensity and the difficulties of finding workers with the right skills. The remedy is supposed to be the substitution of activities more suited to central locations. In New York City's case, headquarters' offices in Manhattan was thought to be the replacement basic industry; but the recent performance of this sector has been very disturbing. Between 1968 and 1974, 40 of *Fortune* magazine's "500" leading corporation headquarters left New York City, reducing its total to 98. About 70 percent of the relocating companies went to the suburbs of the region (especially Connecticut and New Jersey) rather than to other cities. The impact was serious, since the headquarters' offices provide about 45 percent of central business district employment. An estimate relating to the 1968-72 period suggested that these relocations vacated 8 million square feet of office space and resulted in a loss of about 10,000 jobs per year and a fall of tax revenues of about $35 million per year.[10]

The reasons for the relocation are not hard to find. Labor supply was important since the scarcity of qualified clerical workers in Manhattan contrasted with the growing labor pools of the suburbs. "Push" factors such as the scarcity and cost of housing, high corporate and personal taxes, schooling, crime, and living costs are relevant, but their relative weight is difficult to ascertain. Perhaps, as suggested by Macrae in Chapter 7, a more significant explanation is that agglomeration economies are becoming "footloose." The "face-to-face" contacts that provided the rationale for spatial clustering of high-level services are being dissipated by advanced communications systems while the need for outside contacts has been reduced by the internalization of experts and technical skills within large corporations. This internalization makes the corporation highly mobile. Another problem is the risk of cumulative out-migration as additional firms learn of the smooth adjustment of the relocatees to their new areas.

Population Stagnation with Income Growth

Urban growth is traditionally measured in terms of population increase. This is a very poor measure of growth, based on old-style mercantilism. We do not judge the wealth of a country by the size of its population, and we should not use this criterion in a metropolitan context. Indeed, recent experience in the United States suggests that high rates of in-migration into the large cities have dampened per capita income growth. This fact is appreciated very well by the "no-growth" movement which seeks not to stop growth but merely to check net immigration.[11] What the no-growth movement desires is a change in the form of growth from *extensive* growth (a larger population) to *intensive* growth (higher per capita incomes and living standards for existing residents).

The problem, of course, is that while population data are relatively copious, there is no readily available and urban equivalent to national income and product accounts which makes comparisons across regions possible. As a result, urban growth discussions have become bogged down in debates about population size or about jobs. Looked at in this way, the evidence on the larger cities, in the Northeast and Midwest at least, has been interpreted very pessimistically. Very slow population growth, stagnation, or even decline and quite dramatic job losses in manufacturing have been standard symptoms. However, as shown in columns 3 and 5 of Table 13-4, even the most "stagnant" of the cities (e.g., Buffalo, New York, and Pittsburgh) have enjoyed a growth in total personal income of more than 5 percent per annum, minus about 3 percent to correct for inflation. Although the gap between them and the fast growers (Anaheim, Phoenix, Tampa, and Miami) remains wide, the generalization of "urban stagnation" requires some qualification. Of course, a major reason why incomes continue to rise in spite of employment, and occasionally population, losses is that in larger, older cities a substantial proportion of income is derived not from employment but from property, profits, interest and dividends, and from transfer payments.

Thus, property income and transfer payments play a major role in maintaining income levels in the large Eastern cities that have suffered most from the out-migration of industry. As shown in Table 13-7, the six major Northeastern cities all have property income plus transfer payment shares in excess of the U.S. average of 25 percent. Conversely, some of the newer rapidly growing cities have low shares (e.g., Atlanta, Dallas, Houston, San Jose), while some thrive on property income (e.g., Tampa, Miami, San Diego).

The amenity-rich retirement metropolises are obviously less dependent on wage income, though their dominant functions require a large service industry. Apart from these exceptions, however, both property income and transfer payments tend to result in some convergence in the economic performance of the large cities. In some cases this is due to a heavy reliance on property income (e.g., New York, Newark, Boston, Cincinnati, Cleveland); in others (e.g., Buffalo, Pittsburgh) transfer payments are exceptionally high. Since nonlocal property income is relatively immune from fluctuations in the level of activity in a metropolitan area's industries, while transfer payments tend to move inversely with local activity, those cities with high property income plus transfer payments shares may be able to remain fairly stable, even in the face of local recessions and the relocation of their industries.

Consequences of Metropolitan Decline

As we have seen, many of the large metropolitan areas, especially those in the Northeast and the Midwest, are in economic trouble. Recent trends and future prospects in their basic industries have much to do with their problems. Yet, whether this matters or not is a serious question. From one point of view, the diffusion of economic activities out of the high-income metro areas into the intermetropolitan periphery and their dispersion into the previously underdeveloped regions of the South and the Southwest may be regarded as a convergence process, with market forces performing a spatial equity function that would be the envy of regional policymakers in other countries. On the other hand, the decline of great cities might be treated, especially if associated with physical symptoms such as inner-city decay, blighted industrial areas, and abandoned neighborhoods, almost as synonymous with the decline of civilization itself.

Table 13-7
Shares of Property Income and Transfer Payments in Total Personal Income, 1972 (%)

SMSA	Property Income	Transfer Payments	Transfers plus Property Income
Boston	15.5	11.4	26.9
Buffalo	13.1	12.3	25.4
New York	16.7	11.1	27.8
Newark	16.0	9.3	25.3
Philadelphia	13.5	11.5	25.0
Pittsburgh	14.3	12.2	26.5
Baltimore	11.4	10.3	21.7
Washington, D.C.	11.2	11.2	22.4
Detroit	11.2	8.7	19.9
Cincinnati	14.9	9.6	24.5
Cleveland	14.8	9.2	24.0
Indianapolis	11.9	8.3	20.2
Chicago	14.1	8.7	22.8
Milwaukee	14.3	9.2	23.5
Minneapolis	13.8	8.7	22.5
Kansas City	11.9	8.8	20.7
St. Louis	14.3	9.7	24.0
Atlanta	11.9	7.2	19.1
Miami	17.1	10.1	27.2
Tampa	18.7	17.0	35.7
New Orleans	14.1	10.3	24.4
Dallas	14.7	7.8	22.5
Houston	13.8	6.8	20.6
Phoenix	13.4	9.8	23.2
Denver	13.3	8.1	21.4
Seattle	14.5	11.1	25.6
Portland	14.0	10.4	24.4
Anaheim	14.4	10.1	24.5
Los Angeles	13.5	11.1	24.6
San Diego	15.3	13.9	29.2
San Francisco	15.4	11.2	26.6
San Jose	11.5	10.3	21.8
SMSAs	13.8	10.4	24.2
United States	13.7	11.0	24.7

Source: U.S. Department of Commerce, Survey of Current Business, vol. 54, No. 5 (1974), Part II.

Hyperbole this may be., but it is implicit in many of the arguments used to justify the revitalization of central cities.

It is not uncommon for people to think of a city as having a life of its own, to speak of it as if it lived and breathed. Such personification, even deification, is tinged too much with romanticism and mysticism; a more realistic view of a city is as a physical, economic, and social form of organization adopted by individuals and groups to satisfy their preferences and to improve their welfare. This implies that the answer to the question, Does it matter?, depends not on population or even employment decline, not on industrial growth rates, and not on indicators of physical decay, but on the impact of these changes on individual welfare and the quality of life.

The influence of a heavy dose of traditional basic industries on these criteria is ambiguous. Many manufacturing industries, especially if centrally located, create a serious air pollution problem at least in respect to particulates; on the other hand, they are frequently a source of high incomes (e.g., Detroit), while the impact on unemployment rates is unclear, depending on industry mix and the phase of the cycle. Thus, quality-of-life effects and economic welfare impacts are a mix of positive and negative influences, the net consequences of which are difficult to evaluate, even if the individual impacts are quantified empirically.

As indicated in Table 13-4, SMSAs have higher per capita incomes than the national average, though their relative superiority fell from a 14 percent point difference in 1950 to 7 points in 1972. This deterioration is common over all the big cities with very few exceptions—Phoenix, Miami, Tampa, Atlanta, and (a geographical surprise) Boston. In some cases, the rate of decline has been very heavy: Anaheim, Indianapolis, Buffalo, Houston, and Seattle. These examples suggest a diversity of reasons rather than faltering basic industry. For instance, high net in-migration rates remain a leading dampening factor on per capita income growth. Moreover, cities that have undergone vigorous growth in the past for reasons unconnected with manufacturing growth (but explicable in terms of "basic" industrial growth in the widest sense) also shared in the convergence toward the national average, for example, San Francisco and Washington, D.C. Furthermore, even those cities with a manufacturing bias and a miserable growth record in terms of population, output, and employment frequently remain well above average in per capita income terms, even in cases of substantial relative decline since 1950 (e.g., Detroit, Newark, Chicago, Milwaukee). Finally, the revival of Boston casts suspicion on the principle of historical, and a fortiori geographical, determinism.

Column 3 of Table 13-4 displays growth rates in total personal income for the large cities since 1950. The results are hardly surprising. Almost one-half of the cities grew more slowly than the national average of 6.7 percent a year, and most of the victims are located in the Northeast and the Midwest. Conversely, all the cities growing at a rate faster than 8 percent per annum are to be found in the South or the West, except for the "border" town of Washington, D.C. Significantly, the two fastest growers—Anaheim and San Jose—were newer manufacturing cities. These findings remain substantially intact when account is taken of differential rates of increase in prices among cities shown in columns 4 and 5 of the table.

Population and Employment Change and the Quality of Life

It is well known that interarea disparities in welfare indicators may differ widely from those in per capita income.[12] The past decade or so has witnessed a rise and then a fall in attempts to develop a "social indicators" approach to welfare measurement, but the value of this method is limited by the intrusion of subjective factors in the evaluation of quality of life and in the inability to devise a satisfactory weighting system. The data of Table 13-8 reflect a more modest objective, since a narrower range of indicators is represented and there is no attempt to aggregate the results into a single overall index.

The important observations to be drawn from Table 13-8 are that no individual city ranks high on all indicators and, even more critical in this context, that the manufacturing cities fare much the same as the service cities. Although many of the manufacturing cities are polluted, they frequently have compensating assets. Some have high incomes and low poverty rates (e.g., Detroit), others have cheap housing and transportation (e.g., Pittsburgh, Detroit), yet others have low crime rates (Milwaukee, Cincinnati, Buffalo, and Pittsburgh), and most of them have an educated citizenry. On critical indicators such as unemployment, manufacturing cities may stand well (Chicago) or badly (Detroit), but the West Coast cities figure among the worst cases.[c] The San Francisco rate has little to do with basic industry, while the performance of Los Angeles might be as much due to the effects of past in-migration as to the state of the aerospace and defense industries. Moreover, even the newer cities such as Houston and Dallas display a mixed performance, though Dallas would rank uniformly high were it not for poverty and infant mortality. It is wrong to equate urban senescence with poor life quality. In fact, it is possible to push the argument a little further and to suggest that there are even welfare benefits associated with metropolitan stagnation. The nongrowing city offers a high degree of stability, relief from upward pressure on house prices, and sometimes low crime rates and strong community ties.[13]

A likely consequence of the deceleration, and occasionally decline, in employment and population growth in large cities is deterioration in their fiscal position, as indicated in Chapter 12. Again, the New York City experience springs to mind, and this has been analyzed in some detail.[14] An important finding is that the loss of manufacturing jobs has a smaller impact on the

---
[c]See further discussion below and Table 13-4, column 6.

Table 13-8
Economic and Social Indicators in Eighteen Large Cities, 1969 or 1970

	Population (million)	% of Population in Central City	Unemployment Rate (%)	$ of Households with < $3000	Real Income per Capita ($)	Cost of Housing ($)	Cost of Transportation ($)
New York	11.529	68.3	4.4 (9)	12 (9=)	4,513 (4)	2,888 (17)	806 (1)
Los Angeles	7.032	40.1	7.2 (18)	15 (14=)	4,635 (3)	2,419 (10)	884 (7)
Chicago	6.979	48.2	3.6 (2)	10 (5=)	4,498 (5)	2,680 (13)	919 (13)
Philadelphia	4.818	40.5	4.3 (7=)	12 (9=)	3,949 (14)	2,351 (9)	834 (2)
Detroit	4.200	36.0	7.0 (17)	9 (3)	4,724 (1)	2,258 (5)	889 (8)
San Francisco	3.100	34.6	6.7 (16)	16 (17=)	4,639 (2)	2,696 (14)	925 (16)
Washington	2.861	26.4	3.2 (1)	9 (2)	4,232 (8)	2,463 (11)	898 (10)
Boston	2.754	23.3	3.9 (4)	8 (1)	3,822 (17)	2,976 (18)	924 (15)
Pittsburgh	2.401	21.7	5.2 (14=)	13 (12=)	3,966 (13)	2,144 (3)	864 (3)
St. Louis	2.363	26.3	4.6 (10)	14 (13)	3,993 (12)	2,344 (8)	922 (14)
Baltimore	2.071	43.7	4.0 (5=)	13 (12=)	3,935 (16)	2,163 (4)	892 (9)
Cleveland	2.064	36.4	4.7 (11=)	11 (7)	4,224 (9)	2,742 (15)	882 (6)
Houston	1.985	62.1	4.0 (5=)	16 (17=)	4,037 (11)	1,980 (1)	928 (17)
Minneapolis	1.814	24.0	5.2 (14=)	10 (4)	4,375 (6)	2,326 (6)	903 (11)
Dallas	1.556	54.3	3.8 (3)	15 (14=)	4,357 (7)	2,076 (2)	878 (4=)
Milwaukee	1.404	51.1	4.7 (11=)	10 (5=)	3,939 (15)	2,757 (16)	878 (4=)
Cincinnati	1.385	32.7	4.3 (7=)	15 (14=)	4,046 (10)	2,327 (7)	906 (12)
Buffalo	1.349	34.3	4.7 (11=)	12 (8)	3,628 (18)	2,591 (12)	968 (18)
Average			4.7	12	4,195	2,455	894

	Air Pollution (% of EPA Standard)			Infant Mortality (per 1000)		Estimated Central City Addition Rate (persons/10,000)	Robbery Rate per 10⁵		Median School Years	
	Particulates	SO₂	NO₂							
New York	140 (10)	266 (18)	144 (8)	21.6	(9)	191	665	(18)	12.2	(9=)
Los Angeles	124 (8)	67 (10)	340 (18)	18.9	(2=)	35	307	(11)	12.5	(3=)
Chicago	180 (11)	213 (17)	100 (5)	24.4	(18)	31	363	(14)	12.3	(7=)
Philadelphia	170 (15)	83 (13)	44 (2)	23.4	(17)	—	173	(6)	12.1	(13=)
Detroit	154 (14)	63 (9)	220 (16)	22.2	(12)	—	649	(7)	12.1	(13=)
San Francisco	72 (1)	17 (4)	176 (10)	18.9	(2=)	59	348	(13)	12.6	(2)
Washington	102 (3=)	33 (7=)	74 (3)	19.8	(5)	61	504	(15)	12.7	(1)
Boston	114 (5=)	87 (14=)	94 (4)	20.2	(6)	44	136	(3)	12.4	(6)
Pittsburgh	192 (17)	90 (16)	206 (15)	22.1	(11)	—	145	(5)	12.1	(13=)
St. Louis	248 (18)	87 (14)	240 (17)	21.8	(10)	32	280	(9)	11.8	(17)
Baltimore	146 (11=)	70 (11)	182 (11=)	23.0	(15)	—	564	(16)	11.3	(18)
Cleveland	150 (13)	80 (12)	188 (13)	21.3	(8)	—	288	(10)	12.2	(9=)
Houston	114 (5=)	13 (2=)	192 (14)	23.1	(16)	—	335	(12)	12.2	(9=)
Minneapolis	94 (2)	33 (7=)	138 (7)	18.6	(1)	—	179	(7)	12.5	(3=)
Dallas	102 (3=)	10 (1)	136 (6)	22.8	(14)	—	206	(8)	12.5	(3=)
Milwaukee	146 (11=)	20 (5)	164 (9)	19.2	(4)	—	53	(1)	12.3	(7=)
Cincinnati	138 (9)	30 (6)	182 (11)	20.3	(7)	—	120	(2)	12.1	(13=)
Buffalo	114 (5=)	13 (2=)	50 (1)	22.3	(13)	—	145	(4)	12.2	(9=)
Average	138	70	160	21.3			303		12.2	

Source: M.J. Flax, *A Study in Comparative Urban Indicators: Conditions in 18 Large Metropolitan Areas*, Washington, D.C.: Urban Institute, 1972.

Note: Ranks in parentheses with "best" ranked as 1 and "worst" as 18; equal sign indicates two or more cities tied in rank.

property tax base than the loss of other types of jobs. The explanation is that other jobs, such as office jobs, require more and dearer floor space per worker. Thus, in New York City the flight of corporate headquarters is a more worrying trend than the decline or relocation of manufacturing firms.

Rapidly growing cities, of course, are not without fiscal problems since per capita service outlays increase as their populations expand via in-migration. However, since migrants still tend to be younger and more educated and earn higher lifetime incomes than on-movers, they create more revenue to help pay for their service demands.

The large declining cities have the more serious economic problems, and face the unpalatable choice of cutting expenditures (the preferred course) or raising taxes. Neither strategy will increase the stagnating metropolis' power to retain people and industry. However, their prospects look a little rosier than they did a few years ago. Expenditures have been trimmed, municipal employment growth has been stabilized, and the federal and state governments have stepped in to offer substantial and growing financial aid.

Another reason making it difficult to be sanguine about the consequences of job losses in the large cities is the metropolitan unemployment problem, as indicated in Table 13-4. If allowance is made not only for the higher incidence of "official" unemployment but also for the out of work not captured in the unemployment statistics, the actual rates in the ghetto and inner-city areas will typically be two to three times the average city rate, and even higher among ghetto youth. Policymakers frequently link the out-migration of industry and central-city unemployment closely together, and the pressures for policy measures to retain industry and to woo it back are closely tied to the unemployment objective.

I do not wish to challenge this conventional wisdom, but there are some important qualifications to the general picture. The higher unemployment rates are not found in the older Eastern cities but in the West (San Diego and San Francisco) and in Florida (Miami and Tampa). Conversely, most of the older cities have unemployment rates *below* the national average (the exceptions are New York, Detroit, Buffalo, Philadelphia, and Newark). Second, the implications of the data given in Tables 13-1 and 13-2 are that the million-plus cities are performing rather better in terms of employment than population. This tends to alleviate the problem of unemployment, though its darker side is the possibility of an adverse impact on residential property taxes, especially for those who subscribe to the hypothesis that suburbanite commuters "exploit" the central city.

Third, we are not going to develop effective spatial policies unless we become more realistic about unemployment objectives. It should now be obvious to all that the American economy in its present form is incapable of generating full employment, on any acceptable definition of the term. If Americans wished to transform the social system or if we resorted to grotesquely wasteful public works policies, this conclusion might be different. Assuming such changes are neither desired nor desirable, unemployment rates are going to remain rather high nationwide and, inevitably, will be much higher in areas where average skills, educational levels, and work habits are poor. In view of the powerful economic forces in favor of diffusion and decentralization out of the large metropolises discussed above, it is impractical to expect that policy instruments that are feasible in the U.S. institutional environment are going to reverse these trends; Chapter 10 presents some of the reasons for the high resistance to change of local institutions. Entry-exit studies show that even when firms relocate in central cities they tend to avoid sites in or near ghetto neighborhoods.[15] I do not wish to imply that urban policymakers should throw up their hands in despair. Employment subsidies to central-city firms that are willing to increase their proportion of ghetto workers and upgrade the labor force of the inner city to meet the needs of the service and government jobs that have continued to grow at centralized locations are two of many possible strategies. But it would be foolish to expect more than marginal achievements. In any event, the evidence does not point to a close link between inner-city unemployment rates and the demise of the metropolises' traditional basic industries.

Since 1970, the populations of the large metropolitan areas have grown much more slowly than in the previous decades. In some cases, mainly in the Northeast, the large cities have experienced a sharp decline. Although their employment performance has been a little more respectable, there has been a striking difference between the cities of the Northeast and Midwest and those of the South and West. This distinction is even sharper in manufacturing than in total employment, with the contrast between massive manufacturing job losses in New York, Baltimore, Buffalo, St. Louis, Boston, and other cities and rapid gains in Dallas, Houston, Miami, Denver, San Jose, Anaheim, San Diego, and Phoenix. The interregional differentials override other influences such as the dependence of a metropolitan area on manufacturing; manufacturing cities figure among the gainers as well as the losers. However, like many generalizations, the interregional contrast has its exceptions, such as Seattle, at least for a time, the mediocre performance of San Francisco and Los Angeles in the West, and the buoyancy of Washington, D.C., in the East.

Three major sets of forces explain the poor basic employment experience of the older large cities. The first is national economy constraints; employment in manufacturing has been declining nationally, with very few bright spots. Output projections over the next decade suggest substantial increases in production for some sectors, but these will be insufficient to outweigh their productivity gains or to compensate for stagnation in other industries so that employment will continue to fall. The implications of these trends for large metropolitan areas will be exacerbated by the failure of the older cities to perform an "incubator" function for new industries.

Second, the older manufacturing giants are losing out in the scramble for manufacturing jobs to both large and small cities in the more rapidly growing regions of the South and West. The interregional dispersion of manufacturing is now much more important than its decentralization into the suburbs. The decentralization phenomenon is much more critical in the case of nonmanufacturing basic sectors such as corporate headquarters. The strength of this third force may be the "swing" factor in the performance of the large metropolises over the next decade. The New York City experience illustrates what might happen in other cities. Chapter 7 points out growing competition from abroad.

The causes of these dispersion and decentralization processes are imperfectly understood, but the jobs are undoubtedly following population movements, stressing the importance of labor supply considerations and cost differentials with respect to sites, labor, utilities, and other aspects of production. General living costs are unfavorable in the big cities and agglomeration economies have become more "footloose"; in addition, the locational pull of amenities, including climate, has become very strong.

In spite of bleak prognosis, it is wrong to expect the big cities to come tumbling down. Nonlocal property income and transfer payments buffer the fall. Per capita incomes remain relatively high and unemployment rates are below the national average in many of the *older*, if not the newer, cities. The fiscal implications of metropolitan decline are probably more serious, though solutions are not beyond the imagination of man though perhaps beyond the pale of political feasibility. Moreover, metropolitan stagnation has surprising compensations in many instances—cheap housing and transportation, relief from pressure on education and social services, a stronger sense of community, and low crime rates. If the aim of metropolitan policymakers is to promote higher incomes for their citizens and to improve their quality of life, it is not clear that they should be too concerned about the size of the metropolitan population or even about the number of jobs.

For all these reasons, it is not clear that the diagnosis of current trends requires drastic medicine. The interregional dispersion process in particular is nicely contributing to the achievement of spatial equity objectives. One can readily understand why the mayors of some of the big cities are worried, but their problems are not necessarily those of society at large. In any event, the forces at work are probably too strong to be reversed, or even contained, by the type of policies that are feasible in the prevailing institutional environment and current climate of opinion. Perhaps, as Thompson implies, conditions in the large metropolitan areas have to get worse before they can get better. The cost differentials that presently handicap the big cities will converge as the new areas grow and expand. I remain optimistic; the site advantages of the big cities, the quality of their infrastructure, the adaptability and resilience of their populations and their contribution to civilization are too valuable to be thrown away. It is much too soon to accept Engels' prediction that "the great towns will perish."

Notes

1. R. Lamb, *Metropolitan Impacts on Rural America*, Chicago: University of Chicago, Department of Geography, RP 162, 1975.

2. W.R. Thompson, "Economic Processes and Employment Problems in Declining Metropolitan Areas," pp. 185-96, in G. Sternlieb and J.W. Hughes, eds., *Post-Industrial America*, New Brunswick, N.J.: Rutgers University, Center for Urban Policy Research, 1975.

3. G.A. Carlino, "Agglomeration of Manufacturing Activity in Metropolitan Areas: Theory and Measurement," Miami: Department of Economics, Florida International University, 1976; T. Kawashima, "Urban Agglomeration Economies in Manufacturing Industries," Papers of the Regional Science Association, vol. 34, 1975, pp. 157-75; and D. Shefer, "Localization Economies in SMSAs: A Production Function Approach," *Journal of Regional Science*, vol. 13, 1973, pp. 55-64.

4. W.R. Thompson, "Internal and External Factors in the Development of Urban Economies," in H.S. Perloff and L. Wingo, eds., *Issues in Urban Economics*, Baltimore: Johns Hopkins Press, 1968, pp. 43-80.

5. Alan Pred, *The Interurban Transmission Mechanism in Advanced Economics*, Laxenburg, Austria: International Institute for Applied Systems Analysis, 1976, Report RR-76-4.

6. E.M. Hoover and Raymond Vernon, *Anatomy of a Metropolis*, New York: Doubleday & Company, 1962.

7. A.M. Hamer, *Industrial Exodus from Central City*, Lexington, Mass.: Lexington Books, 1973; and L.N. Moses and H.F. Williamson, Jr., "The Location of Economic Activities in Cities," *American Economic Review*, vol. 57, 1967, pp. 211-21.

8. J.F. Kain, "The Distribution and Movement of Jobs and Industry," pp. 1-39, in J.Q. Wilson, ed., *The Metropolitan Enigma*, Cambridge, Mass.: Harvard University Press, 1968.

9. M.R. Greenberg and N.J. Valente, "Recent Economic Trends in Major Northeastern Metropolises," pp. 77-99, in G. Sternlieb and J.W. Hughes, *Post-Industrial America*.

10. W. Quante, *The Exodus of Corporate Headquarters from New York City*, New York: Praeger, 1976.

11. W. Alonso, "Urban Zero Population Growth," *Daedalus*, vol. 102, 1973, pp. 191-206.

12. O.J. Firestone, "Regional Economic and Social Disparity," in O.J. Firestone, ed., *Regional Economic Development*, Ottawa: University of Ottawa Press, 1974, pp. 205-67.

13. See E. Rust, *No Growth: Impacts on Metropolitan Areas*, Lexington, Mass.: Lexington Books, 1975.

14. R.W. Bahl, A.K. Campbell, and D. Greytak, *Taxes, Expenditures and the Economic Base: Case Study of New York City*, New York: Praeger, 1974.

15. K. McLennan and P. Seidenstat, *New Business and Urban Employment Opportunities*, Lexington, Mass.: Lexington Books, 1972; and R.J. Struyk and F.J. James, *Intrametropolitan Industrial Location*, Lexington, Mass.: Lexington Books, 1975.

14

The Economically Disadvantaged in the Mature Metropolis

Marcus Alexis

One issue on which most urban economists agree is that poverty is a problem of fundamental importance affecting many residents of our cities. In addition to the widespread view of poverty as the fundamental urban problem, Banfield observes:

It is clear, . . . that crime, poverty, ignorance and racial [and other] injustices are among the most important of the general conditions affecting the essential welfare of individuals. It is plausible too, to suppose these conditions have a direct bearing on the good health of the society.[1]

Poverty and Female-headed Households in the Inner City

Poverty is widespread in the mature metropolis, but it is a mistake to assume that all groups are affected equally. Within the metropolis poverty is concentrated in the central city, and even here poverty is concentrated in distinct pockets. Members of minority groups and those in female-headed households are most likely to have incomes below the poverty level. U.S. census data are illuminating on this point. In 1970 there were 12.9 million blacks living in the central cities of this country, 25 percent of these residents or 3 million had incomes below the povery line. In 1974 the number of blacks in central cities below the poverty line had increased by a million, and the fraction of black inner-city residents living in poverty had increased to 30 percent. Whites, on the other hand, experienced poverty at a much lower rate. Of the 48 million whites living in central cities in 1970, approximately 4.8 million (10 percent) had incomes below the poverty level. In 1974 the number of inner-city whites had decreased by over 2 million to 46.8 million, and the number of whites living below the poverty line in central cities declined to 4.5 million; the fraction of inner-city whites in poverty remained at 10 percent. Thus, we see that inner-city blacks are three times as likely to have incomes below the poverty level as their white counterparts. Indeed, between 1970 and 1974 the ratio of black to white probability of living in inner-city poverty increased from 2.5 to 3.0.[2]

The incidence of poverty in female-headed families, both black and white, is higher than in the total population. In 1974, for the United States as a whole, 8.6 million of the 23.2 million persons in families with female heads (37 percent) were in families with incomes below the poverty levels. For whites the relevant numbers are 4.3 out of 15.5 million (28 percent). In black families with female heads, 4.2 of the 7.5 million persons (56 percent) had incomes below the poverty level. The situation for persons in female-headed households in SMSAs closely parallels the results for the country as a whole. In 1974 there were 6.2 million persons residing in metro areas who were members of poverty level female-headed households; this is 36 percent of all such households. Of the 11 million white persons in metropolitan areas living in female-headed households, 2.9 million (27 percent) were below the poverty level.

For blacks the numbers are 5.9 million persons in female-headed households, of which 3.2 million were below poverty level (54 percent). In central cities the proportion of female-headed households below the poverty levels are somewhat higher than in either metropolitan areas or for the United States as a whole. This is true for all families, and for white families and black families taken separately. For all families, 4.2 of the 10 million persons (42 percent) were below poverty. In white families, 1.5 of the 5.2 million (29 percent) were below poverty. There were 4.8 million black persons in female-headed households living in central cities in 1974. Of these, 2.7 million (56 percent) were in households with incomes below the poverty level.

The extent of poverty in female-headed households, both black and white, needs to be put into perspective. For the United States as a whole, only 11 percent of all persons were in households with incomes below the poverty levels, as indicated in Table 14-1. In white households the proportion was 9 percent, and in black households it was 31 percent. Whites in female-headed households experienced poverty at a 27 percent rate (see Table 14-2), more than three times the national average for all whites. Among blacks, the relative concentration of poverty in female-headed households is 1.8 times the average for all blacks. The poverty rate in black female-headed households was 56 percent, whereas the rate for all blacks was 31 percent. When we look at metropolitan areas, taken together black and white female-headed families have three times the incidence of poverty as all families; the same relative rate applies for central cities. For blacks alone, the ratio in metropolitan areas is 1.94:1, and in central cities it is 1.89:1. Thus, we can conclude that the probability that a person will be in a family below the poverty level is three times the national poverty rate for both races taken together and for whites, and about two times for blacks in both the metropolitan area and in central city (see Table 14-2).

Income and Employment of Blacks and Whites

Blacks are greatly underrepresented in the private business sector. Of the more than 7 million firms in existence in 1972, only 191,000 (2.6 percent) were black-owned. The share of gross receipts going to firms owned by blacks

Table 14-1
Persons by Low-income Status, 1974[a]

Residence, Region, and Family Status	All Races Total	All Races Below Low-income Level Number	All Races Percent of Total	White Total	White Below Low-income Level Number	White Percent of Total	Negro Total	Negro Below Low-income Level Number	Negro Percent of Total
All Persons									
United States									
Total	209,343	24,260	11.6	182,363	16,290	8.9	23,788	7,467	31.4
65 years and over	21,127	3,308	15.7	19,206	2,642	13.8	1,722	626	36.4
In families	190,471	19,440	10.2	166,111	12,517	7.5	21,440	6,506	30.3
Head	55,712	5,109	9.2	49,451	3,482	7.0	5,498	1,530	27.8
Related children									
Under 18 years	65,802	10,196	15.5	55,348	6,180	11.2	9,376	3,819	40.7
Under 6 years	19,451	3,294	16.9	16,226	2,089	12.9	2,883	1,141	39.6
Other family members	68,957	4,135	6.0	61,312	2,855	4.7	6,567	1,157	17.6
Unrelated individuals	18,872	4,820	25.5	16,252	3,773	23.2	2,347	961	41.0
Metropolitan Areas									
Total	142,399	14,588	10.2	121,814	9,232	7.6	17,878	4,985	27.9
65 years and over	13,429	1,743	13.0	12,079	1,356	11.2	1,174	347	29.5
In families	128,688	11,491	8.9	110,229	6,889	6.2	15,984	4,304	26.9
Head	37,741	3,073	8.1	32,850	1,941	5.9	4,240	1,060	25.0
Related children									
Under 18 years	44,075	6,259	14.2	36,257	3,537	9.8	6,928	2,591	37.4
Under 6 years	13,120	2,073	15.8	10,691	1,243	11.6	2,151	787	36.6
Other family members	46,872	2,159	4.6	41,123	1,411	3.4	4,816	654	13.6
Unrelated individuals	13,711	3,097	22.6	11,584	2,344	20.2	1,893	681	36.0

Source: U.S. Bureau of the Census, *Current Population Reports*, Series P. 60, No. 102, "Characteristics of the Population below the Poverty Level: 1974," Washington: Government Printing Office, 1976.
[a]Numbers in thousands; persons as of March 1975.

Table 14-2
Persons by Low-Income Status in Female-headed Families, 1974[a]

Residence, Region, and Family Status	All Races Total	All Races Below Low-income Level Number	All Races Percent of Total	White Total	White Below Low-income Level Number	White Percent of Total	Negro Total	Negro Below Low-income Level Number	Negro Percent of Total
Persons in Families with Female Head									
United States									
Total	23,245	8,563	36.8	15,480	4,279	27.6	7,485	4,186	55.9
Head	7,242	2,351	32.5	5,212	1,297	24.9	1,940	1,024	52.8
Related children									
Under 18 years	10,458	5,387	51.5	6,294	2,680	42.6	4,062	2,668	65.7
Under 6 years	2,859	1,754	61.4	1,630	933	57.2	1,207	813	67.3
Other family members	5,545	825	14.9	3,972	302	7.6	1,483	494	33.3
Metropolitan Areas									
Total	17,078	6,201	36.3	10,955	2,947	26.9	5,893	3,183	54.0
Head	5,368	1,710	31.9	3,733	807	24.0	1,565	792	50.6
Related children									
Under 18 years	7,682	3,963	51.6	4,369	1,867	42.7	3,227	2,065	64.0
Under 6 years	2,126	1,296	60.9	1,150	657	57.1	962	636	66.1
Other family members	4,029	528	13.1	2,852	183	6.4	1,100	326	29.6
Inside Central Cities									
Total	10,203	4,239	41.5	5,238	1,513	28.9	4,821	2,695	55.9
Head	3,135	1,134	36.2	1,800	453	25.2	1,288	671	52.1
Related children									
Under 18 years	4,805	2,737	57.0	2,078	964	46.4	2,675	1,756	65.6
Under 6 years	1,417	901	63.6	597	336	56.3	812	563	69.4
Other family members	2,263	368	16.3	1,359	96	7.0	857	267	31.2

Source: U.S. Bureau of the Census, *Current Population Reports*, Series P. 60, No. 102, "Characteristics of the Population below the Poverty Level: 1974," Washington: Government Printing Office, 1976.
[a]Numbers in thousands; persons as of March 1975.

amounted to $5 billion, while the receipts of white-owned firms was $289 billion; black receipts were 1.7 percent of all firm receipts.[3]

Blacks are more dependent on employment for income than are whites, but wage rates are lower for blacks and unemployment rates are higher. One of the reasons given for the low-wage rates of blacks is the smaller endowments of human capital, formal schooling, and acquired skills desired in the marketplace. This is by no means uniformly accepted as explaining the size of the differential in black and white wage rates. Thurow, for example, presents evidence that the returns to black investments in education and training are less than they are for comparable whites.[4]

The higher unemployment rates of blacks, as shown in Table 14-3, are to some extent related to the age distribution within the black population. One black male in eight is between the ages of fifteen and nineteen; among whites, one male in ten is in that age group. Similar differences in the distribution of ages among black and white females exist. One out of nine blacks (of both sexes) but only one out of eleven whites is between fifteen and nineteen years of age.[5]

The significance of the age distribution is clear in current unemployment statistics. While the age group to represent teenagers used in the Bureau of Labor Statistics is sixteen to twenty-one, it illustrates the point well. For all people in the full-time labor force in March 1977 the unemployment rate was 7.4 percent (see Table 14-3). For men it was 6.9 percent and for women, 8.2 percent. White men and women had unemployment rates of 6.2 and 7.5 percent, respectively. Blacks, sixteen and over, experienced unemployment rates of 12.6 percent, and black women sixteen and over had a 12.7 percent unemployment rate. The unemployment rate for sixteen to twenty-one year olds, both black and white males and females, was 17.7 percent, or 2.5 times the unemployment rate for all persons sixteen or over.

Unemployment rates for males sixteen to twenty-one was 17.6 percent, which was also 2.5 times the unemployment rate for all men sixteen and over. Females sixteen to twenty-one had an unemployment rate of 17.7 compared to 8.2 percent for all females sixteen and over; this rate is 2.16 times the rate of all women sixteen and over. White men, sixteen to twenty-one, had an unemployment rate of 15.2 percent; this compared with 6.2 percent for all white males sixteen and over. White females sixteen to twenty-one had an unemployment rate of 15.3 percent, compared to 7.5 percent for all white females sixteen and over. The respective ratios of the unemployment rates of sixteen to twenty-one year olds, to all workers sixteen and over, for white males and females are 2.45 and 2.04.

Black workers in the sixteen to twenty-one age group, both male and female, did significantly worse than their white counterparts. The unemployment rates for black males sixteen to twenty-one was 35.7 percent and for black females in the same age group, the rate was 37.3 percent. Black males and black females, sixteen and over, had unemployment rates of 12.6 and 12.7 percent,

Table 14-3
Full-time and Part-time Status of the Civilian Labor Force by Sex, Age, and Race[a]

March 1977

Race, Sex, and Age	Total	Full-time Labor Force — Employed Full-time Schedules[b]	Employed Part Time for Economic Reasons	Unemployed (looking for full-time work) Number	Unemployed Percent of Full-time Labor Force	Part-time Labor Force Total	Employed on Voluntary Part Time[b]	Unemployed (looking for part-time work) Number	Unemployed Percent of Part-time Labor Force
Total									
Both sexes, 16 & over	80,453	71,083	3,446	5,924	7.4	15,318	13,686	1,632	10.7
16 to 21 years	8,129	5,991	700	1,437	17.7	5,828	4,841	987	16.9
16 to 19 years	3,759	2,538	443	778	20.7	4,654	3,785	870	18.7
20 to 24 years	11,861	9,692	659	1,509	12.7	2,194	1,977	217	9.9
25 to 54 years	53,425	48,453	1,872	3,100	5.8	5,604	5,223	381	6.8
55 years and over	11,409	10,401	471	537	4.7	2,866	2,701	165	5.8
Males, 16 & over	51,265	46,089	1,649	3,526	6.9	5,131	4,442	689	13.4
16 to 21 years	4,538	3,383	354	801	17.6	2,905	2,392	512	17.6
16 to 19 years	2,110	1,452	237	421	19.9	2,361	1,891	469	19.9
20 to 24 years	6,742	5,498	338	906	13.4	936	864	73	7.8
25 to 54 years	34,737	32,082	822	1,833	5.3	691	626	66	9.6
55 years and over	7,676	7,057	252	366	4.8	1,143	1,061	81	7.1
Females, 16 & over	29,188	24,994	1,797	2,398	8.2	10,187	9,244	943	9.3
16 to 21 years	3,591	2,608	347	637	17.7	2,924	2,449	475	16.2
16 to 19 years	1,649	1,086	205	358	21.7	2,294	1,893	401	17.5
20 to 24 years	5,119	4,194	321	603	11.8	1,258	1,114	144	11.5
25 to 54 years	18,688	16,370	1,051	1,266	6.8	4,913	4,598	316	6.4
55 years and over	3,733	3,343	219	170	4.6	1,723	1,640	83	4.8

White							
Males, 16 years & over	45,879	41,635	1,398	2,846	6.2	4,022	592	12.8
16 to 21 years	3,990	3,074	311	605	15.2	2,646	436	16.5
16 to 19 years	1,893	1,362	212	320	16.9	2,153	395	18.4
20 to 24 years	5,893	4,909	292	693	11.8	849	70	8.3
25 to 54 years	31,087	28,890	668	1,528	4.9	591	53	9.0
55 years and over	7,005	6,474	225	306	4.4	1,022	74	7.2
Females, 16 years & over	24,986	21,674	1,450	1,862	7.5	8,506	806	8.7
16 to 21 years	3,192	2,400	305	488	15.3	2,280	396	14.8
16 to 19 years	1,489	1,011	181	297	20.0	1,777	329	15.6
20 to 24 years	4,434	3,733	274	428	9.6	1,015	128	11.2
25 to 54 years	15,675	13,868	826	981	6.3	4,248	279	6.2
55 years and over	3,387	3,061	169	157	4.6	1,467	70	4.6
Black and Other								
Males, 16 years & over	5,385	4,455	251	680	12.6	516	97	18.7
16 to 21 years	548	310	43	195	35.7	258	76	29.5
16 to 19 years	217	90	25	101	46.6	207	74	35.7
20 to 24 years	849	589	46	213	25.1	88	3	3.0
25 to 54 years	3,650	3,192	152	305	8.4	100	12	12.0
55 years and over	671	583	27	61	9.1	121	7	5.8
Females, 16 years & over	4,203	3,320	347	535	12.7	875	137	15.7
16 to 21 years	399	208	42	149	37.3	248	79	32.0
16 to 19 years	160	75	25	61	37.8	188	71	38.1
20 to 24 years	685	462	47	176	25.7	115	16	13.7
25 to 54 years	3,013	2,501	225	285	9.5	386	37	9.6
55 years and over	345	282	50	14	4.1	186	13	7.0

Source: U.S. Bureau of the Census, Bureau of Labor Statistics, *Employment and Earnings*, vol. 24, No. 4 (April 1977), Washington: Government Printing Office, 1977.

[a]Numbers in thousands.

respectively. Thus, the younger blacks had unemployment rates of 2.8 and 2.9 times the rate for sixteen and over black males and females, respectively. Interestingly, while the ratio of black to white unemployment for those sixteen and over, in the case of both males and females, is 2:1, the ratio of black to white unemployment in the sixteen to twenty-one age group, again both for males and females, are both about 2.4:1.

Black and white youth are at a disadvantage in seeking employment. Two factors tend to result in higher unemployment rates for inner-city blacks. The first is that a larger percentage of the black population falls into the young worker category. Second, unemployment rates among black youth are more than twice as high as they are for the comparable white worker.

Manufacturing jobs have been moving out of the cities in growing numbers since the end of World War II. Many observers have noted that new industry has located on the periphery of cities since at least the turn of the century. What is new since the end of World War II is that cities are no longer annexing the areas into which new industry is moving, as indicated in Chapter 2. Central-cities' share of metropolitan manufacturing jobs has been declining, at least since the end of World War II. In the period 1900 to 1918 the central-cities' share of manufacturing jobs in eight SMSAs was 87 percent; from 1919 to 1938 that percentage dropped to 77; from 1939 to 1958 it dropped to 76. A large decline in the central-cities' share occurred between 1959 and 1966; in that period it declined to 67 percent. When the 1959-66 period is adjusted to be equal in length to the two previous periods, the rate of decline is over 21 percent. This is almost twice as large as the 11 percent decline from 1919 to 1938. The decline in central-cities' share in 1967 was six percentage points, a very substantial one-year decline. From this we can conclude that although the central-cities' share of employment in manufacturing has been declining for at least sixty years, there appears to have been an acceleration in that decline during the 1960s.[6]

We get some picture of the types of enterprises which were either relocating or expanding in central cities by noting the percentage of new, private, and nonprivate nonresidential building outside central cities. In the period 1954-65, the majority of new industrial and retail store construction was outside central cities; the proportions are 63 and 53 percent, respectively. New buildings for educational, amusement, business, and community purposes are almost equally divided between central cities and the metropolitan area outside the central city; here the percentages were 50, 48, 46, and 45, respectively. Central cities were able to maintain a commanding lead, however, in new office building and hospital and institutional construction. Only 27 percent of new office buildings and 36 percent of hospital and institutional building was done outside our central cities.[7]

Was the expansion outside the central cities the result of relocation of firms formerly located in the central cities or of new firms? Some insight into this question is given by a study of industry relocation from Chicago's black community. Christian and Bennett studied 458 firms located in Chicago's black community in 1969 which had moved by 1971. Only 237 of these moves could be traced; of these, 35 firms (15 percent) relocated into predominately black areas within the central city. There were seventy-one firms which relocated to nonblack sections of the central city. By far the largest number, 105, relocated to the suburbs and other areas within the state of Illinois. A very small number, twenty-six, relocated outside of Illinois. The 105 firms relocating outside of the central city represent 44 percent of all relocations from Chicago's black community in this sample. They constitute half of all relocations within the state of Illinois. From 1947 to 1963, approximately 147,000 jobs in manufacturing were lost from the central city, and the largest and most consistent declines occurred within the highly concentrated black residential areas and those adjacent to it.[8]

Manufacturing jobs have received most of the attention of analysts concerned with job losses in central cities. It is often assumed that what is true of manufacturing jobs is also true, to a greater or lesser degree, of nonmanufacturing jobs. The information cited above, that new construction outside of central cities outpaced new construction within central cities in only two categories—industrial and retail stores—should be sufficient for us to look more closely at other categories of employment. In a study of employment in eleven large cities, it was found that while employment in manufacturing declined from 28 to 22 percent of total employment, and that total employment in manufacturing declined from 2.2 to 1.8 million, total employment increased from 7.0 to 8.3 million. Employment in several fields either held its own or increased; the largest gains were in service and government employment. Employment in services increased from 1.1 to 1.5 million; employment in government, from 1.1 to 1.4 million. The respective employment shares of these two industries went from 14 to 18 percent, respectively, from 1950 to 1967. In these eleven cities, total employment and employment in selected industries is increasing, while employment in manufacturing is declining. There are jobs being created in the central cities but they are different from those which existed at the end of World War II, according to Ganz and O'Brien.[9]

Ganz and O'Brien also note that in the severely depressed city of Newark, total employment increased between 1948 and 1967 from 235,000 to 248,000. In St. Louis, another severely depressed city, employment declined slightly from 454,000 to 446,000. In both cities the usual pattern of manufacturing job decline is observed but, again in both, the number of workers in services and in government is rising. In Newark there were 14,700 service workers in 1948 and 24,700 in 1967; government workers were 31,800 for 1948 and 46,300 for 1967. The St. Louis pattern is very similar; there were 33,200 service workers in 1948 and 73,000 in 1967, and government workers increased from 45,000 to 62,600.

While employment in our larger cities has increased since World War II, the composition of that employment has changed, moving from manufacturing to services and government. The question still remains, Who is being employed in these jobs? Unemployment of inner-city residents is known to be high. Many of the new jobs being created in the central city are being filled by noncity residents. Thus, while the total employment figures for large cities appear at first glance encouraging, there is no evidence that these increases in employment are benefiting central-city residents. Indeed, if Webber is correct, there is good reason to suspect that many of these newly created central-city jobs are going to workers with specialized skills who are likely not to be central-city residents:

The explosive progress in the arts, sciences, and technologies has triggered an unprecedented rise in the scale of the national society, one marked by even finer divisions of labor, calling for even higher levels of education and training: by the shift from extractive and manufacturing industries to service industries that require long periods of preparation; by increasing complex organization of the economy and polity; and by the expansion of the spatial and cognitive fields within which human interaction and economic transaction take place. Specialization, interdependence and integration are definitive traits of today's urbanism. This new skill of complexity distinguishes modern urbanism from earlier forms.[10]

Living Space for the Poor

Anthony Downs graphically depicts the housing conditions of millions of poor Americans living in cities:

Americans have no conception of the filth, degradation, squalor, overcrowding, and personal danger and insecurity which millions of inadequate housing units are causing in both our cities and rural areas. Thousands of infants are attacked by rats each year; hundreds die or become mentally retarded from eating lead paint that falls off cracked walls; thousands more are ill because of unsanitary conditions resulting from jamming large families into a single room, continuing failure of landlords to repair plumbing or provide proper heat, and pitifully inadequate storage. Until you have actually stumbled through the ill-lit and decaying rooms of a slum dwelling, smelled the stench of sewerage and garbage and dead rats behind the walls, seen the roaches and crumbling plaster and incredibly filthy bathrooms, and recoiled from exposed wiring and rotting floorboards and staircases you have no real idea of what bad housing is like.[11]

Housing conditions of the urban poor have long been a matter of public concern. In the 1930s the federal government entered the low-income housing field. The record of government activity in this field has been disappointing. The Douglas Commission reported in 1968 that governmental action resulted in the loss of approximately a million low-income housing units; in the three decades of public housing programs less than 700,000 units were built, resulting in a net decline of 300,000 units. Many critics have charged that the beneficiaries of public housing programs, allegedly designed to help low-income individuals, have been middle-class and upper-class persons. Banfield is particularly harsh in his criticism:

> ... in effect, then the FHA and VA programs have subsidized the movement of the white middle-class out of the central city and older suburbs while at the same time penalizing investment in rehabilitation of run-down neighborhoods of these older cities. The poor—especially the Negro poor—have not received any direct benefits from these programs.
> In practice, however, the principal objectives of the renewal programs have been to attract the middle class back into the central city (as well as slow its exodus out of the city) and to stabilize and restore the central business districts. Unfortunately, these objectives can be served only at the expense of the poor. Hundreds of thousands of low-income people, most of them Negroes or Puerto Ricans, have been forced out of low cost housing—in order to make way for luxury apartments, office buildings, hotels, civic centers, industrial parks and the like.[12]

Housing discrimination has slowed the ability of nonwhites to move up into the better, older housing in many neighborhoods.[13] A model has been formulated which shows that high levels of residential segregation by race are possible, even if racial preferences for neighbors are not strong. One example is a situation in which both black and white residents are willing to live in integrated neighborhoods as long as more than half the residents are members of their own race. In other words, if each race has the mild preference that it be a majority in any neighborhood, the only possible equilibrium is one in which all neighborhoods are composed of members of the same race. This model does not take into account differences in incomes and preferences for neighborhood attributes such as schools, public transportation, proximity to the central business district, and the like.[14] Banfield's view stated above, however, seems sounder.

A recent development of considerable importance in many of our older cities is the phenomenon of abandonment. The National Urban League identifies five stages in the abandonment process. The stages are (1) decline in an area's socioeconomic status, (2) racial or ethnic change, (3) property speculation and exploitation, (4) weakened market conditions, and (5) disinvestment.[15] A study by Sternlieb identifies the abandonment process in terms of (1) reduction in maintenance procedures; (2) permitting the structure to become tax delinquent; (3) virtual termination of all reinvestments for maintenance, usually coupled with increased tax delinquency; (4) cessation of vital services throughout the structure, particulary utility and heating; and (5) arrangements by the landlord through a paper sale to avoid any level of legal liability for the structure.[16] Sternlieb and Burchell give some indication of the scope of abandonment in their report of estimates that in New York City 2 percent of structures were abandoned. In the most affected sections of St. Louis about 16 percent were abandoned. And in the East New York section of Brooklyn, the abandonment rate ranged between 6 and 10 percent. In the Woodlawn and Lawndale sections of Chicago the rate of abandonment was about 20 percent.

Dependency of the Urban Poor

Increasingly, the older metropolises are dependent on grants and aid from Washington and from state governments. Prior to general revenue sharing, most revenue coming to cities was in the form of categorical grants-in-aid for such purposes as education, housing, law enforcement, urban transportation, anti-poverty efforts, employment, training, and other expansions of "merit goods" programs. A wide spectrum of observers have commented on the fiscal dependence of the nation's cities. Ganz and O'Brien find: ". . . large cities were the sources of $10 for every additional $1.00 of Federal and state aid to large city governments and for every additional .90 dollars the cities themselves were able to raise in local taxes."[17]

In another vein, Banfield observes that the fiscal condition of cities could be improved if they were allowed to charge nonresidents for services they received, or if they were allowed to redraw boundary limits so that those living in metropolitan areas would be taxed on the same basis as those residing within the city. On a more pessimistic note, Norton Long dismisses revenue sharing as a "transfer payment from the outside society," and as an "act of pure charity." To be sure, Long sees the contemporary city as hopelessly dependent on federal and state aid. To him, however, the solution to the financial plight of cities is not more aid, but less: "The city's best present hope—if hope is possible at all—may be to resort to something on the order of Lenin's New Economic Policy, in which self-help and self-interest might restore a functioning economy and avert the Indian reservation destiny."[18]

New York City's financial problems have drawn attention to the precarious fiscal conditions of many other old cities. In a front page article titled, "After Daley," the *Wall Street Journal,* April 18, 1977, points to several serious problems facing Chicago. Cited are an influx of blacks, Latins, and other minorities with less education and fewer job skills than the whites who are leaving; high crime rates; and deteriorating housing. The article points to a loss of 200,000 manufacturing jobs and a population decline of close to 500,000 in the period from 1960 to 1970. It also speaks of a school board deficit and financial arrangements which have staved off a fiscal crisis in the city.

Race as an Artifact of Metropolis

The results of racial isolation can only be speculated upon. But it is a contributing factor to an absence of a sense of community: what Banfield refers to as the consensual bonds that hold together. A study of racial exposure found there was very little change between 1960 and 1970; in some cases, there was decreased racial exposure over the decade.[19]

The racially segregated lives of most Americans—and for meaningful contact all urban residents must be included—means that for all practical purposes our cities are enclaves of racially or ethnically distinct composition. Interactions which would promote a sense of community and better understanding in the interest of both races are stifled in such an environment. The extent of racial discrimination in American life is a subject of great controversy; opinions range from the denial of its existence to assumptions that it is universal and virulent. It has been given as an explanation for the relatively low wages and incomes of black workers and has been said to be a working out of the power relationship between blacks and whites.[20]

A recent study comparing the effects of racial discrimination and social status on the earnings of young men concludes that racial discrimination has a much larger negative effect. It finds that the elimination of employment discrimination could raise the earnings of low-status black males by more than 25 percent. When looking only at the effect of social status on earnings, they find it to be negligible.[21]

Prospects and Policies for Metropolitan Human Resources

There is no doubt that since World War II the central city has been declining, in economic terms, relative to the rest of metropolis; as indicated throughout this volume, the causes are complex. Of fundamental importance has been the progress in technology in communication and transportation, which has reduced the central-place importance of cities. Scales of operations and the ability to decentralize production and distribution have placed much of the growth that formerly would have taken place in the central city either in the suburbs of metropoles or in other nonmetropolitan areas.

Scale economies do not seem fully to explain the changing composition of central cities, despite their importance, as indicated in Chapter 13. One would suppose that economies of scale are more prevalent in manufacturing than in either services or government, yet it is precisely services and government which have been gaining in employment in the central city. Perhaps it is true that spatial agglomeration permits reduced costs of interaction by more than the advances in communication and transportation, halting the outflow of such enterprises from the central city. More likely, the new technologies require large scale for efficiency.

The minimum volume for efficient operation on a large computer, for example, could encourage the consolidation of many government offices, while at the same time field services are more and more scattered. Location of government activities in central cities can also be attributed to government policies aimed at stimulating local economies. A case in point is the New York state office building located in Harlem during the Rockefeller administration. Concentration of some activities of government, such as record keeping and courts, make it convenient for some types of service providers to locate close to them, lawyers for example. A better understanding of the comparative advantage which central cities still seem to enjoy for services and government activities requires microlevel analysis.

Employment, Income, and Quality of Life for Disadvantaged Metropolitan Labor

Between 1950 and 1967 total employment in the eleven large cities studied by Ganz and O'Brien increased from 7.8 to 8.3 million. Almost 70 percent of this gain—363,000—came from increases in government employment. An amount equal to 95 percent of the total gain in employment is accounted for by the increase in employment in government and services other than FIRE; the latter account for another 175,000 jobs. When government, services, and FIRE are taken together, they represent over a million more jobs. Since this number is larger than the total increase in employment, there has to have been substantial decreases elsewhere. In construction, manufacturing, and wholesale and retail trade combined, there is a decline of 400,000 jobs. If one adds the losses in transportation, communication, and public utilities, the number of lost jobs climbs to 428,000.

Since 1967 many of our larger cities have reduced the number of public employees. Teachers, policemen, social workers, clerks, and others either have lost their jobs or seen the number of positions decline through attrition. There is no reason to believe that there has been a reversal of the exodus of manufacturing jobs from the central city. Therefore, the prospects are for reduced rates of growth in central-city employment or actual declines over the next decade. To make matters worse, the 1960 boom in office construction in central cities is not being repeated in the second-half of the 1970s. Many headquarters companies are departing the cities for the more spacious, aesthetic settings of suburbia and exurbia. The flight of headquarters companies from New York City has grown to the point where a special effort by the mayor's office has been launched to halt the decline.

The advances in technology, described in Chapter 7, have made it possible for firms to communicate with their manufacturing facilities, employees, and customers from remote locations. Transportation costs, rather than being a deterrent, encourage the movement of office staffs outside the city where a large pool of skilled workers can be found in easy commuting distance. The likelihood of higher energy costs will probably encourage workers to seek employment closer to home. Congestion on the roads leading to the central city and the high cost of downtown parking, together with some efforts to discourage the use of automobiles altogether, could well result in the further decline of the central city, but not the discouragement of automobile use. Job seekers and shoppers will reduce their trips to the CBD and increase the frequency of shorter trips to suburban employers and regional shopping centers.

Public employment has long been the vehicle for upper mobility of new arrivals to the cities. Witness the examples of the Irish and Jews. In cities in which they are large in number, both groups have used such jobs to move up the social and economic ladder. The new immigrants, the blacks and Hispanics, will find it more difficult to imitate this pattern. As central-city jobs become more scarce, one can expect employers to become more selective. Jobs will be rationed on the basis of formal educational requirements and "aptitude" tests which may bear no relationship to ability to perform satisfactorily. High school graduation will indicate, more than it does now, eligibility for employment. In a tight labor market one can expect pressures for professionalization to increase. One need only look at the increased requirements for new applicants for public school teaching positions, in most cases at least a Master's degree, and the requirements of many municipal police departments for two years of college. The effects of this are likely to increase the isolation and hostility of blacks, Hispanics, and Appalachian whites, who will be cut off from employment in disproportionate numbers.

Pressures are now being felt in many cities to require either that city employees live in the city or that job-related testing determine eligibility. If these movements gain momentum, the prospects for blacks and Hispanics in the central cities will be improved. It is not likely that the forces that led to the movement of middle-class and upper-class whites to the suburbs will be less important than keeping a municipal job. These efforts to require city residence for city employment and to replace general aptitude tests with more specific job-related tests are to be applauded. They will do much to heighten the sense of community and to give a psychological lift to city residents that they can provide the basic services required in their cities. Nothing could be more despairing than the thought, current in many central-city communities, that city residents are incapable of efficiently performing for themselves tasks now done by "outsiders." On this subject Long speaks directly to the point: "Could people in the city be prepared for and permitted to fill the jobs still in the city, much of the problem would be solved."[22]

One suggested avenue for improving the employment attractiveness of disadvantaged city residents is through education. As discussed above, much is made of formal education which is not required for the job already available. Furthermore, the education currently available in the public schools does not provide young people with the skills which will be required in the marketplace. There seems considerable merit to the concern held by both Long and Banfield that an essential goal of schools should be to provide a set of habits, skills, and attitudes which make it possible for young people to function in an adult world once their schooling is completed. Interpersonal relation skills are surely among these, but discipline, self-respect, and respect for others—as well as reading, writing, and arithmetic—are minima that should be expected of the schools. Unfortunately, many of the schools concentrate on preparing students for college and a life which they and the school know will not be theirs. This can only create frustration, lack of self-respect, hostility, and a conviction that what goes on in school is not serious business.

It should also be noted that general education skills are important in securing jobs which have potential for growth in skills, responsibilities, and earnings. There is considerable evidence which shows that blacks do not benefit from formal education to the same extent as whites, given the limited career paths available even for blacks with training. This can only result in a downgrading of the value of education and a reduced interest in it by young blacks. While the benefits to blacks from increased education may not be as large as they are for whites, there is no doubt that for blacks, education does have positive marginal benefits; higher levels of educational attainment are associated with higher levels of earnings and lower levels of poverty. Creating a labor market environment in which young blacks will find it worthwhile to increase their investment in formal education and marketable skills will be one of the major challenges of the balance of the 1970s and 1980s. If we are successful in that endeavor, the disparity in black and white incomes will narrow and give hope that it will shortly disappear.

One of the reasons why education is important is because training and education are complementary. More sophisticated job training requires higher levels of formal education. There is, thus, a chicken-and-egg situation; the better-skilled jobs will be closed off from disadvantaged minority youngsters until their formal achievement levels reach critical thresholds. At the same time, the absence of minorities in these jobs may be taken as a signal by minority youths that these positions are not available to them.

Whatever the education and training endowments of disadvantaged minorities may be, general economic conditions in the nation and the state of their own local economies will have powerful influences on their income prospects. There is what might be called "magic number 2." This is the ratio of black to white unemployment rates, in good times and bad. Thus, when the economy is operating at high levels of plant utilization and the unemployment rate in general is low, the unemployment rate for minorities is also low. In the late 1960s, when the national unemployment rate was in the 4 percent zone, the unemployment rate among minorities was about 8 percent. Now that unemployment is running at the 7 percent level, the unemployment rate among minorities, notably blacks, is 14 percent.

Access to jobs is as important as national and local economic conditions. Barriers to employment arise from three principal sources: (1) discrimination discussed in sufficient detail to make it unnecessary to go into it again,

(2) unions, and (3) governmental licensing. By restricting job entry, unions have increased wages of their members, but forced other workers to compete for lower-paying nonunion jobs. Union membership among minorities is lower than it is for whites. Minorities also are more underrepresented in the unions representing workers in the higher-skilled better-paying jobs. Whether union officers are themselves biased or not, racial prejudice by workers can effectively reduce the market demands for minority labor. A high-level economy in which jobs are abundant is likely to make union members less resistant to new minority employees, as long as there are sufficient jobs for those already in the unions. Therefore, an economy expanding in areas in which unionization is important is likely to increase minority job access.

Licensure and certification are government contributions to reduced access by disadvantaged workers. Requirements of formal education, training, and experience, before workers can be licensed to perform certain jobs, works to the disadvantage of the less well educated and to the advantage of incumbent jobholders. One need not think of licensing in the professions to come face to face with restrictions on job entry. In most American cities, Washington, D.C., being a notable exception, perfectly able men and women are denied entry into the taxicab industry because of licensing and strict controls on entry set by local government. Interestingly, in many of these same cities, white taxicab operators avoid the minority sections of the city. Thus, these residents are doubly hurt. First, they are denied opportunities to earn incomes in a lawful occupation; second, these very services which they could provide even on a segregated basis are denied to residents of their communities.

Earnings from property are small to nonexistent in disadvantaged communities. The statistical data cited earlier in this chapter indicate how small the black share of private businesses is in our economy. A viable black business community is important to the life of the central city, not only because of the additional income that it might generate but because there are skills to be acquired which are difficult, if not impossible, to gain elsewhere. Blacks are moving in larger numbers into beginning level management positions; many of these young blacks are products of college programs in business. Such an activity as the Consortium for Minority Management Education now prepares more than ten times as many young minority MBA students as were in all the collegiate schools of business a decade ago. A major problem facing black entrepreneurs is the acquisition of equity capital. Other ethnic groups have been able to increase their capital funds by leveraging real estate and moving their capital to other fields as new immigrant groups replaced them in the central cities. Blacks and Hispanics are the last of the new migrants, but they have inherited a real estate market in which housing is being abandoned and there are no new immigrants on the horizon. Black enterprises which serve a local, segregated market only, will not do as well as black entrepreneurs with access to a larger, more affluent total market. For this to happen, there must be reduced discrimination on the consumers' side and reduction of capital market imperfections, such as lender discrimination.

The least fortunate of central-city residents must continue to depend, at least in part, on some form of transfer payments. These funds, coming from federal, state, or local government, are sources of great friction between the disadvantaged and the more affluent members of society. They also may contribute to a sense of dependence which stifles initiative. It may be that public assistance programs allegedly designed to help the least fortunate are having perverse effects. When taken together with other governmental programs, such as minimum wage laws, the total effect may be to remove marginal workers from the private labor force.

Most studies of market intervention focus on the short-term effects. More attention needs to be given to the longer-term effects of employment and income on the quality of life of the disadvantaged workers. Loury has formulated a model which explicitly takes into account family characteristics, including parents' incomes, on the income of offspring. He shows that in a world in which blacks and whites have different initial incomes and the same endowments of abilities, the long-term equilibrium income of blacks could still be less than that of whites.[2,3]

Some Policy Implications

Feedback effects play a critical role in many dynamic interpretations of the interplay of changes in educational and skill endowments, employment, income, and living environment. As income rises, individuals are able to purchase more of all desired commodities and services. At some point, an income is reached which makes possible the movement into a more preferred neighborhood. This neighborhood may have better schools, in the sense that students score better on standardized tests; and residents are able and willing to allocate more of their income to activities which improve school performance of their youngsters. Peer pressure, reinforced by parental intervention, makes the average performance in such a school higher than in the previous neighborhood. As a consequence of better performance on standardized tests, opportunities are available to the youngsters whose families' incomes have risen that are not available to those whose incomes have not. This permits them to further increase their income, and the gap between them and the children they left behind in the old neighborhood is likely to increase in the next generation. One could add to this, acquisition of attitude, work habits, and graces, which further increase employment and income advancement opportunities, and changes in life-style and mind-set which are more in keeping with the mainstream society. One could argue that this is the traditional American path of advancement. The disadvantaged young can be trapped in a cycle because of failure to meet a basic requirement for passing on to the next stage. But this failure to improve their opportunities may be taken as evidence of the futility of effort. In a community in which this is widely felt and communicated to other youth, chances are increased that they too will fail to acquire the minimum skills necessary for breaking the cycle.

What, if anything, should the role of public policy be in disadvantaged inner-city communities? From what has been argued earlier, one important role to be played by the central government is to pursue monetary and fiscal policies which promote high levels of employment and income. The evidence is very strong that minorities improve their relative economic positions during periods of economic expansion. As the demand for labor increases and competition drives up intramarginal wage rates, the gap between market wages and imposed minimum wages rises, and workers who were formerly unprofitable now become employable. During this period of employment many workers acquire training, experience, and work habits demanded in the marketplace. For many, it is an opportunity to overcome the failures of youth. In a tight labor market employers are also less likely to depend on nonjob-related characteristics of workers, such as scores on standardized tests. The increase in relative earnings of blacks during periods of vigorous economic activity also suggests that discrimination has less impact on employers and employees; some gains won during this period become permanent.

Unless employers are able to capture the benefits of training that workers receive, they are unlikely to be willing to make the investment in them. This may represent a conflict between the private interest of the employer and the interest of society at large. From society's point of view, a trained worker, assuming this means he is more productive, contributes to increased output of valued goods and services. The potential GNP from such a worker could be reduced or lost if the cost must be fully borne by employers. This potential market failure—discrepancy in the private and social benefits and costs—presents an opportunity for government policy. In the case of young inexperienced workers, an inducement can be offered to employers in the form of training grants (or forgiveness of the employers' share of the young employees' Social Security contribution) for a period long enough to make such employees attractive. We have a tremendous stake in our youth; we should not permit them to waste productive years because of a quirk in the market. To ensure that employers are not merely substituting younger workers for older, more experienced ones, it could be stipulated that the Social Security tax forgiveness, for example, applies only to increases in total employment over some base period. This arrangement possibly could take some of the sting out of the minimum wage imposed on employers in interstate commerce, and achieve some of the advantages expected by some from a two-tier minimum wage. The suggested arrangement is also less likely to be challenged by organized labor.

At some point we must face up to the reality that there will be some persons who either will not or cannot work, even in a full employment economy. The present welfare system is almost universally denounced as unfair, inefficient, unworkable, bureaucratic, and, in the words of President Carter, a "disgrace." We should, as soon as possible, move to some form of guaranteed minimum income such as the negative income tax. One thing on which most economists, liberal and conservative, are agreed, is that such a program is preferable to the present hodgepodge of federal, state, and local public assistance and subsidy programs. One of the difficulties in constructing an equitable plan with incomes sufficiently high to provide minimum decent standards of living is that there appears to be evidence that such high benefits discourage labor supply; another concern is the potentially high cost. On the other hand, a plan with very-low-income guarantees could make many poor persons worse off than currently. Attention of the ablest members of the professions must be directed to the development of a workable, politically acceptable plan. One characteristic of such a plan should include, it is to be hoped, strong incentives to increase income by participating in the labor market. A just, negative income tax arrangement would go a long way toward eliminating poverty in the central cities and could shift a major budget burden of a city like New York and permit it to put its fiscal house in order, starting the long road back to budgetary and financial respectability and providing the local public goods that will make it a desirable place in which to live.

Many of our central-city neighborhoods can best be categorized as prisons, holding unwilling residents who have no better place to go, but who despise their surroundings. It is misguided to pursue policies designed to attract higher-income residents of the metropolis back to the cities. What the cities can do is to make life within them tolerable and provide mobility opportunities for those whose education, employment, and income require that they inhabit the least expensive, most densely settled urban real estate. There has been too great an emphasis on central business redevelopment and office building construction. Industries should be attracted which match the skill of the local residents; the educational system in the cities should be directed to provide all students with an education which will prepare them to cope as adults. For those who will not be going to college, preparation for the world of work should be the order of the day. These jobs need not be menial, low-paying, dead-end jobs. Already the median years of schooling of minority youth is more than twelve years. But postsecondary educational facilities, with strong vocational orientation in the developing areas of job growth, should be the adjunct to the basic twelve years of elementary and secondary education instead of academic post-high school curricula.

Most of the disadvantaged youths who are going on to postsecondary education are now doing so in two-year and four-year public institutions. While it may be a source of pride to educators to prepare a small minority of today's youth for the most elite institutions of higher education, it is a poor investment of public resources. The net returns, in a financial sense, from college education have been estimated to be evaporating. There are, however, potentially large benefits to be reaped from high-quality technical education that builds on a solid foundation of general education. Confidence in the schools and the benefits they accord can come only from connecting the life and world of the disadvantaged central-city youth with what goes on in the classroom and school-related job training. Quality college preparatory education should be made available to all who seek it and are able to benefit from it, but it should be made clear that job-oriented education is not a mere consolation prize.

Finally, we must deal with the problem of racial discrimination and racial isolation. The core of the central city can and must again be a place of hope. Whatever disadvantages the resident population now experiences must be thought of as temporary. The way must be prepared for them to enter into the great mainstream of American society. In spite of the relative and absolute improvements in the income of nonwhites since 1940, the percentage of black suburban residents is virtually unchanged. Many economic opportunities exist outside the central city; disadvantaged nonwhites seek access to them. Proximity to manufacturing jobs and to information about jobs, as well as higher levels of public services, are available in many working-class suburbs. Incentives to make the sacrifices that will improve their employability are blunted by barriers to enjoy a better life that their higher income should permit. Failure to provide these opportunities is a capricious and cruel form of taxation.

Notes

1. Edward C. Banfield, *The Unheavenly City Revisited*, Boston: Little Brown, 1974, pp. 9-10.
2. Data taken from U.S. Bureau of the Census, Current Population Reports, Special Studies, Series P-23, No. 54, *The Social and Economic Status of the Black Population in the United States 1974*, 1975; and *Current Population Reports*, Series P-60, No. 102, "Characteristics of the Population below the Poverty Level: 1974," 1976, table 3, p. 19, Washington: Government Printing Office.
3. Bureau of the Census, *Economic Status of Black Population*, p. 85.
4. Lester C. Thurow, *Poverty and Discrimination*, Washington, D.C.: Brookings Institution, 1969, pp. 76 ff.
5. Bureau of the Census, *Economic Status of Black Population*, p. 17.
6. The data have been adjusted in terms of 1965 city boundaries; the error made in many studies which does not reflect the changed city boundaries is thus avoided. See Bennett Harrisson, *Urban Economic Development: Suburbanization, Minority Opportunity, and the Condition of the Central City*, Washington, D.C.: Urban Institute, 1974, chapter 2.
7. Ibid.
8. Charles N. Christian and Dari J. Bennett, "Industrial Relocations from

the Black Community of Chicago," in W. Patrick Beaton, ed., *Municipal Needs, Services and Financing: Readings on Municipal Expenditure*, Brunswick, N.J.: Rutgers University Press, 1974.

9. Alexander Ganz and Thomas O'Brien, "The City: Sandbox Reservation or Dynamo?," *Public Policy*, Winter 1973, pp. 107-123.

10. Melvin M. Webber, "The Post-City Age," in James W. Hughes, ed., *Suburbanization Dynamics and the Future of the City*, Brunswick, N.J.: Rutgers University Press, 1974, p. 258.

11. Anthony Downs, *Urban Problems and Prospects*, Chicago: Markham, 1970, p. 116.

12. Banfield, *Unheavenly City Revisited*, p. 16.

13. Marcus Alexis, "Segregation and Discrimination in Housing: The Case of Chicago," Inter-University Committee on Urban Economics, Economics of the Ghetto, Madison: University of Wisconsin, May 8, 1975 (unpublished).

14. Thomas Schelling, "On the Ecology of Micromotives," *The Public Interest*, No. 25, Fall, 1971, pp. 61-98.

15. National Urban League, *The National Survey of Housing Abandonment*, New York: Center for Community Change, 1971.

16. George Sternlieb, *Some Aspects of the Abandoned House Problem*, Rutgers University, Center for Urban Policy Research, 1970.

17. Ganz and O'Brien, "Sandbox or Dynamo?," p. 115.

18. Norton E. Long, "The City as Reservation," *The Public Interest*, Fall 1971, p. 32.

19. Frank deLeeuw, Anne B. Schnare, and Raymond J. Struyk, "Housing," in William Gorham and Nathan Glazer, eds., *The Urban Predicament*, Washington: Urban Institute, 1976, pp. 119-178, table 10, p. 158.

20. Gary S. Becker, *The Economics of Discrimination*, Chicago: University of Chicago Press, 1957; Marcus Alexis, "A Theory of Labor Market Discrimination with Inter-dependent Utilities," *American Economic Review*, vol. 63, No. 2 (May 1973), pp. 256-302; also by Alexis, "The Political Economy of Labor Market Discrimination: Synthesis and Exploration," in Ann R. Horowitz and George von Furstenburg, eds., *Patterns of Racial Discrimination,* Vol. 2: *Employment and Income*, Lexington, Mass.: Lexington Books, 1974; "Two Theories of Discrimination," in Peggy Reeves Sanday, ed., *Anthropology and the Public Interest: Fieldwork and Theory*, New York: Academic Press, 1976.

21. G. Donald Jud and James F. Walker, "How Racial Bias and Social Status Affect the Earnings of Young Men," *Monthly Labor Review*, April 1977, pp. 44-46.

22. Long, "City as Reservation," p. 27.

23. Glenn C. Loury, "Notes on a Dynamic Theory of Racial Income Differences," in Phyllis A. Wallace, ed., *Women, Minorities, and Employment Discrimination*, Lexington, Mass.: Lexington Books, forthcoming.

**Part VIII
Policy for the Mature
Metropolis**

15 Agenda for the Mature Metropolis

Robert C. Holland
and *Charles L. Leven*

At many places in this book recurrent warnings were offered about overreacting to current declines in population in the mature metropolis. In Chapter 7, Macrae put this in terms of his concept of the "law of opposites," which is rather analogous to the principle of making high profits by always planting whatever was in the greatest excess supply last year, knowing everyone else will turn away from it. The law of opposites clearly is a dramatically oversimplified idea, but an idea with a substantial kernel of truth nonetheless. Its general conclusion, namely, that every policy should contain within it a provision for self-destruct—sort of a functional zero-base budgeting concept—seems to the point. In the days of the "exploding metropolis" many spoke and planned as if metro growth would go on forever; and that was less than twenty years ago. Now in the era of the "mature metropolis" it would seem equally foolhardy to plan on decline as something to be with us forever.

This caution notwithstanding, however, this volume also has offered very substantial argument for believing that metropolitan maturity will be with us—and in an increasing number of metro areas—at least for the next decade and likely through the 1990s as well. That we can be so sure that this will be the general nature of urban development for the rest of this century comes out of the understanding of the emergence of contemporary trends as a logical consequence of the forces leading to industrialization. As early as 1937, the National Resources Committee understood and saw the coming of maturity, as indicated by the quotation from their report cited in Chapter 5. The committee did not see that World War II was about to arrive and that it would insert hypereconomic stimulation and a "baby boom" that would delay things; but their analysis was sound, if their timing was off. Similar foresight also can be seen in the quotation from H.G. Wells in Chapter 3; as early as 1901, Wells seemed to understand what was coming, though he really did not seem to know just when. And so most of the scenarios sketched in this book really are consistent with the major idea suggested in Chapter 2, that maturity of metropolis, along with the rebirth of nonmetropolitan America, is likely to continue. Thus, understanding the current declines as a manifestation of a very entrenched historical process may be the first and perhaps the most fundamental item on the agenda for leaders of the mature metropolis.

Particular policies for particular places will depend on particular conditions. Concrete recommendations for individual problems in individual metropolitan areas cannot be derived from the discussion here. Mainly this is because there are significant diversions from the general historical trend in various places, with some aspects of maturity much more advanced "here" and much less advanced "there." On the other hand, while specific prescriptions must await the attention of local groups who possess detailed knowledge of the particular facts of particular locales, three valuable building blocks for effective public policy in this area can be provided: a set of guideposts to strategy, an agenda for the effective concern of those local groups, and a discussion of just why public and private concerns must be mustered.

Strategies for Expanding Employment Opportunities

A systematic concern with trends in employment and a surveillance of options for expanding it must be the beginning of concern for the mature metropolis; here we are in step with the spirit of most local development organizations. But concern with "finding more jobs" can only be the beginning, not the end of concern.

The real question is not really, How can we find more jobs?, but rather, Why do the obvious mechanisms for finding more jobs produce so few new ones in the mature metropolis? This seemingly slight twist of phrase is important; it underscores the need to understand the unfolding dynamic of the mature metropolis as has been indicated many times throughout this book.

Traditionally, industrial development has been the economic force associated with metropolitanization, so it should be no surprise that it is to manufacturing possibilities that most metropolitan development agencies turn their attention; and, as indicated earlier, there may be manufacturing opportunities in the mature metropolis. Vacant land and even vacant usable factories and lofts may be an attraction; so too may be the ready supply of labor, though the unemployed are likely to be of only from low to moderate skill. As metropolitan fiscal pressures continue and the competition of nonmetropolitan areas becomes more manifest, it may be that employers will face less trade union pressure in metropolis than elsewhere.

Paradoxically, it may be the most mature metropolises which develop the greatest attraction for manufacturing, and more in their central cities than in their suburbs. Exploring these opportunities is an important item on the agenda for the mature metropolis; but the warning of this book is loud and clear, namely, that as a general rule there is little prospect for expecting any net growth in industrial employment in the mature metropolis. Ultimately, it is for this reason that a more sophisticated agenda must be forged if maturity is to be turned into something other than stagnation.

Development of potential employment opportunities in parts of the service sector might seem much more likely; but even here caution is in order. Public service employment, for example, probably is in for very hard times, with absolute reduction in numbers the most likely outcome. Retail trade activity is likely to follow population with only limited room for developmental leverage. Wholesale and routine business service employment is likely to mirror trends in industrial employment, again with limited room to maneuver, except to correct for present underdevelopment. Construction opportunities may be more buoyant than at first anticipated due to the demand for a larger number of housing units stemming from shrinking average family size, but it would be unwise to depend on this trend as a very durable feature of metropolitan development.

As pointed out in Chapter 6, it is in the "new" services, and mainly in particular sectors, that real expansion opportunity is likely to be found: knowledge industries, central offices, data and information processing, health, recreation, tourist, cultural, and education services, including a possible renaissance of arts and crafts. For the most part, however, expanded opportunities in these areas require careful nurturing; much more is involved than just looking for a possible customer for an industrial site. Working through this part of the agenda will call for careful and sustained study of the detailed economic structure of an individual area and a sustained surveillance of the relationship of that structure to technical and new market opportunities emerging nationally as well as locally.

Human Resource Strategies for the Mature Metropolis

The symposium on which this volume was based certainly was not necessary to emphasize the need for better and more extensive education. For at least a few decades, their low human capital endowment has been identified as the major problem of the economically disadvantaged. But here, too, we may have produced an important if subtle change of focus, with the question now being seen as: Why, after so many years of seeing the problem as one of human capital accumulation, and after so much determination and so many programs for improving the situation, does so much disadvantage and so much difficulty in absorbing the labor force into meaningful employment persist?

An important thrust of earlier discussion, especially in the preceding chapter, was an attempt to establish a new kind of concern with human resources in the mature metropolis; not necessarily to replace the old concern, but at least to supplement it. As Alexis so aptly put it in Chapter 14, we must learn how to prepare the disadvantaged for the world of work that can be theirs, not an imaginary world that they, the schools, and the larger society know will not be theirs. And this principle does not apply only to black teenage males; it applies to everyone whose skills are in danger of obsolescence. Conventional education is not necessarily to be replaced, but the answer to those for whom conventional education has not produced employability is not more conventional education.

There is another side of the coin of human resource strategy. Besides more realism in building human capital, there is a need for more realism in the search for private business capital. For example, development agencies in many mature metropolises have taken to sending delegations to Europe and the Far East in search of "reverse investment" industrial locators. This is not a foolish endeavor; reverse investment is taking place and some areas are going to get new industrial facilities as a result. What is foolish, however, is to put any great reliance on this kind of technique or expend much developmental attention on it. The overall national volume of reverse investment is likely to be modest, and the small or nonmetropolitan areas will have a clear edge in capturing it.

The leaders of an individual metropolis probably know more about their area and its advantages and disadvantages than do outsiders. It is they who probably could best estimate the kinds of new activities that really would be profitable in their area. If they could convince themselves of an opportunity's merit, they probably could find the necessary capital and even recruit the entrepreneurship themselves. Of course, this calls for much harder work and more careful analysis than taking a trip to Japan or opening an office in West Germany, but the lessons of this book strongly indicate it is more likely to produce success, especially since the successes for the mature metropolis are likely to be in a series of fairly small and innovative individual events.

Human resource strategies should not be confined to the qualitative matching of labor force characteristics and employment demands; the question of total population size and composition is terribly crucial to the future of metropolis. Changes in U.S. population hang on a very delicate balance between decisions on marriage and childbirth, incidence of disease, and official vigilance with respect to illegal immigration. At a metropolitan level the addition of internal migration considerations makes the balance even more precarious. As pointed out in Chapter 2, it was the shift in birthrate which alerted us to the underlying historical evolution of metropolis which has been underway for some time. Admittedly, it was a big shift in the birthrate; and it produced a correspondingly big jolt in our consciousness. But much less dramatic shifts, say in illegal immigration situations, could make the difference between growing or declining population for individual SMSAs. Such demographic forces mainly are far beyond the control of an individual metropolitan area, but the agenda of every area should include a careful and ongoing analysis of trends in population and its components. Serious work does need to be done to accomplish this, but it may be one of the most accessible "early-warning systems" that a metropolitan area can develop.

Physical Planning in the Mature Metropolis

In earlier chapters, especially in Chapters 7-10, it was noted that substantial changes are in prospect for the spatial organization of metropolis. The mature metropolis will be much more spread out than the contemporary one, but not at all in the sense of the sprawling suburbia we associate with Los Angeles of the 1960s. Rather, we should expect, as in Los Angeles, many centers, but with much denser development around each of them and considerable open space and absence of continuous development between them. People will be much more likely to live, work, and shop within the same subcenter, with occasional commuting or more frequent telecommuting to another more distant subcenter. Transport is likely to focus on the private automobile—probably a much smaller and lighter one—or buses, using pretty much conventional hardware, but likely with more flexible dispatching capability.

The metropolitan area will be much larger than now but it will be interspersed with agricultural, mining, and other open-space functions so that the correspondence between metropolitan activities and exclusively metropolitan territory will be blurred, increasingly to the point of extinction. Oddly enough, even though the area of the whole system will be bigger, average travel distance is likely to be shorter. In part this will be reinforced by a decline in the quality of the metropolitan road system which can be expected. In part, it will be reinforced by the more limited role for mass transit given the more dispersed pattern of settlement, though possibilities for mass transit over *limited* very highly dense corridors may emerge.

Part of the physical planning agenda for the mature metropolis is implicit in the description just given. An important item would be a systematic survey of available technology and possibilities for application in particular areas of more energy-efficient, cheaper, and more convenient modes of short-distance transport, typically with high use rates per day, but with a need for more time-of-travel and specific route flexibility. The other demand will be for nonautomotive transport over longer distances, with less need for flexibility, but at lower densities.

Land-use control will be easier to achieve in the maturing than in the exploding metropolis. Mainly this will be because of the underlying pressures moving the system to denser, more compact settlement in more widely scattered centers. Accordingly, pressures for movement to more global land-use control systems should be weak. For example, the recent congressional interest in statewide zoning systems already has abated; it is not likely to reemerge with any force. At a more immediate neighborhood level, however, zoning control pressures may become stronger, as life at a scale larger than a suburban neighborhood but much smaller than a city becomes typical, and with more aspects of people's lives focused at that one level. In the older central cities, planning at a neighborhood level will become more important as the central cities come to resemble the new suburban system itself. Finally, as indicated earlier, maintaining environmental quality through environmental control will continue as an important item on the agenda, but in the mature metropolis probably not one of growing importance.

The Need for Public Concern and Private Response

In this concluding section we would like to reiterate briefly the kind of concern from private as well as public leaders which has been alluded to at so many places throughout this book. The agenda for concern with regard to public sector aspects of the mature metropolis, for example, calls more for caution than imagination.

The one major functional shift that seems noncontroversial is the need to transfer fiscal responsibility for health and welfare from local to higher levels of government. State governments already have shown increased allocations to metropolitan areas, at least where they are showing maturity, but the capacity of state government probably is inadequate to the problem at hand. Ultimately, the federal government is likely to assume much greater responsibility in these areas, but unfortunately it is not likely to do this in a big way very rapidly. Just what local areas can do about this problem besides complain and wait impatiently is not clear, but at least the concern should be on their agenda. Aside from taking over existing health and welfare burdens, it would seem unwise to look for new federally financed programs in the mature metropolis; federal interest in subsidizing such things as suburban residential development or intraurban mass transit will not disappear but is likely to be weaker.

So far as local government itself is concerned, the main item on the agenda would seem to be improved management. A call for more efficiency in city hall is hardly new, but it takes on added importance in the context of metropolitan maturity since there is hardly anything else available as a constructive object of concern. As indicated, except for existing health and welfare burdens, it seems pointless to look to the federal government for new resources, or to the states for much more than they already are giving. Local tax reform probably still is worth considering and is of real concern on equity grounds, but it is unlikely to lead to much expanded fiscal capacity of local government. Thus, the major concern of the local public sector must be with careful allocation of local public funds, limited ambitions in the provision of local public services, and, maybe most of all, control of skyrocketing local government personnel costs.

With the very limited scope for local government leadership, and except for transfer of health and welfare burdens to higher levels of government, if anything, a smaller total role for state and federal government, the need for business leadership is emerging as more critical. Business views on urban matters, however, have not always been so clear or so constructive. That partly explains why they are sometimes given less credit than they deserve in the court of public opinion. At the most elemental level, of course, we find a business attitude toward the metropolitan dilemma that is one of simple indifference: the view that city problems are not the business of business. This attitude probably is not characteristic of the majority of today's business leaders, but it has been displayed by a distressingly large number of businessmen in many American cities at various times in their history.

A more responsive but self-protective business point of view is *avoidance* of urban problems—packing up and moving a business out of town, to the suburbs, or even out of state, to try to escape some particularly troublesome urban headaches. Some of the proudest names in American industry have done just this within the past decade or two. This is an essentially passive urban strategy, resorted to as a vehicle for attempted circumvention of city problems which have come to exceed the firm's own ability or willingness to cope. A strong impression is developing, however, that a good many firms that have moved out of the city are finding that some metro-style problems follow them. In such instances, there is no escaping the need to face the issues. If for no other reason, a higher-order business response to the problems of the mature metropolis now seems to be the order of the day; this involves a commitment to participation, and even to leadership, in attacking attackable metropolitan problems.

The motive for such commitment varies a great deal, of course, among business firms. Sometimes it is a matter of simple civic pride. Sometimes it has rested upon a feeling of paternalistic responsibility for the surrounding community. As indicated, though, recently it has been based more often on the realistic discovery by many businesses that they will suffer serious damage, directly or indirectly, from an unhealthy urban environment. Whether or not they themselves are located in the city, many businesses find they need features traditionally associated with the big city: big centralized markets, concentrated know-how in production design, technical facilities for distribution and financing, and the intellectual and cultural ambience needed to attract high-quality professional and managerial talent.

For these or other reasons, working to preserve the availability of big-city features has become a matter of enlightened self-interest for many business leaders. But as emphasized over and over again in this book, the face of metropolis is changing. Most particularly, the close correspondence of metropolitan *activities and facilities* and metropolitan *territory* is rapidly fading. In that sense, the focus of appropriate governmental attention may be harder to achieve; it is for this reason that an effective private sector response is needed by the larger community as well as being vital to the business interests themselves.

We must acknowledge that there are great differences in attitudes among private sector leaders, with contrasts that have ebbed and flowed over time. And just as there was and is a hierarchy of urban views among businessmen, there is a similar hierarchy of views toward business on the part of the community. One view sees business as the *exploiter* of other groups in the community; another view, popular among some political interests, sees business as the *exploitee*—a kind of captive golden goose that can be squeezed, via taxes and other methods, to impel it to lay more and more golden eggs for the rest of the community. Juxtaposed against these views is a third one that emphasizes business as the essential job creator in the urban setting. Not surprisingly, among state and local governments there has been a consequent proliferation of offices of economic development designed to entice more and better business firms, but surprising to many, the results have been very mixed. In some cases perhaps the bait has been wrong. It other cases, businesses have been understandably nonplussed by their contrasting treatment by different departments of the same government—like a meal ticket in one office, like a Simon Legree in another.

The "truth" about the relationships between the private and the public sector may have elements of most of these views in it. What is more certain is that important *differences* exist among branches of the private sector in their relation to the urban environment—differences in objective, motives, capabilities, and consequences. Urban policies that cannot take account of these differences are bound to cause problems in their own right in urban-business relations. Still more certain, and more important, is that major *similarities* exist in some of the basic interests of business and other major groups in most communities. Policies for the mature metropolis that fail to seize upon these similarities of interests might well miss an effective shortcut to success.

In truth, this situation of the mature metropolis is one in which the private and public sectors really need each other. The ingredients are present for a successful outcome of this effort. It is hoped that the discussion in this book has tagged some of the key ideas that can be followed up in most situations of the mature metropolis. But we must put aside any aspirations for a standardized formula that can be uniformly applied to all areas. The diversity of conditions among the major metropolises underlines the need to develop individualized approaches, sensitively tailored to each case, hopefully using this book as an agenda. That makes our task harder, but it can make the results much more useful.

About the Contributors

Marcus Alexis is professor and chairman of the Department of Economics, Northwestern University. He has taught at the University of Rochester and University of California. Professor Alexis is chairman of the Committee on the Status of Minority Group Members of the American Economic Association, director of the Summer Program for Minority Students, and consultant to The Urban Institute. He is the author of several books and numerous professional articles. He attended Brooklyn College and Michigan State University and received the Ph.D. in economics from the University of Minnesota in 1959.

William Alonso is Richard Saltonstall Professor of Population Policy and director of the Center of Population Studies at Harvard University. He held faculty appointments at the University of California at Berkeley and Harvard University, is a member of the Inter-University Committee on Urban Economics, and consultant to numerous government agencies both here and abroad. Professor Alonso is the author and coauthor of *Location and Land Use* and *Regional Policy,* as well as numerous other books, monographs and professional articles and is a member of the editorial board of several leading journals in urban economics and regional science. He received his education at Harvard University and the University of Pennsylvania where he received the Ph.D. in regional science in 1960.

Alex Anas is assistant professor in urban and regional planning, Department of Civil Engineering and faculty associate of the Transportation Center, Northwestern University. He has taught at the University of Pennsylvania and is the author of several articles in professional journals and a technical research study for the Regional Transportation Authority in Chicago. Dr. Anas attended Carnegie-Mellon University and in 1975 completed the Ph.D. in city and regional planning at the University of Pennsylvania.

Alan K. Campbell is chairman of the U.S. Civil Service Commission. He was dean of the Lyndon B. Johnson School of Public Affairs, University of Texas, and of the Maxwell School of Citizenship and Public Affairs, Syracuse University. Dr. Campbell was on the faculties of Harvard and Hofstra Universities and is a member of numerous governmental committees both in New York State and nationally, including past membership on the Advisory Committee to the Secretary of Housing and Urban Development and a consultant to the Advisory Commission on Intergovernmental Relations. He is a member of the Governing Council of the National Municipal League and the National Academy of Science and has authored numerous books, monographs and articles including *The Political Economy of State and Local Government Reform* and *Metropolitan*

America: Fiscal Patterns and Governmental Systems. Dr. Campbell was educated at Whitman College, Wayne State University and received the Ph.D. in political economy and government from Harvard University in 1952.

James S. Coleman is professor of sociology at the University of Chicago and has taught at Johns Hopkins University. Professor Coleman is a member of the National Academy of Sciences and National Academy of Education and is the recipient of the John Dewey Society Award in 1969 and the Nicholas Murray Butler Medal in 1970. He is a member of the President's Science Advisory Committee and Chairman of the Panel on Youth and author or coauthor of well over a hundred books and articles including *Equality of Educational Opportunity* and *Power and the Structure of Society.* Professor Coleman attended Purdue University and Columbia University receiving the Ph.D. in sociology in 1955.

Anthony Downs is Senior Fellow, The Brookings Institution, and was chairman of the board, Real Estate Research Corporation and adjunct professor of urban studies, University of Illinois at Chicago. Dr. Downs was on the faculty of the University of Chicago, lecturer at numerous universities, and consultant to many governmental agencies and private corporations. Dr. Downs was a member of the National Commission on Urban Problems and has authored numerous articles in nonprofessional as well as professional publications and several books, including *An Economic Theory of Democracy* and *Urban Problems and Prospects.* Dr. Downs attended Carleton College and received the Ph.D. in economics from Stanford University in 1956.

Daniel Feenberg is a native of St. Louis and received the A.B. from Washington University. He is now at Princeton University where he is writing on the demand for clean water to complete his dissertation for the Ph.D. in economics.

Peter Geoffrey Hall is dean of the faculty of Urban and Regional Studies, University of Reading (England). He has held faculty appointments in geography at the University of Reading, London School of Economics and Political Science, and the University of London. Dr. Hall was visiting professor of city and regional planning at the University of California at Berkeley and is a member of numerous governmental advisory committees in the United Kingdom and former member of the Council of the Royal Geographic Society. He is the editor of *Regional Studies* and author of many books and articles including *London 2000* and *The World Cities.* Dr. Hall was educated at Cambridge University where he received the Ph.D. in geography in 1959.

Robert C. Holland is president of the Committee for Economic Development. Formerly, he was a member of the Board of Governors of the Federal Reserve

System and vice president and senior economist at the Federal Reserve Bank of Chicago. Dr. Holland has written numerous technical reports and articles and a member of advisory boards of several non-profit organizations. He attended the University of Nebraska and received the Ph.D. in economics from the University of Pennsylvania in 1959.

Piotr Korcelli is associate professor at the Institute of Geography and Spatial Organization, Polish Academy of Sciences. Formerly a lecturer at the University of Warsaw and a visiting scholar at the University of Maryland, and the University of Washington, and more recently the International Institute for Applied Systems Analysis (Vienna), Professor Korcelli serves on the editorial board of *Geographia Polonica* and is a member of the Polish National Committee of the International Geographic Union. He is the author of *Evolution of Spatial Structure of Metropolitan Areas in California* and *Theory of Intra-Urban Structure* in addition to almost two dozen published articles. He received his training at the University of Warsaw and the Polish Academy of Sciences where he earned the Doctorate in geography in 1968 and the degree Dr.(Hab) in 1973.

M. Leanne Lachman is vice president and director of Public Sector Studies, Real Estate Research Corporation. She is a consultant on neighborhood and other community studies and project coordinator of a number of projects involving neighborhood preservation, urban renewal, and abandonment and is author or coauthor of several books and articles including *Achieving Effective Desegration: A Handbook* and *Tax Delinquency in the Inner City: The Problem and Its Possible Solutions.* Ms. Lachman attended the University of Southern California and Claremont Graduate School where she earned the M.A.

Norman Macrae is deputy editor of *The Economist.* He has written hundreds of economics articles for this and other newspapers around the world. Winner of the Wincott Award as British Financial Journalist of the Year in 1973, he is author of numerous pamphlets on economic affairs as well as several books, including two on the U.S.A.; *The Neurotic Trillionaire* and *America's Third Century.* Mr. Macrae was educated at Cambridge University where he completed the economics tripos and two years of additional research in 1949.

David Metcalf is professor of economics, University of Kent. He was on the faculty at London School of Economics and has held visiting appointments at Washington University and Princeton University. Dr. Metcalf is a member of the editorial board of *British Journal of Industrial Relations* and is the author of a number of professional papers on urban labor markets, including "Earnings Changes: A Regional Analysis for the U.K., 1960-1968" and "Urban Unemployment in England." He attended the University of Manchester and the University of London where he received the Ph.D. in economics in 1971.

Edwin S. Mills is professor in the Department of Economics, Princeton University. He has held faculty appointments at Johns Hopkins University, Massachusetts Institute of Technology and University College of North Staffordshire (England), and was a member of the senior professional staff of the U.S. Council of Economic Advisors. Dr. Mills is a consultant to a number of public and private groups, including The Urban Institute and the U.S. Department of Housing and Urban Development. He is a member of the Inter-University Committee on Urban Economics, and is editor of the *Journal of Urban Economics*. Dr. Mills is the author or editor of several dozen books and articles including *Studies in the Structure of the Urban Economy* and *Economic Analysis of Environmental Problems*. He attended Brown University and the University of Birmingham (England), receiving the Ph.D. in economics in 1956.

Leon N. Moses is director of the Transportation Center and professor of economics, both at Northwestern University. He taught at Harvard University and the University of Miami and served as a staff economist at TVA. Consultant to several U.S. agencies and to the governments of Tanzania, Burma, and the Republic of Congo. Dr. Moses is a member of the Inter-University Committee on Urban Economics and is past president of the Regional Science Association. Author or coauthor of several monographs and articles including "Thunen, Weber and the Spatial Structure of the Nineteenth Century City" and "Transportation Controls, Travel Costs and Urban Spatial Structure," he attended Ohio State University, University of Buffalo and Harvard University where he received the Ph.D. in economics in 1952.

Dick Netzer is dean and professor of economics at the Graduate School of Public Administration, New York University. He previously was assistant vice president of the Federal Reserve Bank of Chicago. Consultant to numerous governmental and private agencies, including the Regional Plan Association in New York, Dr. Netzer is a member of several advisory boards and commissions and is a member of the Board of Directors of the Municipal Assistance Corporation. Dr. Netzer is chairman of the Inter-University Committee on Urban Economics and is author of several dozen books and articles including *Economics and Urban Problems* and *The Property Tax*. He attended the University of Wisconsin and Harvard University where he received the Ph.D. in economics in 1952.

Harvey S. Perloff is professor and dean of the School of Architecture and Urban Planning, University of California at Los Angeles. He was formerly Director of the Program of Urban and Regional Studies, Resources for the Future, Inc., a U.S. Member of the Committee of Nine of Alliance for Progress, on the faculty of the University of Chicago, an economist on the Board of Governors—Federal Reserve System. Consultant to and member of numerous national and international advisory commissions including past chairman of the Committee on

Urban Economics and of the Advisory Committee, United Nations Program of Training and Research in Regional Planning and Development, Dr. Perloff is author and coauthor of more than a dozen books and several dozen professional articles including *Modernizing the Central City: New Towns Intown... and Beyond* and *Issues in Urban Economics.* He was educated at the University of Pennsylvania, the London School of Economics and Harvard University, where he received the Ph.D. in Political Economy in 1940.

Harry W. Richardson is professor of economics and urban and regional planning at the University of Southern California. His former faculty appointments were at the University of Pittsburgh, Universities of Kent and Newcastle upon Tyne (England) and Universities of Aberdeen and Strathclyde (Scotland). He is a consultant to numerous international agencies and visiting scholar at several universities, is a member of the editorial board of several leading journals, and author or coauthor of more than a dozen books and sixty articles including *The Economics of Urban Size* and *Regional Growth Theory.* Professor Richardson attended Manchester University (England) where he received the M.A. in economics in 1961.

Randall Zisler is assistant professor of urban planning at Princeton University. He received his undergraduate degree from Princeton in 1968, the M.S.E. in structural mechanics and systems analysis from the Catholic University of America, the M.A.U.P. in architecture and urban planning from Princeton University, and the Ph.D. in urban planning from Princeton University. His research interests are primarily in urban economics and finance.

About the Editor

Charles L. Leven is professor and chairman of the Department of Economics and Director, Institute for Urban and Regional Studies at Washington University. He has held faculty positions at the University of Pittsburgh, University of Pennsylvania and Iowa State University. Dr. Leven is author or coauthor of numerous professional articles and several books including *An Analytical Framework for Regional Development Policy* and *Neighborhood Change* and has served on several governmental advisory boards. A past president of the Regional Science Association Dr. Leven attended Illinois Institute of Technology and the University of Illinois and received the Ph.D. in economics from Northwestern University in 1958.